THE SPORTS AFIELD

FISHING ALMANAC

THE
SPORTS
AFIELD

FISHING ALMANAC

Compiled and Edited by
FRANK S. GOLAD

**A FISHERMAN'S TREASURE-TROVE OF TIPS, TECHNIQUES,
TACKLE, FACTS, AND MORE, FROM THE CELEBRATED
"ALMANAC" SECTION OF *SPORTS AFIELD MAGAZINE***

Introduction by
TOM PAUGH
Editor in Chief,
SPORTS AFIELD

L&B

Lyons & Burford, Publishers

PRINTED IN THE UNITED STATES OF AMERICA
10   9   8   7

Library of Congress Cataloging-in-Publication Data

The Sports afield fishing almanac.

   "A fisherman's treasure-trove of tips, techniques, tackle, facts, and more, from the celebrated 'almanac' section of Sports afield magazine."
   1. Fishing.   I. Golad, Frank S.   II. Fishing
(New York, N.Y.)
SH441.S76   1989   799.1   89-2353
ISBN 1-55821-020-2

CONTENTS

FISH COOKERY AND RECIPES

ODDS AND ENDS

INTRODUCTION

In May of 1972 the *Sports Afield* Almanac was born . . . on eight pages of pink, high-bulk stock, printed in orange and black inks. *Gaudy* is not exactly the right word (*god-awful?*), but it was loaded with bits and tips and facts and fancy about hunting, fishing and the out-of-doors. The Almanac proved to be an instantaneous smash hit.

Just how popular it actually became surfaced about five years later when an enterprising new editor decided to change it. He cut the eight pages back to four and did away with the high-bulk stock in favor of normal run-of-the-book, white-coated paper. Readers were enraged, wrote threatening letters, canceled subscriptions by the hundreds and generally carried on, until eight months later the editorship changed hands and the Almanac was wisely restored to its former glory. And so it remains today, though the high-bulk paper is currently a subdued tan and the inks an attractive but rugged russet and navy blue.

The original *Sports Afield* Almanac was the brainchild of Ted Kesting. Ted, who had been the editor of *Sports Afield* for 25 years, took on the job as the first Almanac editor at the time of his semiretirement—and found himself busier than ever.

The Almanac's present editor, and the editor of this book, Frank Golad, is highly qualified for the position, being a man for all seasons, a jack-of-all-trades. He is a writer, an artist, a designer, a collector of books, stamps, coins and, above all, bits of information of interest to outdoorsmen. Mr. Golad is Mr. Almanac.

The Almanac has always been a potpourri of outdoor-related subjects, everything from nature quizzes, to wild game recipes (like antelope enchiladas), to bad jokes about game wardens, to how to call predators by sucking the palm of your hand. The hunting and the fishing is always judiciously mixed in with all the other goodies. Now, for the first time, all the best of the wonderful fishing-related subject matter has been rooted out by editor Golad and is concentrated between these covers. *The Sports Afield Fishing Almanac* has information on all your favorite game species, including bass (largemouth, smallmouth, striped, you name it), the trouts, panfish, walleyes, the pikes and numerous saltwater species. The book tells you how to catch them by multitudinous methods. All you want to know about tackle and gear and boats, on *ad infinitum* and, of course, how to prepare, store, and cook your succulent catch in a variety of ways. If that does not seem to be enough you will also find informative nuggets about weather, safety, health, fishing regulations, travel tips for fishermen and even fishing quizzes. No one has actually counted (who has the time?), but there are obviously far more than a thousand valuable bits and pieces of angling wisdom to rummage through.

Finally, a word of thanks to the hundreds of contributors who have been sending in these items over the years. They are the true heroes of this book, submitting a new fishing knot here, a homemade lure design there, a tried and true family recipe, an old angler's secret tip hidden for years but here rediscovered. These are the little but important stories of sportfishing. Now they have been collected. Now they are yours to keep.

TOM PAUGH
Editor in Chief,
Sports Afield

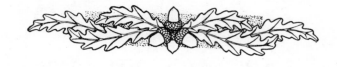

POPULAR
GAME FISHES

POPULAR GAME FISHES

LARGEMOUTH BASS

BETTER BASS BUGGING

When fishing bass bugs, most flyfishermen manipulate the baits with their rod tips. The problem is you do not have full control of the bug; should a fish hit, slack line makes it difficult to get leverage for setting the hook. It is better to fish the bug with the line.

After you cast, hold the rod parallel to the water and wrap the forefinger of your casting hand around the line, holding it lightly against the rod handle. With the other hand, tug on the line to move the bug, either hard jerks or more subtle maneuvers. The direct line link between hand and bait gives you complete control of the bug.

If a fish strikes, the forefinger presses hard on the line, holding it firmly against the handle to keep it from moving, and the rod tip is raised sharply. With all slack eliminated, the odds of setting the hook solidly are much improved.

LONELY LUNKERS

A lunker bass is one that lives for over five years. A good old lunker, ten pounds or better, isn't too sociable and has horrible dining manners with his friends and relatives, so much so that about three lunkers will share an acre of water. They get that big because of their genetic hardiness and the fact that they learned to avoid the hook. Lunkers just happen to be a little more intelligent.

BASS FISHING

Tempting Bass

When fishing for bass, your choice of tactics depends largely on the season of the year.

In the early spring and in fall bass will smash topwater lures, such as floating propeller types and poppers. Occasionally they will hit on the surface at any season, especially in early morning and late afternoon. They are also likely to take surface lures when found in shallow water, such as along shorelines near overhanging trees.

Under these conditions, you will soon learn that you can't cast too close to shore. You'll be surprised at how many rod-jolting strikes you'll get when you place the lure next to the bank.

As the temperature rises and bass have moved back to the cooler, deeper holes, you must change your techniques. You usually need something to dredge bottom. The plastic worm is ideal for this; even the most apathetic bass will respond when one is dragged slowly past its nose.

Don't make the mistake of striking back as soon as the fish clamps the worm. He needs time to work it into his mouth. When the line grows taut, let him move off a few feet, then strike hard. Power is needed to set the hook properly because his mouth is tough. Then, keep your rod tip high and enjoy the fun.

BOUNCE BEFORE RECASTING

When you reel in a weighted plastic worm, bounce it off the bottom a few times direct-

ly beneath the boat before lifting it out of the water. Very often jiggling the worm this way draws last-second strikes from bass that have followed it in.

THE MAIONE RIG

By now it would seem that just about every imaginable way to rig an artificial worm has been discussed and analyzed in excruciating detail. However, there are countless variations. Each method supposedly offers something just a bit different—and the originators hope superior. So one more rigging—the Maione rig—may seem about as useful as a bluegill gaff.

Named for its creator, Ohio bass angler Hank Maione, this worm hook-up is a variation of the Texas rig, but offers far greater hook-setting power. Instead of burying the hook point inside the worm, the tip and barb are actually brought out of the worm body to nestle snugly beside it. With the hook point exposed, it is easier to set the hook and the worm body acts as a weed guard to prevent snags.

After experimenting with the method, you'll find that it snarls surprisingly little and allows you to hook bass with consistency.

★

The jig-and-frog combination is one of the hottest lures in tournament circles. Experts believe it is effective not because it resembles a frog but because it looks more like a crayfish scuttling over the bottom. And that's how it should be retrieved, in continuous, tiny hops.

BUBBLING BASS

Trailing a fly or two behind a casting bubble is often a very effective way to take fish. Panfish are truly suckers for this method, because they like small bites. Insect-eating trout will sometimes take flies when they refuse everything else, even worms.

If you fish water that possibly contains bass, it seems a shame to waste that possibility by casting a bubble. Instead, try something with hooks hanging from it, such as a floating lure.

Tie your fly leader to the eye of the trailing hook. Make the leader at least two feet long; three is better. Tie one or two flies to the leader.

Cast the rig out and do whatever you would normally do to catch the fish you are after with the flies you are using. Forget about the fact that you are using a lure that might tempt a bass—or even a large trout.

Forget it until the moment the water erupts, and you instantly know that it's not a panfish you are playing.

★

Most bass fishermen put their money on California to produce the next world-record bass, although others say Florida, Georgia or Alabama. But don't overlook Texas which is coming on strong with plantings of Florida's giant strain.

MIXED-UP BASS

In some inland northern lakes, you'd conclude that largemouth bass think they're smallmouth bass and vice versa.

Look for bass in cover favored by both species. Be ready for a smallmouth to come busting out of the lily pads or for a largemouth to wind your line around a gigantic boulder in an underwater rock pile.

Where there's plenty of big bass, they seem to take the best cover available, regardless of what fishermen think bass should do.

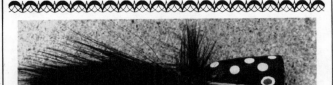

Wine-Cork Bass Poppers

You can make your own bass poppers out of wine corks. If you don't drink the stuff, have friends save corks for you.

Wine-cork poppers are easy and fun to make. You don't have to be an accomplished fly-tier and you probably already have on hand many of the materials needed. The rest can be bought for just a small outlay of cash. The only really expensive item is the electric hand drill.

When making these poppers, it saves time if you make them in lots of six or more.

Select hook for size popper. Select cork and rough-out shape using a razor blade. Make a concave scoop in the front of the cork with the drill and dremel attachment, cut a groove in bottom with hacksaw blade. Make sure the groove is deep enough to easily accommodate hook shank and hump. Mix five-minute epoxy. Apply to shank of hook before inserting in groove. Fill in groove with epoxy. Insert hook. Make certain groove is filled flush with cork. Let epoxy dry. Use medium-grain sandpaper and emery board to smooth out and shape rough-cut popper. Dip cork in Aero Gloss Dope sanding sealer and let dry. Smooth finish with 6/0 sandpaper. Dip cork in clear Aero Gloss and let dry. Paint popper body with Testers Model paints. Use your own color schemes or follow standard patterns. Let dry for 24 hours. Note: Two coats gives a longer-lasting finish. Place popper in tying vise. Tie on hackles for tail and legs.

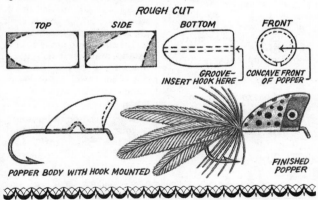

ROUGH CUT

TOP   SIDE   BOTTOM   FRONT

GROOVE—
INSERT HOOK HERE   CONCAVE FRONT OF POPPER

POPPER BODY WITH HOOK MOUNTED

FINISHED POPPER

When you file or hone the hook on a bass lure, dress the hook so its point turns slightly out from, instead of running parallel to, the hook's shank. This causes the point to dig into the tough mouth of a bass on contact.

★

When you're caught without a landing net and your bass is ready to be brought in, here are three ways to do it: 1) reach over the head and compress the gills; 2) lay your thumb over the lower jaw, push up with your forefinger under the jaw, and lift; 3) cradle the bass in your cupped hand and press upwards on the soft belly just ahead of the vent.

THE "WAKE 'EM UP" POLE

When I was growing up in Texas back in the 40s, a lot of my time was spent bass fishing with my aunt. She showed me a unique way of getting fish to hit, a method I've since used with considerable success.

When we went out on the lake, she carried what she referred to as her "wake 'em up" pole: a 12-foot-long rod of unjointed bamboo to which she attached a one-foot length of 20-pound braided line tipped with a snap swivel, the line tied to the tapered end of the pole.

If bass were being finicky, she'd hook a lure, one with propellers on each end, to the snap swivel. As I eased the boat near cattails and lily pads at shore's edge, she would jam the tip of the bamboo pole into the water, then viciously whip the lure back and forth, around and through the structure, the lure and pole tip shattering water and weeds.

Whether the tactic scares lethargic bass into instinctive strikes or makes them so mad at having been unceremoniously disturbed from their rest that they hit in anger, I don't know, but over the years I've witnessed many a bucketmouth fall for the ploy.

Weedless Bass Bugs

Most cork bass bugs can be made weedless: Take a four- or five-inch-long piece of lightweight wire and bend a loop or eye in the middle, like the eye in a safety pin.

Push both ends of this looped wire through holes (made with a pin) in the under lip of the cork body. Pull both through until the wire loop nestles tightly around the hook eye.

This light wire guard rarely interferes with the business of driving the hook home in the jaws of a big bass, yet it is usually sufficient to allow the lure to ride up and over clusters of pads without getting stuck.

SHALLOW WATER CRANKBAITS

Most anglers choose crankbaits to correspond with the depth of water being fished, picking deep divers for water 12 to 15 feet deep, moderate divers for water six to 12 feet, and shallow crankbaits to probe areas thinner than this.

Bass guide Bill Mathias, who fishes Virginia's Lake Anna, claims these are not always the best strategies to employ.

"Deep-diving crankbaits can work wonders on shallow bass," he says. "You have to develop a knack, though, for working these lures gently through the shallows, or else you'll hang up all the time."

Avoid the temptation to set the hook every time you feel resistance, because the deep divers have probably just run into a log or rock. Simply pause and allow the long-lipped lure to back off the obstruction and then resume the retrieve.

A deep diver rooting across the bottom, stirring up mud and kicking up debris can be devastating on shallow-water bass. When a bucketmouth or bronzeback hits your plug, you won't have any trouble telling the difference between him and a rock.

Some bass may be angered into striking the burrowing object invading their territory. Others no doubt mistake the plug for a crayfish, which acts in a similar fashion, scurrying along the lake floor.

"Crawdad" colors of brown and orange usually work best, though chartreuse is productive too.

This tactic works well on both rocky and muddy bottoms, on all species of bass when they're in the shallows. ★

Bass fishing with a flyrod can be as exciting and rewarding as a man can stand. Especially if you stay with a floating deer-hair mouse or moth and tease the fish along close to shore cover such as weeds, lily pads and reeds. You don't need to be an expert—just use short and accurate casts.

Small Bait For More Bass

We've so often read the old admonition "use a big bait to catch a big bass" that many of us are using lures that fish of a modest size will not attack.

There are thousands of lakes, ponds and streams with lots of small and medium-sized bass, but only a few big ones. Of course, if all you want to catch are the big ones, by all means fish with monstrous plugs and spinnerbaits and foot-long plastic worms. But if you want lots of action, then look at the tackle offerings listed for panfish. Hone down your tackle to these smaller lures. Fish them just like the big ones, and the bass will give you plenty of action.

There are two added advantages. First, you will get in some extra panfish action. Second, you're still going to hook the occasional big bass. When you do, you're going to be in for a fine skill-testing fight. Isn't that what the big bass are for?

FATBACK FOR BASS

Doodling a chunk of fatback in brush-choked shallows with a stout canepole and 100-pound-test line is a primitive but deadly way to catch bass.

That's the fishing method one grizzled old-timer from South Carolina used to wrestle nine bass in the ten- to 11-pound-class from a tangle-infested bay of Santee-Cooper Reservoir.

"Don't use light line," the old bass fishermen advises. "Those ten-pounders will break off if you use anything less than 70-pound-test."

Only a foot or two of line is needed. Attach it to the end of a sturdy canepole, tie on a strong hook, and impale a piece of "back meat" on the hook.

Get way up in the brush where the big bassboats can't go, and slap the canepole tip on the surface to make a ruckus and draw the bass's attention. Being curious fish, the big fellows will come swimming in order to see what's going on.

When a ten-pounder lunges at your fatback, you're in for a primitive fishing thrill that's not far removed from wrestling with alligators.

It Was Thisaway

A conservation officer reportedly came across an angler who had one big bass on a stringer. The season was closed on bass.

When asked why he had the bass in possession, he replied: "I'm fishing nightcrawlers and every time I threw out the bait this big old bass nailed it. I just got tired of turning him loose and lousing up my fishing, so I put him on the stringer to keep him out of the way until I'm done fishing, that's all."

Just another reason fishermen are called anglers.

How to Rake in More Bass

You're faced with a huge, matted expanse of thick weeds and just *know* a number of bass are under that carpet of greenery. What you don't know is how to present a lure to them.

Many sly anglers use a trick they call "gardening." All you need is a common rake fitted with a detachable extension handle made from lightweight aluminum tubing.

Ease your boat in close to the very edge of the thick weeds, reach out as far as you can with the rake, and make a three-foot-diameter pothole in the weeds. Now, move your boat a short distance farther down the weedline and make another pothole. Make as many of these intermittent holes as you can.

By the time you've finished raking out the last hole, the first is ready to be fished. Keep your boat a comfortable casting distance away and throw plastic worms, spinnerbaits or weedless spoons. Don't cast right into the pothole, however. Cast several feet beyond, so the lure gently splats down on top of the weeds, then slither the lure across the pothole.

This technique is effective because the raking dislodges minute aquatic organisms and insects that attract minnows and small panfish. Bass then quickly home in on the free eats. In short, what you've created is a temporary food chain.

THINK BIG!

In summer when you fish holes for bass, expect to catch the heaviest fish on the first few casts. The pecking order of bassdom is no different from other forms of wildlife: The biggest and strongest dominate, and they usually hit first.

Bass of various sizes commonly group in or near the same deep-water habitat. The largest fish have the first choice of food or lures dropping into their bailiwick. It is rare for lightweight bass to strike first, so when your first efforts produce small bass, chances are no lunker fish are present.

I have marked this reaction from bass for more than 25 years from Cuba to Canada and from coast to coast. When the first fish boated from a hole weighs, for example, five pounds, others will be about the same weight or smaller.

Thus, that first cast is very important. If you are to catch the heaviest bass, think big each time you begin to explore a new summer fishing hole.

FISHING IQ.: BASSER

If you can match these black bass (genus Micropterus) with their species and subspecies monikers, consider yourself a basser of renown.
1. Alabama spotted bass
2. Guadalupe bass
3. largemouth bass
4. Neosho smallmouth
5. redeye bass
6. smallmouth bass
7. spotted bass
8. Suwannee bass

a. M. salmoides
b. M. treculi
c. M. coosae
d. M. dolomieui
e. M. dolomieui velox
f. M. punctulatus
g. M. punctulatus henshalli
h. M. notius

ANSWERS: 1-g, 2-b, 3-a, 4-e, 5-c, 6-d, 7-f, 8-h.

SMART BASS

Despite studies showing the relative intelligence of simians, porpoises and even pigs, bass fishermen have long held the belief that their quarry possesses an intelligence second to none in the animal kingdom. While fish have never scored well on these animal I.Q. tests, the bass does exhibit traits that may, indeed, set him apart and above his finny counterparts.

According to Ohio Department of Natural Resources, District Three Fishery Supervisor Vince LaConte, the bass shows qualities that elevate him to at least some degree of piscatorial predominance.

"We use nets," LaConte explains, "to determine the population of various fish within particular impoundments. The number of pike, bluegill and other fish are tabulated, and from this an idea of the overall fish population can be estimated.

"A problem arises with bass, however. While other fish will swim up against a net arm and obligingly follow it into the holding net, the bass will not. The bass will simply turn around and swim away from capture."

So, for those bass anglers who come home skunked, blaming the wily foe for lack of fishing success, there does seem to be substantiation to this claim.

NIGHTCRAWLER RIG

A live nightcrawler is a hard lure to beat, especially when you use it on a crawler harness. Simply tie a couple of small bait hooks (usually No. 8s) about two inches apart on your line. Or you can use a commercial harness with a spinner and beads. I prefer a two-hook harness. If all you can find is one with three hooks, cut off the last hook.

Stick the top hook into the head of the crawler and the bottom hook far enough back so there is a good portion dangling to entice a fish. Add a little split-shot about 12 to 18 inches up the line, and you're all set. Cast and then reel in a steady retrieve.

This method takes plenty of nightcrawlers—personally, I never go on an outing with less than four or five dozen. When you get a hit and miss the fish, take off any crawler that has been partially eaten. Only little bluegills will peck at an eaten worm. That's why it takes so many crawlers. Also, make sure your presentation is free of weeds.

This method works from April into early November on a variety of species and in different kinds of water.

You can use it to driftfish for walleyes, entice hungry bass, nail slab bluegills, and even stick on a bobber and haul in perch. Northern pike and crappies have also been taken this way.

The method works well in the early morning or late evening if you're fishing off a dock or just off a weedline. It's worked for me during the dog days of summer. Fish may get finicky in the heat but I landed a dozen bass and an equal number of big bluegills (eight to 10 inches) on a day when the temperature was 80° F at 7 a.m. and more than 100° when we stopped fishing.

I like to fish with artificial bait, but there are times when all the fish want is the real thing. And I always remember a rule of fishing an old-timer taught me: "Give the fish what they want."

DROPPER POPPERS

Both bass buggers and those who use smaller poppers for bluegills can add to their pleasure (and catch) by adding a second lure near the butt of their leaders. This is best done by leaving six to eight inches of the heavier piece of leader in a two-part taper. The overall leader need not be more than five or six feet, but the upper section should be substantially larger than its adjoining taper.

Join the two with a blood knot, being sure to leave the few inches of the heavier piece after snugging the knot tight. Your "dropper popper" can then be attached to this section.

The resulting rig will still cast easily, and the stiffness of the heavier material serves to keep it at an angle to the smaller taper. Handling and casting are easier if the lead lure is either heavier or the same size as the dropper.

Used on bedding panfish, this will produce frequent doubles, and the occasional bass on a flyrod provides true excitement.

NEW BRONZEBACK METHOD

You sneak up to your favorite bass-fishing hole and ease the anchor to the bottom as noiselessly as possible to avoid frightening the fish. Right?

Wrong, according to the latest findings of some Lake Ontario smallmouth fishermen. They use a round cement anchor and let out just enough line so the anchor touches the bottom. Then they drift with the wind, letting the anchor thump along the top of submerged boulders. For some reason, the noise and motion attracts curious bass. Fishermen work hair jigs vertically next to the moving anchor and make outstanding catches.

Exponents of the unique system say that it works better than usual free drifting and traditional silent approach. And the bass run larger.

Reaching for Bass

Canepoles have been with us so long that some fishermen have relegated them to still fishing with a bobber and live bait, where they're dandy.

For a change, try this: Fasten a surface lure to the end of about four feet of monofilament line hanging from the end of your canepole.

With the reach of the pole your lure will easily splash through some tricky shoreline cover on your favorite largemouth bass water. Be ready for instant action.

★

If the spinner on your lure refuses to spin, try bending the blade outward so it offers a greater resistance in water.

BASS GOURMANDS

Most anglers know that largemouth bass are opportunistic in their feeding habits and will eat anything available that looks appetizing. Forage fish, panfish, worms, crayfish and insects are all staples of a largemouth's diet.

However, fisheries biologists with the North Carolina Wildlife Resources commission who have been studying coastal bass are amazed at some of the items that "look appetizing" to these fish. They have found sticks, rocks, broken glass, bird feathers and lead shot in the stomachs of the fish. This information should give avid flyfishermen some intriguing new patterns to tie.

BIRDS ARE BASS MARKERS

Anglers have long watched for swooping gulls to locate schools of baitfish and the larger predators beneath them. Southern anglers have also watched great blue herons for signs of baitfish.

Texan Gene Snider, a guide on Lake Palestine, uses the birds to locate largemouth bass.

"A great blue heron sitting on a stump low in the water is almost always feeding on baitfish," Snider declared. "I motor in to check a bird, and if he lets me get really close or flies only a few feet before landing, it's a good guarantee that there are fish in the area, especially if he returns to the same stump when I back off. But if a bird just flies on down the lake without protesting, there probably wasn't enough food there to hold him."

Snider's partnership with herons began in 1981 with a heron he passed three times in one day—at a distance that normally would spook a bird. When his curiosity finally led him to approach the bird using his trolling motor, a

school of bass surfaced around the heron's perch. Snider took his Texas limit of 10 bass that together weighed 30 pounds from that school while the heron was catching three 10-inch bass of its own.

DOUBLE DEADLY

Two very effective lures for black bass are the plastic worm and the Flatfish. If you want some fantastic action, try teaming them up.

Use the Flatfish that has a spreader bar suspending two treble hooks. Attach one worm to each treble hook by putting the barb completely through the collar end of the worm about one quarter inch from the worm tip. Round-tail worms work fine; those with curly tails are even better.

A very slow two- or three-foot retrieve, a momentary pause, a twitch, another momentary pause, and another slow retrieve will bring your phony worms to life and send bass into action!

Holy Toledo!

A Texas sportfisherman I met in Arizona told me about the giant bass he caught in Toledo Bend Reservoir.

"That fish was so big," he said, "that the lake water receded five inches when I pulled him onto the shore. And he measured exactly three feet—between the eyes!"

"What a fantastic fish!" I exclaimed. "Tell me, did you take its picture to show as proof?"

"I surely did, partner," he said.

"Let me see it."

"Shucks, partner, I don't carry that picture around with me," he said. "It weighs 17 pounds!"

BASS AND THREADFIN SHAD

Texas bass anglers will bombard you with a variety of theories as to why surface schools of black bass are caught during summer and fall months on certain Lone Star reservoirs. According to Texas Parks and Wildlife Biologist Paul Seidensticker, the schooling phenomenon hinges on the life cycle of threadfin shad.

"The threadfin shad feed on algae near the surface and, when bass tear into them from below, they create a surface disturbance easily visible during calm days," Seidensticker said.

The fact that the first schoolie bass of the season are usually very small fish is attributable to the growth rate of the shad. Early in the school season, the shad are tiny and only small bass are interested. As the shad grow, they attract bigger bass.

FISHING BEST NEAR HOME

Where's the best bass fishing in your state? Probably as close as the nearest farm pond. At least that's what a survey by the North Carolina Division of Inland Fisheries found. The farm ponds produced .46 legal bass per angler hour. Next best were rivers and streams at .25 bass per hour. Reservoirs produced .22 per hour and lakes were last with .17. So how come everybody continues to fish lakes?

Brainy Bluegills

Fish researchers have found bluegills to be smarter than largemouth bass. In various "fish intelligence" tests, bass did not learn to do tasks as quickly as bluegills. In hook-avoidance tests bass made more errors than bluegills. In all tests of this nature, researchers found bluegill intelligence to be far superior to bass.

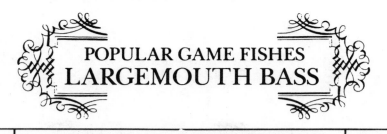
Noisy Worms Catch More Bass

Every dedicated bass angler rates plastic worms among his top offerings. They are bass-catchers of the highest order.

However, since worms are traditionally "quiet" lures, instilling some type of noise-making capability into them will make them much more productive.

The easiest way is to make use of a pair of sliding sinkers on the line instead of one. If you determine that you need one-quarter ounce of weight on the line to take the worm to the desired depth, use two one-eighth-ounce sinkers. Similarly, if one-half ounce is needed, use two one-quarter-ounce sinkers.

Thread the sinkers onto your line in the usual manner, one right above the other. When you retrieve the worm across the bottom, or through cover, the two sinkers will repeatedly "click" against each other, giving bass a sound as well as a visual cue to home in on.

BASS GETTING FLEECED

In sheep country you may run across a sign that reads: "Eat More Sheep—10,000 Coyotes Can't Be Wrong."

Like sheep, bass are in the same stew.

At one southern reservoir, a study during bass spawning showed that bass larva made up 41 percent of the diet of small green sunfish plus 36 percent of larger bluegill food. Bass eggs were also popular items with sunfish, including longear sunfish. In fact, longears were recorded to have stomach contents up to 70 percent of which were newly hatched bass.

Bluegills were the heaviest eaters of bass eggs, consuming 50 percent eggs in their total intake at times.

If bass could talk they'd probably tell fishermen to eat more sunfish, they taste just like bass!

STRIPER STRIFE

The emergence of the striped bass as a major game fish in fresh water has excited many anglers but angered others. Many feel the striper is detrimental to other fishes, especially black bass.

"Yes, a striper might eat a black bass," admitted Bob Kemp, director of fisheries for the Texas Parks and Wildlife Department, "but so will another black bass."

Generally, the striper is no threat to other game species. It is an open-water predator that lives where other fish do not. This is one reason it is stocked in many reservoirs—to take advantage of that unused water. Another reason is it preys on baitfish too large for other predators; its primary food source is gizzard shad, which grow up to about 17 inches.

Florida biologists found that stripers and hybrids significantly reduce the shad population, which in turn helps other game species. In one lake the crappie population almost doubled after the shad declined.

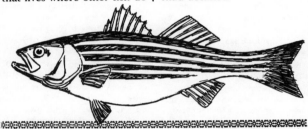

DRAGGING FOR BASS

To stir bass into a feeding frenzy, try this tip used by Lake Ontario fishermen. Drag a light anchor off your boat so that it digs into the bottom, kicking up silt and debris and uprooting crayfish, nymphs and larvae. A short distance behind the anchor, drift live minnows or crayfish on a light line with just enough weight to reach bottom. The cloud of sediment and dislodged food stirred up by the dragging anchor attracts the bass, and it seldom takes long for them to find your bait floating behind the commotion.

★

Nylon monofilament absorbs about 8 percent water, and if you have some old "set" or kinky line, simply take it off the reel, roll it on a stick or spool and soak it in water overnight. According to the Zebco and DuPont people, there's a good chance the line will be limp and supple the next day and ready to replace on the reel.

BE PREPARED

When angling, it's not always possible to take along all the equipment you own, but I usually make sure I bring a couple of flyrods on almost every outing. Sometimes they're never taken out of the car while I'm bass fishing. Other times they've saved me from being skunked.

I recall one pretty October afternoon when my young daughter and I decided to hit a favorite farm pond. While she fished for bluegills, I took my bass rod, but couldn't get a hit. After about 25 minutes, she walked over to the side of the pond I was fishing and scared up some grasshoppers and black crickets. A number of swirls arose in the pond as the bass went for them. I quickly tied a black popper onto a flyrod, and as she scared up the insects, I cast out my popper. It wasn't exactly a perfect way of getting the fish to bite, but I caught 10 bass in an hour.

HIGH-AND-DRY BASS BUGS

Even deerhair bass bugs eventually get waterlogged and refuse to float. Or they soak up just enough water to float in the surface film instead of on it, killing their popping or skipping action.

There is an easy way to postpone this agony. Before fishing any fly with a clipped deerhair body, rub liberal amounts of Mucilin, line dressing, or paste fly floatant into its bottom side. This initial dressing will keep the bug sitting pretty for a long time.

If you are catching fish, or if the bug gets waterlogged without any help, squeeze the excess water out with a handkerchief, then re-dress it with the same floatant.

Night Bassin'

Many bass fishermen head for the barn at dark, thinking that bass do not see well at night and won't strike. Not so.

Even though a bass's vision is restricted at night, its lateral line acts as a kind of radar and easily picks up any disturbance on or in the water. Once the bass has zeroed in on the sound waves, he has a target and will go for it just as he would in the light of day.

Lures that vibrate will, of course, cause the most underwater disturbance, and these are most effective. However, balsa or plastic lures may be drilled to accommodate small BBs that produce rattling noises.

NO HOPE

My wife and I love to fish, and we are constantly on the lookout for good new spots. There is a small pond in southern Oregon that has always looked promising, but a sign posted there read simply: NOPE.

When we heard that the pond had a new owner, we expectantly drove up to see if the sign had been removed. It had. But in its place was a new one reading: STILL NOPE.

FINDING WINTER BASS

When fishing for bass in the winter, there are several ways to find fish: Remember that the southernmost creek will have the warmest water. Try to locate spots on which the sun will shine all day long. Run a lake and look for a long shoreline. Find one big rock, half out of the water. This serves as a break, and the sun will cause the rock to generate heat, making the surrounding water at least 2 degrees warmer. Hunt for boat houses with metal roofs close to the water. They'll also heat up the area. Remember, a 2- or 3-degree change in the water can help everyone's fishing. So look for the hot spots.

★

After bass spawn the big females leave nest-tending to smaller males who will average under four pounds. (There is no record of a male bass weighing over six pounds.) So, the time is comparatively short when you can catch the monster females from a spawning bed.

PADDLE, OAR SHOVEL FOR BASS

Almost every largemouth fisherman has had a trophy fish dive to the bottom after inhaling the lure. If the lake's bottom is covered with weeds, the monster fish will quickly bury itself in the thickest section. Eight- and 10-pound-test line is not designed for uprooting huge clumps of rooted vegetation, and it breaks.

A bass need not be lost in shallow waters. While the angler keeps a firm strain on the line, his fishing companion should take the boat's oar and dig the weeds loose. If done properly, a clump of bass and weeds will come floating up. It is extremely important that the angler constantly keeps a strain on the fish.

The partner will then net the bass with the weeds. The landing method may not be pretty, but it sure is productive.

BASS PROS DISCOVERY

Professional bass anglers fishing the fertile waters of the St. Lawrence River during the 10th Annual Bass Masters Classic may have unintentionally revolutionized northern pike fishing tactics.

For generations the spoon, usually in red and white, has been the favorite lure for taking the long-snouted fish of the weedbeds. Sometimes a strip of porkrind is added, and in recent years anglers have mixed in some minnow-shaped lures such as the Rebel and Rapala with their spoon fishing.

But the bass-fishing pros had trouble keeping the always-hungry pike away from their favorite lure, the plastic worm. Bass fishing guide Zell Rowland of Texas landed 11 unwanted pike the first day of the three-day tournament and five the next—all on plastic worms. Color may or may not be important, but Rowland was fishing grape-colored worms the first day and black ones the second.

In clear water a large or colored bobber may spook fish causing them not to bite. On your next trip to the tackle store pick up some clear plastic floats. Get the bubbles in different sizes, and always use the smallest you can get by with for casting and bait suspension.

Texas-Rig Trick

If you've been working a Texas-rigged plastic worm in all the right places and bass still refuse to pick it up, reverse the bullet-shaped sliding sinker. The concave end that usually fits over the worm head will now drag through the water first, digging up silt and mud from bottom cover. This trick is especially effective during spawning, when the sinker stirring through a spawning bed will draw strikes from enraged bass. But it works just as well later on in the season when a silent, crawling worm isn't quite enough.

MODIFY YOUR BUZZBAIT

Have you ever been fishing with a buzzbait and just can't seem to get those bass to hit consistently, even when using a trailer hook or porkrind trailer? Put a Rapala or imitation minnow on the end of the buzzbait. Tie it about a foot behind the buzzbait. The noise the buzzer creates should attract bass, and the trailer should be too enticing for them to refuse your presentation.

A MATTER OF DEGREES

Bass fishermen know the importance of water surface temperature when on the trail of trophy fish. There are several good electronic surface temperature gauges on the market, but they all have a common flaw as far as I'm concerned: The cost is in excess of $75. You can get the same information a cheaper way.

Photographers use a dial-type thermometer when they are processing film or prints. It is extremely accurate, and it responds within four to five seconds. It features a two-inch dial that is easy to read, has a five- to six-inch probe for easy measurement, and is made of stainless steel so that it can be kept in your tacklebox. Most also have a loop so you can attach a lanyard or cord to keep from losing it overboard. Best of all, it costs around $15.

★

On a calm day when you just know topwater lures should be taking bass but aren't, try a plastic worm rigged without any weight so it will float on top. Snake it over, around and through shore cover bordering deep water.

WILD SHINERS

It's no secret that large shiners take large bass, but the shiners must be kept lively. Although small hatchery-raised shiners bought in bait shops are easy to keep alive, wild shiners are not.

When catching shiners, handle them very, very carefully. If you let a shiner flop about on the bank or in the boat, it will soon die. Do not handle them with bare hands—especially dry hands.

I use a trout net to lift the shiner out of the water. After closing the net around the fish, I hold it gently with one hand while removing the hook with the other. Then I put the shiner directly into a livewell or large aerated bait bucket. Don't try to keep more than a few at one time.

DON'T BE CAUGHT SPEEDING LURES

High-speed reels have been a boon to fishermen who enjoy casting artificial lures. Lures requiring a speedy retrieve are worked almost effortlessly with reels possessing the high gear ratios.

However, with certain lures there are times when speed is not desirable. A case in point is the spinnerbait, which will run shallow on fast retrieves. If the fish are down several feet, the fisherman might be retrieving the lure too quickly. What seems a correct cranking speed can actually be running the lure too shallow.

Many times, especially in hot weather, the fish are deeper. To reach these fish with lures such as spinners and spoons, the angler must consciously think about reducing his speed. This enables the angler to reach the big ones lurking in deep water.—

★

Pork rind used by fishermen is a by-product of meat packers dealing in hogs. Also, it's an old standby of anglers who add a strip to a weedless spoon for added attraction.

PIONEER OF BASS PLUNKING

"Inch for inch and pound for pound the gamest fish that swims," wrote Dr. James Henshall, acclaimed as the father of black bass fishing.

Born in Baltimore, Maryland, in 1836, James Henshall graduated from medical school and eventually moved to Cincinnati, where he established a medical practice. In addition to being a physician, he was also a naturalist, fish culturist and angling writer. His classic *Book of the Black Bass* was published in 1881.

Dr. Henshall worked with the U.S. Bureau of Fisheries from 1896 to 1917 helping to develop improved methods for the propagation of black bass and other gamefishes. His fondness for sportfishing resulted in the development of many fine fishing rods.

POWERFUL BASS

There are any number of reasons why trophy bass are so hard to catch, including the fact that giant largemouths are relatively rare to start with and tend to eat less often than do smaller fish.

Elroy Krueger agrees with those theories; but he also knows firsthand about the sheer brute strength of monster bass.

Krueger, who owns Elroy's Fishing Hole, a tackle store at Universal City, Texas, has a 10-pound bigmouth finning in an aquarium in his store.

The bass is a popular attraction for customers, but Krueger dreads the periodic cleanups and water changes required by the aquarium.

"You can't believe how strong a totally green 10-pound bass is," Krueger reports. "In the aquarium, it's easy enough to hem the bass up and pin him against the wall, then get your thumb onto his lower lip; but I don't think there's a man alive who can hold onto that bass."

Big bass are hard to hook in the first place, and their strength makes them hard to land even when they're solidly hooked.

TOPWATER TIPS

When searching for topwater schooling stripers, wear polarized sunglasses and a hat with a brim as a shield against the glare from the sun. Wide-angle binoculars of 7X to 10X are also useful for spotting thrashing fish and shad skipping on the surface, which can indicate stripers lurking below. Sea gulls can tip you off to feeding striped bass, too. Keep conversation to a minimum when searching out schooling stripers, and you might hear them gulping down shad.

When you locate feeding fish, get to them quickly and throw bucktails, topwater plugs or shallow-diving minnow imitations. Hold onto your rod tightly. The strike of a surface-feeding striper can be savage.

When fishing for freshwater striped bass remember that this landlocked oceanic species is a roamer, apt to be anywhere, so you've got to keep moving and searching. The hybrid striper is more stationary and will hang out in much the same cover as largemouth bass.

Avenues to Bass

A knowledgeable angler takes more than a passing interest in the muskrat. The constant swimming of muskrats creates a channel that many times leads to a large, deep hole in the bank. Cast right to the hole and let your bait sit there a moment before moving it. You might find more than a muskrat there. These muskrat runs create convenient openings when fishing thick, weedy areas. So, look upon the muskrat as the architect of avenues to bass.

The Crazy Bass

Recently a young lady took her mother for a rowboat ride on one of Virginia's scenic lakes. All was peace and quiet until suddenly the water erupted and a four-pound black bass jumped into her arms. She dropped the oars and, after a brief struggle, subdued it. When she told the story back at the dock and displayed her trophy, her audience grinned. Here was a fish story that topped all others. They suggested that the girl had an overactive imagination. Finally, angry because no one would believe her, she yelled, "It's true. Ask mother. She doesn't even drink!"

CONTROLLED TROLLING

In Texas, where black bass are the monarchs among freshwater gamefish, fishermen who troll are generally held in contempt by purists. So guides at sprawling Toledo Bend Reservoir on the Texas-Louisiana border have worked out a trolling-drifting method they call "strolling."

"We first started strolling for crappies over thick moss beds," explains veteran guide Bill Fox of Hemphill. "Then we discovered it is effective on striped bass.

"Strolling is nothing but a controlled drift, using an electric motor to move and guide the boat. For crappies you stroll over submerged moss beds where the vegetation is several feet under the surface. Use small jigs tossed out behind the boat. Experiment with line length and boat speed until you find the combination that keeps the jig just above the moss."

To stroll for Toledo Bend's abundant striped bass, Fox first locates a school of the big bruisers on his graph recorder. He lowers a one-half- or three-fourths-ounce jig down to where the fish are and strolls.

CATCH MORE SMALLMOUTHS

The most productive smallmouth baits on streams are hellgrammites and crayfish. These may be presented in various ways. Here is the method that many Susquehanna River anglers use to increase their catches:

Cut off the tip of the hellgrammite's tail to keep it from anchoring itself in the bottom and then hook it under the collar.

With a crayfish, remove the claws to prevent it from holding fast on the bottom. Run the hook through the back just in front of the tail and bring the barb out through the first or second tail segment.

Rigged this way, these baits will move freely with the current. Fish them deep for best success.

POPULAR GAME FISHES

TROUT

TERRESTRIAL TIME

Trout fishermen fully recognize terrestrials as a major food source for trout: Grasshopper, cricket, woolly worm and ant imitations are popular fly patterns, but they are only part of terrestrial fishing.

Beetles, horseflies, bees, jassids, deerflies and leaf hoppers are readily eaten by trout. Though more prolific in the South, these land-based insects are abundant from early summer through fall in most regions. Terrestrial patterns are often favored when other well-known fly hatches subside.

Deerfly, horsefly and large beetle patterns, Size 12 through Size 8, are good flies to rely on. Their large silhou-

ettes attract large trout.

Before loading your fly boxes with counterfeit terrestrials, check the water you plan to fish for their equal: Certain terrestrials appear more frequently on some streams than on others.

When fishing terrestrials as drys, a gentle twitch may occasionally be necessary to urge sluggish trout into striking.

Finicky trout such as the wild brown might demand your matching the natural in size and color as closely as possible. Try a smaller size fly if you get many refusals.

Though easy to tie, terrestrial patterns do not require expensive or the best dry fly hackle, since they float in the surface film rather than on it.

Trout Unlimited's Philosophy

We believe that trout and salmon fishing isn't just fishing for trout and salmon. It's fishing for sport rather than for food, where the true enjoyment of the sport lies in the challenge, the lore and the battle of wits, not necessarily the full creel. It's the feeling of satisfaction that comes from limiting your kill instead of killing your limit. It's communing with nature where the chief reward is a refreshed body and a contented soul, where a license is a permit to use—not abuse—to enjoy—not destroy our cold-water fishery. It's subscribing to the proposition that what's good for trout and salmon is good for the fishermen and that managing trout and salmon for themselves rather than for the fishermen is fundamental to the solution of our trout and salmon problems. It's appreciating our fishery resource, respecting fellow anglers and giving serious thought to tomorrow.

Soft-Mouth Myth

Many flyfishermen believe that grayling have soft mouths. In fact, the mouth of a grayling is as hard and bony as that of a trout. The myth came about because of the way a grayling takes a fly.

In most cases, trout will suck a fly in from below and the rise form indicates a take. Grayling, on the other hand, have a habit of rolling on a fly, that is, coming out of the water next to a floating fly and taking it on the way down. Many anglers strike too soon and miss the fish or hook it poorly, and the hook comes out.

Learn to wait that extra split second before setting the hook. With a little practice you'll get the hang of it.

MYSTERY TROUT

The case of the silver trout has been argued for decades in New Hampshire. Its continued existence is dubious, and some even question whether it ever existed. But the silver did exist—and in great numbers, though its range was extremely limited. It was found only in New Hampshire's Dublin Lake, at the foot of towering Mount Monadnock. It has never been discovered in any other body of water. Doubtless the extraordinary depth and cold temperatures of Dublin Lake created an environment made to order for this opalescent fish.

The Dublin trout was not inclined toward runtiness—many specimens of five pounds or better were taken throughout the last century.

It was described and cataloged by naturalist Louis Agassiz in 1884 and named in his honor, *Salvelinus agassizii*.

While silver trout numbers steadily declined at the turn of the century, it was still common as late as 1912.

The silver was not fished to extinction, nor was pollution the cause of its disappearance. The voracious yellow perch—noted eaters of the spawn and fry of trout—caused the disaster.

Many claim that the silver trout still survives and has moved to greater depths.

From time to time there are rumors of someone catching one of these rare fish, and two years ago a strange "green-and-yellow trout" was taken through the ice. Unfortunately it was not observed by scientists.

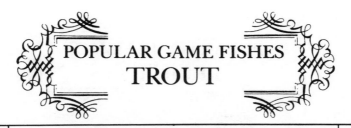

O Sir, doubt not that angling is an Art; Is it not an Art to deceive a Trout with an Artificial Fly? A Trout that is more sharp-sighted than any hawk you have named!
—*Izaak Walton*

Izaak Walton, who wrote the centuries-old classic *The Compleat Angler*, was a wealthy, self-made man who retired in 1643 when he was 50 years old. He spent the rest of his life fishing and lived to the age of 90.

So keep fishing. It could be that angling is the secret to longevity.

HOMEMADE SPONGE BAITS

One of the most popular bait imitations used in drift-fishing for rainbows and steelhead is cut sponge. Various colors are used, from hot pink to yellow, depending on water conditions and the fish's preference. You can buy precut, packaged sponge balls, but with the nature of driftfishing—lots of snags—it can be expensive.

For my home-cut baits I buy two big, medium-coarse sponges used for car washing in canary yellow and pink. That size lasts a couple of seasons.

First run them under the faucet, then wring them out. This eliminates static cling. Then slice the sponge as if it were a loaf of bread. Cut the slices into half-inch cubes, then round them out with a sharp pair of sewing scissors.

In muddy water the sponge will often work better than real spawn bags, and an added bonus is that it is very durable.

The Scholarly Flyfisherman

To flyfish with a modicum of intelligence one must know something about meteorology, optics, hydraulics, chemistry, biology and entomology. Even so, a trout with its little fish brain can make a fool out of man.

Pursuing the meteorological approach, it is usually a waste of time to fish on a falling barometer. The ideal water temperature is from 50° to 65° F. You might as well give up if it hits 74° F. or over. As the water temperature rises the oxygen content of the water is reduced, and our finny friend gets sluggish and loses interest in feeding.

Entomology explains why fish will rise to flies or why they won't.

A female fly deposits her eggs on the water. They sink to the bottom and hatch into larvae which at times attach themselves to submerged objects. The young insect or nymph rises to the surface to get air. The artificial wet fly imitates this action.

Once on the surface the nymph unfolds its wings and it at times floats downstream quite a distance while drying or developing. This action is imitated with a dry fly.

The art is in the way we present the fly. The slightest cross-pull or drag motion imparted to the fly will usually make the fish refuse it. A cast should lay the leader on the water in a loop causing the fly to drift naturally over the fish ahead of the line.

A trout usually points upstream into the current, and a fisherman approaching from downstream has a distinct advantage. Now in optics the surface of the water looks like a mirror to our fish, with underwater objects reflected in it everywhere except in a circular area directly overhead. This area is like a window to the trout. The closer the fish is to the surface the smaller the window and likewise the smaller the chance that he sees you.

Bending of light by water—refraction—makes a man standing six feet above the surface, and 15 feet away, look approximately 15 inches tall. At 30 feet he looks about nine inches tall.

A fish has no eyelids and is blinded when the sun shines in his eyes. The smart fisherman uses the sun so that the fish is blinded to you, but not to the fly.

SPOOK FISHING

Trout streams dependent on snowpack are noticeably low and extremely clear by late summer and early autumn. It makes trout wary and difficult to catch, and many anglers don't try, believing that when leaves turn gold, trout go cold. Too bad. With a different approach, this time of year can offer exciting trout action.

Toward the end of summer, trout pool up where water is deepest, seldom venturing into runs, which are no more than trickles. Just the hint of a shadow on the surface of these clear pools and trout panic.

Let them! In fact, encourage it by walking up on a pool and letting the trout spook. They'll dash for the protection of undercut banks. Once they have, move off 10 to 20 feet, take a comfortable squatting position, and wait. If you can see the pool's surface, you're too close. Move back farther. It takes about 15 minutes before trout start budging. Still cautious, they'll hang close.

Don't bump the ground. Sound waves will send trout scrambling again. Maintaining a low profile, cast just to the water's edge, letting the fly flop over the bank and into the water. Keep false casts close to the ground. All the trout should see is the fly. Strikes are felt, not seen.

As a rule, you'll take no more than one trout per pool, without giving the pool a half hour or so to settle.

Brownie Points

Some brown trout enthusiasts in Ontario fought bitterly to keep migrating rainbow trout below dams in Great Lakes streams, fearing the rainbows would wipe out the browns. Now that rainbows and browns share many of the same waters, biologists checking found no browns in the rainbows' stomachs, but plenty of small rainbows in the stomachs of the browns.

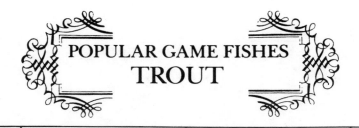

GLUE LEADERS TO FLYLINES

One hassle for flyfishermen is attaching the leader to the flyline. It involves fish-scaring loops or the difficult-to-tie nail knot. Both hang up on rod guides constantly. Here is a better method.

You will need a tube of waterproof superglue (my preference is Duro-brand Super Glue made by Loctite Corporation), a dubbing needle and, of course, a flyline and leader. The needle should be slightly larger in diameter than the leader butt.

Begin by clipping any loop off the leader butt and the tip of the flyline down to sound material. Push the end of the flyline over the tip of the needle until a minimum three-eighths-inch penetration is achieved. Remove the needle. Coat the end of the clipped leader butt with glue and insert it into the cavity in the end of the line. Roll the connection between the thumb and index finger. Let set a minute. Pull on the line and leader to check the bond. If the connection fails, reapply the glue and roll the bond. Some glues need a precoat of glue to achieve a lasting bond.

FISH BEHIND SPAWNERS

When trout are spawning (brookies and browns in the fall, rainbows and cutthroats in the spring) they can often be caught on streamer flies, which they probably take more out of territoriality than hunger. But there's another trick to fishing a spawning run that many anglers are not aware of.

In a stream with two kinds of trout, fish that aren't spawning may lie just downstream of a spawning area to pick off eggs that have been washed free in the current. For instance, when rainbows are spawning in the spring, look downstream for lurking browns. The best flies to use are patterns tied in pinks and yellows.

Flyfishing Puzzle

You're fishing for wild brown trout in a clear stream under a bright summer sky. Tapered down to a 6X tippet, you've caught and released a few eight-inch fish on a No. 20 Cinnamon Ant. Suddenly you notice several large trout move into open water and hold there. Meanwhile, the small trout start feeding greedily. To hook a couple of those big trout, you should:

a) *go right on fishing the Cinnamon Ant.*
b) *switch to a No. 20 Black Ant.*
c) *use a No. 16 Adams fly.*
d) *use a No. 12 Ant and sink it.*
e) *snip back to a 3X tippet and use a No. 6 nymph or streamer.*

ANALYSIS: Your best bet is d) followed by c), a), b), then e). Some unseen event—a sudden shower, cows fording the stream, a gust of wind—has launched extra food downstream. As opportunists, brown trout feed hardest when food is easiest to get, which explains the appearance of the big fish and the excitement in the small fish. Trout, however, prefer to feed economically, taking the most food for the least effort. Large trout usually leave the tiny morsels to the small trout, preferring bigger bites.

Nevertheless, while a large nymph or a streamer might work in turbid water, it would probably spook these clear-water trout. You could continue to take small trout on the Cinnamon Ant with a slim chance at a big one, but switching to a Black Ant would cost you time without improving your chances.

The No. 16 Adams might work. It's between tiny morsel and big bite. But the No. 12 Ant is just the sort of big bite large trout like, and bringing it to them underwater would help them conserve energy.

FLYLINE STORAGE

Line driers aren't particularly popular today, largely because today's flylines rarely require drying. But there's a good reason why every serious fly angler should have one: Good lines are expensive, and they deteriorate if kept on the reels at the end of a season.

There's no better way to store flylines than to wind them on a drier, particularly if you have several lines. Most driers can accommodate about eight lines without crowding. If you put a tag on the end of each line or its backing, you can easily identify both the line weights and the reels to which they belong.

BRANCHING OUT

Every angler experiences a bad day of fishing once in a while. During a hot morning on the Big Hole River in Montana a few years ago, I was having just this problem.

After three hours of hard fishing, with only three small rainbows and a whitefish to show for my efforts, I spied a stream feeding the river on the opposite bank. With nothing to lose, I waded across and began fishing the 12-foot-wide stream.

The next hour and a half produced 23 fish, 16 of which were browns. The smallest fish I landed during that time was a 10-inch rainbow, and many of the fish were in the 15- to 16-inch range.

Upon further exploration, I found that my new stream wasn't that at all, but simply a branch of the Big Hole that separated from the main river, flowed some 250 yards and then rejoined the main channel, forming an island but looking like a feeder stream.

Since then, I have rescued similarly poor days on the Bitterroot, Henry's Fork and others by seeking out "branches."

Wading Staff Cache

After experimenting with various shoulder straps and harnesses designed to carry wading staffs between periods of use, I concluded the simplest thing to do was discard them when they are not required.

During the next few trips to favored steelhead haunts I carried a sharp hatchet in the pouch of my fishing vest. With it I fashioned a half dozen sturdy staffs at each main crossing point and concealed them where my companions and I could find them easily. This gave us a double supply since we did not always return by the same route.

Many of those original staffs are still in use to this day.

PRACTICAL LEADER CONNECTION

A smooth connection between leader and flyline is an important factor in the flycaster's presentation. Most commonly it is achieved by nail-knotting the two together, and while the end result is good, changing leaders in this manner is a pain.

The Orvis Fly Fishing School in Manchester, Vermont, teaches a better way. They simply nail-knot a six-inch piece of 25- to 30-pound leader material to the end of the flyline. A loop like those found on snelled hooks is then tied into the opposite end. The connecting leader must also have a loop (most commercially tied leaders come that way).

To connect the leader itself, pass the loop attached to the flyline through the loop on the leader; reaching through the flyline loop, grab the butt section of the leader and pull the leader up through, until the tippet passes the loop. Now just pull the loops together by tugging on the flyline and the butt section in opposite directions.

The result is a smooth transition from line to leader, one that can be easily changed.

THREADING WITH E STRINGS

When musicians replace the steel strings in a guitar, they must clip the excess string from the tuning gear. The fine wire of the B or E strings, when looped, makes an excellent flytier's threading tool. The ends can be glued into a pin-sized hole made in the end of a section of small dowel. The dowel becomes a handle.

The extra clippings from one guitar restringing will provide you with enough wire for many threading tools.

Net Results

Most of the "big ones that got away" were lost during netting. The following tips will make landing fish easier.

Pick a landing net with a dark nylon netting—the dark color is less likely to frighten the fish.

If a second person is doing the netting, place the net in the water well in advance of bringing the fish alongside the boat. Always try to net the fish headfirst, never tailfirst. Normally it is best to wait until the fish is well played out before trying to net it. Don't make wild sweeping motions with the net; make a slow sweep or leave the net stationary. Instinctively fish look for cover to escape and will often swim into the net.

Once the fish is in the net, lift it onboard, keeping the handle of the net vertical. This serves two purposes: It causes the netting to close in around the fish and it also prevents leverage working against the fisherman.

I have seen many net handles break under the weight of heavy salmon when an angler tried to lift the fish from the water with the handle held horizontally. Consider the mathematics: Weight × the arm = force. If the fish weighs 25 pounds and the fisherman is holding the net handle at four feet, it takes 100 foot-pounds of force to lift the fish if the net is held horizontally. Lifting the net straight up vertically requires lifting only 25 pounds and is a lot easier.

TROUT ID

The trout, a member of the family Salmonidae, has one feature not present in many fishes: the adipose fin, a fatty flap without rays between the dorsal and caudal fins.

Differentiating among the chinook, coho and rainbow mouths. Coho salmon usually have a black or very dark gray mouth and tongue, while their gums are grayish-white. The chinook has a black mouth, tongue and gums. The confusion usually comes when trying to determine

trout when they are in the silvery stage is difficult for some anglers. Most trout have white which is a rainbow and which is the coho salmon. The answer lies in the mouth.

A LITTLE DAB WILL DO YA

Flyfishermen who use color codes to mark loose leader tippets by size or flyreel spools with the AFTMA weight of the line are on the right track. But it's a mistake to use an arbitrary code that has to be memorized and thus can be forgotten at a critical moment. It makes more sense to have the number of letters in the color the same as the number to which the color has been assigned: red for No. 3, blue for 4, green for 5, yellow for 6, and combinations of these four colors for higher numbers.

The lack of colors for 1 and 2 is no problem; the finest leader diameter is .003, and those who use the rarely seen No. 2 flyline can leave that reel spool unmarked.

If you like to know the X rating of your leader as well as its diameter, simply subtract the diameter from 11. When using two colors for designating an even number above 6, it may be less confusing to use different colors than two marks of the same color (e.g., red and green rather than blue and blue for No. 8).

Those with color vision problems may want to select a different set of colors or shades, say tan for No. 3. Any grouping is okay as long as the number of letters is the same as the number to which it is assigned.

The small bottles of colored enamel sold in model stores are excellent for marking. Only the four basic colors need be bought. On a reel spool, clean off a one-quarter-inch spot with some alcohol and apply a dab of color with a toothpick. For leader tippets, dip about an inch of the end into the bottle. It will be cut off when tying in the tippet. It may seem unnecessary to mark spooled leader material, but a spot of color in a recess on the back of the spool will come in handy if labels come off.

TINSEL TIES

The story goes that a fly-tier, feeling melancholy at Christmas time, plucked some garland from the tree and wrapped it around the shank of a salmon fly.

A few years later an enterprising tier produced his own tinsel that was superior to the original in both strength and resistance to corrosion.

Today most every mail-order fly shop lists tinsel in various colors, sizes and textures, at a profitable price.

However, the development of another synthetic has made the original tinsel—the kind that can be plucked from the tree and never missed—useful again. That product is head cement, or lacquer.

After the Christmas-tree tinsel is wound on the shank, apply a liberal coat of lacquer. It forms a protective coat that prevents breakage and seals out tarnishing from water.

Since most tiers recommend a coat of lacquer over fly-tying tinsel, the only thing a tier who uses tree-trimming tinsel is missing is the expense.

Open and Shut Case

Northwest steelheaders use pencil lead as a sinker weight because it resists snagging on the gravel stream bottom. The soft cylindrically shaped lead can be obtained as a bulk coil. Cut varying lengths to obtain more or less weight.

Some pencil lead has a hollow center, making it easy to slip onto monofilament line. To cut lengths of pencil lead without closing the hole with each cut, use a pair of dog toenail clippers. These make a clean cut with a center hole open and undistorted. Toenail clippers can be purchased at pet shops.

More Trout, Less Money

During the dark ages of fishery management, when rainbow and brown trout had to be captured and hand-squeezed for eggs and sperm in order to provide fish for stocking, about 50 percent success in hatch rate occurred. That was just before 1950.

Since then, a test showing when trout were ripe was standardized: when fish held in natural spawning positions leaked eggs without any human pressure, they were ready.

Eggs and sperm are currently being taken using an air method. About four pounds of compressed air is injected into ripe female trout and eggs get pumped from the body. Suction is then applied after eggs are extracted to remove air in the belly. Sperm too is taken by suction from males.

Eggs taken this way flow into a soft net. By mixing eggs and sperm in a basin with a feather and placing fertilized eggs in a hatching jar, 90 percent hatch rate can be achieved.

Despite inflation, it's possible we're now getting more trout for less money.

THE DISAPPEARING SIX

Six different species of rare western trout that seldom make headlines are fighting for their small niche against total extinction.

One, the *Arizona native trout*, is gold to olive-yellow with a yellow cutthroat slash; most fin tips are white. Larger roundish spots decorate its sides. This fish possesses the largest dorsal fin of any American trout.

Lahontan cutthroat trout have large spots distributed evenly on the entire body. The gold, crimson and orange colorations of Lahontans are dull, if present at all. Nevada and California have limited populations.

New Mexico and Arizona harbor very few of what are called *gila trout*, which were only recognized as a new species in 1950, as they were on the brink of extinction. And the brassy yellow-sided *Colorado River cutthroat*, which sometimes has red or pink bands under large spots, is found only in a small area divided by Colorado, Wyoming, New Mexico, Arizona and Utah.

The *Greenback cutthroat trout* of central Colorado, which displays strikingly large round and oblong spots, sometimes with a blood-red coloring, is another priceless fish getting more scarce. So is the nearly spotless California *Paiute trout*.

Pure-strain populations are undermined by breeding with other trout species; habitat destruction creates unfavorable conditions for rare ones. Even trout that can't breed with endangered fish keep numbers down by competing for food.

ATTRACTOR TACTIC

One of the more frustrating experiences encountered when casting hardware lures in clear water is to see a big trout or bass following but not striking your lure.

If changing lures and retrieve speeds doesn't produce more strikes, here's another tactic that may bring dramatic results: Rig a trailing wet fly, nymph or streamer 18 inches or so behind the hardware lure. Remove the treble hook from a spoon, tie on a length of leader material and your fly. Fish are attracted and aroused by the flash of the hardware lure and slam the smaller, more natural-looking trailing fly.

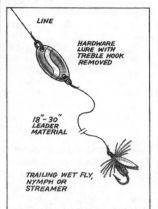

This is also an effective method for fishing wet flies, nymphs and streamers with a spinning outfit. Besides serving as an attractor, the lure provides the weight for making long casts and getting the fly to the desired depth.

Greasing the Front Helps

Greasing a flyline was once both a tradition and a necessity. The modern dry flyline floats very well but will pick up the fly even better if the first few feet above the leader are greased. Greasing helps attain a longer drag-free float in streams where the current tends to suck the front of the flyline under. Don't use too much flotant or it will pick up dirt.

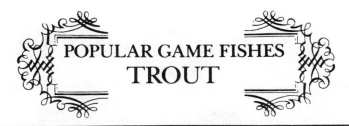

Trout Bonus

With the huge number of people angling for trout, there just aren't enough fish to go around. The solution can very well be catch-and-release.

Statistics provided by Herm Covey, a district wildlife manager from Massachusetts, indicate that in a catch-and-release-only zone, managers can conservatively expect an average of 2½ fish catches per trout stocked. This number is even more impressive when compared to a Michigan study that estimated only 40 to 45 percent of stocked trout were caught each year in open waters. The comparison between the two management practices translates into more than five times as many trout catches in catch-and-release-only waters as in open waters.

Covey points out that in appropriate waters, a catch-and-release philosophy also promotes the reestablishment of a native, self-regenerating population of wild trout.

Catch-and-release is even being practiced where it is not required by law. Quality trout fishing is becoming more widespread, larger trout are available, and the numbers of catchable fish are increasing dramatically.

FISHING I.Q.: TROUT WATER

Browns, rainbows, brook trout: You can find one or more of these species in each of the rivers listed here. Now, can you locate the rivers?

(1)	Ausable	A.	New Hampshire
(2)	Babine	B.	New York
(3)	Batten Kill	C.	Pennsylvania
(4)	Beaver Kill	D.	Michigan
(5)	Chimehuin	E.	Montana
(6)	Gacka	F.	British Columbia
(7)	Itchen	G.	California
(8)	Klamath	H.	England
(9)	Letort	I.	Yugoslavia
(10)	Madison	J.	New Zealand
(11)	Tongariro	K.	Argentina

ANSWERS: (1) D; (2) F; (3) A; (4) B; (5) K; (6) I; (7) H; (8) G; (9) C; (10) E; (11) J.

Go Small

A friend and I were fishing a small lake for trout. I was flyfishing, he was spinfishing. I was catching fish; he was casting and retrieving—endlessly. When we laid our two lures side-by-side on the boat seat, what struck us was the difference in size. I was using a relatively large fly, he was using a relatively small spinner. Still, his lure was four to five times larger than mine.

Action, color and weight of lures are important. But when selecting spinning or trolling lures, keep in mind the size of the trout's last meal: It was probably an insect or small baitfish. You will have a better chance of making your lure his next meal if you go small.

•

The quickest way to set the hook when fishing a nymph is to snap the rod tip down. It's faster than trying to lift the rod and much more effective.

FISH SHELTERS

Scattered through streams and lakes there will be a number of small holes or shelter locations where a good fish or two will make its headquarters. Try them on days when the more obvious places fail to produce.

In fast water, it is easy to locate these shelter spots—just look in white and tumbling water for the dark-surfaced areas. It will be quieter and perhaps deeper. Trout lurk in such spots because food is washed into them or along the outer edges. Also, the fish can rest without battling the current all the time.

A short line is called for here. The rough water surrounding the hole means that you can get in close, without too much fear of detection, and be in a good position to work it thoroughly. Float a dry fly or manipulate a spinner in the manner intended for these lures—a feat that is almost impossible when fishing a long line in fast water.

Often a trout that ignores flies floated over it will rise to a fly dangled provocatively from the side of a rock. Thus presented, the fly has the advantage of being free from conflicting currents that interfere with the natural drift of a cast fly. Also, the fly touches the water lightly for brief intervals, and most of the time no leader shows at all. It has the completely detached look of a natural insect—and thus is deadly.

TROUT FISHING PARTNERS

A simple, effective way for leapfrogging trout fishing partners to mark their points of entry to the stream is to use a piece of plasticized surveyor's ribbon. This material, in highly visible colors such as red, yellow and orange, is both lightweight and durable. A single length of two or three feet is all each needs (although anyone who fishes with others should place a length in his fishing vest).

When two people are fishing together, one normally walks a few hundred yards upstream (or downstream, depending on the technique they are using) from where his friend began casting. He should tie the ribbon on a convenient limb in a prominent place where it is certain to be noticed by his partner when he reaches that spot. Upon reaching the spot, the fisherman unties the ribbon and carries it with him as he

leapfrogs his partner.

Two fishermen can thus move around each other all day and always be certain they are fishing undisturbed water. This is much simpler than old standbys such as breaking a limb and leaving it on a midstream rock or looking for signs of where one's partner has been wading.

SNEAKY SINK-TIP

When you're fishing with a sink-tip flyline and the wind makes the lake or river choppy, place the rod tip slightly under the water's surface when you retrieve the fly. With the floating portion of the line just under the surface, wave action on the line is removed, and a strike is transmitted more efficiently to your line hand.

NYMPH INDICATOR

It is difficult to fish a nymph and detect delicate takes. This is especially true when fishing upstream with the dead-drift presentation, which is so imitative of the way natural trout foods really behave. As many as four or five fish might inhale and reject the fly before you are sure you have one.

An indicator will help you spot those surreptitious takes. A bright floating focus for your eyes, it will make a small movement each time a fish stops your fly, enabling you to set the hook before the fish can spit it out.

An indicator can be a bit of bright yarn tied to a leader knot coated with fluorescent paint. Or you can buy indicators backed with waterproof stickum to fold over the leader.

One of the best indicators is a Worden's Corky. Designed for steelhead fishermen, it is round, floats, and comes in bright colors. It has a hole drilled through the middle, and you can run it up the leader to any depth and set it by jamming the tip of a toothpick into the hole.

It won't move on the leader, but you'll see it move in the water when a fish takes your nymph. It's about the best indicator you can buy.

★

Most fish should be netted head first. Since they don't swim backward, any surge will carry them deeper into the net. The only exception is when you are using a treble-hooked lure and the fish is big. In that case, the hooks can snag the net and you can't get the fish inside.

GORDON'S QUILL

The still popular Quill Gordon fly was created by Theodore Gordon of New York sometime around the turn of the century. Gordon is considered by many to be the father of American dry-fly fishing, and the Quill Gordon is one of the first American patterns.

The Series Fly

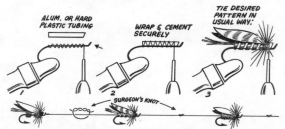

ALUM. OR HARD PLASTIC TUBING

WRAP & CEMENT SECURELY

TIE DESIRED PATTERN IN USUAL WAY:

SURGEON'S KNOT

4 'THREAD' FLIE(S) ON LEADER & USE A PIECE OF MONO & SURGEON'S KNOT FOR 'STOPPER.'

Fishing two or more flies at once is nothing new. However, the droppers are troublesome to tie and prone to tangle. If these are the only reasons you have for avoiding such rigs, here is a solution:

Aluminum tubing available from hobby shops, or hard plastic tubing such as the spray extension that comes with a can of WD-40, serves as a body through which the leader can be passed. The hook to use is a standard Turned-Up Eye.

The flies can be held in place with a short piece of monofilament and a surgeon's knot, or you may add them to the sections when you tie a tapered leader.

•

Standard advice is to fish a fly upstream against the current. However, an eddy will often turn and reverse, in which case a trout will sometimes face downstream when feeding.

MATCHING FLY TO TIPPET

One of the old-fashioned ways to decide what fly size to use for a particular tippet is to multiply the tippet size by four and use a fly of that size or one step larger or smaller. For a 6X tippet, sizes 24, 22, and 26 would be the traditionally recommended flies for this leader.

Unfortunately, this calculating technique and the published charts found in most fly-fishing books were compiled when the strength and quality of tippet materials was far below today's standards. Also, most of those earlier flies imitated mayflies, which tend to twist light, fine leader tippets. Many of today's popular fly patterns imitate terrestrial insects and caddis flies, which generally lack the projecting wings that twist fine tippets. These two factors often make it possible to use far lighter tippets with a given size fly than is normally recommended by the published charts. The converse is also true: you can use much larger flies on lighter tippets than is traditionally suggested.

The table below suggests tippet and fly sizes adapted to today's strong, thin-diameter leader material. Of course, the final test is in the twist. If you tie a No. 14 fly on a 7X tippet and it twists the leader, you have two recourses: cut back to a heavier tippet or go to a smaller fly. For most fishing situations and patterns, however, this chart is a valuable guide.

TIPPET SIZE	DIAMETER	FLY SIZE
4X	.007	6, 8, 10, 12
5X	.006	8, 10, 12, 14
6X	.005	10, 12, 14, 16, 18
7X	.004	14, 16, 18, 20, 22, 24
8X	.003	18, 20, 22, 24, 26, 28

WOOLIES UNDER WADERS

Half the fatigue and half the discomfort we get from wearing waders for a day—or even an hour—comes from the way pants stick to the inside of the waders. Denim is especially bad: blue jeans, when damp with seepage or sweat, stick to rubber, chafe you, and reduce your ability to move comfortably.

The problem is easy to cure. For an all-day trip, especially if a lot of walking is involved, leave the jeans in the car. Wear cotton long johns or woolies, or both if the weather demands it. For short trips, an hour or two of fishing without a lot of walking, slip a pair of athletic sweat pants over your denims. They will not only reduce sticking and chafing, they will add a layer of fine warmth.

One caution: Do not try to increase warmth by wearing down-filled garments under waders. When you are out of the water, they will steam-heat you. When you are in the water, the pressure against your legs will collapse the down, and you will, essentially, be wearing nothing warmer than a pair of nylon stockings.

DRY-FLY ATOMIZERS

As every dry-fly fisherman who has done much wading will know, sooner or later he is going to take a tumble. This is an accepted occupational hazard. When such a dousing occurs, it is important that all equipment be thoroughly dried as soon as possible. This is especially true of dry flies. Failure to do so can result in rusted hooks, and it doesn't take much corrosion to ruin flies tied on tiny hooks.

As protection against such rust, try to get your hands on an old perfume atomizer, or buy a new one. Fill the atomizer with liquid flotant and give your flies a good spraying.

Doing this after every outing will guarantee both longevity and maximum buoyancy of the flies, and they'll be ready to be fished when you are next casting flies at streamside.

POPULAR GAME FISHES
TROUT

ASSET OR LIABILITY?

Many trout anglers blame live-bait fishermen for the introduction of suckers into favored trout waterways. The actual facts disclose that suckers are native to most of the West's better streams and reservoirs and are of some benefit to sport fisheries.

Suckers are despised as being competitors with trout for available food, but a study made by scientists in Wyoming established that a population of white suckers, the most common fish east of the continental divide in that state, probably directs more useful force into the trout population, as nourishment for the trout, than they take from it by the consumption of food that trout would normally have eaten.

Since research shows that suckers help improve the quality of trout waters, anglers may have a change of heart regarding these rough fish. The slimy creature with the permanent pucker is doing its part to provide a better trout habitat.

Stop Those Snags

Fishing nymphs with spinning gear has become a popular sport in some areas. But the split-shot required to cast with such tackle will not move with too slow a current. This trick can solve that problem.

Just tie a No. 6 bait hook on the end of your line and thread a fat night crawler onto it. Then attach the nymph on a dropper. The worm provides weight enough to cast and is heavy enough to drag the fly near the bottom of the stream, yet it is buoyant enough to keep from snagging easily.

Sometimes this rig provides a handsome bonus—like a nice trout that couldn't resist the juicy crawler.

Catch/Release Casualties

A report by the Washington Department of Fish and Game cites more than 30 studies concerning catch-and-release trout fishing that indicate up to 50 percent of the fish caught with bait die upon being released. Those caught on any kind of artificial lure—spinners, plugs, spoons or flies—suffer a mortality of only 5 percent when they are let go. It doesn't matter if the hooks are barbed or not.

The only exception is steelhead. They are not usually hooked in vital areas, even with bait, and so aren't wounded as severely when caught with bait.

New Ranking for Bull Trout

Arctic char (bull trout) and Dolly Varden are so closely related that resident Alaskan anglers refuse to treat them differently, even though biologists say there is a difference, be it ever so slight. Now, Dr. Ted Cavender, an ichthyologist at Ohio State University, has also established a difference between Dolly Varden and bull trout, previously thought to be the same species.

Because it is extremely difficult to distinguish between the two, identification will be based mainly on location and size of the catch. The Dolly Varden is generally an anadromous, coastal species, seldom exceeding six or seven pounds. The larger bull trout tend to be found inland.

Dr. Cavender's discovery has resulted in a shuffling of world records within the last few months. N.L. Higgins no longer holds the all-tackle world record for Dolly Varden. His 32-pound fish, caught in 1949 in Idaho, is now the all-tackle world record for bull trout.

STREAMSIDE CADDIS COLORS

For the ultimate in streamside matching of the free-living caddis larvae, so well imitated with latex bodied patterns, pre-tie your flies in different sizes with natural-colored latex bodies. Finish them off with a short hare's ear thorax, with a few fibers picked out for the legs. Carry a few Pantone markers in your portable flytying kit or the glove box of your car. When you get to your favorite river and collect a sample of the naturals, you can choose the right color and mark your imitations on the spot.

This will cut the number of flies you need to tie: you won't need an assortment of colors on hand. The best waterproof colors to carry: green, brown, tan and orange. With shadings these match almost all caddis larvae.

HOOK THREADER

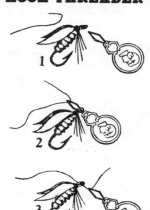

Threading fishing line through the eye of a small hook or fly is no great problem if you use a needle threader. The tiny tool is especially handy when fingers are cold or light conditions are poor. Just follow the three steps shown: 1. Poke wire tip of threader through eye of hook. 2. Insert line into wire tip. 3. Pull threader and line back through eye. Needle threaders are available in the sewing supplies section of most fabric or department stores.

WARY CREEK TROUT

Next time trout refuse to take that bait or fly, try this old trick:

Find a flat piece of bark from the streamside debris and place your offering on it. From an out-of-sight spot upstream, float the bark to the waiting fish. Be sure to allow plenty of slack line.

The idea is to present the food in as natural a manner as possible and ring the dinner bell for a hungry trout.

Since many forms of insects infest dead wood, such debris is usually scrutinized by trout as it passes in the current. The bait is usually nabbed the instant it tumbles off the wood into the pool.

Give it a try. You may find that your next big trout is only a few bits of bark away.

FRAGRANT FLIES

Trout are no different from bass in their response to odors. They will sample a scented fly at times when they refuse all other offerings. I have found that they usually nip and reject so quickly that it is very difficult to hook them.

Do not add the attractors to dry flies, because whether they are rejected or taken usually depends only on their visual appeal.

On days you have promised

a friend a couple of trout and they stop hitting, choose a fuzzy-bodied nymph or Woolly Worm and soak it with scent. Work it slow and deep, and you will have a better chance to fulfill your promise to your friend.

HOMEMADE SINK TIPS

When flyfishing with nymphs or streamers in big water, a sink-tip flyline is often the only way to go. You'll probably find, however, that you'll need several different densities for varying conditions, and at something like $20 per line this can get expensive.

A cheaper and easier way to fish sink-tips is to get a spool of lead-core trolling line and cut it into sections of varying lengths, from six inches to two feet. With perfection loops tied on each end of the sections, you can attach one end to a loop in the leader butt and loop a short leader to the other. A whole selection of lead-core sections can be rolled up and stored comfortably in a vest pocket.

Using this method, you can turn a standard floating flyline into whatever density sink-tip you need, quickly and easily, and save yourself a lot of money to boot.

Fishing I.Q.: Flying Tackle

It takes more than a bit of feathered fluff to bedazzle a bluegill or beguile a brown trout; It takes tackle and technique. Test your skill in both areas with these 12 questions.

1) The double haul is a casting technique that facilitates long casts. True/False?
2) Mending line means to: A. remove "line belly," B. excise damaged line sections, C. strip line in.
3) A fly's free float is most important in: A. dry-fly fishing, B. nymphing, C. wet-fly fishing, D. streamer fishing.
4) Such free float is achieved by the: A. Galway cast, B. roll cast, C. serpentine or S-cast, D. bow-and-arrow cast.
5) False casting is another way of describing a multiple cast. True/False?
6) WF-6-ST refers to: A. rod style, B. reel configuration, C. leader taper, D. line type.
7) Strike indicators are most helpful when working subsurface flies. True/False?
8) Weight-forward lines are primarily designed to present flies delicately. True/False?
9) In wet-fly or streamer fishing, strikes often come when the line tails out downstream from the angler. True/False?
10) An OX leader tippet is normally much stronger than a 6X tippet. True/False?
11) Fish are sometimes attracted to several flies attached to the same leader. The added weight of such extra flies increases casting ease. True/False?
12) When using a flyrod, the longer the rod is the more leverage the angler can apply to the fish. True/False?

ANSWERS: 1) True. 2) A. 3) A. dry-fly fishing. 4) C. the S-cast. 5) False. False casting keeps a fly moving through the air. A multiple cast uses two or more flies on the same leader. 6) D. 7) True. A dry fly itself acts as a strike indicator. No other is needed. 8) False. They put casting weight into the air sooner than level or double taper lines, but some ease of presentation is lost. 9) True. 10) True. 11) False. In flycasting, it is the line and not the lure that provides casting weight. Usually, more flies mean more awkward casting. 12) False. Many anglers agree that a long rod gives the leverage to the fish.

GET THE BANK RIGHT

Which side of a stream, river or brook is the right bank?

No, not the side where the fish are biting. According to the federal government, every waterway has permanent right and left banks, and they're not interchangeable.

The designations are constant whether you're flying 3000 feet overhead, going downstream in a canoe, or standing on either shore.

Give up? The right bank is always on the right side of the *direction in which the water is flowing.*

STRANGE LIMIT

The Test River in England is probably the world's most famous trout stream. Historically, it is the place where trout fishing began with Izaak Walton, and where it still prospers over 400 years later.

In many ways, the Test has set the standard for the rest of the trout-angling world, yet its current limit structure is in direct opposition to the American approach.

At a time when Yankees are promoting practices like reduced limits, trophy fishing only and catch-and-release regulations, you cannot release a trout on the Test. The limit is seven fish, and once you have caught that many— that you must kill and keep— you must quit.

According to John Birth, a sporting entrepreneur who books anglers into beats on the Test, these limits ensure against leader- and hook-shy fish, and establish an accurate mortality rate that is unclouded by the speculative results of mishandling and deep hooking. They also encourage anglers to fish to the more difficult trout—to be more selective in their quarry— rather than hooking every trout in the stream.

Carry Fewer Flies

Aquatic insect nymphs, the major food source for most trout, come in a wide variety of colors, and if you imitate them all your fly selection can get out of hand. One way to cut down on the number of flies you carry is to tie, or buy, all your nymphs in a light tan or cream color and carry a selection of waterproof marking pens. This way you can make whatever color nymph you need on the spot and carry fewer flies.

BUILD A TROUT HOUSE

Do you know of a stream that is cool and rich in oxygen throughout the year, yet the trout disappear when summer arrives? It could be that heavy pressure has fished out the stream, but it is more likely that the streambed structure does not provide critical cover in low water.

A trout house is a simple but effective habitat improvement device. It requires little more than a willing spirit, a pry bar and large, flat rocks.

Pick out a section of the stream that is deep enough to hold trout but has little visible structure or flow variation. Find a large rock or boulder in the stream, and pry up the downstream side of it. Wedge a smaller rock underneath the boulder so that it stands at a 45-degree angle, and presto, you have a trout house!

The trout house must be secure enough to withstand high water. If there is a crevice on the upstream side of the main rock, the current will dig underneath and dislodge it over time. To avoid this problem, place a smaller rock in front of the larger rock to divert the current.

The house provides trout with a natural feeding station and cover. Trout will feed in the eddy behind the boulder and move up alongside it when danger approaches.

Trout can be encouraged to move into an area by placing several houses in a pool. Keep them about five feet apart to avoid territorial conflicts.

LEADER REPAIR

Flyfishermen must often repair a broken leader on the stream. If the break occurs anywhere above the tippet, knowing how many strands to replace is sometimes hard to figure out. Here's one solution: Put a dab of black lacquer on the knot that connects the .011 to the .010 strand (or the OX to the 1X, if you use the X system). It's rare to break off above that joint, and the painted knot is a fast and reliable guide in helping you find the needed replacement.

The Tiger Trout

The tiger trout is a cross between the eastern brook trout and brown trout. It is not common but can be found in lakes containing both parent species. The cross occurs only by chance and subsequent generations are inferior and biologically unable to reproduce successfully.

The tiger trout is an exceptional sportfish. It strikes hard near the surface and puts up a determined battle once hooked. Several states have raised them in hatcheries to determine their potential as a put-and-take fish. A few sporting clubs have already stocked them in small private ponds.

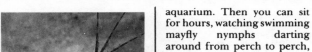

NATURAL BEHAVIOR

It is relatively easy to collect an underwater insect and select a nymph or wet fly pattern to match it. But how do you decide what manner of presentation best suits the behavior of the natural? Does it swim and should the imitation be fished with a fast retrieve, or does it crawl so the imitation should drift dead along the bottom?

Such questions are hard to answer by looking at an insect in the palm of your hand. The best way to see how a natural behaves is to observe it under natural conditions. You can duplicate these in a household aquarium. Then you can sit for hours, watching swimming mayfly nymphs darting around from perch to perch, clumsy cased caddis larvae clambering over vegetation, and quiescent dragonfly nymphs lying in wait for some luckless victim to come too close.

A few ideas for stocking an aquarium: 1) Use lake or slow-stream insects; they adapt better and survive longer. 2) Take water from the stream or lake where and when the insects are collected. This exposes them to less rapid temperature and chemical changes. 3) Use a vigorous air pump to keep the insects well supplied with oxygen. With few exceptions, they take their oxygen from the water, just as fish do, and need to have the water constantly aerated. 4) Use a charcoal filter to keep the water clean. It will also prevent algae blooms, which cloud the water and cut visibility.

Aquarium set-ups need not be expensive. For less than $15 you can get a tank, air pump and filter outfit that will be more than adequate. If you would like to spend more, you can rig up elaborate systems with flowing water and duplicate the conditions found at streamside.

UPTURNED FLIES

Believe it or not, there are places where there are so many fish in a particular river that you are worried about foul-hooking a fish. In some salmon streams, for instance, the fish are stacked up in holding pools. If one fish makes a move for your fly and you miss setting the hook, you may snag the fish next to it.

Trying to bring in a tail- or dorsal-fin-hooked fish can take a lot of time and often results in a lost fly and damaged or lost leader.

Here's a method that has worked well for me over the past couple seasons. I tie some of my salmon flies upside down, in the same manner as bonefish flies are tied. With a little experimentation, you can get your artificials to ride point up. Not only will they ride over the backs of salmon but they also have less affinity for bottom debris and log-jams. The upside-down salmon flies are just as easy to construct as regular flies, and in addition, their hooking capabilities are equally effective.

DOUBLE STRENGTH

Two problems flytiers sometimes encounter while tying bass bugs and saltwater patterns or spinning deer hair are running out of 4/0 or larger thread and breakage that may occur when a substitute is used. Even though today's prewaxed nylon is strong, it can also break if too much pressure is applied. Mono-Cord, frequently used for more durable patterns, has its limitations too.

The solution is to pull off twice the amount of thread you would normally use and attach both free ends to the hook shank simultaneously. You now have double-strength thread capable of withstanding most heavy tying.

This double strand may require spinning with hackle pliers and waxing to ensure coherence.

Tie 'Em Up

Nymph bodie are easily and effectively tied when winding saddle hackle on backwards. The tip of the feather should be tied in as you would any body material, wind forward. For a tight body, twist the feather. Wind the last portion on straight (without twist) and leave the soft hackle fibers sticking out for swimming legs. Wooly worms are tied by winding the entire hackle on straight (without twist). This is a good way to use up the abundant soft fiber saddle hackles most flytiers have lying around.

GOOD CATCH PARADOX

An unusually abundant catch of lake trout can be a sign that the lake is becoming lethally acidic—and is running out of fish.

The reason behind this paradox lies in the food chain that is slowly destroyed as a lake becomes more acidic. To unravel the puzzle, fisheries biologists began adding sulfuric acid to a lake in northwestern Ontario in 1976. By 1983, it was 47 times more acidic.

Kenneth Mills, a member of the team from Freshwater Institute, a government agency, supplemented the team's scientific research with his own rod and reel. Mills says when the experiment began, he was catching four or five fish an hour. By 1983, he was hooking 20 per hour.

The increasing acidity of the lake was killing the food fish needed to survive. The trout grabbed at the bait.

Trout about 2.2 pounds at the beginning of the summer lost up to 14 ounces by the end of the season.

Stomach Info

Checking the stomach contents of trout is a well-known ritual among flyfishermen, but it also works for other species. When fishing on a lake, open the stomachs of the fish you catch and try to identify the contents. More than just revealing what the fish are feeding on, this will also tell you where to find them.

For instance, if you find mud minnows you know that the fish are feeding in the debris close to shore, whereas the presence of log perch would indicate the fish are on weedy sandbars at mealtime.

Also study the characteristics and habits of some of the important forage species. Next time you go fishing you'll know exactly where to look for gamefish instead of spending your time over empty water.

A TIME-SAVER STREAMSIDE

Most snags resulting in broken line are caused by the weight getting hung up on or between rocks on the streambed. A simple rubber band can correct the problem and reduce the amount of time you spend repairing your line by 50 percent.

Simply apply the desired amount of split-shot to the rubber band and attach the band to the swivel. (Either a snap swivel or a three-way barrel swivel will do for this type of rig.)

When the shot becomes snagged, apply moderate pressure and stretch the band. Then quickly release the pressure. The action of the rubber band should dislodge the hung-up shot.

ANTIREVERSE STRATEGY

One of the most frustrating problems a baitfisherman will encounter on a stream is the inability to fish a tailout from an upstream position. At a point roughly 20 degrees downstream from the angler, the current will lift the bait from the bottom and drag it crossways away from the desired position.

The trick to mastering the tailout drift is to fish with the reel's antireverse set to the Off position. With the gears thus disengaged, you can control the movement and depth of the bait at any part of the tailout.

As the current begins to lift the bait from the bottom, crank the reel backward, slowly. This keeps the bait in position. If you decide to move the drift a little closer, you need only stop reeling backward and let the current move the terminal gear. When the bait is in the desired position, simply begin reeling backward again.

A word of caution: Do not reel backward faster than the current is moving; you'll lose valuable fishing time removing snarls from monofilament.

Once a fish is hooked, the antireverse is flipped to the On position to prevent backlash during the ensuing battle.

RUBBER BAND

Neat Nets

Most flyfishermen have had their net snag on brush as they walk the banks of a stream. One way to minimize this is to tuck the net bag under a rubber band stretched around the handle. It's easy to slip the bag out when needed.

REVIVING THE OLD SNELLED FLY

Snelled trout and/or salmon flies, once very popular, are wet and dry patterns dressed on hooks pretied with four- to six-inch snells or leaders made of so-called catgut, a forerunner of monofilament.

Snelled flies have advantages. One, two and even three of differing patterns are easily arranged at intervals on the leader. Indeed, a three-fly cast can catch more than one trout simultaneously.

Some of today's fishermen are reviving the snelled fly. They tie their own patterns or have commercial tiers dress them directly onto nylon-snelled bait hooks.

The point, or end, fly is often a nymph pattern. A wet pattern is placed at, roughly, midpoint, and a dry fly is tied onto the uppermost dropper strand. All three phases of fly-fishing incorporated into a single cast! A strike can occur on any fly, but the dry fly, when skittered across the surface, often brings spectacular results.

SALMON EGG SAVVY

Much has been written about the importance of making worms and other live baits behave naturally. But what about salmon eggs, which have no life?

Salmon eggs too should be attached to the hook so they bounce and drift realistically with the current. This works in streams and lakes that have minor up-and-down currents caused by water temperature changes. These drifts often make it appear that the egg is moving freely. That's exactly the impression you want to create.

The choice of color and type, of course, is the major decision a salmon-egg fisherman has to make. They come in singles and clusters, and in a variety of colors and scents. Cheese-flavored and fluorescent red eggs probably are the most popular among trout anglers.

I'm inclined to believe that if a trout is stung by the hook in a red egg, it will refuse another red egg. So it is good insurance to have two or more colors of eggs with you whenever fishing for trout.

RECOATING FLYLINES

Any brand-name flyline will perform well throughout the first year of use. Unfortunately, after two or three seasons of fishing, most lines begin to show their age. They no longer slide through the guides smoothly and the pickup from the water requires more effort. A thorough cleaning helps, but the like-new feeling is gone.

One successful way to rejuvenate a worn flyline is to apply a silicone-based waterproofing agent. The aerosol used to spray spark-plug wires works very well and is available in any automotive store. Take care to wipe off any excess, and permit it to dry thoroughly before rewinding onto the reel. Both floating and sinking lines can be treated in this manner and the like-new coating will last a full season or more.

TROUT LEADER FORMULA

Leader formulas abound, but the flat-butt system offers many clear advantages. The flat butt straightens out more quickly and easily than round monofilament. It provides tighter leader loops when casting (flat mono bends more, like the flyline), inexpensive material to work with (50 yards costs around $3, the cost of two factory leaders), and a butt section that is good for an entire season.

This leader formula also employs a midsection (preferrably tied with Maxima) with the proper amount of stiffness, excellent durability and stretchability, and low cost (27 yards for $1.50). With it, the angler has options such as changing tippet length and/or length to suit the prevailing fishing conditions.

All tippets should be at least 24 inches long to provide the proper shock absorption from striking fish. The following formula chart is for floating lines, and it uses Cobra flat monofilament, but Amnesia (a stiffer material) can be substituted. The remaining sections of monofilament are Maxima. The tippet should be tied using a very soft and supple monofilament.

A nail knot or needle knot works well for attaching the leader to the flyline. Covering the finished knot allows it to slide in and out of the flyrod guides smoothly. A blood knot or surgeon's knot works well to attach leader sections and tippet together. Don't be misled by the abrupt change in poundage rating from the butt section to the first length of leader. The monofilament ensures a smooth transition without any hinging effect while casting.

LEADER FOR NO. 3 LINE: 64", 15-lb. flat butt; 12", 6-lb. Maxima; 12", 4-lb. Maxima; 12", 3-lb. Maxima; 24" tippet (optional size).

LEADER FOR NO. 4, 5, OR 6 LINE: 64", 20-lb. flat butt; 12", 8-lb. Maxima; 12", 6-lb. Maxima; 12", 4-, 3-, 2-, or 1-lb. Maxima; 24" tippet (optional size).

LEADER FOR NO. 7 LINE: 64", 25-lb. flat butt; 18", 10-lb. Maxima; 18", 8-lb. Maxima; 12", 6-, 4-lb. Maxima; 24" tippet (optional size).

★

An effective deepwater trolling lure for lake trout can be made from an ordinary metal fish stringer. Just attach a flashing spoon or large spinner in front and a treble hook or bait fly on the end. Troll the rig in the usual manner.

Match The Hatch

The serious trout angler strives to imitate the insect life on any given stream as closely as possible. A caddis? A stonefly? Usually he chooses correctly. But how many can identify the insect's common name with its scientific counterpart? Try this quiz, scoring one point for each correct match. A score of 9-10 makes you a purist; 6-8 a serious flycaster; 2-5 average; and 0-1 a worm dunker.

1. Black gnats	a. Ephemeridae
2. Caddisflies	b. Mecoptera
3. Damselflies	c. Diptera
4. Grasshoppers	d. Trichoptera
5. Water beetles	e. Hymenoptera
6. Stoneflies	f. Odonata
7. Ants.	g. Hemiptera
8. Scorpion flies	h. Plecoptera
9. Mayflies	i. Sialidae
10. Alder flies	j. Orthoptera

Answers: 1-c, 2-d, 3-f, 4-j, 5-g, 6-h, 7-e, 8-b, 9-a, 10-i.

BEHIND THE WATERFALL

Why is it so many anglers never fish behind waterfalls—even the tiny ones common in any fast-water stream?

Perhaps they go by surface appearances, without considering the setup: Behind each waterfall there is usually a gouged-out backwater that acts as a natural repository for food. Small minnows often frequent these backwaters and are an added attraction for gamefish.

Bait is usually the best medicine for behind-the-falls work, although flies and other lures will work if they are manipulated properly. The important thing is to keep the bait behind the falls long enough for a fish to see and take it.

FABRIC STORE FLIES

A fabric store or a yarn shop offers some great deals for flytiers. A remnant or scrap table is the best place to start looking for natural and synthetic materials, but don't overlook other items in the store. Yarns that can be wrapped or dubbed for fur bodies are very inexpensive when you consider the number of fly bodies you can get out of one skein.

Be sure to check out secondhand stores and flea markets also. On several occasions I've found old stoles, coats or fur hats, and the amount of usable fur remaining on them would have brought a much higher price at a specialty fly shop. I doubt you'll find a dry-fly cape or a box of salmon hooks, but you may find good substitutes for other materials.

NYMPH RIGS

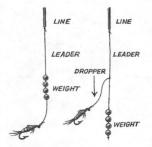

Flyfishermen who want to work a nymph right on bottom in deep water typically add some lead, either split-shot, fuse wire, or twist-ons, to the leader about a foot above the fly. This is a very effective way to fish nymphs, but it can cost you a lot of flies as you hang up on the bottom. (If you're not hanging up, you're probably not fishing deep enough.)

A good way to save flies is to put your weight at the tip of the leader, above a small knot so it doesn't slip off, and attach the nymph to a dropper a foot or so up the leader. When you hang up, you'll break off the weight and not the fly. This rig also gives you a more direct connection between the rod tip and the fly, which makes detecting those delicate strikes a bit easier.

ATTRACT A TROUT

When you are fishing on the bottom for trout in lakes and strikes come few and far between, the fish may not be finding your bait. Replace your lead sinker with a shiny No. 3 wobbling spoon weighing anywhere from one-sixteenth to one-quarter ounce.

Remove the spoon's barbs and loop a two-foot leader to the hook ring. Tie a hook to the end of the leader. Bait it, and you are in business. The shiny spoon attracts trout to the area and they soon locate your bait. It's still fishing with an attractor blade, which is a method popular among knowledgeable trollers.

Tunnel Fishing

Don't overlook small, brush-clogged feeder streams when searching for good trout locations. Many of these little streams run through swamplands and are choked by overhanging clumps of alders, willows, briar bushes and other growth, hence the term tunnel fishing. To fish such streams, regular methods have to be discarded.

Because of the challenge these feeder streams afford and the singular lack of other fishermen, I love to try my hand in such areas. In the junglelike growth there is usually no space in which to make conventional casts or work a lure, so the best method is to poke your fishing rod through an opening in the growth (if you can find one), drop a worm into the head of a pool, and let the worm slowly drift with the current.

To get the bait down to where it will do the most good, I use one or two small split-shot clamped onto the line about a foot above the worm.

While many of these little streams are inhabited only by brookies, there are some waters where rainbows or browns may be present.

When fishing low, clear streams and rivers during summer, wear drab-colored clothing that blends in with the brush and vegetation along shore. Camouflage isn't a bad idea, either.

NEW LIGHT ON RAISING TROUT

Utilizing an innovative technique to improve the output of its hatcheries, Colorado is producing greater numbers of trout for its put and take program. Through artificial daylight, the ripening of adult breeders for egg production is adjusted to fit rearing schedules.

In nature many animals experience physical changes triggered by the changing length of daylight between seasons. The change in color of a hare's fur from brown to white as winter approaches is an obvious illustration.

Like the hare's color change, trout reproduction is controlled by day length. Photosensitive pigments in the trout's eyes react to the total hours of daylight. A message is sent to a center in the brain that stimulates reproductive development and spawning behavior. The maturing of egg and milt is then accomplished by a chain reaction of hormones released by internal glands.

A genetic factor also exists, which explains varying breeding schedules and fall-versus-spring spawning within a species of trout.

Colorado hatcheries have designed a method of regulating light to alter natural breeding dates. Holding tanks are covered completely to shade out all light and equipped with rows of incandescent lights. Exposure of breeders to light and darkness is strictly controlled. The trout are actually fooled into fall reproduction months in advance of the normal November spawn.

This technique allows eggs to be produced over two or more separate time periods. If necessary, incubation nurseries can be filled repeatedly. In turn, more fingerlings are hatched each year. The problem of limited space, which would occur if a large number of eggs were produced at one time, is solved.

Larger trout is another benefit of this procedure. Fingerlings begin development two or three months earlier, and they are a good size when stocked into waters during the prime fishing months of spring.

Reading the Rise

The next time you see trout feeding, look carefully at the way the rise disturbs the water. With a little practice you'll be able to tell whether the fish are taking floating insects or subadult bugs just under the surface. Then you can match your fly to the conditions and catch more fish.

When a trout takes a floating insect such as a mayfly dun, it slurps it in with an audible *plop*, usually leaving bubbles and telltale concentric rings on the surface. This is the classic surface feeding rise that tells you to match the hatch with an appropriate dry fly.

Another type of rise is made by trout feeding just below the surface on subadult insects swimming up to begin their winged adult phase. This type of rise is characterized by a bulging of the water's surface as a trout rolls porpoiselike to capture the emerging insect. You can frequently see the fish's dorsal fin breaking the water. These rolling trout seldom take dry flies, but will strike an emerger pattern fished a few inches under the surface.

Reading the rises is a subtle bit of fishing savvy that can turn a fishing experience from a total bust to bonanza.

THE REAL THING

Although dry fly purists may cringe at the thought of using live bait, there is nothing I have found yet that is as effective during a mayfly hatch as the real thing. Simply catch the live mayflies as you need them, impale them on No. 8 or 10 hooks and deliver with flyrod or lightweight spinning gear. Keep live mayflies on your hook, not dead ones. The small hooks are so light the mayflies will still float. The artificial enthusiast may keep up for a while, but you'll still be catching fish long after they have ceased hitting his imitations.

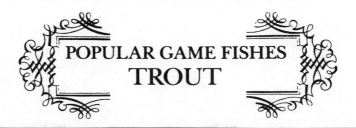

THE TELLTALE TAIL

Is that trout you just caught wild or was it planted? There are all sorts of myths and prejudices about planted trout. If it fights like a dishrag, then it must be planted. If it won't bite, then it's certainly planted ("They breed 'em not to bite"), and on and on.

You probably have some notions of your own about hatchery trout, but what proof do you have? Take a closer look.

The tail of a hatchery trout is different from that of a wild trout. (Wild means born in a body of water or released there a season or more ago. There are few truly wild populations anymore.) The tail fin of a hatchery trout is worn and rounded; that of the wild trout is sharp and angular.

The difference can be quite pronounced and is due to environment, not genetics. Trout in a hatchery are raised in cement ponds and raceways, constantly swimming, tail to snout with other trout; their fins are nibbled on, and scraped and rubbed against pond walls, thus losing their sharpness. Once the fish are released into the wild, the tail fins regenerate and become sharp and angular. Depending on the growth rate, this can happen within the season.

BAIT 'EM WITH BEETLES

Along about July, when insect hatches are sparse, garden pests become dandy trout baits—especially Japanese beetles. Carry a jarful in your creel. Flip several at a time onto riffles that usually harbor trout. After a parade of beetles floats past, the trout often become interested in surface feeding and will readily take a fly imitation.

A bagful of Japanese beetles can be trapped with no effort on your part by hanging up bags, baited with sex attractants, in the garden. The trap is an effective alternative to harmful pesticides. Not at all surprising, river smallmouths feed on beetle baits also.

FISHING I.Q. — FLIES

Writing about 200 years before the birth of Christ, Aelian noted that the Macedonians used artificial flies to take fish. Since then, it would be hard to say whether more fish or fishermen have succumbed to these sometimes subtle, sometimes flagrant concoctions of fur and feathers. Test your fly I.Q. with these ten questions.

(1) Thor, Skykomish Sunrise and McLeod's Ugly are flies designed to attract: A, black bass; B, Atlantic salmon; C, golden trout; D, steelhead.

(2) The Silver Doctor, Jock Scott and Blue Charm are wet-fly patterns for: A, steelhead; B, pike; C, Atlantic salmon; D, brook trout.

(3) The Parmachene Belle, Montreal and Alexandra are best known as attractor patterns for: A, brook trout; B, rainbows; C, king salmon; D, grayling.

(4) Brown and rainbow trout anglers should recognize the Adams and Blue Dun as _____ imitations.

(5) They should also know the Royal Coachman is: A, a dry fly; B, a wet fly; C, a streamer fly; D, all of these.

(6) Other than as an egg, the mayfly has three basic life stages. To an entomologist, they are known as _____, _____ and _____.

(7) Tied as flies, these same stages are called _____, _____ and _____.

(8) Recent design innovators, Carl Richards and Douglas Swisher, have created dry flies which remain buoyant without traditional: A, dubbing; B, hackle; C, wing material; D, none of these.

(9) The Cowdung is a wet-fly pattern dating back: A, 20 years; B, to the 17th century; C, to the Macedonians; D, there is no current pattern bearing this prosaic yet repulsive name.

(10) Mayfly and stonefly imitations represent aquatic insects. Flies which mimic tiny land creatures, such as ants, beetles and jassids, are called _____.

ANSWERS: (1) D, steelhead; (2) C, Atlantic salmon; (3) A, brook trout; (4) mayfly; (5) D, it can be any of these; (6) larval, subimago and imago; (7) nymphs, duns and spinners; (8) B, hackle; (9) B, the 17th century; (10) terrestrials.

•

Trout feed on the surface, just below it or near the bottom, so fishing the middle is usually a waste of time.

•

Never walk right up to the edge of a small trout stream. Stay back as far as you can and keep a low, hunchbacked posture. Sometimes it even pays to get down on your knees to keep from spooking the skittish quarry. Wearing drab clothing helps, too.

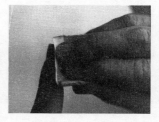

SMOOTH FINGERS

Work-roughened hands can break flytying or rod-wrapping thread at a crucial moment in the tying process. Use a pumice stone or sandpaper to smooth the rough spots on your fingers. Professional flytier Polly Rosborough uses Corn Husker's lotion to keep his hands soft and smooth, but any good hand lotion will help.

SUPER TROUT

Trout are big business in Pennsylvania, and fish hatcheries rear the scrappers by the millions for anglers throughout the state. In hatchery raceways you'll find the usual species as well as blue, palomino and tiger trout.

The palominos are produced by crossbreeding golden rainbow and rainbow trout. The tiger trout is the result of a cross between the brown and brook trout. The blue trout is a mutant variety of rainbow. Besides the curiosity factor, these trout represent important strides being taken in the field of fish research.

It is hoped that new species will be developed to withstand conditions that less hardy fish can't stand.

Sound Familiar?

I was walking along a quiet stream when I passed a fisherman and asked, "Catch anything yet?"

"No," was the answer.

"That's strange," I said. "I heard this was a fine place for trout."

"It must be," was the answer. "They refuse to leave it."

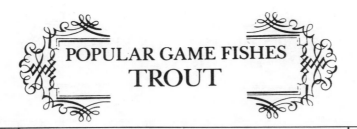

HIGH RIDERS

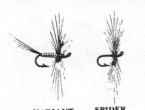

VARIANT   SPIDER

On days when the best of the basic, time-tested dry-fly patterns fails to get a rise, the smartest thing a dry-fly purist can do is switch to spiders and variants. Both have brought me astonishing results at times. While they can't be called infallible—no fly can—they definitely have earned a place beside the best patterns.

A spider or variant often will bring trout to the surface. Then you can switch back to a conventional dry fly, if need be, and go to work on them. Some fly anglers prefer to go to wet flies or other sinking lures to accomplish the same results, of course.

The action you get from spiders and variants is completely unlike that of ordinary dry flies. They drop to the water with exceeding delicacy, often somersaulting or jumping after touching it. Fish find that extremely attractive. Often, during a strong wind, these light flies will skitter over the surface, interesting observant fish, though they may not actually rise to the lure.

High-riding is another attribute of these flies. When tied properly, their hackles support the hook above the water's surface, thus imitating a natural fly much more closely than the ordinary fly does.

The wings of the variant make it rest just a bit lower than the spider, which may account for its better hooking record.

Anglers who tie their own flies generally use spiders more than they do variants, because spiders are easier to tie. Sometimes, though, it is necessary to switch to variants in order to catch any fish.

Be a Quick-Change Artist

If you have carefully stalked a surface-feeding trout only to have it rise short and miss your presentation, here's what to do. Quickly change to a wet fly. Wait a few minutes and make the presentation again. Chances are the trout will accept the underwater tie even though reluctant to begin surface feeding again. This may not succeed every time it is tried, but it's a tip worth remembering when, for some reason, you have put down an active feeder.

HENSHALL ON GRAYLING

"The grayling was named by the ancients *Thymallus*," wrote James Alexander Henshall in 1903, "owing to the smell of thyme that was said to emanate from the fish when freshly caught."

Although history remembers Dr. Henshall for his classic angling treatise, *Book of the Black Bass* (1881), it should be noted that while in charge of the U.S. Fish Commission station at Bozeman, Montana, he was first to propagate grayling eggs artificially.

Henshall's bass records are impressive considering rod, reel and line technology was in its infancy in the late 1800s. He took a 14-pound largemouth bass on a fly, and caught a 20-pound largemouth on bait.

The good doctor caught other big fish, too. His biggest crappie weighed three pounds. He boated muskies up to 40 pounds. And in Florida, near Naples, he took a 60-pound jewfish on rod and reel.

What did Henshall think grayling smelled like? He thought the fish smelled like cucumbers.

BASS FLIES FOR BIG TROUT

As trout grow bigger, they require more and larger meals to maintain their strength. After reaching a certain size, they reduce their intake of small insects and begin to prey on small fish, mice, salamanders, snakes and even birds. For fly anglers, this means that the biggest fish in a stream may no longer be interested in the traditional fur-and-feather imitations of stream insects. Also, big trout grow wary and feed mostly at night or during dark, cloudy days.

A switch to flies designed for bass may be the ticket for these big fish. Hair mice top the list, followed by bulky streamers and frog patterns. At night, a cork popper retrieved noisily across a deep pool may bring a strike.

WEIGHTY PROBLEM

After making only a few casts with the flyrod that I purchased last summer, I suddenly became arm weary. The rod was much too heavy.

If you, too, have an arm-busting flyrod, try what I did: make the rod lighter by making it *heavier*.

Fit up rod, line and reel, then hold the rod horizontally and hang sheet lead or lead wire over the middle of the reel until the outfit balances on a finger somewhere not far ahead of the grip—exactly where is a matter of taste. Then remove the line, wind the lead onto the reel arbor, and wind the line over it.

A fly outfit fixed up this way feels gosh-awful heavy when you pick it up. But since it's not tip-heavy and has the balance near your hand, you'll find your arm far less tired at the end of a hard day's casting.

GO LIGHT FOR LAKERS

Peter Hurley, a top rod at Moosehead Lodge in Messines, Quebec, makes deepwater trolling for lake trout a lot sportier by lightening his terminal tackle. With a swivel, Peter attaches 15 feet of 30-pound mono to his spool of steel-core line. Then he attaches 15 feet of 15-pound mono to the heavier mono with another swivel. He also uses a light seven-foot spinning rod with his baitcasting reel instead of a stiff boat rod.

Having located fish with sonar, Peter calculates a 10-foot drop for every 100 feet of line and trolls to depths of 60 feet directly from the stern. At greater depths he relies on small downriggers.

Peter shuns the heavy Christmas-tree attractor spinners typical of lake trout fishing, sticking to large wobblers and jointed pencil lures in bright or fluorescent colors. His lake trout fishing stays lively even in the dog days of August and early September, and his action can get downright hectic in June and early July when the fish are suspended in the cold water.

★

Few flyfishermen carry a steaming teapot along to fluff up bedraggled flies. But, a small bottle of detergent enables you to wash off slime and algae. After false casting to air-dry them they look alive again.

Trout Mallows

Western fishermen know the effectiveness of Velveeta cheese as a trout bait. Another good morsel in which to imbed a hook is a piece of marshmallow. So why not combine the best of two worlds?

It's simple: Place Velveeta cheese in saucepan and heat until melted; cut plain marshmallows into trout-sized bits and blend into the melted cheese until the pieces are completely coated; allow them to cool.

Keep this bait refrigerated until ready to use; when fishing, keep it cool and firm in an ice chest.

MEXICAN TROUT

Native trout in Mexico? You'd better believe it. In spite of the fact that the climate of northern Mexico is famously arid, our neighbor across the border can claim two interesting native trouts.

The Nelson trout, a subspecies of the rainbow, can be found in northern Baja. The Mexican golden trout is a rare species that was "discovered" and officially described only 25 years ago. This beautiful fish exists in a few streams in the mountains of Sinaloa and is the most southerly naturally occurring trout in the continent of North America.

INSECT VIAL BANDOLIER

Shotgun shell webbing from an old hunting vest makes a great addition to a fishing vest. The angler/entomologist can then easily carry a nice supply of vials for streamside insect sampling. The webbing can be sewn in or attached with snap rivets or Velcro for quick removal when not needed. A strip of Velcro will also secure a small aquarium net for collecting the insects.

ROUGH-WATER POPPERS

Trout often feed on the surface of violent, choppy currents where it's nearly impossible to keep a dry fly afloat and in sight. Next time you're in this situation, tie on a tiny, cork-bodied panfish popper, any color, in about Size 12. These unsinkable little lures float high and clear through the worst churning waters and never require dressing. For some reason whitewater trout blast the midget poppers harder than any lure I've ever used. You can drift them "dead," work them cross-current in small pops, or repeatedly jig the lure downstream over one spot until an angered trout charges up through the froth and bubbles and rips it off the surface.

FLYFISHING'S BUGS

Veteran flyfishermen seem to be speaking foreign language as they lapse into two- and three-part Latin names to describe certain aquatic insects on which trout are feeding. This jargon can be very confusing and discouraging.

I found it so until an aging and kindly gent sympathized with my complaining and reduced flyfishing to its most basic elements.

He said that flyfishing in North America is essentially involved with the imitation of three kinds of insects: the mayfly, the caddisfly and the stonefly. Recognizing which of these three the trout are feeding on constitutes 90 percent of flyfishing. And each insect is unique, making identification easy.

The mayfly has wings that stand up on its back, and it usually has three fibers for a tail. The wings of the caddisfly lie back against its body, forming a pup-tent shape. And the stonefly is generally larger than an inch, while the other two are considerably smaller.

Now I catch just as many trout with my mayfly as my fanatic friends with their so-called Ephemerella invaria.

Traveling Tiger

A 19-inch tiger trout that escaped from the Wild Rose Fish Hatchery in central Wisconsin was caught a couple months later 55 miles away.

Apparently the tiger trout, a cross between a brown and a brook trout, migrated over three dams and three lakes, then moved into the upper Fox River to Waukau Creek and into Rush Lake where it was caught just before the lake froze over. Saved from certain death from winter kill, the adventuresome tiger trout was taken to the Milwaukee County Zoo where it is now living.

PRACTICAL FLYBOX

If you're a flyfisherman, chances are that the compartments of your flyboxes that hold a particular pattern have a mixture of used and unused flies. There's nothing wrong with that, except that you might suddenly discover nearly all of a particular favorite are worn out.

HARNESS THE RIVER'S POWER

In fishing a swift stream, your lure often becomes wedged between rocks. Next time, instead of tugging fruitlessly on the line or wallowing downstream to retrieve the lure, stay put and let the river do the work. Pay out enough line to form a long bow below the snag. Then, reel it back in as fast as you can. The drag produced by reeling in, combined with the drag of the current pulling the snagged side of the bowed line downstream, more often than not will whip your hung-up lure free.

To better gauge replacement needs, carry a small "used" box. If, for example, you want to tie on a No. 16 Adams, look for one that's been used before; if you have one, continue using it until it's ready to be discarded; then choose a fresh one to replace it.

HANG A FLYROD

The proper way to secure a flyrod when you stop for a short streamside rest or lunch break is to hang it up. Putting a rod anywhere near the ground or against a tree is not recommended because someone may trip over it. It also risks soiling the reel.

To hang a rod safely on a tree branch, all you need is a small loop of line at rod tip. To get this, attach the fly to the lower part of the reel, wind in all the slack except for the last few inches, then hitch a bit of line from the reel to the handle. The resulting anchored loop of line at the rod tip can then be used to hang up the flyrod.

NIX THE NOISE

Fishing a choice section of stream occupied by noisy anglers can be discouraging. Be patient. When they leave, move in quietly. The fish will be greatly relieved with the commotion now over and more receptive to a bait left still. Be sure not to move it.

FLY HOLDERS

Sew, or glue with epoxy, small cubes of cork or balsa wood to the band of your favorite flyfishing hat. They will serve as holders for your flies, and the hooks are more easily removed than from fabric.

MICRO TIPPET

A flyfisherman's tippet is usually heavier than 1-pound-test, but when an 8X tippet is necessary, a spool of clear or smoke-colored polyester sewing thread works great. It's strong, stretchy, and at 50 cents for 150 yards it costs less than a tenth of the price of regular leader material. Sewing thread spools are small and easy to store in a vest until needed. One word of caution though: length. A 1-pound tippet should be at least three or four feet long to provide a springy shock absorber for strikes and sudden runs.

MAGNETIC SALMON

University of Washington researchers have uncovered evidence suggesting that some salmon may well have a magnetic guidance system, along with chemical and visual clues, that aids their migrations.

Whereas most salmon leave river spawning sites and migrate immediately to the ocean, sockeye fry spend their first year in the lake of their birth, moving in a specific direction that differs from lake to lake. (Although studies have shown that salmon in rivers and the ocean navigate by smell, similar studies have not been done on lake-dwellers.)

Taking sockeye fry from

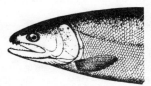

three different lakes and isolating them in separate water tanks, Fisheries Biologist Thomas Quinn noted that they moved in the same direction as in their home lakes. When he changed the magnetic fields around the tank, the fish changed directions accordingly. However, the fish were not affected by the shifting magnetic field when the tank was left uncovered, apparently because their solar navigational ability overrode their magnetic sense.

Preliminary studies have found no magnetic particles in the sockeyes for a direct correlation to changing magnetic fields. How they know which way is north remains a mystery.

★

When bottom fishing in a stream for any species of fish inhabiting fast water, carry an assortment of jig heads weighing from one-eighth through one ounce. Match the weight of the jig to the speed of the current. The faster the water the heavier the jig you'll need to keep it near bottom.

THE TRUTH ABOUT SALMON

Studies in Oregon, Washington and California show that the old story of a steelhead always returning to the exact spot of its birth is often a fish story.

It's true that perhaps 99 percent of the fish return to the same major drainage system in which they were born, but from there on upstream the path becomes murky. The olfactory system of the steelie is sensitive enough to detect the chemical differences between major streams, such as the Salmon and Clearwater rivers in Idaho. However, once the fish enters one of these major rivers, the many small tributary streams are often not sufficiently different in chemical makeup to allow the fish to distinguish between them. Consequently, a fish may end up spawning in any of the streams which drain large areas of similar soils.

There's another reason the fish don't always make it "home." The spawning urge is triggered by increasing day length. If the fish's upstream journey has been held up because of low water temperatures (the fish will hold for weeks in one spot until a freshet raises the water temperature to at least 40°F.), and the critical day-length period is reached while they're still downstream from their intended destination, they'll often turn into the first small side stream they encounter, there to complete their long journey.

LITTLE FISH—BIG LURES

The kokanee, a landlocked sockeye salmon, rarely reaches lengths over 20 inches. It is becoming quite popular as a gamefish in many western states. Gang trolls used to catch them may seem out of place, considering the kokanee is a relatively small fish. However, there's method to this madness.

These salmon do not feed on traditional bait but on zooplankton—microscopic aquatic organisms—and they feed in schools. A gang troll worked at the proper depth will imitate a school of feeding fish, drawing the attention of gamefish, which assume the feedbag is on.

Experienced kokanee anglers often attach an 18- to 24-inch leader and a drift bobber, such as the Spin-N-Glo, to the gang troll as an added inducement. A small bit of worm on the terminal rig is also added by many kokanee fishermen.

Gum to Be Sure

Many anglers have a great deal of difficulty distinguishing chinook salmon from coho salmon from steelhead trout. The problem is compounded because these three species may be found at the same time as they ascend rivers to spawn.

There is a very easy way to tell these fish apart; look at the gumline inside the mouth. If it is black your fish is a chinook, if gray or silver it is a coho, if pure white it is a steelhead.

It is important to know the difference because limits and seasons may differ for each.

SPOONING FOR STEELHEAD

In steelhead waters of the Pacific Northwest, spooning is not as popular as the other steelheading methods. However, it quite often will outfish eggs or bobbers in certain types of water. Thus, it's a good idea to carry a few spoons in your tacklebox and use them when you find such water.

Look for fast water that is broken on the surface into swirls and boils. A fast riffle that bounces along over rocks with a boulder sticking up here and there is good for a spoon. So are those times when you can't fish with bait or bobber without losing too much gear.

It's possible to fish a spoon through a fast shallow run where your lead for baitfishing would hang up most of the time. With a spoon, you can search out the pockets in this sort of run to find a spot where a steelhead might be resting.

IMAGINING YOU'RE A STEELHEAD

To locate steelhead, look downstream, imagine you are a fish, and pick out the easiest water in which to swim upstream. That is where you probably will find them.

If whitewater covers half the river, fish will likely choose to come up the easier half. Cast your line across the water and let it drift into the fish paths you visualize. Let your lure work its way up that path, even though the smoother water ends somewhere along the way. If a fish decides to go after the lure, it very likely will come up the channel of quieter water.

Steelhead generally follow the same paths and rest in the same places. Thus, once you catch a fish, keep working that same spot each time you return to the river.

Knowing how to locate steelhead is what separates the experts from the tyros.

SULKING FISH

A hooked fish will regain energy and prolong the battle by sulking on the bottom, lying motionless while resting and recuperating. A lunker hooked on light gear requires trick rod handling rather than brawn to bring him to net. Adult chinook salmon are the kings of sulkers, with winter steelhead, hooked in fast water, a close second.

Next time you find yourself fighting a sulker, try twanging the taut line like a guitar string or tapping the rod butt with the side of your hand. It won't be long until you'll feel your opponent's head tossing angrily.

A brushy stream bank can prevent a fisherman from following a steelhead downstream. Sometimes this trick will fool them: Try slackening the line and allowing a belly to form, then bring it taut again and give a few light jerks. This gives a fish the illusion that his opponent is downstream from him and he will resist by swimming upstream.

HOT SHOTTING ON FOOT

Too often fishermen think of the deep-diving steelhead and salmon lures as off-limits to anyone without a boat. Actually, lures such as the Hot Shot, Tadpolly and Hot 'N' Tot, in sizes of one-quarter ounce and smaller, are useful for the wader-equipped early-season angler.

Wading a trout stream, an angler uses the deep-diving lure in exactly the same fashion as driftboating steelheaders. The method is called backtrolling. A fisherman allows about 15 to 20 feet of line to drift downstream (lure attached) into likely trout lies. As each pocket is fished out, the angler moves slowly and carefully a few steps downstream, allowing the lure to drop into the next hole.

To fish a drift again, step from the water and return to the starting point.

Felted waders and an old stick or wading staff are a must when backtrolling.

Spring Teaser

Spring steelheaders face two challenges: cold weather and finicky fish. When water temperatures tumble, instead of packing up and heading for home, try this double teaser to tempt those bottom-huggin' chromers.

Steelhead tend to drift into deep pools to wait for the next warming trend, so getting your offering down to them can be the key to success. First, attach a large-lipped deep-diving plug to your main line. The larger Hot Shot and its double-hook setup will do quite nicely. Remove the rear treble hook. To the split ring left behind, tie on a 30-inch leader. This should be a bit lighter than the main line, in the event you meet up with a bait-grabbin' log. At the end of the leader, tie on an egg hook. Trim out the hook with your favorite spawn bag, and you are ready to go.

The lure will take itself and the spawn bag down to the gravel where the fish are holding. And it waves the spawn bag at the steelhead it manages to wake up.

The rig is fished in the drop-back method from a boat, or can be offered by wading steelheaders standing in the shallows above the deep pools.

STEELHEAD QUICK QUIZ

1. During the summer months when water levels in rivers are low and clear, you'll usually catch more steelhead if you use . . .

☐ *larger lures*   ☐ *smaller lures*

2. Steelhead will mouth a plug, spoon or spinner, giving an angler plenty of time to set the hook.

☐ *true*   ☐ *false*

3. Year-round, 95 percent of fly-caught steelhead are usually taken on . . .

☐ *dry flies*   ☐ *wet flies*

4. When flyfishing for steelhead, the absolute minimum of 15-pound-test backing to use is . . .

☐ *50 yards*   ☐ *150 yards*   ☐ *200 yards*

5. A wet fly for steelhead should usually be fished . . .

☐ *just under the surface*   ☐ *close to the bottom*

1. Smaller lures. 2. False. Steelhead hit these artificials fast and hard, so you must strike fast and hard. 3. Wet flies. 4. 150 yards. 5. Close to bottom.

STEELHEADING WITH A FLYROD

Take along both your fly-rod and spinning gear when you go prospecting for steelies. You'll find quite a few opportunities to put the fly-rod to good use. Your chances of catching steelhead in shallow water or a slow-running pool are better with flies since spinning gear hangs up here.

Try casting flies about five yards from shore, a likely spot for steelhead in shallow water. Use bright flies on bright days and dark flies on dark days. Cast upstream, letting your flyline float down uninterrupted, with the looped line taking pressure off the fly so it can sink.

By keeping the rod low and the tip pointed at the fly, you can bring the artificial across the stream and down close to the bottom. A steelhead very often will follow across the stream and take the fly when it hangs straight down.

Deep holes offer little hope for flyfishermen since there is no movement such as that you get with a spinner or a bright fluorescent lure. That's the spot to use the spinning gear.

★

Flylines exhibit a frustrating tendency to coil around the tip-top of the rod when being reeled in. You can eliminate this problem by pushing the rod tip underwater as you reel.

A & B STEELHEAD RUNS

Summer steelhead migrating up the Columbia River system to Idaho each year are actually made up of two distinct groups of fish. The first usually enters the Columbia in late July to mid-August. Those fish average five to seven pounds and are mainly bound for the Salmon River, a tributary of the Snake River. Fish of the second group average 14 to 16 pounds and are mainly bound for the Clearwater River, another Snake tributary.

Idaho Fish and Game Department biologists traditionally assign a late August date as the end of the A run and the beginning of the B run.

POPULAR GAME FISHES

MUSKIES/PICKEREL/PIKE

MUSKIE MEASURES

The wake of an outboard motor seems to fascinate muskellunge.

Or maybe it's the light flashing off the propeller blades that brings these big gamefish into easy casting range. Any fisherman can benefit from this trait by putting a lure where a muskellunge is likely to be—in the wake about 25 feet behind a boat.

In the weedy South Bay of Ontario's Lake Nipissing, I watched two anglers concentrate on an area 25 feet back in the wake, while both casting and trolling. Each made a muskie-type bucktail spinner alternately skip above and dive below the wake.

On a cast they yanked their fishing rods, almost as though they were trying to jump the lures away from the mouth of a waiting muskellunge. Often enough one was there and, irritated or excited by this tactic, it instantly smashed the lure.

That's when most fishermen would agree with Nipissing, Ontario, angler Ed Yakovac, who warns "25-pound-test line is light tackle for really big muskellunge."

The average number of hours fished per muskie taken is estimated at around 200. You can reduce this considerably if you hire a muskie guide on your first trip to benefit from his know-how. Also talk to veteran fishermen to learn the best lures, how to work them and where to find fish.

MUSKIE MANEUVERS

One of the most difficult jobs an angler faces with the muskellunge is setting a hook properly. When the big fish clamps his powerful jaw on a wooden bait, you must be able to drive the hook solidly into rock-hard bone. The smoother the plug, the easier the task.

For maximum smoothness coat new plugs with several layers of polyurethane varnish. The slick surface will help slip the bait into a good hooking position.

If the lure is a season or two old, it will have grooves worn from the hooks. Fill the slots with mastic epoxy and then sand. Repaint the plug and cover it with polyurethane.

For the ultimate finish, you might even wax the varnished plug to make it more slippery.

HOOK ANGLES

UNACCEPTABLE BENDS — TOO TIGHT — TOO OPEN
ACCEPTABLE BENDS — SLIGHTLY OPEN — PARALLEL

Although most muskie anglers use a file and stone to keep their hooks sharp, few check the angle made by the barb and shank. Most hooks are bent toward the shank and do not sink into the jaw easily. To correct this, use two pairs of pliers and bend the barb outward away from the shank. To achieve best results, bend the point of the hook parallel to the shaft. Anything beyond a 180-degree angle will result in greater hooking qualities, but this will proportionately reduce the hook's ability to hold a fish.

Use the accompanying illustration for proper angles. Always examine any new plug and correct the angles of the hook if necessary.

•

Keeping heavy leader material coiled sometimes poses a problem. Instead of wrapping the tag end around the coil three or four times, use a rubberband. Slip it around the coil and push one end through the other. Pull it snug, and the leader will be secured.

JERK BAITS

Every muskie fisherman knows that jerk baits catch muskellunge with uncanny consistency. Unfortunately, jerk baits are very difficult to work—especially new ones fresh from the box.

Two things can improve the workability of a jerk bait. One alternative is to presoak the bait before casting it. Drop a jerk bait into a live well or minnow bucket an hour before fishing. The additional weight will cause it to dive deeper and be more responsive. A presoaked bait will also rise more slowly, allowing more time in between jerks.

The same improved action can be achieved by drilling two small holes just back of the front hook. Use a three-sixteenth-inch drill bit and sink the holes a quarter inch deep. Fill each cavity with lead, using waterproof glue to secure the lead. The additional weight will not sink the lure, but will cause it to go deeper—where the big muskies hang out.

Sensitive Muskies

Several Ontario fishing guides I have met over the years are adamant in their belief that the smell of freshly repainted lures and plugs is repulsive to muskies.

Tactics to overcome this condition include hanging the lure outside for from one week to a month; burying it in a box of earth for two weeks; and bathing it with scents such as oil of anise, strawberry, vanilla and one evil-smelling concoction brewed mainly from cigarette butts and Canadian whiskey.

MUSKELLUNGE LORE

While a lot of mystery surrounds muskie fishing, old-time 'lunge hunters swear by tips such as these:

● Muskies seem to be aware of boats in their vicinity, but they can't actually count them. A strike often follows if a muskie fisherman drifts quietly near a powerboat and remains in place after the powerboat makes a noisy exit.

● Muskies appear to be turned off by the odor of northern pike. Therefore, when they catch a northern, many veteran muskie trackers carefully put that lure aside and immediately wash their hands with unscented soap.

● Large spinners and spoons often attract muskies without tempting them to strike. Some fishermen toss around spinners and spoons until a muskie follows. Then they quickly switch to a large floating or diving plug.

● Muskies seem to hate stiff currents almost as much as the suckers they feed on do, so experienced river fishermen look for muskies first in slack water and in slow eddies near a dropoff.

★

Choose a lure to fit the fish you're after. Muskies go for big lures, bass for middle-sized lures and panfish for tiny ones. For super sport try a ¹⁄₆₄-ounce jig with a hair, feather or soft plastic body, with an ultralight rod on 2-pound line.

WORM POWER

A worm-baited lure often has that something-extra in fish appeal, especially on slow days.

When a three-pound brook trout north of Sault Ste. Marie would only tap my orange Abu Reflex spinner, a small piece of worm brought a solid strike.

In Ontario, fishermen often bait a Flatfish plug with a dew worm, especially for French River muskellunge, and in the warm-water Kawartha lakes, some of the most successful fishermen use a worm-baited Mepps spinner for bass, walleye and muskellunge.

Muskie Watch

Much of the fascination of muskie fishing is visual. The thrill of seeing one of those "living logs" stalk a bait causes the heart to hammer. To enjoy the sport to the fullest, the angler's eyes should be glued to the plug. But if you're using a dark-colored bait, you will have difficulty picking it up in the water.

To eliminate the problem, try painting a small patch of phosphorescent color on the front portion of the plug. Select a color that contrasts with the basic color of the plug. Be sure to use white enamel as a primer-base coat for the sharpest results.

Another aid to seeing bait in the water is the new "glowing" line. Monofilament manufacturers have produced brightly colored lines. Tie a plug to one of these; you'll have a direct-sight line to your lunker muskie.

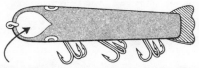

PHOSPHORESCENT PAINT ON HEAD OF MUSKY LURE.

Muskies usually prefer deep water, but in the late afternoon and on windy, cloudy days they will often come into the shallows. On such occasions you can sometimes seduce them with a fast-moving surface lure.

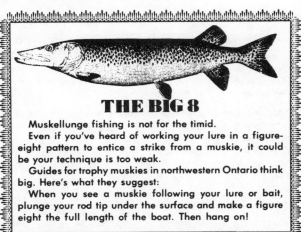

THE BIG 8

Muskellunge fishing is not for the timid.

Even if you've heard of working your lure in a figure-eight pattern to entice a strike from a muskie, it could be your technique is too weak.

Guides for trophy muskies in northwestern Ontario think big. Here's what they suggest:

When you see a muskie following your lure or bait, plunge your rod tip under the surface and make a figure eight the full length of the boat. Then hang on!

REARING MUSKIE FRY

Fisheries biologists have made great strides rearing muskie fingerlings successfully in hatcheries where conditions are carefully controlled for maximum production until the fish are six to 12 inches long and ready for release. But nature still interferes from time to time.

Hatchery men sometimes have to cope with abnormally cold weather. That keeps pond water frigid enough to prevent the development of tiny aquatic organisms which the newly hatched muskies rely on for food. Any shortfall in this early food supply could kill the fingerlings.

Once there was a heavy loss of muskies at a north-central Wisconsin hatchery site after heavy rains during the pollen season. Fisheries experts concluded that the rains washed airborne pollen into the rearing ponds, and the pollen irritated the gills of the young fish.

SMART ANGLER

For years, my husband had fished with little success. Then, suddenly, he started coming home with a full string. This increased his appetite for the sport, and he went more frequently.

I was with him one day when he tried an unfamiliar lake in the Rocky Mountains. He assembled his gear and stood looking all around the lake. "What are you looking for?" I asked.

"The old man."

"What old man."

"When I go fishing now," he said, "I always look for an old man. He has more time to figure out where the 'holes' are, and when he catches a full stringer and leaves, I take his place."

He then trudged off in the direction of a solitary white-haired man fishing in an unlikely looking spot. In an hour he returned with his limit.

Open Wide

Treble hooks are great for catching muskies and northerns, but are difficult to dislodge without destroying delicate gill tissue or having the teeth of the fish slash your hand. A good way to remove a plug is to first open the mouth wide with a spring-type mouth-opener. Keeping the line taut, insert your hand through the large gill cover of the fish, then back the barbs of the hooks out of the gills. When all the hooks are free, drop the lure through the gill opening and disconnect it from the leader. Now the fish can either be put on the stringer or it can be returned to the water unharmed.

FULL FISH MEASURE

My father often told of the big ones that got away, but he would also brag about some of the 12-inchers he had caught. When someone would question this, saying that 12 inches wasn't very big, Dad would simply explain that he always measured his fish between the eyes.

WEEDLESS JITTERBUG

The big three-hook Jitterbug is a deadly lure for giant bass, muskies and pike. It's all but useless, however, in thick weeds where these fish often hang out. To alter it for fishing in thick vegetation, take a small rubberband and loop the two side hooks together over the top of the plug. Remove the back hook. The hooks on top will still hold a big fish but won't snag as it's brought through grass and brush.

Pike Quiz

Their large ducklike snouts and elongated shapes distinguish pike species from other freshwater fish. But confusion often prevails when identifying the various members of this family. Three of the more popular species are shown here. Markings and scale patterns identify these as:

(1) _____
(2) _____
(3) _____

Answers: 1. Northern pike. These have scales on cheek but lower half of operculum is scaleless. Has light oval spots on dark background. **2. Muskellunge.** These have no scales on the lower half of both cheek and operculum. Coloration consists of vertical bands or dark spots on light background. **3. Chain pickerel.** This species has both cheek and operculum completely scaled. Color pattern consists of dark chain-like markings on lighter green background.

After you finish scaling a northern pike or pickerel, scrape the skin thoroughly with a knife blade and then swish the fish in cold water to get rid of some of the strong odor and taste that some find objectionable.

FRESHWATER BARRACUDA

The following is a tip that is guaranteed to improve your muskie-fishing success:

Muskies have a coldwater preference. In lakes, this means, of course, deep water. In most rivers, however, muskies have no deepwater retreat. So look for coldwater springs. Any water entering a river that is several degrees cooler than the river water will attract muskies. And believe me, it's most enjoyable receiving those quizzical looks from old-timers when you keep landing 15-pounders throughout the hottest days.

MUSKIE MASTICATION

If a lure spit out by a terribly irritated muskie is any criteria, lures may not cling very long to jaws of fish who break off.

This lure, found in a Pennsylvania lake heavily stocked with muskellunge, was chewed to pieces. By actual count, 64 tooth marks, some protruding entirely through the bait, were found in the balsa wood crankbait. The one remaining treble hook, hardly rusty at all, was straightened out. It seems obvious that the muskie broke the line and, with temper flaring, went to work mean-mouthing that bait clinging to its jaw and then spit it out.

Not all fish are able to dislodge and spit out lures this easily. Some, with lures lodged deep in the esophagus regions, may not survive. Others, however, hooked in the lip region apparently rid themselves of the lure somehow, usually in a day or two.

★

When fishing for bony-mouthed fish like pike, muskies and big bass, you'll discover they can straighten out your hook unless it is properly tempered.

When fishing for pike, pickerel, muskellunge or other sharp-toothed fish, include in your gear a pair of medium-weight leather gloves—or at least one for your left hand. A leather glove will help you get a safe, firm grip on a fish when boating it. The glove protects your hand while the lure is disengaged, and should you wish to return the fish to the water a firm (not tight) grasp—preferably around the gills or in the mouth—is less likely to harm the fish.

EXCLUSIVE MUSKIES

The muskie can at times be truly called the fish of 10,000 casts. During Memorial Day weekend there was a muskie-fishing tournament on the Spider Lake Chain in Sawyer County, Wisconsin, where 65 experienced contestants fished diligently for three solid days. Not a single legal fish was taken.

Think about that for a minute: 65 anglers at ten hours per day on the water for three days. That comes to 1950 fishing hours.

Fishy Story?

There are as many fishermen in the world as there are fish stories, but it isn't very often that you hear of a dog that's tried it. At any rate, there was one water spaniel who covered his name with glory. Sitting in the bow of his master's boat one day, he saw the man's rod fall into the water. He jumped in, grabbed the rod just as it started to sink. As he swam towards shore, a passing pickerel struck his lure. The dog, who had been fishing with his master many times, alternately tugged and rested, slowly heading for shore. He played the fish for 15 minutes, got the upper hand and beached it—a five-pounder.

QUALITY OR QUANTITY

An angler was dragging a fish twice his size from the end of a fishing pier when he passed another fisherman with a half-dozen small ones on a stringer. "Howdy," said the first, pausing for a comment. The second fisherman stared calmly and said, "Just caught the one, eh?"

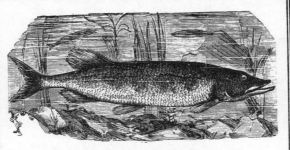

BEST BAITS FOR PIKE

In an elaborate study conducted several years ago, researchers at the University of Missouri tested 14 different fish to determine which were the most vulnerable to predation by northern pike. Pike ranging in size from four to 40 inches were kept in ponds and pools under varying conditions and given unlimited opportunities to feed on small 1.3- to 6.4-inch fish presented in mixed lots. The testing was done between June and September.

The list below shows which fish pike went after most often. Results were the same for both ponds and pools and variables such as water turbidity. Age/size of pike did not show up as significant. You can use this as a guide for selecting minnows and lures to catch pike.

Highly vulnerable to northern pike: *1. gizzard shad, 2. small carp, 3. bigmouth buffalo, 4. fathead minnow, 5. smallmouth bass.*

Moderately vulnerable: *6. white sucker, 7. green sunfish, 8. largemouth bass, 9. golden shiner, 10. yellow perch.*

Least vulnerable: *11. channel catfish, 12. small northern pike, 13. bluegill, 14. black bullhead.*

•

A red and white spoon is a favorite lure for large pike. When you cast the spoon, don't reel it back immediately. Let it sink just short of the bottom before you start the retrieve. Then lift your rod and let the lure flutter down again.

•

Make Mine a Double

Muskies and pike react fast when they spy "double-take" lures. We're referring to the rigging, used by some experts, which places two lures in tandem. The rig consists of a large minnow-shaped plug trolled 18- to 24-inches behind a big spinner-and-bucktail combo. The result appears to be a large minnow chasing a smaller bait. Few pike will allow the plug to catch and eat that smaller lure.

A 30- to 45-pound-test wire leader with a swivel-snap connects the plug and spinner combo. Add a three-ounce sinker above the spinner to sink the double rigging to desired depth.

Troll near weed beds. About 75 percent of the time pike will hit the trailing plug, while the spinner will account for the other 25 percent of the strikes.

STINGERS FOR TOOTHY FISH

Fish with teeth can wreak havoc on monofilament line, as well as the nerves of anglers. They do not quit when the weather becomes cold, either, but switch tactics to nip at the tail end of a jig or minnow. The remedy for such behavior is commonly called a stinger: a short piece of line with a treble hook hidden in a baitfish's tail. But then again, there are those teeth to contend with.

A solution to "bite-off" by the likes of pike, muskies or pickerel is steel leader material without the normally necessary swivels, sleeves and snap lock. I like Steelon, which has a plastic coating over the wire that melts from the heat of a match or lighter.

All an angler has to do to come up with a dentureproof stinger is wrap an appropriate length of Steelon at the bend of the jig's hook and heat it until the plastic melts into one solid mass. The same procedure is repeated with the smaller treble hook.

Make sure you do not melt the plastic off the wire by getting it too hot.

This setup works for some sharp-dentured saltwater species as well.

A Mecca For Pike

Pennsylvania is the only place in the world where pursuers of the pike can find all six species of this scrappy fish.

Five of these are natives. The sixth, the Siberian muskellunge (Amur pike), was imported by the Pennsylvania Fish Commission from Russia in 1968. The commission's experimental planting of this species of pike is doing well in the waters of Prince Gallitzin State Park, Cambria County.

Teamwork

Mr. and Mrs. Harry Reinfelder believe in teamwork when it comes to fishing. They were angling for walleyes with nightcrawlers in Munuscong Bay, off the eastern end of Michigan's Upper Peninsula, and cast their lines at the same time.

A lone muskie promptly grabbed both baits. They battled the fish together until his line broke. Hers held, and she eventually landed the 37-pound fish. Incidentally, an 18-inch sucker was found in the muskie's stomach.

Use a pair of needle-nose pliers instead of your fingers when you want to tie a really snug, nonslip knot in monofilament fishing line. This works well with the standby knots such as the blood knot and the nail knot. You will find the pliers especially helpful on a cold day when your fingers have become stiff.

★

When fishing at night, remember that pike, pickerel, muskies and yellow perch are poor night feeders while bass, walleyes, catfish, trout, bluegills and crappies are active nocturnal feeders.

Pickerel Tip

Chain pickerel generally display exceptional appetites. It's not unusual to find a three-pounder with a six-inch sunfish stretching out its thin-walled stomach. But when the jack pike prove finicky, try tiny minnows measuring a mere inch or two. This strategy can pay off handsomely, particularly during winter, and often yields a stringer of arm-sized chainsides.

Waders and Walleye Nights

Walleyes favor low-light conditions. Day-in and day-out fishing after dark will bring the most chances for a full stringer, and the odds get even better in autumn. That's the time when Old Mooneyes can often be found in waters no deeper than three or four feet, searching for emerald shiners or perch, and you can get at them if you're equipped with a pair of waders.

Use a light spinning rod with 8- to 12-pound test and a variety of minnow imitations, both surface and shallow runners. More fish will choose natural-looking thin shapes over standard fat plugs—Rebels, Rapalas, Long As Devil's Horses, etc. Jigs with plastic shad or marabou bodies tipped with live minnow can also be counted on to do a good job.

Look for night walleyes in the late fall on shoals, flats and points where deep water is nearby. It's often a good idea to scout an area after dark to find emerald shiners. On calm nights they can easily be spotted by their wakes as they search just below the surface for plankton dinners. Where they congregate, walleyes usually appear sooner or later.

Even though spotting baitfish calls for calm, you can fish with wind as long as the whitecaps aren't big enough to bowl you over. Weather makes no difference to the walleyes. They may decide to hit a topwater lure twitched just enough to spin its propellors, or grab a skinny minnow slowly wobbling along a foot down.

TRADERS FAVOR WALLEYE EGGS

Walleyes, walleyes, who's got the walleyes? One state that has them in abundance is New Mexico, and state game and fish department personnel there view walleye eggs taken during the spawning season at Ute Lake as a valuable commodity on the gamefish trading block.

In 1978, for instance, New Mexico Game and Fish Department personnel obtained about 23.5 million walleye eggs during egg-taking operations at Ute. Dick McCleskey, hatcheries section administrator for the Department, says some of the eggs were traded to Texas for blue catfish and striped bass fingerlings, some went to Colorado in return for rainbow, cutthroat and kokanee eggs, and still more were traded to Utah for rainbow trout eggs.

Anybody want to swap for three Mickey Mantle baseball cards?

★

When fish appear to have lockjaw, try reeling a floating-diving lure barely under the surface so that it makes a V on the water. Look out!

Walleyes at Night

Many fishermen are skeptical about catching walleyes on a surface lure, but they will surface with great gusto for topwater lures after sundown.

Those that hide in weeds during the day and those on deep, gravel bottoms move in to feed along shore after sunset. Poppers, chuggers and lures with spinners fore-and-aft to create a good disturbance on the surface will attract walleyes when used at a slow pace. All-white lures, or those of light colors often out-produce more somber colored lures. Walleyes have good night vision and can readily see such lures.

Most anglers know that walleyes are neither bottom- nor surface-dwelling fish. They live and feed somewhere in the middle. And knowing exactly where in the water walleyes are is a major factor in knowing how to catch them. Now, thanks to studies done by the Winnipeg (Canada) Department of the Environment, anglers can better judge.

When scientists examined the eye structure of walleyes they found these facts. First, their eyes are located and set for looking up and out toward surface light. In this way they are able to monitor the amount of light above them. Secondly, their eyes are equipped primarily with nerve cells that favor dim light.

All that remained to be determined, after these initial findings, was how walleyes reacted to different light intensities from above. In bright light, the walleyes reacted by going deeper in a water column. In darkness, the fish tended to rise toward the surface. Walleyes tried to find light conditions which favored their dim light capabilities.

Anglers can easily take advantage of these new findings. Fish deep on bright days, and more toward the surface on cloudy days or at night.

WALLEYE CASH CROP

Minnesota anglers are wild about leeches, reports a study by the Minnesota Department of Natural Resources. Leeches are deadly baits for walleyes, and state anglers spend over $2 million every year for the slippery critters.

How many leeches does $2 million buy? Well, the DNR folks figured it out to be an estimated 45.9 tons used annually. That's about 1,194,180 dozens of leeches. Incidentally, the DNR explains that the ribbon leech (Nephelopsis obscura) is the kingpin species used for bait. Although about 30 other species of leeches inhabit Minnesota waters, they are rarely used by anglers.

THE STING

Coldwater, boat-spooked and overfed walleyes are often notorious for picking up a minnow by the tail and testing it—even carrying it around—while your jig dangles harmlessly two inches from their mouths. The solution to this frustration comes in the shape of a little No. 10 treble hook—a stinger!

A stinger puts a hook back at the minnow's tail, so short-nipping walleyes get a little more than they bargained for. Using a piece of monofilament about 2-pound-test lighter than your fishing line, tie one end to the little treble and—allowing for the extra length you'll get when you pull the knot tight—the other end into the eye of your jig. Then trim off the excess.

A little practice should give you a stinger hook that reaches back to where the minnow's body ends and the tail fin begins. Stick one hook of the treble into the minnow and fish your jig as usual.

If you're going to tie your stingers on demand, practice at home first to find how much line you need and a convenient way of working with it.

To avoid tying more than one knot per stinger, I carry a bunch of trebles with the piece of line already tied to them.

With a stinger hook the short hitters are about to become fillets instead of frustrations.

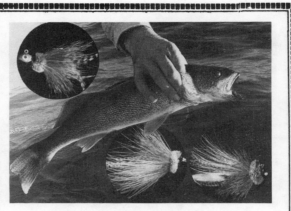

Greatest Walleye Fly

The lead-headed fly, generally referred to as a jig, is one of the all-time great lures for walleyes. But one pattern is truly outstanding—the muddler minnow. The pattern is very suggestive of crayfish and darter-type minnows—both walleye favorites. With or without a worm or pork-eel to sweeten the lure, this pattern really excites walleyes in deep water.

The pattern looks complicated, but it is not. Tie several long hackle feathers to the hook shank. Over these, tie on bunches of deer body hair; the ends flare upward as the tying thread is pulled taut. The hair is trimmed to form a fat collar—the main feature of this pattern.

Tie some of natural tan color, others all white and all black. These three colors outfit you well for a lively season with walleyes.

Walleyes are notorious short strikers. They will often nip at a plastic worm or pork-rind trailer. In such cases, a tail hook added to the end of the lure will often succeed in hooking them.

•

When casting a jig for walleyes, fish it slowly and deep, letting it sink to the bottom. As you retrieve the jig, reel in the slack while raising and lowering the rod tip, letting the jig hit bottom each time.

WALLEYES

1. Walleyes usually feed better on the windward side of a reef than on the lee side.
   ☐ True   ☐ False
2. Walleyes in a school are usually all of the same size. Thus, if you want big ones you'll first have to catch a big one.
   ☐ True   ☐ False
3. The best fishing for walleyes is usually . . .
   ☐ during the day   ☐ at night
4. The best fishing for walleyes in lakes is around . . .
   ☐ deep, rocky ledges   ☐ deep, sandy bottoms
5. Walleyes cruise around a lake searching for bait-fish. They are too energetic to stay in one spot waiting for food to drift toward them.
   ☐ True   ☐ False

1. True. 2. True. 3. At night. 4. Deep, rocky ledges. 5. False.

WALLEYE HOTSPOT

When a research tagging study was completed on a number of popular Minnesota walleye lakes, it revealed two things that should help anglers immensely.

First, walleyes spend 90 percent of their time associating with structure and bottom features in midlake regions that are not connected to the shoreline.

Second, there was one type of bottom feature they distinctly preferred over all others: a rock-capped island or hump that tops off about eight feet beneath the surface, with surrounding water that averages 20 feet deep.

Finding these walleye hotspots is not easy, which may be exactly why they are walleye hotspots in the first place. You'll need an accurate bottom contour map and some type of depthsounder, plus plenty of patience.

A Lot Of Eggs!

Walleyes in Oneida Lake, New York, produced 12 to 18 *billion* eggs each spring during an eight-year study. With a start like that the lake should be knee-deep in walleyes, right? Well, a lot of things happen twixt the egg and the stringer.

Oneida is a walleye-yellow perch lake and the site of some extensive research in "year-class strength" in the jargon of the fishery biologist. More than 99 percent of the walleye mortality took place before the fish were one-half inch long, and probably occurred during the egg stage. Cannibalism by older walleyes appeared to be an important factor. It was most intense when young perch were scarce. When abundant, perch buffered the predation on fingerling walleyes.

The five year classes that were monitored for four years each produced from 12,000 to 478,000 adult fish. This study, while certainly not providing all the answers, sheds additional light on the intriguing question of what happened to those billions of eggs.

WEEDBED PANFISH

The favorite haunts of panfish are often in the hides and holes right in the midst of the thickest weedbeds. These tough places to fish drive most anglers off the best waters when weeds reach within a foot or so of the surface. But that's when the fishing can be at its best, since fish are getting used to taking floating terrestrial insects.

To entice fish from weedbeds, find the smallest torpedo bobber that your outfit will cast and tie it to the end of your line. Tie two feet of 3-pound leader to the back of the bobber. Add two feet of 2-pound leader to this, using a blood knot and leaving one tag of leader about five inches long.

Now tie a cork bug to the dropper and a small dry fly to the point. If the weeds are a foot or more deep, you can even use a wet fly or nymph at the point; the bug will hold it up.

Cast to open pockets in the bed, or if the weeds don't reach the surface, cast above the bed. Let the rig sit a long time. Then retrieve with gentle twitches, *very* slowly. When you see a swirl, set the hook.

Also set the hook if the bug or the bobber makes an odd move. When this happens a fish has taken the point fly.

FLOAT YOUR POPPERS

For sunfish, rock bass and smallmouths, try drifting small poppers down a lazy river on hot days. Use an old eight-foot flyrod with about 10 feet of ordinary 4-pound mono as a leader and a few bugs in Sizes 10, 12 and 14.

Wade the shallow stretches where the river is slow and gradually pay out 15 or 20 yards of line, letting the current carry your popper downstream. Now and then hold the popper still and twitch your rod tip. It's not fancy, but it's a great way to relax and cool off on a hot day.

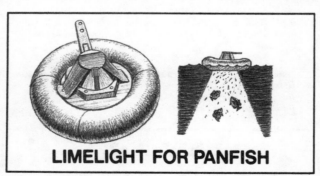

Instant Bluegill Bug

The next time you encounter surface-feeding bluegills and your fly boxes lack bluegill bugs, don't feel frustrated. It's easy to construct a realistic substitute. Here's how you do it. Take a dry trout fly, clip the hackles evenly off the bottom—and with no more effort you have a low-riding bluegill bug.

Clipping the hackle accomplishes two things. It lets the fly ride flush in the surface film, presenting a buggy outline. And it exposes the hook point, making it easier to hook bluegills, which have tiny mouths.

Dress your dry fly as you normally would. To help keep it afloat, dress the leader, too. A floating leader will not disturb bluegills; the V of its wake may even attract fish to the fly.

LIMELIGHT FOR PANFISH

Fishermen who prefer to get away from the crowds and still catch plenty of crappies should try night fishing. Using either a commercially made floating crappie light or a homemade version from an auto spotlight mounted in a boat-trailer innertube and pine board, night crappie fishermen can literally create a dining room for panfish.

These floating lights, which run on 12-volt marine batteries, draw plankton to the side of the boat. The tiny creatures swarm under the lights and in turn attract baitfish, such as emerald shiners, that are crappie tablefare.

At first fishing is done a few feet off the bottom with either slip bobbers, plain line, or small jigs, all baited with minnows. Later in the evening, crappies usually move upward.

This method works whether you fish big lakes where crappies grow to trophy size or small lakes and ponds.

TWO OLD-TIME BLUEGILL BAITS

It seems as though I've spent just about as much time in bait-shops for angling necessities as I have fishing. Every so often I'll hear an old bluegiller come in and ask the owner if he has cress bugs or perch bugs. Most of the time the answer is no, but the idea is a sound one. In the old noncommercial days when baitshop owners fished and gathered their own live bait, these live baits took their toll on many a gamefish.

Cress bugs would probably be more recognizable today if they were called caddis larvae, the preadult form imitated by flyfishing trouters. The caddis spends its intermediate stage of life in portable housing: hollow plant stems or tiny twigs, stones, shells and leaf pieces held together by silk produced by the larvae. Clinging to rocks, logs and other current-washed debris in rivers and streams where oxygen abounds, cress bugs can easily be harvested with seines or small nets or simply hand-picked.

Perch bugs, being hardier, spend their juvenile days in lakes, ponds, swamps and the slower, less-oxygenated rivers and streams. They are the nymph stage of both dragonflies and damselflies. These meat-eating larvae are a special treat for all panfish and both basses. Being efficient predators, most notably of mosquito larvae and adults as well, perch bugs attack from ambush sites in weeds, sunken leaves, etc.—places where anglers with seines will find them.

Both of these insects can be kept for long periods by storing them in plastic foam coolers or buckets with some of their natural habitat. Water should be changed daily or aerated with an aquarium pump. Putting the container in a cool place lessens the chances of having a hatch before a fishing trip.

Both baits are workers year-round, whether you're pushing water with oars or walking on it with ice creepers—truly worth the time and effort in harvesting them.

PREDATOR ALERT

Should a sudden lull develop when you are panfishing, it does not necessarily mean the school has moved on or simply lost interest in your bait or lure. It could well be that a predatory fish has moved into the area intent on a snack. Having a suitable outfit rigged up and sitting by will give you the chance to take full advantage of the situation. Over the years I have seen hefty Dolly Varden char caught by panfish anglers in the West and pike, muskie, bass and walleye by others in the Midwest.

Attempt to judge beforehand which species are most likely to play the role of predator: if the water is shallow and weedy, perhaps pike; rocky outcroppings or wharf pilings, smallmouth bass; steep dropoffs nearby, muskie or walleye. Then rig an outfit for that fish. When the wee ones stop biting, grab the heavy outfit and make a few random casts. You may discover the reason for the disruption is very interesting.

Flies are fine for bluegills, especially in Sizes 10 and 12. But they are markedly better when tipped with a tiny tad of worm, a maggot or shrimp. Try it, bream like it!

A WINNER IN WINTER

Goldenrod grubs are a popular panfish bait in the Midwest, and they're just about unbeatable for winter fishing. The grub is the wormlike larval stage of a fly that lays its eggs in the stems of goldenrod during the summer.

When the fly inserts the eggs in the stem tissue, the plant reacts by forming a rounded growth around them called a gall. The grubs hibernate in winter and come out as adult flies in the spring. Anglers collect and harvest the galls from along secondary roads in September or October and store them in a refrigerator or freezer.

When it's time to go icefishing, remove the galls from cold storage, cut them open and remove the grubs that are found inside. It's a dynamite bait.

EMERGENCY JIGS

1. Heat shank.

2. Twist eye and bend shank up.

3. Squeeze on split-shot.

4. Bind on dressing of feathers or hair.

When my partner and I lost the last of our small jigs during a crappie fishing spree, he quickly saved the day by whipping up a new batch right there in the boat. Long-shanked bait hooks were gripped by the bend with a set of pliers while the shank behind the eye was heated cherry red with the flame of his lighter. Each hook was allowed to cool slowly. Then the eyes were twisted sideways 90 degrees and the shank bent upward at an angle of 45 degrees. He then pinched a splitshot over the bent shank and scraped the metal shiny with the point of his knife.

A large walleye jig supplied more than enough marabou to dress the four ultralights that got us through the rest of the day. He happened to have a spool of heavy thread in his tacklebox, but light fishing line would have done just as well for binding the plumage to the shanks.

Quick Time Spiders

When it comes to being tough on an angler's offerings, bluegills rank right up there with the likes of pike, muskies and barracuda—especially if you are talking flies and panfish bugs.

Since they like fake spiders, try carrying a box of different-colored old plastic worms and grubs of the floating variety, a supply of rubber leg material, a small needle with eye large enough to accommodate several strands of rubber at once, and a tube of Crazy Glue. With this paraphernalia, you have the makings of a veritable bug factory on board.

When an old spider or bug looks impossibly decrepit, strip away what is left of the body and discard it. Pinch off a suitably sized section of one of the worms or grubs and run the bare hook through it. Apply a drop of the glue fore and aft, then use the needle to run a few strands of leg material midway through the middle of the body, and trim to size. Using a match or lighter, heat the needle tip and touch the entry and exit points of the legs to help keep them in place at the insistent tugs of fish.

★

For years it was believed that yellow perch wouldn't take artificial lures. Now fishermen take limits on tiny hair jigs. The secret is to retrieve slowly and set the hook automatically every turn of your reel handle. This hooks sneaky perch you can't feel taking the lure.

★

A can of corn, opened and carefully lowered into a midlake hole, will attract bluegills and catfish if left there for a few hours. Fish around the can, and the best bait to use is (you guessed it), kernels of corn.

KEEP THE KEEPERS

It's only natural for the nimrod to want to exercise his prowess and stalk the larger panfish. But once in a while he should take home a few of the smaller panfish, especially those that have been badly hooked. It will, if only on a small scale, help reduce the stunting of fish, which, as most fishermen know, is caused when there is an overabundance of fish and too little feed.

TOP TIPS FOR SPRING PANFISH

● **Bank-fish for bluegills** when waters reach the 50s, for crappies when water is near 60°F, and perch when water hits the 45° to 50°F range.
● **Clear spin bubbles,** used with light leaders and wet flies such as black gnats, allow casting of tiny baits having little weight.
● **Bluegills spawning in and around lily pads** and other heavy cover can be taken efficiently with old-fashioned canepoles, short lines and small hooks baited with leaf or red worms.
● **When shallow-water panfish get spooky** after a number have been caught on flies or rubber spiders, add a waxworm or piece of earthworm to entice a few more.
● **Fish the north shore in early spring** where waters warm the quickest.
● **Fishing right after ice-out** is often productive if you jig vertically using tiny icefishing spoons tipped with the grub baits.
● **Flyfishing rubber spiders** and poppers in small sizes on islands just beneath the surface and off points is often excellent weeks before bluegills actually invade these areas.
● **When searching for productive fishing spots** during bluegill and crappie spawns, look for reeds and arrowhead weeds. Both grow in the firm bottoms that spawners prefer.
● **Tiny crayfish in the inch-long range** are deadly for spawning bluegills, which aggressively inhale the tiny crustaceans.
● **After a long winter,** panfish fall easy victim to nymph baits such as wigglers (mayfly nymphs), cress bugs (caddis larvae) and perch bugs (the larvae of the dragonfly).

THE CHANNEL CAT

If Nature had set out to design the ideal sportfish, she could hardly have improved upon the channel cat. You may disagree, but think about it. A dogged scrapper that often rolls on the surface and has been known to leap free of the water when hooked, the channel catfish will strike anything from dry flies to plugs and spinners, to crawlers and stinkbaits. Sleek and attractive, it prefers a clear-flowing current but inhabits all kinds of water.

Children love to catch small catties on canepoles. Specialists rig up stout tackle for 20- and 30-pounders. Displaced flyfishermen in the grain belt call them "prairie trout."

The next time you're enjoy-

ing a meal of deep-fried channel cat fillets—the most popular freshwater food fish in the country—reflect for a second on the many virtues of the tasty fish you're eating. Few of our native American fishes provide as much all-around pleasure.

DREAM STREAM

When I was visiting ir. Wyoming, a native asked me to go fishing. He wanted to get away from the mob, although by my eastern standards there wasn't any crowding on the streams around Laramie.

Jim drove toward Lander and turned into the Red Desert country. He left the main highway for a secondary macadam road, from that to a dirt road and then onto a cattle trail. Finally he left all semblance of a pathway, cut across open country and pulled up on the lip of a promontory from which we could see up and down a winding stream for miles and miles. At a point some three miles below, two cars were parked.

"Darn!" said Jim in disgust. "This place is taken!"

He threw the car in gear and headed across the prairie for some privacy.

Cat-Catching Capers

Large catfish seem to fascinate people. The first question they usually ask after admiring a slick-skinned specimen is, "How did you land it?"

Rod-and-reel anglers usually employ one of two methods. They play the fish with savoir faire; or, as soon as they horse the fish into the shallows, they clamp down on the line and run backward until a tree stops them.

A variation of the latter method: As soon as the fish is in shallow water, drop rod and reel, rush into the water and bulldog the fish.

The angler who uses a trotline is more apt to land a larger fish than the rod-and-reeler because his tackle is heavier, and the fish often has worn itself out fighting the strong nylon line. If the trotliner does not have a dip net large enough to handle the fish, he can ease it alongside the boat, dip the gunwale and ship a little water along with the fish, then remove the hook. If, however, he has an excitable companion who inadvertently shifts his weight to the side being dipped, the boat usually turns turtle smack dab on top of the trotline.

There is another method called the "belly tickle" in which the trotliner eases the boat alongside the hooked fish, reaches under the cat and gently massages its stomach. I have it on good authority that this will lull even the biggest catfish into an almost hypnotic state, at which time the fish can be hoisted aboard with little tail flapping. I have neither witnessed nor tried this method, primarily because the catfish I have hooked on trotlines have always fit inside my landing net.

There is another method of calming a catfish. This one works so long as the fisherman's hand will fit around the tail of the fish (see photograph). Pressure must be applied from top to bottom, not side to side, at the base of the tail of the fish. When pressure is applied, the fish becomes temporarily paralyzed. Bear in mind, however, that when the pressure is released, the fish will be just as mobile and powerful as ever.

A REMINDER

When wearing glasses afield, it's a good idea to get an elastic cord or band that fastens across the back of your head. On a boat, for example, glasses can fall off while you lean out over the water to land a fish. Losing your glasses can turn the trip into a disaster.

STOP THE SPITTERS

If the fish are spitting out your lures before you can set the hook, switch to a soft plastic lure about the same size. The plastic feels more natural, and a fish will take longer to reject it.

DOUGHBAIT

Looking for a good effective bait for catfish? Try this recipe my grandmother swore by back in the 1930s. Catfish was a main staple of our diet, and we always had a platter of golden-fried fillets on the table after fishing with her "dugh."

Add one pound of chicken livers, including blood, to one cup of yellow cornmeal. Using your hands, mix thoroughly, squeezing the chicken livers and cornmeal together. Don't be gentle. Squeeze hard. Once mixed, add more cornmeal until a sticky paste is formed.

To this mixture add pulled cotton (my grandmother used raw cotton straight from the field, but cotton balls will do). Pull each ball apart, adding small clumps of cotton to the mixture; about a dozen balls are needed. The cotton holds the mixture together in the water.

Add cornmeal until individual balls of the mixture can be rolled without sticking to your hand.

Store in plastic containers until ready for use. The mixture can be frozen. My grandmother never did, though. She made up a batch, let it age for three or four days, then headed for the lake.

To use, bait each hook with a small doughball pinched from the dough—then get ready to reel in those catfish!

Buccal pertains to the mouth.
Caudal pertains to the tail.

PADDLEFISH

The long, sharklike body of a paddlefish has few scales, and the vast mouth is toothless. A freshwater giant weighing up to 200 pounds, it feeds primarily on microscopic zooplankton.

The most remarkable part of the paddlefish, however, is the large, snoutlike appendage that gives the fish its name and precedes the large mouth and body as it moves through the Mississippi, Missouri and Ohio river systems. The "paddle" is covered with taste buds and comprises about one-fourth to one-third of the fish's length.

Often called the "spoonbill cat," the paddlefish is among the last survivors of a primitive family. Its one close relative inhabits China's Yangtze River system and reportedly grows to over 20 feet.

Protect Your Catch

Turtles, particularly snappers, can be devastating to fish kept on live chains or stringers suspended from your boat, especially on small ponds. The turtles attack and bite out chunks of flesh from the catch without your knowing it. Keeping fish on live chains in water overnight is an open invitation to turtles to dine.

Where turtles are abundant, keep fish in a live net made of wire that is easily collapsed for storage, or keep them safely in a livewell within the boat, or in a moistened burlap bag on the boat floor.

Stink Stuff

Catfish often go on a feeding spree as a stream begins to rise or subside after heavy run-off. One reason is that flooding waters wash a lot of food into the stream. Another reason is the catfish can locate this food—or a fisherman's bait—with its amazing "smelling" apparatus, even if the water is muddy. In one study at the University of Michigan's School of Natural Resources, it was discovered that a blind bullhead could detect food from a distance of at least 25 fish lengths away. This is why at times a malodorous bait like coagulated blood or commercial stink bait will catch more catfish than will something natural.

In the United States there are seven popular native catfish species: channel cat, blue cat, flathead catfish, white catfish, black bullhead, brown bullhead and yellow bullhead—and each one possesses the uncanny ability to home in one food by smell rather than sight. The ultra-sensitive "taste buds" cover the fish's whiskers, commonly called barbels. There are eight of these appendages: one long pair trails from each corner of the mouth, two more are stationed near the nostrils, and four project from under the chin. The flathead catfish is the aristocrat of the clan, preferring food that is alive or at least fresh. The others are primarily scavengers and will dine on most anything that is found or falls into the water, even the rotting carcass of a fish, bird or mammal. Stink turns a catfish on, not off.

BLACK DRUM FACTS

The black drum, Pogonias cromis, largest member of the drum family, is an important gamefish along much of the Atlantic Coast from New York south, being most abundant in the Gulf of Mexico. Pogonias, from Greek, means bearded and refers to the conspicuous chin barbels, or whiskers; cromis, also from the Greek, means to grunt or to croak, and refers to the drumming noise (made by the air bladder) produced by a school of these fish.

Black drum spawn near the mouths of rivers, bays or sounds. The fish spend their early lives in estuaries, and as adults they frequent shallow coastal waters.

Growth rates vary, but a one-year-old fish is usually eight to 10 inches long, a five-year-old about 30 inches and 19 pounds, and a 10-year-old is 46 inches and 60 pounds.

Almost any bottom-dwelling invertebrate serves as food. Fish may also be eaten. The strong crushing teeth allow the black drum to handle crabs as well as mussels and oysters.

The flesh of the black drum is good table fare. However, the fish is often infested with a parasitic nematode—the "spaghetti worm"—which, while not harmful to man, does nothing to enhance the flavor.

Sluggish strikers but strong fighters, the fish are often taken on the bottom with baits such as dead mullet, crab or shrimp, but jigs, spoons and bucktails are also effective.

DOUBLE PACK STINKBAIT

A great many of the cheese baits, blood baits and stinkbaits used for catfish and carp that are sold in various aromas and consistencies come in glass jars. Sealable plastic pouches can prevent a jar from breaking and rolling around in the trunk of your car or spilling on the seat or the floor.

They have another advantage, too. If the bait that you are using separates, you can use the pouch to knead it back together. If you are using rubber worms that are dipped in the bait, you can spread the bait on the worm easily through the plastic without getting it all over yourself.

An easy way to handle this type of bait is simply to bag up the amount of each kind that you need. Put the assortment in a plastic bucket and wedge the bucket in a corner of your vehicle. The bucket is also handy for bailing water.

I use Ziploc bags. Do not overfill. Leave a little airspace at the end of the lock if the stuff you are going to use is still "working." This will prevent an explosion of stinkbait in the trunk of your automobile.

FISHING TECHNIQUES

FISHING TECHNIQUES

ANGLING HINTS AND TIPS

LONG-RANGE RELEASING

While fishing Vancouve Island's brawling Gold River, our group was confronted with several dead-end situations where hooked steelhead could not be followed downstream because of steep cliffs. Dr. Ken Hampson came up with a solution that, while not guaranteeing we could land hooked fish, gave our quarry an opportunity to escape without breaking the line.

We simply increased the breaking strain of our leaders and switched to light wire hooks that were further softened by annealing. This was accomplished by holding the bend of the hook over the flame of a lighter until it became red, and then allowing it to cool slowly.

Pinching barbs closed further ensured hooks would straighten and pull free with relative ease.

Most fish hooked were landed without incident, but on those occasions when strong steelhead managed to gain the heavy rapids, we were able to affect a long-range release by simply lowering the rod tip and increasing pressure on the reel spool until the hook straightened and pulled free.

In none of the cases did the leaders break, proof that "Doc's" idea was a boon to both fish and fishermen alike.

★

At times, porkrind will outfish anything else you can hang on a spoon, jig or spinner lure. Maybe it's the "live feel" or sinuous action, or even taste—no one really knows.

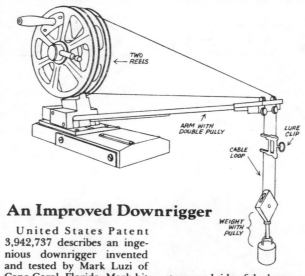

TWO REELS
ARM WITH DOUBLE PULLY
LURE CLIP
CABLE LOOP
WEIGHT WITH PULLY

An Improved Downrigger

United States Patent 3,942,737 describes an ingenious downrigger invented and tested by Mark Luzi of Cape Coral, Florida. Mark hit on the idea of an inexpensive, hand-operated downrigger that would permit fishermen to crank up only the lure— not the eight- or 10-pound stabilizer weight—whenever they miss a strike, change rigs, or adjust for depth. Mark's downrigger uses a closely set pair of reels to lower a weight on a cable loop rather than a single cable strand. Once the weight is at the desired depth, Mark clips his lure to the sternward side of the loop and lowers it while the weight stays in place.

Those who have fished with Mark on the Great Lakes and along the Florida coast say his downrigger works easier and quicker than a lot of the expensive electric models. And it cost him only a few dollars in materials and a couple evenings in his workshop. As Mark puts it, "Why work so hard at something that should be fun?"

DON'T MIX 'EM— MATCH 'EM

For greater casting distance, always match lure weights with line tests. Use 6-pound line or lighter for ⅛-ounce lures, 8- or 10-pound line for ¼-ounce lures, 12-pound line for ⅜-ounce lures, and 15- to 17-pound line for ½- or ¾-ounce lures. More accurate casts, fewer snarls and less arm fatigue will result.

Here's another tip: When fishing in a current at a time when the fish tend to bite very gently, it pays to use the lightest line possible. Six-pound-test line or lighter will relay the slightest nudge if a fish mouths the bait or lure.

PINPOINT CASTING

Many fishermen look upon pinpoint casting as an art impossible to master. If the boat is a fair distance from the shore, the casts come up short. If they move in too tight, the lure ends up hitting the bank or trees. No matter where or how they vary the boat's position, the casts are less than desirable. A great part of the problem is that these anglers are constantly varying the distance of the boat from the shoreline. If the moving boat is always kept the same distance from shore, the casts will start becoming very accurate. By keeping the distance constant, the fisherman's body will soon become attuned to accurately hitting the shore's edge every time. Each cast is made at the same exact distance. By not having to think about the distance, the fisherman now only has to concentrate on pinpointing his casts to the precise spot.

IT PAYS TO ADVERTISE

Sign at a bait shop in Laguna Beach, Calif.: "Our Minnows are Guaranteed to Catch Fish or Die Trying."

DISCOVER NEW STREAMS

Now is the perfect time to set a goal for yourself to find one new stream to fish this coming summer.

Get topographical maps from libraries or sporting goods stores. The U.S. Geological Survey sells them: USGS, 1200 S. Eads, Arlington, VA 22202 (east of the Mississippi) or USGS, Federal Center, Denver, CO 80225 (west of the Mississippi). Write for an index map of the state you are researching, then order the specific maps you want.

Do a map search. Look for streams with unfamiliar names or for tributaries to popular streams. Locate access to streams in agricultural areas—these are often overlooked. Two hints for most types of terrain: Pick streams that have watersheds at least two miles long (or they'll be too small). And, pick streams that don't cross a lot of contour lines on the map (or they may be flowing down cliffs).

Choose two or three streams when you do your map search because not all will pan out. When the season opens, pack a good lunch, get out your felt-soled hip boots, pick up your favorite short rod and go exploring.

The stream you find might not hold trophy-sized fish. But, almost always, its fish and its fishing will truly be your own.

HIGH FLOATING BOBBER

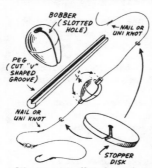

Western steelhead anglers have long used a high-floating bobber to guide lures or bait through difficult stretches of water. The type most commonly seen is constructed of hard foam plastic and shaped like an egg. A slotted hole through the center of the body accepts a flexible plastic peg with which the bobber can be adjusted. You can modify this float and convert it into a highly efficient sliding bobber, thereby extending its usefulness a great deal.

First cut a V-shaped groove the length of the peg. It should be deep and wide enough to allow free passage of the heaviest line you expect to use. Insert the peg into the hole and trim the protruding ends one-fourth of an inch from the body of the float.

To make this outfit totally convertible, you need stopper disks or bumpers. These are fashioned from soft plastic such as snap-on coffee-can lids. A number of holes are burned through the lid with the aid of a hot nail or straight pin. The size of line to be used will indicate the size of the hole. Using a sharp pair of curved manicure scissors, cut tiny disks around each hole. Size or shape of the disk is not important, but try to keep them fairly small. Grip each disk firmly with a pair of pliers and use a sharp razor blade to make an angled cut through the disk. The angle of the cut should be as acute as possible, then when the disk is slipped onto the line it should remain in place throughout most fishing conditions.

The final step of the conversion is to tie two sliding knots onto the mainline. Either the nail or the uni-knot may be used; I prefer the former with five wraps. The first knot is tied into position approximately six inches from the swivel. This is merely a safety knot in case the mainline happens to break off at the swivel, and can mean the difference between retrieving your bobber or having to replace it. As this knot is not adjustable it should be tied snugly.

The second knot should be tied only tight enough to allow it to be adjusted under slight pressure. A word of warning here: The knot should only be adjusted while the line is wet.

•

Crappies prefer a slow-moving lure—the slower, the better. Just twitch the rod slightly to give the lure a little action.

•

JIGGING SHALLOW WATER

Often the bouncy movement of a leadhead jig is the only thing that will entice feisty panfish. But just about as often, the water where a jig works best is so shallow or so snaggy that you can't catch a fish because you catch a snag first.

One way to solve this is to tie your jig, or a pair of them, *ahead* of a casting bubble. The bubble will keep the jigs from sinking too deep. You can hop them along with lots of action, or you can fish them as slow as the fish prefer. Either way, you'll be able to keep the jigs above weeds and snags.

As a bonus, you will never have trouble detecting the light take of a fish, the kind that often results in the fish spitting out the jig before you can set the hook. Your bubble will bounce when a fish hits, though you will have to get used to the idea that it bounces toward you rather than away when your bubble is ahead of the jigs.

IT'S A REAL DRAG

Boat-fishing techniques often dictate a slow drift, and there are times when conditions refuse to cooperate. Strong winds or tides and swift river currents can rush you by the best holes, or concentrations of fish.

When you want to slow down a drifting boat, but don't want to anchor, use a drag. The most practical drag amounts to three lengths of heavy chain, connected by spring-loaded snap locks. The size of each length should be determined by the size of your boat. A 14-foot cartopper is served best by two-foot lengths.

Depending on the strength of the blow or push of the current, attach one, two or three lengths of the chain to your anchorline. The chain snakes along the bottom, curls around and over rocks without hanging up, and will cut your drift speed to a crawl. It will also keep your bow headed into the waves or the current, and eliminate the tendency to yaw, correcting two other annoyances common to boat fishing.

Chain drags stow easily and take up little room; always keep one on board. Should you forget or lose yours, you can create the same effect by tying a large bucket to your anchorline, though this trick isn't nearly as efficient or as adaptable to a variety of conditions as multiple lengths of chain.

★ ★ ★

PERIMETER FISHING

Instead of casting a lure or tossing a bait to the center—where you think the fish should be—try the edges or perimeter first.

Often fish are loosely schooled at some structure. A fish hooked in the middle of such a school can scare the rest. They may move out, or just quit biting.

These areas can be "milked" by catching the fish on the outer edge of the school, then going for the ones that are in the middle.

TREES TO FISH BY

Tree overhangs have long been known as a prime source of fish fare in the form of insects that drop off into the water. The following tips will help you search out the best trees.

• Trees with conspicuous flowers. Both the insects that pollinate them and the insects that consume the pollinators (wasps, praying mantises, etc.) will make their way into the water and into the mouths of fish.

• Defoliated trees usually indicate the presence of moths, sawflies or beetles in the larval stages.

• Trees cracked by lightning or severe winds provide housing for many insects.

• Woodpeckers signal the presence of tree insects.

• Hardwood forests harbor more insect life than evergreens.

• Trees pollinated by insects include cherry, horsechestnut, apple, dogwood, hawthorn and catalpa. Pines and hardwoods use wind pollination.

• When angling near trees, use the wind to your advantage—fish areas where it is blowing from shore.

★

When wading and fishing a stream, the farther you hike from a bridge, or entrance point, the better your chances to find bigger fish that haven't been spooked too much.

Sharing Lunch

Have you ever been on a bass-fishing expedition and come across a likely bluegill hole you'd like to try but didn't have suitable bait or artificial lures? If you happened to bring along a sandwich for lunch, you're in luck. Select your longest and lightest rod and tie on a No. 10 or smaller hook. Then moisten your thumb and first two fingers, pinch off a bit of bread, and roll it into a ball. Place this doughball on the point of your hook and drop it over. The bluegills will literally "eat it up!"

Fishing for the Birds

Weekend anglers who fish for gray trout (weakfish) and blues in the vicinity of Virginia's Smith Point on Chesapeake Bay use three methods to find fish: They use a recording fishfinder; they watch for feeding birds; or they tag along behind the *Don-El*, which is skippered by one of Smith Point's ace charterboatmen, Don Kuykendall.

Over the past 4th of July weekend Kuykendall was treating his party to extraordinary fishing, finding school after school of hefty trout. Unfortunately, every time the *Don-El* stopped to fish it was harassed by a half-dozen private boats.

After a half day of this Kuykendall decided that he had had enough. As he looked for another school, he surreptitiously crumbled up the entire contents of a large box of crackers and spread them on the water, attracting every gull and all their cousins from miles around. Every private boat in sight was drawn to the spot as if by a magnet. As the *Don-El* continued on, Kuykendall raised his binoculars for one last look. His jaw dropped: Most of those boats had one or more anglers into fish!

Apparently, the fish came to the birds.

•

When planning a float trip, it is better to pick too short a stretch of river than one that's too long. To extend a short drift, you can use your anchor and thoroughly fish the territory. But choosing too long a section can leave you paddling furiously through strange water, trying to reach your take-out point before dark. That's never fun, and it can be dangerous.

Bridge Hopping

Float trips for fishing, hunting and pleasure boating are among the finer things of life—except for the overland transportation problems.

As usually conducted, float trips require two vehicles. You leave one at point B (a bridge or access point) downstream and drive upstream to point A, put the boat in at A, float down to B, take out, and drive back to A to get the other vehicle. That's a lot of driving.

Another method is for one or more boaters to drive to A and fish downstream. Another party meets them at point B and then drives them back to the vehicle at point A. That's also a lot of driving and means someone hasn't enjoyed the float trip.

A fishing partner and I use a simpler method that requires only one auto. We take two small boats (canoes) on one pickup. (Cars can be used if racks are installed.) We choose a suitable stretch of river or creek with three bridges or access points, and drive to point A upstream where one of us puts in. The other drives the truck down to point B, where he puts in and fishes down toward point C. Meanwhile, the first angler fishes down to point B, takes out, and picks up the other angler at point C.

Simple! The same scheme will work for hunting and for wading a stream as well as floating. It can also work for more than two people—all manner of variations are possible for larger parties. The savings in gas and travel expense can be considerable when the float trip is made a good distance from one's home.

CLINCH KNOT STRATEGY

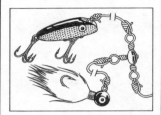

Tests have shown that the improved clinch knot is strongest when tied with five or more wraps of the tag end of line around the standing portion of line. When fishing with complex terminal rigs, such as a plug with a dropper jig, or tandem shad darts, the canny angler can vary the number of wraps used in this knot to reduce both the amount of gear lost when breakoffs occur and fishing time spent rerigging.

By reducing the number of wraps of the tag end of line around the standing part of line, the strength of the improved clinch knot can be lowered slightly where desired to increase the likelihood of line breaking at a particular joint. By tying the outermost clinch knots in your rigs with fewer wraps of line you can increase the chances of these breaking first if you hang up on the bottom. This then eliminates the need to retie a whole new complex rig, perhaps involving leaders, droppers, and extra lures. You simply tie on a new lure where the knot broke at the end of the leader.

INTO THE THICK

Try casting a shallow-running Heddon Wood Vamp or weedless Johnson Silver Minnow into the middle of a reed bed instead of trolling just around the edge of the weeds.

Working from a wind-drifted boat, a fisherman can drop these lures into open pockets of water inside reed beds. The muskellunge, largemouth bass and walleye hiding in reeds are often much bigger than fish of the open lake.

FLAGS UP FOR SMELT

By freezing smelt in the spring icefishermen are assured the best northern pike bait available. Freeze them whole in packages containing enough for a day's fishing. Then all one has to do is remove a pack from the freezer the night before and by morning they're thawed and ready to produce. A smelt will take a second freezing if necessary, but they often become too soft, smell strong, and are not the appealing bait they once were.

Preformed smelt hooks are most commonly used, but the common straight-shank fishhook is also popular. A preformed hook holds the smelt horizontal, while the regular hook, planted in the back balances the bait.

Setting the hook differs between these two hook styles. With the preformed hook the secret is getting there quickly to set it immediately. With the regular hook wait until the pike has finished its final run and has settled down to enjoy your tasty snack. Now gently retrieve line until you feel the slightest resistance. At this point set the hook heavily and keep hauling in.

LOCATING THE SCHOOL

Ever fish for schooling fish such as perch, white bass or crappie and have all action stop because the school left the area? Your chances of relocating the moving fish are slim. Here is a tip that can keep you in the midst of the school: Take one of the liveliest fish that has been caught. Hook a large snap through its bottom lip. Tie about ten feet of line to the snap and attach your largest bobber (or a balloon) to the other end of the line. Place the fish in the water and chances are he will follow the school. The bobber will pinpoint the area.

SUBMERGE A SURFACE LURE

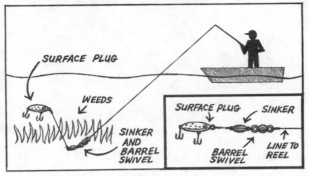

Buoyant surface plugs can be fished below the water's surface with surprising effectiveness. The doctored plugs are particularly useful when you are trying to maintain a certain lure depth above submerged weeds.

Tie one end of a barrel swivel to the end of your line. Then to the other end of the swivel tie a length of monofilament about a foot longer than what you estimate the distance to be from the top of the weeds to the bottom depth you are fishing. Slip an egg or cone sinker over this end piece of line, and then tie on your favorite surface plug. When you cast, the sinker will easily carry your topwater plug under the water, but above the weeds.

Retrieve with short wrist snaps. Pop your lure back toward the boat or shore. If you're going to use a steady retrieve to bring the lure back, you will have to make the terminal line longer. The faster your retrieve the longer this line must be to prevent it from hanging up in the weeds.

HIDDEN HOTSPOTS

If you live near farm country, there's probably a lot more good fishing around than you think because many farmers keep ponds for watering animals and fighting fires. Some of them stock these and some don't. But couple days of labor for access to his pond. He warned me that he hadn't stocked it, but the bass and bluegills I caught there more than made up for the few hours I spent digging postholes for him.

A particularly enjoyable

sooner or later fish find their way into the ponds anyhow—washed in by floods, carried in by children, or flown in as eggs sticking to the feet of herons and ducks.

I once traded a farmer a way to locate farm ponds is from the air. Schedule a short excursion flight some weekend, take along binoculars, and watch for mature ponds lined with cattails, brush and trees.

Hold on There

Holding an open-face spinning outfit with two fingers in front of the reel's "foot" or "leg" is not the only correct way to grip the rod, according to tackle officials at James Heddon's Sons. Women, kids and others with small hands should use a different grip, for greater casting control.

The proper grip is actually determined by positioning the index finger of the rod hand over the lip of the reel's spool; that finger is used to "feather" the line during the cast (to slow the cast, if necessary) and is also used to apply pressure to the spool when "extra" drag is needed.

Small-handed people may actually have to use three or even four fingers in front of the reel foot to allow their index finger to reach the spool lip. Conversely, people with large hands may have to place three fingers *behind* the reel foot.

★

If you are catching fish on a particular lure and the action dies suddenly, try a larger artificial. Sometimes the bigger offering will turn the fish on.

MUSICAL RETRIEVE

My wife, Emilie, quite by accident came across a rhythmic retrieve with a topwater lure that sometimes teases bass into striking when my own scientific approaches fail.

She calls her method "The Topwater Waltz." The favored lure is a chugger. Its concave head makes a distinctive "bloop" noise as the lure is pulled through the water.

Emilie casts the lure out and retrieves it with the slow cadence of an old-fashioned waltz. Sometimes I can hear her counting the beat aloud: "Bloop, two, three, bloop, two three."

A fish usually hits between the bloops, while the lure is at rest. I believe it's the unvarying cadence that makes the retrieve effective, but then I always try to figure out reasons why fish do what they do.

NET RESULTS

There's an art to netting fish that many anglers never seem to learn.

The most common mistake is working a big fish up to the side of the boat and then repeatedly jabbing at it with the net. All this accomplishes is spooking the fish, causing it to about-face and streak away on another run.

A better way is to have on board a net that's large enough to handle the biggest fish you're likely to encounter. Then, when your partner begins working his trophy in close to the boat, lower the rim and bag of the net into the water on the *opposite* side of

the boat and hold it still.

Now, your partner can lead his fish around the bow or transom to your side and guide it headfirst into the open bag. When the front half of the fish is safely through the rim of the net, you can now simultaneously move the net toward the tail and lift the whole works.

Stumpy Fish

Most artificial reservoirs and man-made lakes scattered across the country cover what were once vast sections of woods that were cleared before flooding began. Never fail to fish these stumpy areas. The stumps may be visible above or just under the surface.

Many state fish and game commissions provide maps of these areas. Also, some states prepare underwater shelters of logs and brush for fish.

Learn the locations of these spots, especially if you are seeking panfish or bass. Other good bets are small coves where logs and driftwood have created log jams. Fish under the jams with natural baits for best action.

DEADLIEST LURE PRESENTATION

Despite the efficiency of skilled baitcasters and flyfishermen who drop lures into cup-sized pockets, there is a more efficient method of presenting artificial lures.

It's called by various native names like tule dipping, jigging, spat fishing, dunking, etc. It involves a ten- to 15-foot cane pole or tubular-glass telescopic. Attached to the tip is a piece of six-pound mono equal to the length of the pole.

Attached to the end is a small jig, spinner or spoon. This is quietly lowered to the bottom, near any shore cover, and eased along until a fish inhales it. It's sporting, requires skill and is deadly!

•

A profitable time for fishing is after a heavy rain muddies streams flowing into a lake. Fish will often be waiting for food, such as crickets and grasshoppers, as it is washed into the mouths of these tributaries.

Clothespin Downrigger

A simple clothespin can become a very useful fishing aid now that downriggers have become so popular for deepwater trolling. After a few easy modifications, this common household item will allow two lines to be fished from a single downrigger unit. My cartopper is large enough to hold only one downrigger, and with one of my kids along this rig means both our lines can now reach the cooler temperature zones. It provides the fish with a choice of lures at slightly different depths.

All you have to do is cut the "legs" off a wooden or plastic clothespin at the indentation where the clothesline fits. (This is just excess material and adds unnecessary drag in the water.) Then drill a single 1/32-inch hole about a 1/4 inch from the tip of one of the arms (the part you squeeze to open the clothespin).

To set up for trolling, thread your monofilament through the hole, tie on your lure, and pull through the length of line at which you want your lure to run behind the boat (I use eight to ten feet). Then twist the pin four or five times and snap anywhere along your downrigger wire.

I usually place the second line about ten to 15 feet above the main line, which is hooked to the release on the cannonball. The spring in the clothespin is strong enough to hold the wire firmly and allow the rod to be tightened into a sharp bend, yet release cleanly with the pull from any fish over a pound or so.

Facts for Future Success

Keep a fishing log book. It's a relatively simple project requiring little effort and expense. After a couple of seasons it can be one of your most valuable pieces of "equipment."

Here are a few ideas you may want to incorporate into your log. Make a separate entry each time you go fishing. Include the name of the lake or river, your location, approximate depth, cover, date, time of day and weather conditions. These entries can be as detailed as you like. Take information on the weather as an example. You may just want to note "sunny and warm" or the entry can include air and water temperature, cloud cover, wind, precipitation and even the barometric pressure. It is important that you gather the same type of information at each outing so you have a basis for comparisons.

You can learn a great deal from the data in your log book. Besides, it's just plain fun to keep one and be able to read it during the midwinter doldrums. Your entries can include insect hatches, prevalent baitfish types and productive lures you used.

My log book contains detailed sketches of productive waters so I can easily find them again or show them to a friend. Where appropriate I have information on boat rentals, access points, parking areas and the phone number of a local fishing enthusiast to contact for current water conditions—facts that can be forgotten between seasons. I jot down equipment problems or needs that can be taken care of during the off-season.

If a lure with sensitive action does not have a split ring in the line tie, do not attach line with a jam knot because it can adversely affect the lure's action. Either add a split ring to give free movement, or use a loop knot.

PRE-RUNOFF FISHING

It is impossible to mark down the exact dates of top-notch pre-runoff fishing in rivers across the country. The hot fishing can come as early as March or as late as June, depending on snowmelt and rainfall.

Pre-runoff fishing should be undertaken after winter releases its grip on the land and just before consistently warm weather and spring rains trigger high, muddy water. Good timing often guarantees the best fishing of the year. The hint of spring triggers feeding frenzies in all species of fish. Where trout and warm-water species like bass, walleye and pike were concentrated in a few deep holes during winter, they invade the shallows and become more accessible.

Pre-runoff fishing does not constitute the main spring runs which draw hordes of anglers to river banks each season. The fast, pre-runoff bite lasts only a couple of weeks during fairly stable weather and is often missed, for the most part, by the majority of anglers who are waiting for the main runs of fish.

How do you determine the prime time? Personal investigation of the river is the best way. When the extremely low, clear water of winter gives way to a clear, but rising river, pre-runoff conditions exist. Fish should be aggressive. The rising water is usually a result of two or three days of unseasonably warm temperatures. However, a cold snap usually checks the heavy melt and clear, but high waters continue.

Confine Yourself

Often fishermen tend to cover as much stream as possible in a day. In so doing, they pass over many good fish, some of trophy size.

Try limiting your fishing to a predetermined course. Set up visible markers from point A to point B and restrict your fishing to that site. Probe every pocket and holding area. If time remains, return to point A and fish that area again.

This ploy has other advantages. There's less walking, hence less exhaustion at day's end. Water is read more thoroughly. Usually at least as many fish will be creeled as if you'd explored additional miles.

Thermometer Fish Finder

Fishermen are continuously reminded to carry a pocket thermometer, but those who do are in the minority. A small pocket model can help increase your catches. With one, surface temperature of water can be checked before commencing to fish, and the reading will reveal where fish are located at that moment and where time should be spent fishing. For example, surface temperatures immediately tell the following:

TROUT: *50° to 68° F. (10° to 20° C.) Found in three- to six-foot depths. Over 20° C. will seek deeper, cooler depths.*

PIKE and MUSKIES: *60° to 75° F. (16° to 25° C.) Found in four- to ten-foot depths. Over 25° C. will seek depths from 15 to 40 feet.*

LARGEMOUTH BASS: *60° to 75° F. (16° to 25° C.) Found in two to six feet of water. Over 25° C. will move to 12- to 25-foot depths.*

SMALLMOUTH BASS: *60° to 70° F. (16° to 23° C.) Found in two- to 10-foot depths. Over 23° C. found in 20- to 40-foot depths.*

SPOOKY TACTIC

For years anglers have been cautioned to be especially quiet when out on the water. After all, it's pointed out, fish can sense noise and any sound could negatively affect the day's fishing. Yet, some successful anglers purposely spook fish.

These fishermen scour the lake and actually move right on top of likely spots in the hope of arousing a few fish. When boils or other signs of fish are detected, the anglers continue on, giving those spooked areas a rest. Later, they return and carefully and quietly work the spot.

ENTICING WOBBLE

A fish-attracting wobble can be imparted to a lure or fly and bubble by lightly holding the monofilament above the reel as it is reeled in. The line is held just tight enough to unbalance the spinning reel, causing it to jerk, which sends a small shock wave down the line to the lure or spinning bubble. The erratic behavior causes a fly behind a bubble to hop and bounce, thus driving a fish crazy.

RIVERBANK TROLLING

A clever new device called a sideplaner is currently selling like hotcakes to western steelhead bank fishermen. The idea of the floating plastic contraption is literally to plane a trailing lure from shore out to midstream, then suspend the lure in the current until a migrating steelhead or salmon smacks it. At that point a release trips, and the planer slides down the line to interfere less with the fight.

Sideplaners enable shore-bound anglers to back troll diving lures downstream and cross-stream as though from a boat, but with a good deal less fuss and expense.

THE WIND AND FISH

The effect of wind on fishing—often underestimated or ignored by anglers—can be seen in this example. During a hot August in western New York, Lake Ontario shoreline fishing was excellent when strong north winds blew in cold offshore water from the depths. The temperature change drew smallmouth bass and jumbo yellow perch into water three- to five-feet deep only a short cast from the beach. Salmon and brown trout that had been at the 90- and 100-foot level for weeks moved to 30-foot depths when the winds brought in 54°F. water.

Two days later, offshore breezes pushed the cold water out, replacing it with 70°F. water. The fish disappeared.

Wind can matter even when water temperature remains unchanged. Minnows and baitfish move to the downwind side of a lake on breezy days to gorge on insects blown into the water. Gamefish follow and cruise just under the surface. On days with whitecaps you will often see big fish splash on the surface as they lunge for insects.

Remember this the next time you are tempted to fish the lee side of a lake to get out of the wind. You may be more comfortable, but your chances of catching fish will be lessened.

★

A simple and very effective lure desnagger can be made from any stiff, coiled spring. Tie a strong cord to one end, slip the coils over your line, lower it until one of the coils engages the hooks of the snagged lure, then jostle or jerk it loose.

FLY-RODDING WITHOUT FLIES

Many fishermen shy away from owning a fly rod because they feel it is a tool for expert fishermen; a delicate wand for placing dry flies on the surface of crystal clear trout streams or for casting salmon flies across broad, pine-shrouded rivers.

Yet you can catch any freshwater fish on a fly rod without flies . . . or fly casting.

Catch bluegills by slowing drifting your boat just off weedbeds. Tie six feet of 4- to 6-pound-test monofilament to your fly line and use a size 10 or 12 hook with a long shank and baited with angle worms. Let the bait drift naturally along the bottom. If you find a hotspot, anchor. If the bluegills are deep, add one or two split-shot. For crappies, switch to minnows and a Size 4 hook. Panfish are great little fighters, particularly bluegills, and nothing brings this quality to the front better than a fly rod.

Its longer length gives a fly rod the edge when it comes to baitfishing for trout in small streams. You can also use one on larger streams for coho or steelhead. Get distance by stripping slack line from your reel and swinging the end of the line like a pendulum, then releasing the slack. With practice you can gain fair accuracy.

Trolling, drifting and still fishing with a fly rod for walleyes is a fun way to take these tasty fish. Carp, catfish, suckers and a variety of other bottom-feeding river roughnecks can provide many hours of fun for the fly-rodder. For these bottom feeders, use six feet of 10- or 12-pound-test monofilament. Slip this through a sliding sinker then tie to a Size 4 hook. Pinch a split-shot ten inches above the hook to hold back the sliding sinker. You can get this rig out a fair distance by stripping line from the reel and using the side-arm swing. Favorite baits are whole kernel corn for carp, sharp cheddar cheese for catfish and nightcrawlers for suckers.

Depending on where you live and the conditions particular to your area and type of fish, you will probably be able to think of other ways to utilize and enjoy fly-rodding without flies.

Weedy Fishing

Most anglers feel it makes good sense to seek gamefish in weeds at certain times. What some do not realize, however, is that *not* all weeds are prime fish-holders. Weeds in relatively deep water are often good, but those in extremely shallow water generally aren't productive. Also, some weeds (such as arrowhead and water milfoil) are good oxygen producers while others (such as cattails and water lilies) are not. Further, some plants provide good fish cover (coontail is an example) while others (such as big duckweeds) do not. It just makes good sense to fish the best weeds first instead of haphazardly trying to find fish within or near any type of aquatic plant growth you happen to come upon.

HANDY MARKER BUOY

A marker buoy is a valuable tool both for drift fishing and trolling. While they are easy to assemble, many of the colorful containers used—such as antifreeze jugs—are cumbersome for the small-boat fisherman. Many of the smaller plastic containers are hard to spot in the water since most are translucent. It's simple to color your buoy so it will be highly visible even in choppy seas.

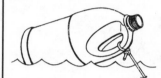

Take an empty ammonia or fabric-softener bottle and rinse it out thoroughly. Add less than half-an-ounce of bright paint—yellow or orange is a good color. Fluorescent paints used for jig heads are ideal. Run several ounces of warm tap water into the bottle, cap it and shake it vigorously until the paint has covered the bottle's inside. Empty the excess and let the container dry. Cap the bottle tightly after the paint has dried and you've got a brightly colored buoy that won't lose its color while in the water.

VISIBLE LINES

When fishing a plastic worm or jig in medium or deep water the use of high-visibility line is not critical. Most strikes are detected by feel, the tell-tale tap, tap. But when using unweighted worms over lily pads, stickups and grassy shallows, or light jigs in the same areas, the lack of weight on the lure reduces the messages sent up the line by a taking fish. In these situations the only sign of a pickup will probably be a slight movement of the line, and if it is not of the high-visibility type, many fish will taste your offering and reject it before you know it happened.

CAST A CROOKED LURE

A problem with modern crankbaits is they don't always run straight.

Instead of correcting all your crooked lures by bending the wire or screw eye where the line is tied, set a few aside, noting on the lure which way each runs off—an *L* for left and an *R* for right marked on the bill with a magic marker.

The next time you fish near a large object such as a bridge piling, boathouse or rocky ledge, try those erratic crankbaits.

Tie on a lure marked *L* and cast down the right side of the structure. The lure will track left, coming much closer to the structure than it normally would. To fish the left side, tie on a lure marked R.

Buzzbaits, those big-bladed surface-disturbing spinnerbaits, can also be made to track left or right. Bending the lure's wire arms slightly will cause the bait to track back in a semicircle. Don't bend too much, or it will roll over and lose its buzz.

Cast the crooked buzzbait alongside a pier, boathouse or overhanging limb, and its semicircular path will take it into and under the cover where the bass are found.

WINTER SCUBA FISHING

There is a small group of Idaho fishermen who don scuba gear—instead of down jackets—when they go after mountain whitefish in winter. Among them is Stacy Gebhards, Bureau of Fisheries Chief with the Idaho Department of Fish and Game.

Catching whitefish underwater is not only *possible*, says Gebhards, but it's productive and rather simple to do. He claims that a good scuba diver can submerge, select a choice whitefish from a school, hook it on a stonefly tied to a short handline, and surface again all in 22 seconds flat.

STOP THAT RETRIEVE

It's happened to every angler—fish follow the lure all the way back to the boat but refuse to strike. Some authorities recommend speeding up your retrieve to elicit a take from such trailing fish. Others say slow down your retrieve. Still another school of thought suggests making a figure-eight with your rod tip at the side of the boat to draw a strike from these reluctant specimens.

All of these tactics work on occasion, and they're certainly worth trying on nonbiting fish. But the procedure that I find works most often involves simply stopping your retrieve entirely.

Many fish, particularly panfish such as crappies and bluegills, will strike the dropping lure with a vengeance. Big freshwater stripers often fall for this technique too, as do walleyes and bass at times.

If the water is clear, let the lure drop until you see it hit bottom—if a fish doesn't suck it in before that. Some fish will even pick up the lure off the bottom while it's sitting there inert.

In murky water, let the lure drop for several seconds if you sense a trailing fish and watch for the slightest twitch in the line. If you see it, set the hooks fast and hard.

This tactic works with all types of lures, but it's especially deadly with jigs, plastic worms and spinnerbaits.

CHUMMING FOR SHAD

White shad on both coasts are known to hit small leadhead shad darts and small gold spoons. They will not hit bait. Even though they only hit lures, there is a chumming method for shad almost forgotten except for a few old-timers at the sport.

About the turn of the century, fishermen cleaning fish along the banks discovered that shad are attracted to and will more readily hit around shad scales washed into the water. Thus, they would often scale shad into the water to increase their chances of a hit.

The next time fishing gets slow, try scaling shad in the current so the scales drift back into those spots where shad normally hit lures. The only problem is that, like the old joke about rabbit stew, first you have to catch a shad.

Penny Wise/Pound Foolish

When live-bait fishing in choice water and the hook becomes fouled, don't attempt to retrieve it by wading or motoring to it. Simply break the line as quietly as possible, wait a few minutes, then try again with a new bait. The trophy that's waiting could be a priceless experience, so don't reduce the odds of obtaining it to save a few cents.

SUMMERTIME STREAM ANALYSIS

Many fishermen miss a great opportunity to understand their favorite trout streams better by not visiting them in late summer. This period of high heat and humidity, coupled with low, clear water, may not afford the prime fishing of spring, but it does allow the angler to examine structure that can't be seen in high, murky water. With water levels low and clear, the best lies and most hazardous snags are easily spotted.

This information can be stored in the memory, recorded on film, or charted by hand. In any event, the knowledge gathered by a summer visit to a favorite stretch of river will enable a fisherman to cover it better in the prime high-water fishing that is found in the spring and fall.

USE A FLOATFISHING INFORMANT

The worst fate that can befall a floatfisherman is to travel a great distance to a favorite stream, only to find the river discolored with mud and raging out of its banks. To avoid wasting the time and gas, establish a local source on the river—a tackleshop, warden or farmer who lives nearby—and contact it before leaving home.

Cold-Weather Casting

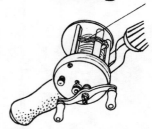

The normal oil or grease used in lubricating casting reels may become stiff in cold weather —which can lead to problems. If the spool doesn't revolve easily when it's necessary to strip out line in a hurry the hook could pull out, or light monofilament line could snap. To prevent this from happening, disassemble the reel and clean it thoroughly. Then lightly lubricate it with Anderol synthetic oil or with powdered graphite. Both lubricants are sold by better gun dealers.

MAKE THE MOST OF A MISS

Even the most proficient caster misses the target from time to time. When you are fishing visible cover, a miss may seem as good as a mile. For this reason, after an errant toss many anglers will quickly reel in line in preparation for another cast.

There are at least two reasons *not* to do this. First, by speeding up your retrieve, you may throw off your timing and find the next cast off-target as well. More important, by slowing down your retrieve instead of speeding it up, you'll have a much better chance to catch a fish. When a poor cast lands, allow extra time for the lure to descend. This gives the fish extra time to move out of cover toward the bait. Then slowly retrieve the lure, stopping (or killing) its action occasionally. Give the fish every possible opportunity to get out from the cover and strike your bait. On the next cast, you will be more composed and can fully concentrate on hitting the target.

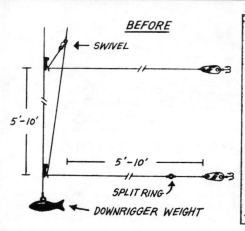

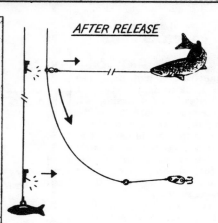

BEFORE
← SWIVEL
5'-10'
5'-10'
SPLIT RING
DOWNRIGGER WEIGHT

AFTER RELEASE

Cheater Rig

In our Great Lakes states, where trolling is a way of life to the salmon and trout angler, the use of more than two rods per man is prohibited by law. With fish often suspended at anywhere between five and 150 feet, a great deal of time can be wasted trying to determine the proper depth to fish. Local fishermen have overcome this handicap by fishing a "cheater."

The cheater rig allows anglers to fish two (or more) lures off a single rod. Thus, a man can fish two rods with four lures, covering depths from 20 to 40 feet (with lures spaced from five to 10 feet apart).

To rig the cheater, first slide a barrel swivel onto the main line and tie a split ring or swivel at the end. Next, tie a short length (one or two feet) of monofilament to the ring and add your main lure. The split ring will stop the second line from sliding all the way down onto your main lure. After the main lure is attached to the downrigger release, lower the rigger five or 10 feet and tie on the second line. To do this, tie a five- or 10-foot length of mono to the barrel swivel and attach the second lure to the end of this. Secure this second line to another release and lower the downrigger to the desired depth.

Obviously, some sort of stacking release must be used to utilize this technique. The Roemer release is favored by many Great Lakes trollers.

When a fish strikes one lure or the other, both lines pop free of the releases and the second line slides down the main line, allowing plenty of room to bring that trophy to the boat. The rig can also be used with planing boards.

EDDY MAGIC

For successful driftboat fishing, you must be able to row into places where fish gather without frightening them, which is not always easy in a rigid boat. Fortunately, a raft is quiet, even if it bumps a rock en route to the selected area. For this reason, a good place for rafting fishermen is the midstream eddy. Some of the best fishing in rivers is found on the downstream side of big boulders that create calm eddies where fish like to rest and forage.

It takes a fast, backward pull of the oars at the right moment to reach an eddy. Once there, drop anchor so that everyone can concentrate on fishing.

Try fishing under and around the raft. And remember that sometimes fish are frightened by the intrusion of a raft and need time to recover before they'll strike.

One especially productive area to try is the downstream end of a V-shaped eddy—the eddy tail. In a rocky river, you may be able to cast from one eddy into others—and into other tails—without moving the boat. That's a boon to the oarperson who may also want some fishing action.

DOUBLE THEIR PLEASURE

Everyone knows the value of the spinner as a fish-catching lure. You are also aware that plastic grubs, with curly tails, can produce some really nice fish.

By combining these two baits, you can create a dynamite lure. The enticing flash of the spinning blade coupled with the tantalizing wiggle of the grub tail is more than many fish can resist.

One word of advice: Not all tails are created equal. Some simply sit there with nary a twitch. Others move so actively they seem likely to self-destruct. These lively ones are the ones to use.

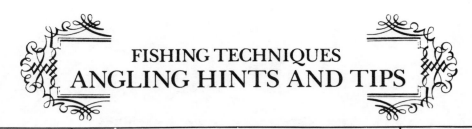

THE STRIPPER

Once in a while we fishermen want to use live bait in an area with rock or fallen wood on the bottom. Then the first thought that comes to mind is,

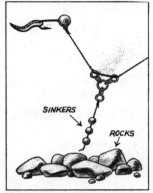

SINKERS

ROCKS

"How am I ever gonna drag a sinker through that mess?"

Here's a good live bait rig you can put together quickly and cheaply. Just run the line from your rod through two of the three eyes of a three-way swivel so that it can function as a regular slip-sinker.

Next, tie on about a six-inch dropper line for the sinkers. (Ideally, this should be a slightly lighter test than your main line.) Then pinch on split-shots and add a floating jig head.

The floating jig head keeps the bait above the snags, and if the sinkers hang up, a strong steady pull will just strip them off the dropper line. Put on some new sinkers and you are back in business.

It's a lot cheaper and faster than breaking off your rig and having to retie a whole new setup.

SCOUT FROZEN STREAMS

This winter take a leisurely walk along your favorite ribbon of fishing water, making notes as to where the spring holes are—places where the stream is not frozen over.

During hot summer days these are the coolest spots in the stream and may offer you the hottest angling action. Fish seek out springs, and when all other holes fail to produce, holes with springs should prove to be far better.

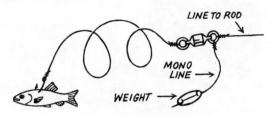

LINE TO ROD

MONO LINE

WEIGHT

NO-TWIST DRIFT RIG

"Live lining" a bait is an established technique for presenting live or dead baits. It involves drifting a bait out to your quarry. When strong currents or rough water make the addition of weight necessary, the usual procedure is to pinch a weight to the line, but there are two liabilities in following this procedure. First, the pinching often weakens the line. Second, unless the weight is perfectly streamlined, it often adds extra twist to the line as you retrieve. Even if your setup is perfect, the bait often causes considerable twisting as it rotates in the current.

There is a better way that involves a minimum of hardware. Tie in a barrel or crane-type swivel about two feet up from the hook. Knot about six inches of mono to the loop of the swivel that is closer to the rod. Now you can pinch the weight onto the mono dropper as needed, and it will act as a keel to keep the gyrating bait from twisting your line.

Over a snaggy bottom, the weight will strip off the dropper before the line breaks. As added protection, you can use a strand of mono that has a lower breaking strength than that of the line.

Use the smallest black swivel that will do the job. Ball bearing models are the most efficient, though more costly.

You know that a fish will surge when it sees the boat or when you are about to drag it ashore. Be ready for this moment. To avoid breakoffs when the fish makes its final bid for freedom, drop the rod tip and allow line to slip from the reel. Otherwise, the impact could snap the line like bakery string.

PREFISHING HINTS

Helpful hints to make your fishing and boating more enjoyable:

(1) If your boat motor is key-operated, hide an extra key out of sight somewhere in the boat. It could be a lifesaver if you're many miles from home and discover you forgot the key.

(2) When backing a boat trailer into the water, try to stop just short of entering the hubs. This will help reduce the amount of water that is drawn into the wheels when the bearings are hot.

(3) Keep a daily diary on fishing and accurately mark hotspots on maps. This will help in planning future trips.

(4) Long before you take a youngster on that first fishing trip, let the little guy or gal practice tossing a dummy plug at an empty pail in the backyard, preferably with his own outfit. If the yard's too small, pack a lunch and hike to an open spot. It's important to explain that while fishing is a wonderful sport, hooks can be very dangerous if used carelessly. Also, get a child in the habit of looking behind each time he makes a cast to be sure the coast is clear.

(5) When storing your motor for the winter, turn it over several times to get rid of excess water that might cause damage by freezing. Also drain grease from your motor's lower unit to get rid of water, then refill with new outboard grease that is recommended for the motor.

★ ★ ★

MAKING CATFISH BAITS WORK

There seems to be a new homemade or commercial catfish bait coming out each year. If you've tried—and failed—to score with these concoctions, this may be why:

Cats are attracted to appetizing new aromas but, since they've never tasted the product before, they're far more wary, afraid of getting sick from it (you would be too if someone offered you some).

Edward E. Little of Florida State University found that catfish rarely ate strange food-gel cubes when first exposed to them. Response increased after repeated experience—up to 100 percent over five feeding sessions!

Also, his observations uncovered how catfish orient themselves to food by barbel (whisker) contact, biting, chewing and swallowing or regurgitating it. They touch unusual food longer with their whiskers before mouthing it.

To get the most from modern catfish baits, try chumming small bits (if legal where you live). This accustoms fish to smelling and eating the product.

Don't get impatient for action. Let the bait sit 15 minutes before reeling in to check it.

Since cats will play with untried bait, use smaller hooks and bury them deep in the food so the fish won't be pricked during his taste testing. A light line also helps to avoid suspicion.

Finally, let catfish play with a new bait longer than you are used to before setting the hook. He's going to take awhile before deciding what you have is okay to eat.

DOUBLE-DUTY CHICKEN

If you don't eat those livers, hearts and gizzards that come with chickens bought for family fare, wrap, lable and freeze them for use as a surefire catfish bait. They keep for months.

FISHING TECHNIQUES

ICE FISHING

EASY ICE CHISELING

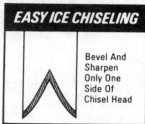

Bevel And Sharpen Only One Side Of Chisel Head

'f you happen to be an old-.hioned ice fisherman like myself who still insists on hand chiseling his fishing holes, here's a handy tip for easier and faster chipping. As you know most chisels have a flat, single bevel cutting edge. But I suggest that you convert your present one by cutting or burning out an inverted V (see diagram). You'll find it cuts much faster with less effort, due to its point and knife-blade design. Remember also that a heavier head is to your advantage as compared to a lighter

ICE ANGLER'S SHOULDER SAVER

For those times when ice anglers must shoulder their sleds over rough spots on the ice or carry them into a lake

or pond, a piece of rubber-backed carpet slipped onto the rope will make for less wear and tear on one's shoulder.

Ice-Fishing Essentials

Those new to the sport of ice fishing often show up with equipment more suited to warm-weather fishing. Pictured here are a few basic items. (1) Ice chopper. This chisel or a power-driven auger is necessary to punch holes through ice that sometimes is 12- to 20-inches thick. (2) Skimmer. To skim off chipped ice from the newly punched hole, thus keeping hands dry. Skimmers are ladles or spoons with drain holes. A small fish net used by aquarium hobbiests, works fine. (3) Folding seat. This does away with the need to stand or kneel on the ice. (4) Hand rod. Short sticks, sometimes referred to as jig-rods, with a few yards of line wound on blocks, are better for hand-line fishing. These don't freeze up as do rod guides and reels. (5) Tip-ups to suspend live bait through the ice hole. Some states allow as many as five or more to be operated.

Add to these a portable shelter or shanty for protection against the biting wind, a charcoal grill or stove for warmth, and layers of warm clothing.

★ ★ ★

ON THE ROCKS

Many icefishermen take great pride in removing all the ice from their ice hole. This is good on cloudy days, but on bright sunny days leave some ice chunks in the hole. If the water is shallow, the clean hole allows sunlight to travel through the hole unhindered. Since the rest of the ice blocks out sunlight, this unnatural beam of light will at times make the fish nervous. By keeping some ice in the hole, the light is refracted, and the fish are less likely to be spooky.

SHALLOW ICE-FISHING RIG

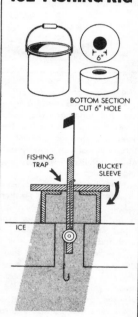

BOTTOM SECTION CUT 6" HOLE

FISHING TRAP

BUCKET SLEEVE

ICE

This set-up is very effective, especially in windy and snowy conditions. Cut off the bottom section of an industrial-sized white plastic bucket, one-third up. Then cut a six-inch hole in the bottom. Push the rod of a standard fishing trap through the hole and down through a hole in the ice.

This set-up blocks the sun's rays from penetrating shallow water, and the fish see only the bait and not the distracting reel.

Don't hesitate to fish in less than a foot of water. I have received five state awards using this method.

TIPS FOR WINTER FISHING

Here's a handful of tips for hard-water fishing this winter:

* Try fishing two ways at once. Jig for panfish and set out tip-ups for larger fish. If the law allows, bait one or two tip-ups with the smaller perch or bluegills you catch jigging.

* Fish migrate vertically more in the winter than at other times. Start fishing just off the bottom and raise your bait one foot for every 15 minutes you go without a bite.

* Never look directly down on a cocked tip-up. A gust of wind, a nudge, or a sudden bite can flip the flag up into your eyes.

* Once off balance on slippery ice, chances are you'll fall backward and give your skull a nasty whack. I've seen more ice fishing outings ruined this way than any other. Relax, and always move cautiously on slick ice.

* The best day to go ice fishing is Monday. The weekend fishermen leave behind them all the auger holes you'll ever need.

* The big fish you catch will surely draw curious skaters who will, just as surely, chop to bits with their skates any fishing line left lying on the ice.

* On blustery days, aim a tip-up so that the wind blows the flag against its ratchet. The mark of a novice ice fisherman is a day full of "wind bites."

* Before you ever set foot on the ice, make sure you've left your vehicle where you can free it from the mud, snow, or slush that alternately thaw and freeze as the day goes by. If possible, park downhill facing a cleared section of road or parking lot.

NO LIE

It may mean nothing, but . . . the Fisherman's Information Bureau located in Chicago, Illinois, which is devoted to preserving fishing records of all kinds, is known as FIB.

PUSH, DON'T PULL

Ice fishermen often have the problem of pulling their equipment through piles of deep snow. They put a rope on their sled or shanty and tug and yank their equipment through the drifts. By putting a discarded lawnmower handle on the sled, shanty or toboggan, the fishermen can push the load much easier. This allows all of the body to be used. Since the fisherman is leaning forward, the chance of slipping on the ice is less than if he were pulling the load.

The use of the lawnmower handle on a toboggan can solve many a drift problem. Take a 2x2-inch board and cut it one-half inch shorter than the distance between the open forks of the handle. Bolt both of the forks to the ends of the 2x2. Cut the head off of one of the bolts if it is for a toboggan. This allows the person to slip the board through the ropes and reattach to the headless bolt on the other side. If it is for the shanty, remove the heads of both bolts and screw the 2x2 to the back of the shanty.

START WITH A SPUD

At the onset of icefishing season, before a foot or so of ice accumulates, you'll find an ordinary bar spud easier to use for hole cutting than a manual or power auger. You can buy a spud cheap or make one by firmly seating a broad-edged wood chisel in a piece of pipe. Or you can ask a machinist to cut off an old trenching iron.

Remember to attach a handle or rope to the spud to keep ahold of it when cutting your holes. The classic icefishing blunder is to send a spud plunging down through a hole.

DOUBLE DUTY

This handy ice-fishing sled serves to move gear, minnow pail, ice chisel and other equipment out to your favorite hotspot on the lake. Then when tipped on end, you have a fish house.

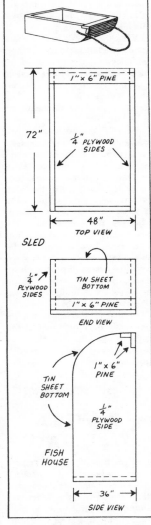

Added Punch

Use a leather punch to produce small circles of red or orange adhesive fluorescent tape then stick them on some of your fishing spoons or plugs for added flashes of color. Your lures should look like a small brook trout, a favorite food of other gamefish.

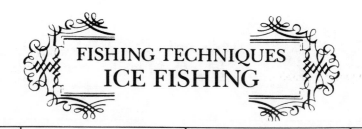
STORAGE ON ICE

Ice fishermen who ply their sport without the luxury of a comfortable ice-fishing shanty should become acquainted with the plastic garbage pail. These containers offer substantial lightweight, waterproof storage, and do it inexpensively. As there are several sizes, the angler can select that which best fits his needs.

We often bring two or three (one inserted inside the other) with food and gear loaded inside the inner one. It is easy to pull them along on an icy surface. If snow covers the ice, they can be lashed to a small sled for a lengthy hike.

Usually the early mornings are colder, and we're dressed for maximum warmth. However, once activity commences (boring holes, setting tip-ups, running to flags) and the day warms, we often find that we're overdressed and sweating. Thus we shed garments into the extra pails, where they stay dry and organized. Then, as the late-afternoon chill arrives we simply reverse the procedure. This permits us to wear the proper amount of clothing regardless of weather changes.

Finally, for the trip home, we generally designate one of the pails to carry the fish. How can anything so useful be called a garbage pail?

WINTER FISH BAIT

If you burn firewood, it's possible you have a decent source of winter fishbait. I discovered this when a friend said he had found large grubs while splitting punky old elm logs. I volunteered to split some and picked punky blocks that looked as if they had been drilled lengthwise several times by a quarter-inch wood bit. Each drill hole when split led to a larger chamber that was filled with treasure: plump golden grubs one and a quarter inches long. It took only a few minutes to collect several dozen specimens of this high-quality winter bait.

Tin Can Warmer

Icefishermen can make a dandy hand-warming stove from an ordinary No. 10 tin can.

An old bottle opener is used to make two or three holes for air draft along the bottom edge. Several more cuts bent inward around the top edge will support the lid. And in the lid itself, a V-shaped cut folded over a large metal washer forms a handle.

Fuel the stove with charcoal briquettes or charcoal pressed into egg-carton sections.

Place a wood block between

stove and ice. Set near the fishing hole, its radiant warmth will dry wet hands and remove much of the winter chill.

Eggshells make a great chum for both icefishing and open-water angling for panfish. Crumble the shells up and sprinkle them occasionally in the area you are probing.

•

Some fish grow lethargic during cold weather, but pickerel become quite active. Use live two- to four-inch baitfish, silver spoons or minnow-imitating plugs to fool these toothy battlers.

ICE-FISHING ANTIQUES

In recent years antique sporting items have risen sharply in value. Consider antique duck decoys, firearms and outboard motors for example. And now, following the trend, there is yet another antique collectible of sporting origin—ice-fishing decoys.

Ice-fishing decoys are essentially hookless, brightly colored, carved wooden fish. They are equipped with fake fins, and assisted by weights they are lowered into ice-fishing holes where they can then lure fish to nearby baited hooks.

The decoys are a midwestern phenomenon. Their exact origins are unclear, but scholars believe they were invented by native North American Indians. Although plastic versions are marketed today, the old, crudely carved decoys (with genuine leather fins) are the ones that collectors of Americana are now after. A rare 19th century decoy can be worth up to $100.

FLY-LINE ICE FISHING

A Montana fisherman says he uses old flycasting line for ice fishing. Once the fly line has become too beat up for good fly-fishing, he puts it aside for winter fishing only. The fly line runs freely through an ice fisherman's tip-up, resists kinking, won't freeze and sheds snow. What more could you ask for—other than fish where you cut a hole through the ice?

FINDING FISH

If you can find them you can catch them—so say the experts in ice fishing. Here's the trick you can use to put the odds in your favor. Don't put your fishfinder away after the rod-and-reel season ends—you can use it during the jigging and tip-up season. You'll find the fishing action fast at the right spot and the right depth. Just dunk the transducer in the hole and watch for the flashes. You'll know when to stay and when to move. It beats waiting for a bite by a country mile.

ICE JIGS FOR TROUT

Many ice fishermen know that small ice jigs or flies are excellent for perch, bluegills and crappies. Not many realize that these tiny slivers of metal will also catch trout. I like to use them with ultralight spinning tackle and 2-pound-test line when stalking stream browns and brookies.

When using worms, sometimes only a hint of weight is needed for the proper presentation. So rather than pinch a split-shot to the line, I tie on an ice jig and hang a worm on the fine wire hook. Unlike the shot, which may be crimped on the line eight or more inches from the bait, the jig forms one unit with the worm, which allows neater, more precise casting.

Ice jigs come in an array of

colors, and you may choose a color depending on water clarity and light intensity. In discolored water and/or low light, use bright shades—yellow, red or chrome. In clearer water and/or bright light, try green, brown or black.

★

Before inserting a leadhead or hook in a plastic grub, bait tail, or worm, position it precisely on the outside. Clamp the plastic tidbit with thumb and forefinger to mark the exact location where the bend of the hook will be. Make sure the point exits at that spot—and the tail will lie perfectly flat.

POP-CAN ICE FLIES

The fact that zooplankton play a very major role in winter food chains has finally been recognized by most of the icefishing fraternity.

One of the most realistic and easily concocted plankton look-alikes can be made from an aluminim can, some epoxy glue, paper punch, scissors, hooks and paint.

Cut strips from the sides of the can. Use the paper punch to pop out some disks, which in turn are folded to resemble half moons. A small No. 10 or 12 hook is slipped into the fold—point away from the round edge—and glued into place. Once the adhesive has had time to set properly (wait 24 hours), each tiny aluminum spoon can be painted the desired color.

If you want, eyes can be added with the aid of a point-sanded toothpick dipped in paint and barely touched to the sides of the attractor. The result is a dead ringer for a Daphnia.

For Icefishing Jigging Rod

Most anglers have at least one broken fishing rod around the house that could be converted into an icefishing jigging rod with very little effort.

First remove the rod from the handle. If it cannot be pulled out, cut it off flush with a hacksaw. Next, shorten the tip portion—18 to 24 inches is about right. Measure the diameter of the tip's butt end. then drill a hole the same size, about three inches deep, into the front end of the handle.

Apply epoxy to the butt end of the rod and hole in the handle. Insert the tip's butt end into the hole, align the line guides with the reel seat, wipe off any excess epoxy, and allow it to dry.

Your custom-made jigging rod can be used with any type of reel.

Black Ice Savvy

As many veteran ice anglers have discovered, fishing early ice (sometimes called black ice) frequently provides better pickerel and perch fishing than later in the season. It's also less work—less ice to bore through. However, black ice is black because it's thin, therefore potentially dangerous. To minimize risks, heed the following:

1. Never go black-ice fishing alone.

2. Never venture on less than three inches of well-formed ice. Take measurements in several places.

3. If you're a heavy person, don't assume the ice is safe because you see others on it.

4. Avoid lakes known to have underground springs (warm water spots) until the ice is thicker.

5. Avoid lakes subject to drastic, unpredictable draw-downs, as this can break up the ice.

6. Stay well away from any open-water areas, or ice adjacent to running brooks or streams, and get off the ice if it appears to crack under your weight.

7. Don't run on thin ice, don't stand with your friends in concentrated groups, and space out your gear.

8. Though you might feel silly, wear a personal flotation device, at least until you're positive the ice you'll be fishing on is safe. Keep it on if the temperature is much above 32°F.

9. Bring a 50-foot coil of rope with a large loop (big enough to encircle an adult) tied to one end.

10. Fasten two screwdrivers somewhere on your body (waist or strapped to your forearms). In the unlikely event you break through the ice, the flotation device will keep you buoyant, and you can plunge the screwdrivers into the ice, using them as handholds to help you climb out.

TWIST IT!

If jigging, slowly raising and lowering the bait, or just plain letting it remain motionless doesn't attract winter fish, some ice anglers have found that twirling the line can be an effective alternative. The twisting action imparted to the bait sometimes triggers cold-water panfish into action when other methods fail. Simply grasp the line between the index finger and thumb and roll it at varying tempos. Be alert for the slightest indication of fish activity, and quickly set the hook when you feel a fish on the line. This new twist may just do the trick on those days when fish seem sluggish.

Kneepads For Icefishermen

More and more icefishermen are learning the advantages of hole-hopping. This is a simple technique that involves punching numerous holes in a given area, then moving from hole to hole to seek out small and isolated groups of fish. It has one noticeable drawback: It is quite inconvenient to lug along a box or pail every time you change holes. Most hole-hopping anglers solve this by abandoning their boxes and kneeling at the holes. This is fine—until water begins soaking through your clothing.

To eliminate this problem, you need only a scissors and a worn-out car inner tube. Cut from the tube two sections (free of large holes or rips) approximately 24 inches in length. Even over the extra clothing worn for winter fishing, the elastic tubes slip on your legs rather easily, but still fit snugly enough so as not to slide down when you walk. Try them once, and they will be a standard piece of equipment on all icefishing outings. Not only do the pads prevent wet knees and shins, they also offer a surprising amount of added insulation from the cold ice and snow.

Two Tips for Ice Fishermen

● Instead of using light fishing line on ice rods, try sewing thread. Not the kind found in a sewing basket, but clear nylon thread used for sewing rugs. It's more supple than fishing line and can handle good-sized panfish. Also, it's a lot cheaper than regular monofilament line.

● While you're on the ice and if you do a lot of hole hopping, don't forget to weight down your other pole. You'd be surprised by the number of veteran ice anglers who have had a fish take a rod into the water while they were hole hopping or talking to other fishermen.

ICE SKIMMER

Skimming ice chips from your ice-fishing hole is a real chore when the water freezes into a chunk on your metal skimmer. And that clumsy skimmer could end up on the lake bottom, if numb fingers lose their grip.

Cut Away Broken Line Area

To make a better skimmer, cut out the bottom corner of a one-gallon, plastic milk jug, leaving part of the jug's handle attached to the cup you've produced. Insert a dowel in the jug handle, perforate the cup with a paper punch—and start skimming.

I prefer the jug skimmer to a commercial metal one, since it's free, unsinkable and sheds ice build-up with a quick tap against your foot.

ICE FISHING SKIS

Many ice fishermen carry their tackle, lunches, camp stoves—even pop-up tents and collapsible shanties—in wooden boxes strapped or bolted to sled runners. This way of moving gear works well most of the time—but not always. Sleds can bog down in deep snow and slush, and they often break through a snow or ice crust. They are also heavy and cold to handle, and they tend to rust when left on a truck bed or in a car trunk.

Try instead an old pair of shortened skis stripped of their bindings and screwed firmly to the bottom of the box. Skis are light, they store cleanly, and they'll go wherever sleds go just as smoothly. They'll also glide across thin crusts, and they'll negotiate soft powder if you distribute the weight in your box evenly.

ICE CLAWS WILL GET YOU OUT

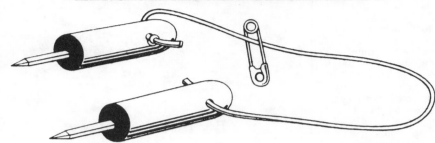

Be prepared! A simple pair of ice claws which you can make will enable you to crawl out quickly and easily if you break through the ice. This is an especially dangerous situation when alone. There is nothing to grab with your hands that will enable you to pull yourself out of the hole. With a pair of ice claws dangling from a lanyard, and within instant reach of your hands, the odds turn in your favor. With an ice claw in each hand, you extend one arm as far as it will reach on the ice surrounding the hole. Then you drive the steel point into the ice and use it to pull yourself partly out of the hole. Next reach out with your other arm and drive that ice claw into the ice, beyond the first claw.

By gripping the second ice claw imbedded in the ice, you can pull yourself completely out of the hole. Should the ice break, the floating claws still attached to the lanyard allow you to repeat the process until solid ice is reached. Once out of the hole do not attempt to stand up and walk. Either sprawl out on the ice and crawl or roll over until safe ice is reached.

A pair of ice claws can be made using ordinary ice picks. With a file, hacksaw or grind-

stone cut off all but two inches of the steel point. Now sharpen the stub to a tapered point.

If ice picks are not available, ice claws can be made from scratch. From a hardwood broom or mop handle cut two pieces four inches long. Avoid pine, fir, redwood or other softwoods because they may split or snap under strain. Suitable stock may also be split and shaped from hardwood fireplace fuel.

Cut the heads from two carpenter's spikes. Do not use nails less than four inches long. Next drill a two-inch-deep hole, slightly less in diameter than the spike, lengthwise through the center of the handpieces.

Grind or file a blunt point on the spike end from which the head was removed. Drive this end into the hole in the handpiece until two inches of the spike extend from it. Then grind or file a tapered point.

Now a lanyard should be made that passes around your neck and down the front of your coat. Secure the ice claws to this. Drill a small hole near the top of each handpiece. Thread a nylon or leather thong end through each of the holes. Make large knots in the ends of the thong to prevent it from pulling out of the holes.

Unless secured in some way, the ice claws will swing and bob and catch in brush. This is easily cured. With the lanyard passed around your neck so it dangles at your chest, use a safety pin to secure the thong to the front of coat or jacket. This should be at the point where the lanyard is attached to the ice-claw hand grip. There is no need to try to open the pins if you fall through the ice. A jerk on the handgrips will force the pins open, freeing the claws.

The sharp points should be covered to prevent an accidental injury. For this, cut 2½-inch lengths of any pithy growth such as goldenrod, joe-pye weed, teasel, elderberry or willow. Slip a section over each spike as a sheath. There is also the alternative of soaking cotton with any glue and rolling it to form a small ball. This ball is pressed on the tip of the claw where it will harden and stick tightly.

Do not try to remove either type of tip protector. Simply drive the claws into the ice—the covers will shatter on impact. Avoid driving the claws close to each other in the ice. This could fracture the ice and weaken it so that it could not support a body weight. Drive the claws at least a shoulder's width apart.

Ice-Fishing Gaff

Ever lost a good fish trying to pull it up through a small hole in the ice? The answer is a gaff to get a firm hold on the fish. In a pinch, all you need is a metal clothes hanger. Straighten it out, except for the curve at the end.

This gaff will do minimal harm to the fish if you wish to return it to the water. If a sharp point is needed, a little work with a file will do the trick.

★

The "sunken islands" you hear fishermen talking about are simply underwater humps which would be islands if the lake receded far enough to expose them. Fish them. They are consistent gathering places for many species of fish.

FUNDAMENTAL ICEFISHING

There's great satisfaction in teaching a youngster the fundamentals of icefishing. To help you along, here are a few guidelines.

• Be sure the youngster is well bundled. Try to fish on a day when the temperature is in the upper 30s or 40s and the panfish have been hitting well. Nothing turns a beginner off quicker than lack of action.

• Don't plan on doing too much fishing yourself. You are there to instruct, to get the neophyte angler squared away, and, above all, to prevent boredom.

• Interject a helpful little tip now and then, but mostly let him do his own thing. Prior to the trip, you might explain the importance of fishing with light tackle in the winter and of removing the excess ice buildup from the bobber, line and rod tip, pointing out that otherwise the whole purpose of fishing light will be defeated. Show him how a bait lowered slowly, with periodic halts, will often trigger a strike, which will be a distinct tick or a sudden slackness in the line. Don't lecture; let things come naturally.

• When the action slows, take a break and go sit inside the tent (if you have one) to warm up a little. Have a sandwich and a cup of hot chocolate or soup. Joke a little, try to create a festive mood, and tell him how much more enjoyable the trip is with him along. Always praise children when they do well.

• Keep in mind that while some kids will take to this wonderful sport, others may not. If yours doesn't, don't try to force it and don't feel bad.

Ice Angler's Carryall

An empty five-gallon plastic bucket of the type used for paint, a driveway sealer or wallboard compound, and a piece of one-and-a-quarter-inch (inside dimension) PVC piping can be made into an ideal icefishing carryall.

Cut several five-inch lengths of PVC. Drill two one-eighth-inch holes about an inch from each end. After finding the placement of the PVC holders, drill matching holes through the bucket.

Fasten the PVC to the bucket with appropriate hardware. A hook to hold your ice skimmer may also be fashioned to fit over the bucket's lip. Small utility handles can also be attached to the bucket.

Tip-ups, snacks, lures and other icefishing gear can be carried inside the bucket. Jigging rods are toted and stored in the PVC holders, handles down. The bucket may also be used for a seat when you get to your favorite fishing spot.

ICE SAFETY

Like blood, ice is thicker than water, but you make sure it is thick enough to keep you alive! The state of Colorado conducted some research and came up with the following safety measurements on *lake* ice:

• Two inches of ice will support one man on foot.

• Three inches of ice will support a group walking in single file.

• Seven and one-half inches of ice will support a light automobile.

• Twelve inches of ice will support a heavy truck.

But remember: Slush ice is about one-half as strong as clear, blue ice. River ice is about 15 percent weaker than lake ice. New ice is generally stronger than old ice, but repeated travel over the same route weakens any ice, as do underwater springs and currents.

Perch Research

Facts about the winter habits of yellow perch that should help increase your catch (the information is from a study done on Lake Mendota, Wisconsin, by the University of Wisconsin):

Daily Activity: Yellow perch start moving at daybreak and increase their activity all morning until a peak is reached sometime between 8:00 and 11:00 a.m. Movement then drops to a low around noon, followed by another rise. A secondary peak of activity is reached sometime between 1:00 and 4:00 p.m. Perch are relatively inactive after dark.

Preferred Depth: Perch tend to stay at midwater levels and seem to prefer the 30- to 60-foot range. They are found most frequently in areas of a lake that have at least 50 feet of water. As the season progresses and oxygen levels decline near the bottom, perch move more toward the top of their preferred range.

Schooling Density: Yellow perch schooling patterns are much more dispersed in winter than at other times. Mean distance between top and bottom fish in a school during winter is 22 feet. This compares with a compact 8.5-foot average that is found during the summer.

LATE-SEASON ICE FISHING

Late in the ice-fishing season, water below thin ice is often most productive. That's because thin ice means either that there is water movement, or that warm water and oxygen levels are high. Ice close to open water is also a great place to cut a hole because oxygen will be in abundance when the rest of the lake might be deficient in this vital element. Be careful, however, and don't venture onto ice so thin that it's unsafe.

FISHING TACKLE
GEAR AND
ACCESSORIES

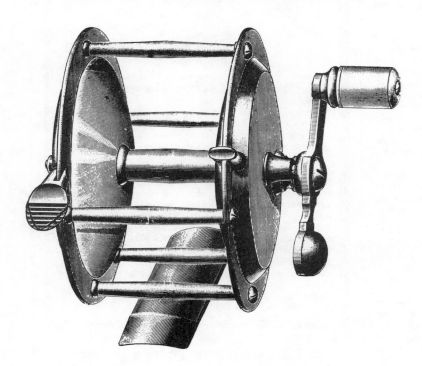

FISHING TACKLE · GEAR AND ACCESSORIES

TACKLE CARE AND REPAIR

STREAMSIDE ROD REPAIR

A broken fishing rod doesn't have to spoil your trip. If you're in pine-tree country, with needle-nose pliers (a must in any fishing vest) and a match, you can repair that broken rod and keep on fishing.

If the rod breaks at the ferrule, the first task is to remove the broken piece of rod. Build a small fire and with the pliers put the ferrule into the flame. Once the metal has heated, it will char the broken piece of rod inside it, so you can remove it.

Next, gather pitch or resin oozing out of a pine tree, or any tree releasing a sticky substance. Place the resin into the cleaned-out ferrule. Holding the ferrule with plier, reheat the metal until the resin is hot. Then place the broken section of rod into the ferrule. Allow the resin to cool, and reassemble the rod sections.

If your hollow rod breaks at the tip or at a section between ferrules, the same technique can be applied in reverse.

This time, square up the broken ends with a hook hone or pocketknife. Whittle a dowel from three-quarters inch to one and a half inches in length and matching the diameter of the hollow portion of the rod. This makeshift dowel will join the hollow ends of the two pieces of broken rod.

Heat the resin, coat the plug with it and slide both hollow ends over the plug, holding the rod in place until the resin cools.

★

To keep a rod from bouncing out when your boat or vehicle is moving, try a tapered door stop wedged in a rod holder aboard the boat or a bumper rack.

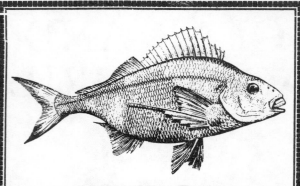

Multi-Use Bags

Heavy-duty Ziploc freezer bags are a boon to fishermen: they are airtight, punctureproof and will prevent freezer burn when freezing your catch. Now you can fillet and package your fish on the spot and will not have to rewrap before freezing.

When traveling from the fishing site, the bagged fish placed in ice will arrive home quite fresh. A bonus feature is that these plastic bags, which are available in several convenient sizes, can be washed and used over and over again.

The smaller sizes of Ziploc bags are ideal for carrying plugs with multi-hooks, and leaders with and without hooks. They are also handy for carrying all types of bait, cut and otherwise, to your fishing site.

Strong and flexible, they can be folded flat to be stored in your tacklebox or in your jacket or fishing-vest pocket where they can be easily accessible.

SURE CURE FOR DIRTY CORK

Fishing is good clean fun but sometimes the cork handles of fishing rods can become so soiled that they are disgusting to look at and even harder to hold. Catfish anglers using chicken livers know what "true grit" is all about.

Cleaning a cork handle or reel seat takes very little time, and everything you need is right in the house. Just douse the cork handle with liquid bleach and use a kitchen brush to scrub the cork clean.

Rinse both the brush and the cork thoroughly with water, then scrub again under the tap water. The results when dried will amaze you, and after you've demonstrated your expertise your partner may let you back in his boat.

Fill It Up!

Much has been said about the retrieve ratios of high-speed reels. Unfortunately some anglers aren't taking advantage of their speed capability. They aren't filling spinning and casting reels to the recommended line capacity. This means that the spool's diameter is smaller, with smaller revolutions that do not pick up as much line as does a filled spool.

Besides hindering the retrieve, a half-filled spool can be less than desirable for long casts. For the openfaced spinning reel, the filled spool is highly recommended. When a spinning reel is only half filled, the cast line hits more of the spool. This slight amount of friction decreases casting distance. The fisherman who tries to save a few pennies by only half filling his reel with line is going to pay a lot more by hindering the reel's effectiveness.

SAVE OLD SPLIT-SHOT

Battered and worn split-shot can be very useful. It can be permanently attached to long-shanked hooks, used in emergency jig situations, or for anytime fishing. You can easily change the weight or even make sets of different weights and sizes. Also, try dipping in colored enamels.

COLOR-CODED BOBBERS

A canny West Coast steel-header I know never has any problems determining how much weight to use with individual bobbers. Each is coded with a dot on the side; small models with red indicate 3/16-inch diameter lead wire; large ones with green are for 1/4-inch.

A short length of fishing line with a large plastic bead tied to one end is threaded through the bobber. A length of lead wire is secured to the line with a small ring of surgical rubber tubing.

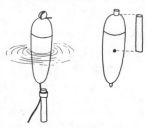

Weight is adjusted by trimming off small pieces of lead until the bobber floats at precisely the desired level for successful steelheading.

The length of the lead wire is then recorded on the bobber's side by measuring from the top of the cap.

Steelhead anglers normally adjust the distance between bobber and sinker until the latter is lightly dragging the bottom; thus the additional weight of bait or lure is hardly noticeable. If, however, bobbers are to be used to suspend bait off the bottom, the added weight must be compensated for.

INEXPENSIVE FISH GRIPPER

Kitchen tongs make handy grippers to hold fish when taking out the hook, especially when ice fishing, since your gloves do not have to be removed. Fish meant for the pan will keep their mouths open wide when grabbed on their sides with the tongs, thus making it very easy to remove hooks.

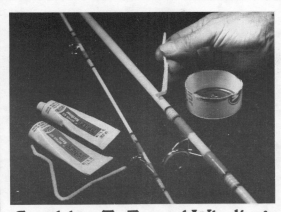

Good-bye To Frayed Windings

Frayed windings on fishing rods can be made to look new and last years longer by coating them with plastic. Mix up a two-part resin and hardener according to directions. Then use a pipe cleaner to flow this material onto the windings at guides and ferrules. Allow to harden several days. The new covering is almost indestructible—it lasts much longer than varnish.

•

When handling monofilament line you sometimes find a white powder on your hands. This is "monomer bleed" and an indication that the line is beginning to deteriorate. When line loses its color and shine, consider replacing it. Nicks or scrapes on the line weaken it considerably, so cut the damaged sections off and discard them.

TACKLE CARE

Many a moan and groan has resulted because some irreplaceable or choice bit of fishing tackle has given out prematurely. Proper storage or, more specifically, proper care taken before storage probably would have prevented the loss.

For those who did that "chuck-it-in-the-corner" act on the last day of fishing season, tackle should get priority treatment. If dirty, give it a thorough washing with mild soap and water, followed by a careful drying. Then inspect the windings. If they are secure, but look a bit worn, touch them up with lacquer. If not, rewind and realign guides to avoid frustration on opening day next spring.

Loose ferrules also should be fixed. If they are only dirty or a bit corroded, clean them with a mild abrasive such as silver polish. Then rub with a slightly oiled rag.

Reels, of course, need some attention. The average single-action flyreel should stay in good condition for a long time if cleaned and oiled after use. But the spinning reel is a horse of another color. It should be taken apart and cleaned, dried and then carefully lubricated before reassembling. Use a slight smear of oil on chrome parts.

Make a note to order any worn parts, using the manufacturer's parts list for identification. If these parts should go bad, you'll have the spares handy for quick replacement.

EASY REEL LOADING

The traditional way to load fishing line onto a reel is to run a pencil through the hole in the new spool of line, brace the pencil between the knees, and use the fingers to adjust the tension as the line is cranked on the reel. If a companion is available he can hold the pencil instead of letting you hold it with your knees.

But Norm Seymour, a Saint Lawrence River guide, has his own pet method, one he has used hundreds of times to fill the big muskie reels and smaller ones he stores on his boat for use by his clients. Seymour drops the new spool of line into a pail or other container of water where it floats and turns easily as the line is wound on the reel. The water also provides enough friction to prevent the revolving spool from overrunning the line to cause a backlash. The line is already wet, well initiated, by the time it rests on the reel spool.

RECYCLE LEAD-CORE LINE

When your old lead-core trolling line gets frayed and cracked, don't throw it out or abandon it in your junk drawer. Recycle it. Cut out all the damaged sections and use the rest to make jig lines for ice fishing.

Being slightly stiff, these lead-core jig lines will rarely get snarled or tangled. And, they'll always be easy to handle, even when you're wearing bulky gloves.

Old flyfishing line can also be recycled to make better than average jig lines.

WORN WADERS

Consider giving waders that are beyond repair a second lease on life. Depending on the nature and location of the damage, you might be able to salvage a pair of slip-on waterproof boots with no more effort than a little scissor work.

If the boot feet are bad, chest waders with the boots cut off make excellent rainpants. If both the boots and tops are beyond help, you can cut a waterproof butcher's apron from the front of the boots, or a waterproof seat for deer and duck season from the back.

Even small strips of this material can be useful. They'll serve as buffers between two abrasive surfaces, such as the gunwale of a light boat and cartop carriers, and combined with a good contact glue, they'll patch virtually any air-or-waterproof material from a rubber raft to the new pair of waders you inadvertently snagged.

★

Why hasn't green ever been a "selling color" in lures? A good guess is that because it matches weedy backgrounds, a green lure is too hard for a gamefish to see. Some greenish colors do sell in plastic worms, however, especially chartreuse.

MAKE A CASE FOR IT

The transport of rods, whether in the back of a pickup or in the trunk of a car, carries with it a potential for possible damage. All quality fishing rods should be transported in a rod case.

Rod cases can be custom-made, inexpensively, from PVC plastic plumbing pipe. The smaller diameters are suitable for individual rods, while larger sizes can accommodate and store a number of rods. End caps are available. One end cap can be secured with glue and the other tethered. PVC pipe is reasonably priced and is available cut to the lengths you need in plumbing supply houses and also many hardware stores.

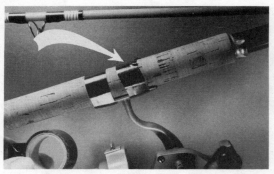

Double Duty Rod

Your seven-and-one-half or eight-foot fly rod can do double duty as a delightful spinning rod for small lures on trout and bass streams. The light-action rod is sheer joy to use with a spin-reel and small lures.

Two or three turns of friction tape will hold a spinning reel firmly to the cork handle enabling you to grip the reel properly. The wire guides on the rod do not interfere with the flow of monofilament line, nor do grooves wear into the wire snake guides exceptionally fast

•

On calm days the underside of a lake surface acts like a mirror, reflecting things that would not usually be within a fish's vision. Fish can often see what is lurking on the other side of a rock or log because of this mirror effect. They can still see through the surface and spot movement above the water very easily. Thus, calm days dictate a more careful approach.

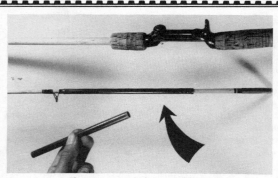

Spare The Rod

Don't discard damaged glass or graphite rods. They can furnish spare parts to repair other rods that may break in the future.

How? Well, let's assume two rods have fractured tip sections. Lay the two fractured rods side by side. Most likely a six- to eight-inch-long section that is undamaged can be sawed from one and slipped like a tube over the splintered portion of the other. Cement in place with plastic resin and hardener. When this dries, the repaired rod is serviceable again.

Save the sawed-apart rod for more spare parts in the future.

Even if you don't know a chipper from a putter, next time you come across a used golf bag at a flea market or yard sale, buy it. My husband thought "Oh no!" when I brought one home, but now he's a golf (bag) lover. It makes a great fishing rod organizer. Standing neatly in a closet corner, it holds nearly two-dozen rods of assorted types and sizes. There they are safe and very accessible. No more uncasing and recasing rods every fishing day. Rods can also be stored with the reels still attached. We've had four bait-casting, two spinning and two fly outfits inside, without overcrowding. Furthermore, a half-dozen or more reels can be kept in the outer ball pouch.

QUICK WADER REPAIR

A little tube of Chapstick or similar lip balm can be a real day-saver when small punctures in your waders threaten to spoil your fun. Just work a glob of the waxy substance in your fingers till soft and then apply to the puncture. It hardens right up again in the cold water, and really works! I have saved many a chilly spring afternoon using this trick.

★

In clear, calm water a noisy lure can spook fish. Try making low, flat casts so that the lure falls lightly on the water close to cover, like some small, injured creature. Then work it slowly, barely dimpling the surface as you bring it back to shore or boat.

HALF A ROD

The whippy top half of an average-size spinning rod makes a quite serviceable—and essentially free—minirod. To complete the ultralight rig, just tape on a miniature reel near the base ferrule. You'll be surprised how well the half-rod action compares with that of a regular ultralight rod.

TIP-TOP TIP

Tip-tops on rods often become grooved, bent or broken and require replacement more frequently than any other rod guide. This is easy to do, but since they are glued in place, care must be taken when removing them to prevent damage to the rod.

Heat-set glues, such as hot-melt glue of ferrule cement are usually used to glue tip-tops in place, and heat is used to remove them. Use a cigarette lighter or alcohol lamp and hold the metal tube of the tip-top to the side of the flame. This will prevent a wide spread of heat and possible rod damage. Rotate the tip-top to heat the tube uniformly, and remove it with a straight pull with pliers. Usually a few seconds of heat are enough to break down any glue.

To protect the rod from excess heat during this operation, wrap the end adjacent to the tip-top with several layers of masking tape.

ALL-AROUND VEST

A shotgunner's vest makes an ideal fishing outfit, especially for flyfishermen, because the shell-holders stretch just enough to hold small containers of flies, hooks, sinkers and other small items.

Gather some containers (35 mm film holders are fine). Color code the snap-on lids with hobby paints used for plastic. I use red for flies, yellow for hooks, gray for sinkers, and blue for swivels.

On the red tops for flies I mark, with black paint, the type of flies in that holder, such as GH for Gray Hackles and RC for Royal Coachmen. The vest has plenty of pockets for a variety of flies.

Weekends are poor times to fish popular places because of the added angling pressure. Your chances of catching fish are much better if you fish an hour at daybreak or dusk a couple days during the week.

Test Tape

As months go by, it's difficult to recall what test line is stored on those spare reels. Is it 8-, 12- or 17-pound test?

A piece of tape placed on the reel seat with line-test marked on it solves the dilemma. Changing reels and lines to match fishing conditions is easy then. If you use more than one spool per reel, mark each spool.

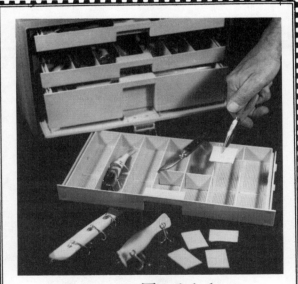

Custom Tacklebox

If large muskie-sized lures do not fit into your tacklebox, customize the trays by cutting out some of the dividing partitions.

Use a sharp knife to score both sides and bottom edges of each partition. Use pliers to crack loose and remove the dividers. It's a simple procedure.

This method of customizing trays to house special bait selections does away with the need to purchase another tacklebox, or to carry more than one box astream.

Rod Grippers

Even with meticulous maintenance, a rod will sometimes refuse to be broken down. The problem is often compounded by wet, cold hands and an equally wet rod. There are textured rubber pads for taking down stubborn rods. Or the enterprising fisherman can purchase and modify a similar item from the local grocery store—a textured pad for unscrewing stuck jar lids.

A light coating of paraffin (candle wax) will help most ferrules slide, but beware of using questionable emollients. One fellow I know used petroleum jelly on his fiberglass rod ferrule and had to send the rod back to the factory for dissection.

MAKE A LEMON FLOAT

An empty, lemon-shaped plastic bottle makes a great fishing bobber. Just loosen the cap, twist your fishing line around the screw threads, and then tighten the cap. The yellow plastic shows up very well in the water.

Ever notice how your line spool distorts from the tension of nylon line? Well, some reel spools can distort also unless you use braided line backing to cushion the compression of nylon mono.

Stuck Ferrule

For fishing-rod ferrules that stubbornly refuse to part no matter what, try some Liquid Wrench. Available in automotive and hardware stores, this product is specifically formulated to loosen items frozen together by rust, corrosion, old grease, etc. Just spray a little around the male ferrule and let it drip down. It takes only a few minutes for the liquid to penetrate. Wipe both of the ferrules clean after pulling them apart.

Fishhook Filer

The best—and the cheapest—fishhook sharpener I have ever discovered is a diamond fingernail file. It costs about 50 cents for the straightforward model that I prefer because of its slim handle and long blade. With this file, I can get a long, fine stroke at the point of the hook. For around $2, you can get an abbreviated model, complete with tiny scabbard, that fits perfectly in a fishing-vest pocket.

To sharpen a hook with this file, hold the hook firmly in one hand, and with the other take two or three strokes from the back of the point toward the eye of the hook; do this to each side. Filing should be in the same plane as the slope of the barb. In essence, you should construct a triangular point by taking metal off each side, at a slant. Avoid taking any metal off the outside of the bend.

Every hook should be sharpened before it is fished. When sufficiently sharp, the hook will dig in when run across your thumbnail.

VENTILATED BOXES

Drilling small ventilation holes in inexpensive fly or lure boxes will allow the artificials to air-dry after use, preventing the hooks and other metal parts from rusting.

Restoring Cork Handles

One way to restore a nicked or gouged handle on an old but serviceable rod is to fill the gaps in the cork handle with more cork. To do this, use a file or rasp on scrap cork products to make a small pile of sawdust. Mix the cork dust with a water repellent or waterproof glue to as thick a consistency as possible. The end result should closely approximate the handle in color and texture.

With an awl or old screwdriver, force the glue/cork mixture into the gouges and nicks in the handle. Build up the filling higher than the cork handle and allow to cure for at least 24 hours. File and sand the whole grip smooth, using successively finer grades of sandpaper. The rod handle will look as good as new.

Emergency Creel

If you ever find yourself on a trout stream and decide to keep a few fish but don't have a creel, don't panic. An adequate creel can be made in just a few minutes. All you need is two square feet of any loose-weave material, like a cotton T-shirt.

Lay the material flat. Pick up the corners and tie them together with a piece of cord or fishing line. This leaves easy access into the sack. Tie this improvised creel to your belt.

When you keep a fish, layer the bottom of the sack with wet streamside grass. As you add trout, separate each fish with additional layers of dampened grass. Keep the sack and contents damp. Air circulating through the wet sack will serve to ensure that everything is kept cool and fresh throughout the day.

THROWAWAY SINKERS

Used spark plugs make great fishing weights over litter-strewn or rocky bottoms. By looping a rubber band through the electrode and then tapping the wire down, the plug can be attached to a loop of monofilament. The rubber band stretches when the plug is hung up, and even if the extra stretching force isn't enough to break free, the band will break before the monofilament.

Used spark plugs are free for the asking at service stations or garages. Smaller plugs are discarded at lawnmower, chainsaw or motorcycle repair shops.

A handy way to carry plugs is in a plastic antifreeze or bleach jug. This has a convenient handle and a small enough opening so that only one plug at a time comes out.

VERSATILE FISHERMAN'S VEST

A lightweight, inexpensive fisherman's vest is ideal for either day or overnight campers. For day hikers, it can hold everything needed with the exception of a canteen. For overnight hikers, it will hold all those items normally used during the day and prevent going into the main pack for often-used items.

Most vests have a large back pocket and several medium-sized front pockets with some small pockets above them. Use the back pocket for a lightweight raincoat, parka or nylon jacket. For day hikers, it will also hold a light lunch.

The medium-sized front pockets will hold a map, hiking guide, bird book, small pair of binoculars, trail snack and extra socks for a midday change.

The small upper pockets will hold a compass, extra film for a camera, kerchief, sunglasses, insect repellent, etc.

The weight and bulk of these items are evenly distributed to make hiking more pleasurable and less strenuous.

RED LIGHT FOR NIGHT

Sportsmen who pursue outdoor activities at night can take a tip from pilots and astronomers, who know that red lighting doesn't hurt your night vision. Covering the lens of a flashlight with a piece of red plastic will provide illumination without spooking game or surface-feeding fish.

There is also a definite safety factor involved with using red light at night. The inner structure of the human eye is made up of rods and cones. The cones, used in bright daytime light, give us color vision, while the rods are used in low-light levels to provide sensitive night vision.

Once the eye is dark-adapted, the iris expands to approximately 7mm to let in the maximum amount of light the eye can detect. If you switch on a white light, the eye reacts by contracting the iris. After the light is switched off, it takes several minutes for your eyes to regain their night vision. The cones of the eye are not as sensitive to red light as they are to white light. So red light helps to overcome this problem, making night fishing or hunting much safer.

QUICK FLOAT TUBE TAKE-DOWN

By replacing the standard valve cap on a float tube with a valve core removal tool, a tuber can quickly deflate it to a compact size for easier transporting. To deflate the tube, the tool is unscrewed and then it is inverted into the valve stem where the two prongs can engage the valve core for easy removal.

Gum Rivets

Bubble gum makes a good temporary repair for a lost rivet in an aluminum boat or canoe. Chew the gum until it's soft, then force it through the hole and flatten it on both sides. In cold weather, warm the surface before making the repair, so the gum won't become too stiff to work through the hole.

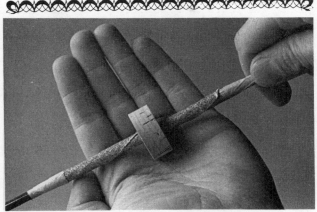

Quick Fix For Cork Rings

When building a rod, the most time-consuming chore is hollowing out the hole in the center of each cork ring to the right size.

A quick and accurate way to do this is to tape medium-grade sandpaper in a strip at the thin end of the rod blank. Tape the sandpaper over a strip of writing paper to keep the grit from marring the rod finish. The sandpaper will go on in a spiral because of the taper of the rod blank.

Use cork rings with holes large enough to fit over the small end of the blank. Slip the sandpaper section through the hole. Now roll the ring back and forth across the palm of one hand, while holding the blank steady with the other. This will make an even expansion of the hole.

Occasionally run the ring down the blank, trying it for fit, until it slides snugly to the place you want it. Leave it there, get another ring, and sand it until it fits against the first. Go on this way until all of the rings are where you want them. Then slide them all up a few inches, and fasten them back in place one by one, with five-minute epoxy. When the epoxy has set, sand the handle to the shape you want.

A warning: Don't try this with preformed grips. It only works with cork rings. With a full-length grip, you might get the sandpaper jammed inside or possibly mar the rod blank.

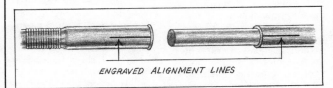

ENGRAVED ALIGNMENT LINES

PERFECT ROD ALIGNMENT

The sections of multiple-piece rods often slip around, causing line guides and tip-top to be out of alignment. It can take you several minutes to get them back in the proper perspective.

Maybe someday rod manufacturers will help us out by producing rods with alignment marks on adjoining sections, but until that time comes, mark your own.

Sit down sometime when you aren't rushed and line up the tip-top and line guides until they are perfect. Then with a sheet metal scribe or other sharp metal object engrave a straight line about one inch in length at the junction of abutting rod sections.

It will take only a glance and a slight twist while fishing for perfect alignment every time.

Depth Marker

When icefishing with tip-ups, resetting your bait at the same depth can be a hit-and-miss proposition. One way to eliminate this is by attaching a reference marker to your line.

First determine the depth at which you want to fish, from the bottom of the tip-up's spool. Next take a small piece of bright-colored cloth or wax paper or cigarette pack foil. Then, using two half hitches (or another knot of your choice), attach the marker to the line where it first makes contact with your spool.

Now when a fish strikes and you pull the line in, setting the bait at the same depth is a snap. Just wind the line around the spool until the marker makes contact with it, place the tip-up in the hole, and set the flag.

The marker can be used as a bite detector when the tip-up flag trips—just look into the hole and see if the marker moves. This will allow you to hook more members of the pike family, since they usually hit the bait, drop it, mouth it again, run, then swallow it.

The marker is also effective when attached to a jigging line, to keep your lure at the desired depth. Simply lower your rod until the marker touches the water, and jig as usual.

★

To make any lure run deeper, just change to a lighter line. Smaller diameter lines offer less resistance and allow any diving lure to drop farther into the depths.

Jiffy Guide Repair

Don't panic if you discover a worn line guide on one of your favorite rods on the eve of that big fishing trip. Carefully build up several layers of nail polish on the inside of the guide. This will prevent it from fraying your line until you can get the guide replaced.

Tripod In The Surf

The trouble with fishing the surf is that there's no place to lay a rod down or hang gear—canvas bags, bait containers, extra clothes and stringers of fish.

A camera tripod propped up on the beach behind you is the equivalent of about four extra hands. You can hang gear on it or lean things against it. All will be held up out of the water. Unless you put it out among the breakers, it will not tip over.

Two cautions: 1) watch the tide and 2) wash salt water off the tripod when you get home.

THE WADER'S WAGON

Wader fishermen have to figure out what to do with all the gear they need in a day of stream fishing. An inner tube, a four-foot piece of rope and a bushel basket will solve the dilemma. Tie the rope around the air-filled tube, push the basket through the tube's center, and you have a wader's wagon. Then fasten the rope to your belt and all your necessary gear can be hauled almost effortlessly. No bulging pockets or bulky backpacks will hinder your fishing style.

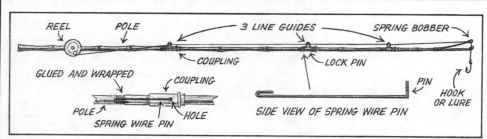

TAKE-APART CANEPOLE

Fish around brushpiles with floating bobbers and you're apt to get snagged. There is a much better way to catch more fish and lose fewer lures and hooks: a long pole poked down to unhook snagged jigs.

Rig up a 12-foot canepole that breaks down into three sections. On the thickest section, tape a single-action reel about a foot from the end. On the side of each coupling, tie and glue a line guide; glue another in the middle of the thin section. On the tip, use a spring bobber, which can be made out of any light spring steel wire (piano wire will do). Most tackleshops have ready-made bobbers, used mostly for ice fishing. The bobber should be lined up with the hole in the pole tip, with as little line rubbing as possible.

To take the pole apart, just reel up line as far as possible, then fold both ends against the middle section and tie to keep the sections together.

Sometimes the tip section will come off when unhooking from a snag. To prevent this, drill a three-thirty-seconds-inch hole through the smaller coupling while the pole is together and properly lined up. Then use a piece of spring wire about six inches long for a pin. One end of the wire is bent at a right angle to fit through the hole in the coupling, and the other end is bent like a hook, tied and glued to the pole. The hook prevents the wire from turning, thus securing the tip tightly in place.

Do not use a line more than 8-pound test. If you do, and hook a big fish, the tip of the pole will break before the line does.

Reel Lube

One of the best ways to lubricate a reel is with a silicone lubricant, usually dispensed in a three-eighths-ounce tube. But a better buy is the larger two-ounce size found at electronic supply shops. Phonolube is a silicone lubricant for phonographs, record changers, tape decks and similar mechanisms. It has exceptional clinging power and it won't change viscosity over a relatively wide temperature range. For only a little more money you get more than five times as much silicone lubricant. You can save and stay slick at the same time.

FLIPPER SAVERS

Swim fins designed for divers and snorkelers also work well for float-tube fishermen and hunters. Good fins are expensive, but a nylon cord secured to the fin and tied to the ankle will keep the fin from slipping off and being lost.

Small leaks in waders or boots can be plugged temporarily by melting the end of a plastic worm and smearing the hot plastic over the hole. It will harden in a few seconds.

Invisible Rod Repair

White silk thread is ideal for reinforcing repairs on bamboo rods, wooden net handles, creels and other similar items when you don't want this reinforcement to be obvious. White silk turns transparent when varnished and stays transparent after the varnish has dried.

White buttonhole silk can be found in many sewing supply stores. This is size E and useful for heavy work. Size A and 2/0, commonly used in wrapping freshwater rods, can be found in many tackle and fly-tying supply houses. Be sure it is not waxed.

Fingers should be as clean and smooth as possible when winding silk.

Before varnishing, quickly pass the finished winding through a sootless flame to remove the fine filaments that could cause bumps in the final finish.

The varnish must thoroughly penetrate the silk to make it transparent. Warm the varnish in a pan of hot water to thin it for proper penetration. Work the varnish into the winding thoroughly with your fingers. When the winding has become transparent wipe excess varnish off the winding and adjacent surfaces. I prefer to do such reinforcement windings separately from the rest of the varnish work on a rod to make sure it is done right.

Let subsequent coats build up the varnish above the thread before rubbing down the winding. When rubbing down, be careful not to cut into the thread. Such cuts turn white and may not turn transparent when re-varnished.

SAFEGUARD YOUR GEARS

Sheepskin cases are great for storing spare spools, but the shearling tends to rub off the protective silicone lubricants that gears and spindle bases need to prolong reel life. A quick remedy is to cover the inside padding of the case with Scotch tape, which is slick so it doesn't absorb the reel lube. Or cement a circle of slick plastic to Velcro. Those little fibers grab the case lining and hold tight.

INGENIOUS RESOLE

Anglers who do a lot of wading know there's no such thing as an indestructible felt sole, and nearly everyone ends up at some point with a pot of sticky contact cement trying to glue indoor-outdoor carpeting to the bottom of their waders. A friend of mine has come up with another solution. He simply buys ordinary waders and slips a pair of felt liners sold for snowmobile boots over them. One set usually lasts him most of the season, but when he does have to change it's a simple matter of just slipping off the old liner and slipping on the new. Take your waders along when you buy the first set of felt liners and try several sizes to find one that fits snugly.

Easy Hook Guards

Treble hook guards are easy to make using the simple design shown here. All you need is a supply of small branches from pine, spruce or any other softwood tree. The wood should be dry with no cracks. Cut a one-quarter-inch-thick disk from the end of a branch, then drill a small hole in the center with an awl or small Phillips screwdriver. Now simply cut a "Pac-man" style mouth in the disk with a thin-bladed knife. To use, just slide the disk on and press the wood firmly into the hook points. Guards can be reused dozens of times before the wood will eventually deteriorate.

Quick Drain Grommets

Nylon-covered float tubes offer a great safety measure against puncture, but when the tube comes out of a pond, a considerable quantity of water is trapped inside the nylon. A series of inexpensive brass grommets inserted in the nylon cover not only allows the water to drain out quickly, but reduces a great deal of strain on the seams of the cover as well.

★ ★ ★

Grass Catcher

Trolling in water containing floating grass and algae can be frustrating. The grass collects on the line and then slides down to build up on the terminal tackle or the lure itself if no leader is used. Eventually it begins to destroy the natural action of the lure, making it necessary for the angler to reel in his line and clear it of the grass.

Norm Seymour, a Saint Lawrence River guide who has spent 30 years trolling for muskies in the grass-filled waters of the international river knows what to do.

Seymour clamps an alligator clip on his trolling line at a point where it will ride just beneath the surface of the water. The clip collects the grass that would otherwise slide down the line to the lure. The grass still has to be removed from the alligator clip periodically, but this can be accomplished quickly by reeling in a short length of line. The lure is not disturbed.

On braided wire line Seymour simply slips a tooth of the clip between the strands, but if he is fishing monofilament he likes to first wrap the line with plastic tape and place the clip tightly over the tape. This will prevent damage to the line.

Ferrule Caps

Ordinary house dust is one of the leading causes of jammed or tight-fitting ferrules. The stuff accumulates when rods are stored and wreaks havoc with the small tolerances that allowed for a smooth fit. To keep dust and other foreign matter out during storage, use caps from discarded felt-tip pens. Experiment with different sizes until you find the best fit. Even large surfcasting and trolling rods can be accommodated using caps from magic marker pens.

★

Reverse one battery in a stored flashlight to keep it from being turned on accidentally.

Which Stringer for What?

Basically, fish stringers come in two types: The chain type with safety snaps at the end that can be pushed through the fish's lower lip and locked, and the type made with a length of nylon cord with a spike at one end and an eye at the other. In most cases, the chain stringer is the simplest and best to use. But there are two species of freshwater fish that shouldn't be kept on a chain stringer.

Channel catfish will often get loose by twisting around and popping open the snaps. Use a nylon stringer, or a sack for catfish. Crappies, especially the smaller ones, have such thin mouths that frequently pulling them from the water will often cause their lips to pull free of the stringer. A wire fish basket is best.

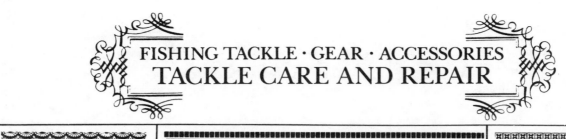

Saltwater Reel Protection

The chromed surfaces on saltwater reels take a beating from the salt water and even with prompt rinsing in fresh water can soon become pitted and old looking. These surfaces, in fact all metal surfaces on reels used in salt and brackish water, can be easily protected and kept looking new by the same method we use to protect the chrome bumpers on our cars—by waxing them. Chrome reel seats will also keep their new look longer as well as work more freely if kept waxed.

Although there are a number of quick-shine liquid waxes, the best protection still seems to be supplied by a good hard paste auto wax, such as Simoniz or Blue Coral. Already discolored surfaces should be cleaned with a combination cleaner wax or chrome cleaner, then coated with a hard paste wax. On dull-surfaced anodized reels you may object to the shine of the wax. If so, don't buff the wax after applying. It will protect just as well. The threads on reel seats need to be waxed more frequently as usage wears the wax off the threads more quickly than off other parts of the reel seat.

Rewaxing should be done two or three times a season, depending on how much you fish and wash the reel. If you wash in detergent, rewax immediately as detergents are pretty good at removing wax.

TEST FOR WORN GUIDES

Years of intensive casting with monofilament lines can wear grooves into metal rod guides. This can cause lines to roughen and weaken, and often break when hooking heavy fish. So check guides regularly. Pull pieces of nylon mesh stocking through each guide. If the stocking catches or pulls, indicating a flawed surface, replace with a new one.

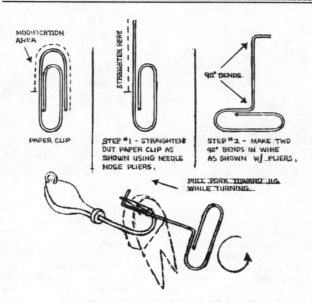

EASY OFF PORK REMOVER

Removing stubborn porkrind from a hook is difficult at best and sometimes impossible without destroying the strip. With the aid of needle-nosed pliers, you can reshape a simple paper clip into a handy pork remover in only a few seconds.

Use the pliers to straighten the paper clip as shown in Step 1. Then simply make two 90-degree bends as shown in Step 2. Presto, you've created a pork remover.

With this little tool, removing pork chunks is a breeze by following these two easy steps:

1) Insert the clip through the pork chunk, keeping the wire to the left side of the hook.

2) Now push down slightly on the clip while at the same time turning it counterclockwise and pulling the pork toward the jig.

This method slips the pork right over the barb and off the hook without enlarging the pre-cut hole in the pork chunk. With a little practice it's easy and effective.

Reels should be wiped clean with a demoisturizing spray when you are finished fishing. Some people run water over them, but this should be done carefully so the flow does not drive dirt particles inside. Don't submerge a reel in water to clean it. Periodically, take the reel apart, remove the old grease, and lubricate it lightly. Adding new oil or grease to the old will create problems.

Stocking-Foot Wader Repair

Lightweight stocking-foot Waders are popular with fishermen and duck hunters. Though comfortable and durable, they have a tendency to leak at the seams.

If the leak is near the bottom of the waders and is slow, there is an easy way to keep your feet dry: Simply pull two or three large plastic trash bags over the leaky leg before climbing into your waders. If the water is cold, wear heavy socks inside the waders and trash bags. This will work as an emergency repair or as a long-term fix to save waders that are beyond repair.

Tackle Care

You know enough to wash your rod and reel with fresh water right after fishing in salt water. But have you thought about your tacklebox? Your baits, hooks, pliers, sinkers, swivels, steel leaders, knife—they are salt-watered, too. Everything should be flushed with fresh water and dried thoroughly to prevent rust and corrosion. Even if it is a plastic box, the salt is there, and the next time it gets wet, the salt will dissolve and redeposit itself elsewhere.

One more thing: If you have driven your car within 500 yards of the beach, wash it immediately. Do not stop with the outer body. Thoroughly hose down the entire underside of the car to wash off the salt.

Salt starts to attack steel, copper, brass and aluminum within hours after exposure and can do considerable damage within a few weeks if it is not eliminated at once.

If you are unfortunate enough to have a high tide saturate the bottom of your car, there is only one thing to do: Wash it off immediately as described above and trade it off within a couple months. Otherwise the cost of repair will be prohibitive within six to 12 months.

USE THE YELLOW PAGES

Loosely wound monofilament on a reel spool can be a frustrating problem. To obtain a tight wind, try the Yellow Pages (or a big dictionary).

When winding new mono on a reel spool, first run it through a heavy book before winding it onto the spool. This will provide tension to insure a tight, even wind.

Apply just slightly less tension than it takes to make the drag whine.

Do not use a favorite text because monofilament creates friction that will fray the pages.

Spool Storage

If you buy monofilament in bulk spools, make this simple gadget for storing and dispensing the lines.

Find the center on a spare piece of wood 1 × 2 inches or 1 × 4 inches.

Length determines the number of spools to be stored. Drill ¼-inch holes in on a slight angle (about 85 degrees) every 5 inches. Insert ¼-inch dowels that have been cut 5 or 6 inches in length. If the dowel rods are snug enough, no glue is needed.

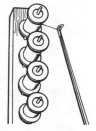

Drill a hole in the top and bottom of the back board for mounting vertically in a place of your choice; or just clamp it to a vertical support for temporary placement.

The clue to the efficiency of this gadget lies in the angle of the spools to the board. Sufficient friction between the edge of the spool and the board prevents the spool from running wild—when you stop winding line on your reel, the spool stops turning. Tape holds the mono end.

GOOD FOR THE "SOLE"

For those of you who apply indoor-outdoor carpet or other similar materials to the soles of your waders to increase traction, I suggest using the glue made for repairing scuba divers' wet suits. It's a fast-drying waterproof contact cement that, as far as I'm concerned, has no rivals for holding power in this situation. Use liberally, following the directions on the can. It's also great for applying a patch to waders, or any other rubber or canvas material. The last can I bought, complete with applicator, cost under $2, and was more than enough for a pair of waders.

Underwrap-Overwrap

Anglers building heavy rods and those concocting decorative wraps are using more and more underwraps on their rods. An underwrap is a solid wrap on the blank that will be under the guide and guide wrap when finished. The underwrap shows under the center of the guide and also at both ends of the guide wrap.

When underwraps and overwraps are of the same size thread, the overwrap will often have slight gaps in it as the thread centers between the rows of the underwrap.

To prevent this, use an underwrap of finer thread. You might use a Size A underwrap and Size D overwrap, or, on heavier rods, a Size D underwrap and Size E overwrap.

To prevent "bleed through" of the colors when finish is applied, make sure the underwraps are lighter than the overwraps covering the guide feet.

If your tacklebox is too crowded and hard to sort through, try breaking down the lures according to species or types of fishing and putting them in several smaller boxes. It's easier to find what you want this way, and you don't have to lug around a box full of inappropriate lures.

Easy Swivel Mount

An inexpensive, 360-degree swivel mount for any gimbal-mounted depthfinder is easily made using a small wooden block, a three-eighth-inch bolt, epoxy, and a three-eighth-inch wing nut.

Drill a three-eighth-inch hole through the center of the block which should be slightly larger than the base of the metal bracket that comes with the depthfinder. Countersink one side of the hole so that the head of the bolt is flush with the block. Epoxy the bolt in the hole. Slip the depthfinder bracket on the bolt and tighten the wing nut over the top. Two washers on either side of the bracket will facilitate turning.

Finally, screw the block to any appropriate place in your boat. Mine is located right on the rear seat for easy access. Here it can be swiveled in any direction for anglers in the front or rear

LONGER WADER LIFE

Waders usually end up in the garbage can, not because of rips and punctures, but because of the checking that occurs along fold creases and at points of stress. These checks are myriad and microscopic, it is difficult to tell which ones are leaking, and they invariably occur in a place that refuses to hold a patch.

Waders can be saved, and their life extended several years by an application of rubbery, tough silicone bathtub caulk. This repair medium can be found on the shelves of most hardware and plumbing-supply stores, where it is sold in a toothpaste-type tube.

Clear, rather than colored caulk is preferable, because when it sets its color will be identical to that of your waders, impossible to see except for a slight sheen.

To make the repair, fold, press or stress the checked area, so the checking is open and exposed. Squeeze out enough caulk to cover the area, and smooth the bead flat with a putty or butter knife, working it into the cracks as you move along.

You will have to work fast; this stuff sets up quickly, and then fully cures in a day. But once cured, it makes a tough, invisible seal that will outlast any other patching method, and stretch the life of your waders.

Marking Buoy

A discarded, yet leak-proof, float bulb from a reservoir toilet makes a long-lasting buoy for marking underwater places. Screw in a float rod, cut to desirable length and attach a ring or bend the end of the rod to form a loop. Paint the buoy international orange.

TEST THE ACTION

Building your own rod has advantages besides the money you save, which is an advantage not to be sneezed at. You can pick the exact action you want, and finish the rod to suit your taste in beauty and handling comfort. By selecting one of the quality blanks, which are made by several manufacturers, you can build a glass, graphite, or even split-bamboo rod.

Books have been written about the basics of rod building. Dale Clemen's *Fiberglass Rod Making* and his *Advanced Custom Rod Building* are available from Dale Clemens Custom Tackle, Rt. 2, Box 860-A, Wescosville, PA 18106. Don McClain's *Fiberglass Rod Making* is published by Frank Amato Publications, P.O. Box 02112, Portland, OR 97202.

Many first-time rod builders select blanks with sweet, crisp, fast actions in the tackle shop, but then find them soft, lazy and slow in use. Remember: Any blank without the weight of the tip guide feels lighter and faster than it will after it is built. The addition of the tip slows the rod down to the action it will have when it is completed.

Whenever you select a blank, fix a tip to it of the type you would use—a flyrod tip on a flyrod, a heavier spinning tip on a spinning rod. Use a small piece of Scotch Tape to hold it in place while you wave, wiggle and wobble the blank to test its action.

Rod-Building Tip

When building a rod one of the toughest problems is shaping the cork rings for the grip to the proper diameter with a rattail file. There's a simple solution. Use a tall, heavy wine bottle with an opening just a bit smaller than the cork rings. Simply place each ring on top of the bottle, and file away. The job goes fast, is easy, and will give you a more accurate diameter for a better fit on the rod blank.

Prolonging Creel Life

Cleaning tends to remove the oils from the leather binding and dry out the reeds of a willow creel. You can extend its life by a simple program of care and repair.

Split reeds can be bound together after coating the insides of the splits with epoxy cement. Broken reeds can be bound to those alongside. Use white buttonhole silk as it will turn transparent when varnished and the repair is not obvious. Use a large needle to pass the thread through the spaces between the reeds.

A couple of coats of good varnish will protect the reeds from soap or detergent. The first coat should be thinned out a little to penetrate. Any good spar varnish that is suitable for fishing rods can be used. Apply thinly to keep from clogging the spaces between the reeds—they are there to supply ventilation. Work the varnish into those spaces behind the leather binding but keep the varnish off the leather. By cutting off most of the handle of a paint brush, leaving a stub just a couple of inches long, you will find it easier to work inside the creel.

Leather dressing compounds such as Snow Proof are better than neat's-foot oil as the latter is apt to soil light-colored tackle vests. Warm the leather before applying and it will absorb more of the dressing. Several applications of dressing should be made during the fishing season to replace the oils washed out by cleaning.

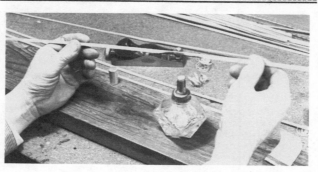

Straighten Bamboo Rods

Vintage bamboo rods may be straightened by carefully heating the "set" over an alcohol lamp. But for rare or extremely valuable rods, consult a professional.

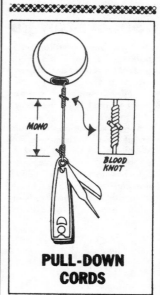

PULL-DOWN CORDS

To keep certain tools handy, such as fingernail clippers or line straighteners, flyfishermen attach them to spring-loaded retractable pin-on reels. However, the pull-down cords begin to fray with use. The life of the pull-down can be prolonged by replacing most of the cord with monofilament leader. The remaining length of cord and the mono can be joined with a blood knot. Use a pair of locking pliers to hold the cord out while cutting it and attaching the mono.

TACKLE RETRIEVER

Keep a chain stringer nearby while fishing, even if you don't intend to bring any fish home. It comes in handy as a grappling hook if a fishing rod or other valuable tackle falls overboard.

Tie it to another rod's line, unsnap all the clips and drag it across the bottom area where the lost equipment went overboard. Don't give up. Sometimes it takes a few tries before one of the open clips snags a line guide or reel brace, but eventually you'll connect.

Once you feel extra weight on the line, retrieve the chain stringer slow and steady until you've retrieved the missing tackle.

TWO-IN-ONE TOOL

The little hole in the end of an inflation valve for basketballs and footballs makes a dandy nail knot tool. And soldering a needle into a valve-core removal tool makes a good hook-eye opener for cemented-over flies and aids in sorting out wind knots. The inflation valve can be screwed onto the valve-core removal tool, covering the needle. Solder a small ring onto the top of the tool for a handy vest attachment.

MONO LINE CARE

Laboratory experiments have shown that monofilament fishing line is not affected if it comes in contact with gasoline, oil, insect repellent, suntan lotion and similar substances that anglers are likely to have onboard.

However, two things can cause mono lines to begin deteriorating: prolonged exposure to heat and direct ultraviolet rays from the sun.

So, never leave rods and reels lying in the bottom of a boat when it is parked in your driveway or moored at a dock. Don't leave them standing on the back porch, sitting on the rear window ledge of your auto or stored in the trunk of a car—the inside of a car trunk can reach 120°F in summer.

The best place to store rods and reels and unused spools of mono line is a cool, dark, dry corner of your basement, in a closet or in a rod-locker in your boat.

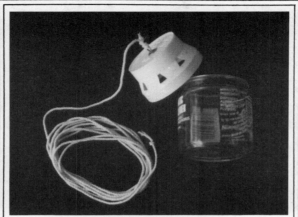

Chumming Jar

Don't throw away those empty automatic bowl-cleaner jars—some of them make great containers for chum. The evenly spaced perforations in the plastic covers let chum seep out to attract fish.

The tops are snap-ons and are easily removed with a screwdriver. Punch or drill a hole in the cover. Insert a cotter pin through it, put on a washer and add another cotter pin. Bend the ends back against the inside of the cover. Tie a line through the loop in the top of the cotter pin so you can raise and lower the container to release the chum.

Rod-Making Tip

Here's a tip from an expert for neophyte rod builders: Epoxy finishes must be mixed exactly as directed, with *precisely* the proper amounts of each liquid. They must be very thoroughly mixed.

If this is not done, the finish might remain tacky.

However, don't despair if a slight tackiness or stickiness persists. Mix another batch of epoxy and do it right this time. Apply a light coat over the slightly tacky stuff. Let it dry the prescribed time, and you'll have a beautiful extra-hard and smooth finish.

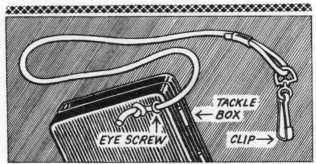

TACKLE
← BOX

EYE SCREW ↑

CLIP →

Pocket Tacklebox Security

Attach a cord to your pocket tacklebox, and you won't have to worry about dropping it in the water or forgetting it on a rock. Simply drill a slightly undersized hole near the back of the box, then insert a small eye-screw. A knot will stop the cord from slipping through the eye. A clip on the other end allows you to secure the rope to a belt loop or buttonhole or even to your belt.

DEPTHFINDER

Having difficulty in maintaining proper trolling depth, but you can't afford a downrigger or electronic equipment? "Kokanee Bill's Field Expedient Trolling Rig" will cure the problem for less than $10.

First cut a series of one- or two-inch lengths of string or thread. At 10- to 25-foot intervals along the trolling line tie on a length of the string using a barrel or nail knot. Next, coat each marker with a liberal application of fingernail polish to secure the knots. A second coating of wax (the kind used for sealing letters) can be applied, but is not essential.

Now, go trolling! Count the number of knots in the water as the line is played out. When a fish strikes, multiply the knots by the distance of their separation on the trolling line and, *presto!* the depth of feeding has been determined.

"Kokanee Bill's Field Expedient Trolling Rig" should not be used on any rig one plans to cast with.

SPOON SCALER

If you ever find yourself without a fish scaler, try using an ordinary tablespoon. Simply grip the bowl near where the handle begins. Now, with the edge of the spoon resting on the fish and the hollow facing toward its head, make a smooth, deliberate stroke. The scales have a tendency to gather in the hollow, making them easy to dispose of. It isn't necessary to lift and strike repeatedly so that scales fly every which way. A smooth, even stroke is all it takes. Also, in any scaling job, you'll find that it helps to keep the fish wet.

ROD RETAINER

Line the entire inside of your boat gunnel with a non-slip material such as a self-adhering weather stripping. It not only keeps rods in place, it also protects their finish and will keep the noise down.

QUICK EMERGENCY REPAIR

Most sportsmen's repair kits include items that you seldom use and that offer only temporary, unsatisfactory solutions to recurring outdoor problems.

There is a quick-fix product on the market that is not only strong, flexible and waterproof, it is inexpensive and easy to use. It will help repair anything from torn waders to leaky canoes, and fits easily into a coat pocket or tacklebox. Its use is not limited to outdoor problems, either.

The magic cure is none other than ordinary duct tape, the kind sold for less than a dollar per 60-foot roll in most plumbing and hardware stores. Just apply to a clean, dry surface and smoothe out any bubbles that may form.

Duct tape will last long enough to let you finish a trip or until permanent repairs can be made. It takes only a matter of a second to apply it.

REPLACING HOOKS

Pluggers often find it necessary to replace the treble hooks on their lures because fish bend them out of shape, they rust or on old plugs, the steel may have become brittle.

When you change a hook, change the split ring as well, because it is also subject to stress and rust. I have found that a good-grade, stainless-steel split ring will help maintain the strength of the assembly. They are inexpensive when purchased by the hundred, and they do not spread or rust as do most of those that come with the plugs.

Stainless-steel hooks are not a good idea. They are more easily bent out of shape by a fighting fish. Also, if a fish gets away with your plug, stainless steel will not rust out as a plain steel hook will.

If you do not own a split ring pliers, buy one. They are inexpensive and they make hook changing a breeze.

Rubproof Rod Case

Aluminum rod cases, unless anodized, will get your hands black. Since handling white fly-lines and cork grips, or reaching into a pocket with dirty hands is not my idea of how to start fishing, I looked for a way to make aluminum rod cases rubproof.

Plastic spray worked only briefly. So I wound my rod cases with colored plastic tape, the kind that can be purchased in any variety store, and my problem was solved. My hands no longer get black; the cases can ride together without rubbing themselves black. Some of the cases pictured have been wrapped for at least ten years, so the tape could be considered permanent.

Added advantages of tape are that the separate cases are easier to identify since the wrappings are different colors; and the tape could be removed at will.

Keeping Fish Fresh

When I go astream prepared to keep some fish for the table, I can completely avoid messy vest pockets and slippery fly boxes, without having to carry a bulky basket or pendulous creel. I keep a paper bag folded flat in the back of my vest. When I kill a fish I clean it immediately, nest it in ferns, and wrap it in the bag. The ferns and bag absorb moisture and keep my vest clean. They also breathe and keep the fish cool and fresh. Plastic bags do not breathe. They leave the fish mushy, like a hatchery fish, after only an hour or two.

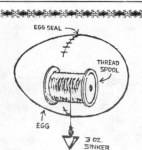

MARKER BUOY

The egg-shaped container for L'EGGS brand panty hose can be transformed into a very functional marker buoy for anglers.

Simply tie a two- or three-ounce lead sinker to the end of a spool of nylon or other strong thread, and place the spool (sinker left on the outside) in the egg. The container will carry the thread to the bottom. Its seal is tight enough to hold the egg together in most situations and prevent additional thread from unwinding. The eggs are large enough to be visible in the water and small enough to let you carry several in a paper bag.

The panty hose buoy is not useful in strong currents.

POPPER BOBBER

Everyone has heard stories of huge bass or pike smashing a panfisherman's bobber. These tales need not end with the big one that got away, if the angler is using a popper bobber. This is nothing more than a large bass popper tied directly to the line with a three- to four-foot leader knotted onto the popper's eye. Add a small hook and bait, and you are ready for any eventuality.

The combination is ideal for panfish since the popper's size offers little resistance to light-hitting fish. When the popper starts bobbing and jiggling from panfish hits, the activity will attract bass, pike or maybe a muskie. The popper will make a loud *glump* when the hook is set on a panfish, which can result in a second savage strike—the big one that didn't get away.

VISE DE-BARBS HOOKS

The use of barbless hooks for flyfishing is becoming more and more popular. Recently I was shown a quick and easy way to bend a barb that eliminates the need to buy various styles of barbless hooks. It also prevents the frustration of breaking a hook—after tying a beautiful fly—when you try to de-barb it with a pair of pliers at streamside.

Before tying a fly, slip the hook point sideways into the jaws of your vise. Then close them gently; it takes no more pressure than that needed to hold the hook firmly. The barb will be flattened neatly. Remove the hook, tie a fly on it, and drop it into your fly box.

A quality vise with fine jaws can bend barbs on hooks Size 20 and smaller. This method adds one simple step to the process of tying a fly. If you like barbless hooks, it is the fastest and cheapest way to get them.

Multipurpose Nail Polish

It's always disheartening to purchase a $1.50 spoon and to find after the fifth or sixth cast that the paint is chipped and broken. Clear fingernail polish, applied to either new or used painted spoons, spinners or plugs, will protect the paint and increase durability considerably. Sometimes it seems to make the lure almost indestructible.

Brass and copper lures can be protected from tarnishing with a single coat.

Chips in rod finish or frayed windings can be quickly remedied.

I carry a bottle in my fishing vest. In a pinch it will even substitute for Loc-Tite.

Ever have trouble with a gun screw backing out under heavy recoil? Take the screw out, paint the threads with nail polish, then screw it back in. It will hold tight for a considerable savings in price over the real thing, and it's invisible.

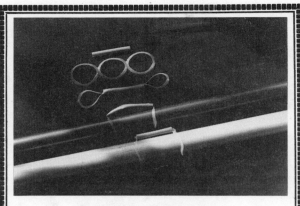

Rod-Case Handle

You can have all the handles you want for free from the throw-away plastic holder that keeps a six-pack of soda or beer together. Cut it in half, as shown, and you immediately have two handles. The elasticity of the loops allows the handle to stretch and fit most rod carriers except the very large.

If you have an old plastic-tube chair, you can doll up the handle by threading the plastic loops through a piece of the tube before you begin to mount it on the rod case.—

•

The guides on a rod help keep the line off the blank and lead it in a smooth arc when you are fighting a fish. To tell if a rod has enough guides and they are properly positioned, run a line through them and have a friend pull on the line while you hold the rod.

•

RESTORING OLD BAMBOO RODS

Handmade bamboo flyrods dominated the market for more than 100 years prior to the early 1940s. Then other materials better adapted to machine production came into general use and the bamboo rod gradually passed from the fishing scene. Although bamboo rods are still being made, their prices, unfortunately, are beyond the average angler's budget.

Many vintage bamboo rods are tucked away gathering dust. Most would require work to restore them, but it's well worth the effort, if not for fishing for their antique value.

All early bamboo rods were handmade. Rods bearing the names of famous rodmakers could warrant restoration depending, of course, on their condition: Gillum, Winston, Thomas, Leonard, Phillipson, Payne, Edwards, Dickerson, Garrison, Granger, Orvis and Powell. These rodmakers frequently engraved their names on the reel seats or autographed the rod shaft.

Rod shafts were made in four, six and eight strips of bamboo, tapered, beveled and glued into tubular shapes. Restoration of such a rod can be enjoyable and relatively easy.

Helpful information on the history of early rodmaking as well as restoration techniques can be found in the following books available at most public libraries: *The Care and Repair of Fishing Tackle*, by Mel Marshall; *Classic Rods and Rodmakers*, Martin J. Keane; and *The American Sporting Collector's Handbook*, Allen J. Liu.

BAIL SPRING SAVVY

Going fishing without an extra bail spring for your spinning reel is like driving across a desert without a spare tire—under Murphy's Law, springs usually break when the fishing gets hot. I always carry extras in a 35mm film canister, and a little homemade screwdriver, which I keep in the pocket of my fishing vest.

The replacement spring is of no use if you don't know how to change it, however, so practice beforehand.

If you break a spring while wading, don't try to fix it standing in the water—you might drop the spare and lose it.

When buying a new spinning reel, get spare springs at the same time. If the retailer doesn't have them in stock, order them from the manufacturer right away. Stow them away in your fishing vest or tacklebox along with a tool to remove screws from the reel (sometimes a dime will do the trick). Thus equipped, it will take more than a broken bail spring to foul up your day's fishing.

STRIPPING SIMPLIFIED

One of the biggest problems with rebuilding a fishing rod is removing the worn-out guides, lacquer and thread without damaging the blank. Sandpaper and steel wool are most often used, but the results usually include scratches.

I've found an easy way to do this job without marking up the rod. First carefully remove the old thread from the guide foot with a razor blade. Unwind the remainder from the blank. Now take one of those plastic-faced sponges used for scrubbing Teflon pots, dip it in lacquer thinner and wring it out. Use the abrasive side to remove the old finish. There won't be a scratch. Do this in an area with adequate ventilation because the fumes from the lacquer thinner can be harmful to your health.

READY ROD REPAIR

Breaking off the tip of a favorite casting rod in the middle of a fishing trip can be downright exasperating; but there is a simple, on-the-spot repair job you can perform that will considerably reduce your blood pressure.

All these essential items will fit neatly into your tacklebox: one roll of plastic tape, one razor blade, one spare rod-tip guide, one book of matches.

Wrap the broken end of the rod shaft with a thin strip of the plastic tape, then cap the taped end with the new rod-tip guide, screwing it down on the shaft to avoid bunching the layers of tape. Line up the guide tip with the other guides on the shaft, apply the match flame to the new tip to melt the tape, quench the tip in water, remove the excess tape with the razor blade, and you're ready to start casting again, your rod good as new, though a few inches shorter.

CORK CLEANER

Use a suede leather brush for cleaning cork fishing-rod handles that have become soiled or discolored. The soft metal bristles will deep-clean into the pits of the cork rather than clogging them with residue; they are much less abrasive than sandpaper.

EMERGENCY GUIDES AND TIP-TOPS

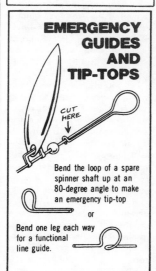

CUT HERE ↓

Bend the loop of a spare spinner shaft up at an 80-degree angle to make an emergency tip-top

or

Bend one leg each way for a functional line guide.

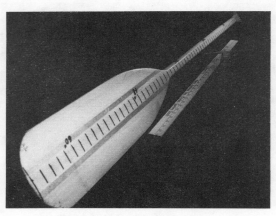

Paddle Measure

Mark your boat oar or paddle to indicate inches (or centimeters if you are so inclined) and you have a handy scale for measuring your catch.

Be an optimist and inscribe marks over the entire length of the paddle. This can be upward of 60 inches or more, but some day you may need this long scale to measure a trophy-sized muskie.

UNSNARLING RODS

When carrying several fishing rods together, even though you remove the lures, the lines invariably snarl over the guides. Try this cure. Pull off enough line to match the length of the rod. Hold the tip of the line in one hand und the rod handle in the other. Rotate the rod and spiral the line around it to bind the main line to the rod shaft.

Take care to wrap the line above and below each guide. When finished, tie a loop in the end of the line and slip it over the reel handle. Do this with all your rods and you can carry or transport as many as you desire without having to unsnarl them.

It takes little time to unwrap the spiraled line and rig each rod for fishing. When through fishing, this procedure allows you to store the rods until next needed without the usual tangling.

Keep Line In Line

Somehow a rubber band is never where you need it when monofilament line, whether on a bulk spool or a reel, starts to do its unwinding trick. Some reels have clips where you can stick the end of the line, but most don't, and bulk spools don't. An easy solution is to drill a $\frac{1}{16}$-inch hole on the lip of the reel or bulk spool. Just run the end of the line through the hole a couple of times and you're free of the unwinding blues.

BURN LOOSE ENDS

After wrapping a rod winding, there is almost always a tiny tag of thread left where the wrap is pulled back under itself and trimmed. The best way to do away with it is to burn the tag off with the flame from a candle.

The heat will be high enough at one-quarter to three-quarters of an inch above the point of the flame. Lower the tag toward the heat until it suddenly shrivels and disappears. The wrap itself should never touch the flame.

After all tags are burned off, run your finger over each wrap, knocking away any little knots of charred thread that are left. Then epoxy or varnish the smooth thread wrap.

Tacklebox Anchor

Two rubber bathroom soap holders on the bottom of your tacklebox will help anchor it in your boat. The disks have strong suction cups on both sides that grip like iron when wet, and your tacklebox will not slide no matter how much the boat rocks. Look for the disks in hardware and department stores. Bathroom soap holders cost about 30 cents each.

HOMEMADE FELTS

Felt soles on hip boots and chest waders greatly increase your stability on slick, rocky streambottoms. Some boots come with felt soles, or you can buy felt sole kits. But there's a cheaper way to do it: Indoor-outdoor carpet glued to the soles of cleat-foot waders works just as well.

Any indoor-outdoor carpet will do; often you can get sample pieces at a carpet store. A typical sample will yield four soles.

First, grind the cleats flat on the soles of your boots. You can usually get this done for free at a tire store or garage, especially if someone who works there is a fisherman. Trace the shape of the boot foot on the carpet sample and cut it out with a pair of heavy shears. Remove the foam backing on the carpet with a wire brush, and glue the piece to the boot foot with Barge (brand name) cement. Tape it on tight with masking or duct tape, and let set for at least a full day. ★

When angling for light biters, use only a hook and bait, no sinker. It takes longer for the bait to sink, but you can feel the fish take it much better.

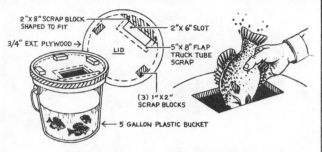

Labels in illustration:
2"×8" SCRAP BLOCK SHAPED TO FIT
3/4" EXT. PLYWOOD →
LID
2"×6" SLOT
5"×8" FLAP TRUCK TUBE SCRAP
(3) 1"×2" SCRAP BLOCKS
5 GALLON PLASTIC BUCKET

MAKE A HANDY FISH BUCKET

Here's a way to make a combination fish bucket and chair. Start with a five-gallon bucket. Cut a lid of three-quarter-inch exterior plywood slightly larger than the top of the bucket. Cut a 2×6-inch hole in the lid near one side and nail a 5×8-inch flap, cut from a heavy inner tube, over the hole. Nail the flap along one side only. Tack on three small blocks to keep the lid from sliding off..

Fill the bucket half full of water and fit the lid into place. You can drop crappies or perch into the bucket to keep them alive, and you can sit on the bucket while you're fishing. The rubber flap moves out of the way as you deposit a fish, and it keeps fish in the bucket from splashing water onto the seat of your pants.

PROTECTING RODS

Equipment that spends a major part of its life bouncing down rivers in a drift boat isn't assured a protected existence, but you can't afford to neglect it, either.

Many professional guides on the western rivers have found that gunwale padding is one of the best insurances against rod abuse. Indoor-outdoor carpet can easily be tacked to wooden gunwales and other contact areas. Aluminum gunwales can be conveniently covered with plastic PVC tubing slit lengthwise. Plastic-covered clothesline wire or nylon rope can then be spiraled around both tubing and gunwale in the same manner in which leather steering wheel covers are secured.

TEST THE FINISH

If you are a neophyte rod maker and aren't sure how your windings will look after the finish has been applied, don't put the stuff on and then wish you'd tried something different. Once on, you can't take it off.

Try a sample first. Use a dowel about the same diameter as the butt of your rod. (A discarded or broken rod can be used instead of a dowel.) Now wind three or four sections of thread on it, each about the same length as it would take to anchor a guide foot. Then apply the trim thread.

On one section, apply varnish only. Put on three or four coats. On the others, apply color preservative, as directed. Then try varnish on one section and, if you like, some of the one-coat, two-part mixes on the others, following directions.

Now you can select the one that pleases you most. You can even enamel the dowel the color of your rod before putting on the sample windings.

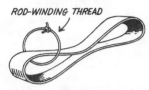

ROD-WINDING THREAD

Here's a simple trick that solves two problems at the same time.

Rubber bands provide a good way to keep line from uncoiling off spare spinning reel spools. Some tackle shops have special bands with a built-in pull tab that makes it easy to remove, but many dealers use the ordinary office type when they refill empty spools. These can be troublesome to take off, particularly when you're in a hurry. Problem Number 2 is remembering which spool is filled with what test line.

Both annoyances can be cancelled out with rod-winding thread. Just make a short loop around the band, as shown, and you have a convenient handle for removing it. The many shades of thread available will permit color-coding the size of each line.

TOOLS FOR SNARLS

A pair of large fabric needles is a real help when working out line snarls. These polished chromed-steel tools allow you to needle your way through tiny, tight little loops so you'll have something to work on. Their smooth finish permits you to tug and pull on the loops without damaging the line.

Fabric needles are six inches long and three-sixteenths inches wide at the widest part of the tip. Most hardware stores sell them for about 50 cents each. They are great for stitching up dressed game, punching holes, etching plastic, and lifting staples. They are well balanced, and with a little practice you can throw them into a dart board. Fabric needles are also handy come time to sew canvas tarp, leather or carpet strips.

PRESSURE GAUGE

Ever wonder how much force is generated when you set the hook? Or how much pressure you put on a fish you are fighting? Would you like to check the strength of the knots you tie? Here's a simple trick that lets you do all that.

Start with a high-quality barrel-type scale such as those made by Chatillion. Wrap a strip of light cardboard—a piece of an old file folder is ideal—around the barrel of the scale a few times. Hold the cardboard firmly while you overwrap it with a piece of tape. The cardboard ring should be snug enough to hold its position, yet loose enough so that the scale's pointer can slide it down the barrel.

You now have an accurate scale that *will hold its peak reading*. To test your hook-setting power, fasten the scale firmly to something solid. I hang it from a big screw hook driven into a tree in my front yard. Tie your line to the scale's hook. Slide the cardboard collar up the scale until its top edge is at zero. Now back off to your usual striking distance with your rod. Reel your line up snug and "set your hook" as you normally would in a fishing situation.

Now look at your gauge. The cardboard ring will have moved down the barrel of the scale, and its top edge will indicate exactly how much force in pounds your strike generated.

Use this same technique with a slow steady pull to measure a hypothetical fish's fighting force. You will probably be amazed just how little pressure is exerted through a rod.

Scientists are measuring water pollution by monitoring the coughing of fish. It seems the more polluted the water, the more fish cough.

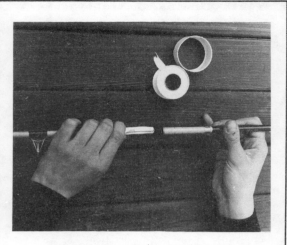

WORN FERRULE REMEDY

When the ferrules of your favorite two-piece fishing rod become worn and the two sections are always parting company, don't cast the rod aside. Here is an easy and inexpensive solution that will add years of service to the rod: Take a three- or four-inch length of Teflon tape (get it from a hardware store), and place it over the end of the male ferrule. While pulling it taut, mate the two rod sections. Then, using a razor blade, cut off the excess tape where the ferrules interface.

MAKING MINI MARKERS

Styrofoam and plastic have all but replaced wood as the material from which thread spools are made. One major thread manufacturer has discontinued small spools entirely and offers only 100-yard spools or larger.

I like these large plastic-foam spools not only because they are light and hold more thread, but also because they are big enough and bright enough to make small buoy markers.

Usually, these markers are shaped like a barbell, or they can be H-shaped. Line is wrapped around the middle, and a weight is attached to the end of the line. At times 15 or 20 mini buoys are needed to map out submerged creek channels and other structure. That's when spool markers come in handy.

Making mini markers from spools is easy. Merely wrap heavy thread or old fishing line around the spool, then attach a piece of lead to the end of the line. Pinch-on pencil lead is ideal.

Obviously a spool has limited line capacity, and heavy monofilament tends to coil off the spool. Use light line.

When dropping a spool marker, I watch the line until it goes slack. Then I pick up the spool and secure the line with a rubber band.

Larger, more stable markers can be made by gluing three or more spools end to end, and then wrapping the line around the middle spool. Also, wooden paddles of some sort can be attached to the spools to make the rig hold better.

Getting a supply of spools shouldn't be a problem. Most anglers know someone who wraps rods or ties Living Rubber skirts onto jigs and other lures. They should have plenty.

Floating Fish Baskets

A collapsible, wire-mesh fish basket is fine as is, but you can enhance its usefulness by placing a 4.00x8-inch inner tube around the upper portion of the basket. This converts it to a floating fish holder.

Using the floating basket with a boat keeps it in a handy position for quick insertion of fish. The tube also acts as a fender to keep the basket from scratching the hull. If you tie a longer line to the tube, the basket may be towed by the boat while trolling.

The floating basket can also be used from a pier in saltwater tidal areas without fear of having the basket hanging high and dry above the water at low tide. Adjust the holding line to allow the basket to float at any tide level.

DEFINE FISH

Fish: A creature that goes on vacation at about the same time that most fishermen do.

LEADER STORAGE

Steelhead and salmon fishermen can go through a lot of leaders in a day's drifting, so premade leaders are helpful. However, carrying and storing them can be a nightmare.

After making your leaders, coil them in two- to three-inch-diameter coils and tape in two places. The tape can be folded to form a tab. Buy some of those transparent plastic envelopes used in wallets and place your coiled leaders inside. When needed, the tab can be pulled so the leader cuts its way through the tape, giving you a perfect leader.

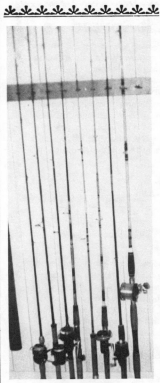

CUP HOOK ROD HOLDERS

Cup hooks with tension springs built into them will hold rods vertically to prevent damage. Just screw the hooks into any piece of scrap lumber and install on a wall, as shown. You can make a narrow shelf to hold rod butts off the floor if you wish. These cup hooks can be purchased in various sizes from most hardware stores and are inexpensive.

SOCK YOUR REEL

Many fishermen, especially in the West, like to leave a favorite fishing rod in the gunrack across the back window of a pickup truck. Besides the rod's being fairly obvious to thieves, a lot of dust and grime is deposited in the gears and working parts if you drive with the windows down. Some sort of cover is the answer.

An inexpensive and always handy reel cover is an old sock. Most people accumulate enough odd socks in a fairly short time to provide a lifetime supply of reel covers.

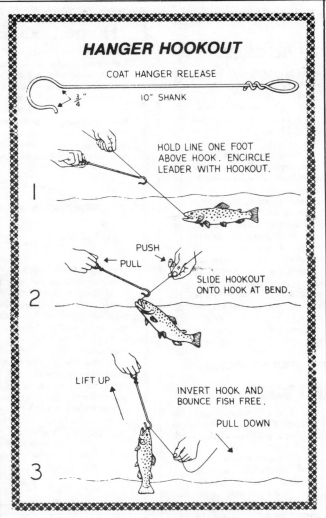

HANGER HOOKOUT

COAT HANGER RELEASE
10" SHANK
¾"

1 HOLD LINE ONE FOOT ABOVE HOOK. ENCIRCLE LEADER WITH HOOKOUT.

2 PUSH — PULL SLIDE HOOKOUT ONTO HOOK AT BEND.

3 LIFT UP INVERT HOOK AND BOUNCE FISH FREE. PULL DOWN

Fisheries biologists in Washington state have found that up to 50 percent of the salmon caught and released die within a few days. Surprisingly, it's not injury from the hook wound that is the villain in most of these cases, but infection that sets in when protective scales and mucous are scraped off by anglers holding the fish to unhook it or scooping the fish up in a rough mesh net. Fish that are released untouched by hands, nets, boats, etc., stand an excellent chance of survival. Most hook wounds heal quickly, with no damage.

The best way to release a fish is with a hook release. You can make one in a few minutes from a standard coat hanger using a pair of pliers and wire cutters.

Cut off a 15-inch section of straight wire. Use the pliers to twist one end into a circular handle by twisting the tag end around the shank. On the opposite end, twist the wire into a hook with a ¾-inch gap between point and shank.

To release a fish, grasp the leader about one foot above the hook and catch the leader in the release hook. Slide the release down to the hook by pulling the leader down and away. When the release is around the bend of the hook, pull the leader straight down and the release up, inverting the hook point. If the fish doesn't slip off at this point snap the hook release up and down to bounce it off. Make sure the fish is over water when released.

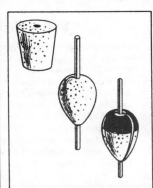

LOW-COST BOBBERS

A cagey West Coast steelhead angler of my acquaintance manufactures bobbers from large corks at a fraction of the cost of store-bought ones. He first drills a three-sixteenth-inch hole through the center, then forces a length of hardwood dowel through the hole. The dowel is then secured in the chuck of a drill press. The spinning cork is quickly shaped with a coarse file, then smoothed with sandpaper.

Prior to sealing the cork with clear plastic varnish a saw cut is made through one side into the hole. Once the varnish has dried the bobber may be painted with a visible color along the top shoulder. The bottom portion should be left its natural color.

The final step is cutting the dowel to the desired length. It should project about one-half-inch through the bottom and one inch through the top.

LURE CONTAINERS

Spare lures can be carried safely in plastic prescription vials and 35mm film containers with snap-on lids. These are reasonably waterproof, and if one slips from your pocket you can retrieve it as it floats.

A film canister will float with about 1¼ ounces of weight inside. A prescription container two inches tall and one inch in diameter will float with a half ounce of weight inside.

Dry Waders Quickly

One problem encountered in the proper care of waders or hip-boots, after they have been rinsed out, is drying them. Try this method.

Go to your local carpet store and ask for one of the cardboard tubes from the inside of a carpet roll. Rolls of carpet usually come in standard lengths of 12 and 16 feet. Try to get a 12-foot roll, because you will need only a total of nine feet to dry your waders. Use a handsaw to cut two 4½-foot sections of cardboard tube without bending it. If the seams of the rolled cardboard are loose, tape them with masking tape to prevent further unraveling.

After you rinse and drain your waders, place one 4½-foot length of cardboard tube in each leg. Keeping them upside down, lean the feet up against a wall in a dry, well-ventilated room. Make sure the open ends of the tubes do not lie flat against the floor or the inside sole of the boot. This allows free circulation of air through the tubes. When the outsides of the boots are dry, reverse the tubes, so that the dry end is now placed inside the boot. Pull the waist section of the waders inside out, over the boots. Loop the suspenders over the feet to prevent the waist section of the waders from falling back over the boots. When the waders are completely dry, roll them up and bag them for proper storage.

SURF DRIVER

I was surfcasting near Ormond Beach, Florida, and making some nice catches. A short distance down the beach a man was trying to fish with a freshwater casting rod and reel with no success. No matter how hard he tried he couldn't land his bait over the sandbar. After about ten tries he picked up and left.

Soon he was back, but in place of a sinker he had attached a golf ball. He reeled off a lot of line and carefully placed it in a shoe box. Next he set a golf tee in the sand, placed the ball on the tee, took a driver and whacked the ball and bait nicely over the bar. Picking up his rod and reel, he took the slack out of his line and in two minutes had a kingfish. This went on until he had five fish. Then he gathered up his gear, held up his string for me to see and left.

Snap-On Bobbers

The photography shop where I buy my supplies often sells the containers for 35mm film cartridges for one cent each. When used as fishing bobbers, these containers have some definite advantages other than their cost.

First, they can be quickly snapped on the line. Just take off the lid, put the line across the top of the container, and snap the lid on again.

Second, you can cast farther with the film container than with regular bobbers. Remove the cap, put some water in the container, and put the cap back on. The extra weight of the water makes casting easy, and you don't need a sinker.

For the personalized touch, and to make them easy to see, paint the container to suit yourself.

Homemade Bait Spreaders

Flounder fishermen: Don't discard the hard plastic tubes from your old Bic pens. They can be made into effective bait-spreaders for bottom fishing for flatties.

Take your old ball-point pen and, with your fingers or a needlenosed pliers, remove the point and the attached ink cartridge, and discard. The hollow plastic shaft must then be inspected for slope and wear at each end. Cut off the sloping point-end of the tube with a coping saw at a 90-degree angle to the axis of the tube. Cut off the butt end also at a 90-degree angle to the axis of the tube.

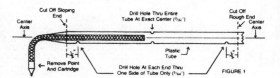

Measure the plastic tube and mark the exact center with a large needle or awl. Enlarge the mark to use as a guide for drilling, to ensure that the drill bit won't slip off the center mark. Drill a hole through the entire center of the tube with a 3/32-inch drill bit. Now make a mark ½ inch from each end of the tube, through one side of the tube only, with a 5/64-inch drill bit. (See Illustration 1.)

Cut a piece of wire coat hanger about six inches and insert it in the center hole. Make a loop in one end, and join a barrel swivel to it with a pair of pliers. The other end of the six-inch wire should be bent in a large loop, to accommodate a bank sinker. Attach two flounder hooks (No. 8 to No. 10 Chestertown, long shank) to the end holes with two 12-inch pieces of monofilament leader material. Use a perfection loop to join the leaders to the end holes of the tube. (See Illustration 2.)

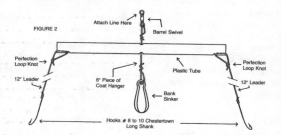

These spreaders have fewer parts than those sold on the market. Their simple construction helps to prevent the rig from getting snagged on the bottom or tangled. In addition, the plastic tubes will not rust.

CLEANING MONO

Monofilament line gets surprisingly dirty, especially in salt water. To clean it, pull the line off your reel and lay it out in a large circle on your lawn or wind it on a spool such as the one the line came on. Wet a small, clean cloth and hold it around the line just in front of the reel. Wind the line back onto the reel, pulling it through the damp cloth. The amount of residue will surprise you. Use oil of anise for a pleasant "worm oil" scent.

GUIDE SELECTION

Any guide can be crushed or broken. The most fragile guides are made of the hardest materials—the rings on carboloy and ceramic guides break easily when banged sharply on hard objects such as boat gunwales or rocks. Stainless steel or plated wire guides will stand more abuse, but being of softer material, they wear out a little sooner.

The actual inside ring diameter of a guide in a given size is often overlooked. The diameter is much smaller on all ceramic guides compared to similar-sized guides of other types. Inside ring diameters are very important in fly-rod stripping guides and guides used on rods where much casting is involved. If you fish during freezing weather, you need the largest ring diameter you can get in a given size guide.

A recent, short session with a variety of guides and a powde. scale revealed several interesting points. Carboloy guides are much heavier than other types. Ceramic guides, however, are not the lightest available. Aetna-type guides are the lightest, but I seldom use them on my custom rods as they wear and groove much too easily. Stainless wire or plated guides are slightly lighter than ceramic guides in the same size.

I match the guide weight to the stiffness and action of the rod blank. Carboloy works very well in softening the stiff action of some graphite blanks. Wire-framed, hard-plated guides will preserve the delicate action of light rods. Industrial chrome-plated snake guides and tip are a must on fly rods. I also use them for the uppermost guides on light spinning rods.

The price of different styles and makes of guides varies considerably, and the price is usually a good indicator of quality. Don't scrimp.

DOUBLE DRAG SYSTEM

Many a taxidermist's delight is lost when a fisherman tries to adjust the star drag on his casting reel while playing a fish. The mechanism which puts pressure on the drag washers and prevents the drive gear from rotating backwards is a simple pin. If this antireverse pin is removed, the drive gear will revolve in either direction and nullify the star drag whenever the fisherman chooses.

To take this pin out, remove the outer cover of the reel on the handle side. Look at the base of the drive shaft on the side plate—the pin rides loosely on a short shaft next to the drive shaft. Pull it straight out.

With this minor modification, an angler can tighten the drag as much as he needs to set a hook. If the reel handle is grasped firmly when the fish strikes, the reel's drag is 100 percent operational. But, if a freshly hooked fish wants to run, the angler can let go of the handle and thumb the spool to feed the fish as much line as he has to.

Handy Storage for Your Outboard Motor

A simple way to store outboard engines involves only a few scraps of lumber, a few nails and 15 minutes of your time.

Using 2×4s for the uprights and wall supports and a 2×6 or 2×8 for the engine bracket, you can make a stand that will keep the outboard clean, safe and out of the way in your garage or storage shed. Make it to accommodate the engine dimensions; allow ample room for the skeg to clear the floor and enough room between the engine support and the wall to fasten and tighten the transom clamps.

Keep the gas can nearby and the safety chain attached to the motor so that you have everything you need for the next fishing trip. The stand comes in handy for minor engine repair or, with a pan under the skeg, to drain and change the grease in the lower unit.

COFFEE CAN DOWNRIGGER

"Necessity is once more the mother of invention," my partner quoted as he lowered the makeshift downrigger weight into the depths. A short while later he was rewarded with a husky walleye—the first of several.

We had trailered his boat to a remote Ontario lake, then discovered the downrigger weights had been stolen. After my friend calmed down and mulled the problem over, he walked over to one of the grub boxes, withdrew a three-pound coffee can and emptied the contents into a plastic bag.

A nail was used to punch two holes, one through the bottom of the can and the other through the plastic lid. A wire coathanger was straightened out, inserted through the bottom hole, and bent back up around the edge of the can. The can was packed with sand and the lid slipped over the wire and seated. The protruding wire was then formed into an eye and the excess trimmed off with a pair of pliers.

Although the jerry-built "cannonball" did not track as well through the water as a smaller and heavier lead weight would have, it let us fish with light tackle instead of heavy sinkers.

ROD GUIDE CEMENT

To hold rod guides in place prior to wrapping, put a small amount of rubber cement *both* on the rod and the bottom of the guide foot. Let it dry. Position the guide as accurately as possible and hold it in place. If necessary the guide can be lifted off without damaging the finish, and reset. Excess cement can be removed by rubbing with a finger. The cement will not interfere with the color permanency of the winding threads or the finish. Rubber cement can be obtained at stationery counters or displays.

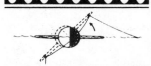

TWO ENDS BEST

Some anglers aren't certain which end of a spherical bobber should be attached to the line. Actually, the best procedure is to attach the line to *both* ends with the raised center point facing the rod tip. This will cause the float to lie on its side in the water with the center point facing the angler. When a fish lightly nibbles the bait, the stem will move upward. That's the time to set the hook!

WADER TIPS

Try using a belt instead of suspenders. The increased freedom of arm and shoulder movement makes shooting easier and reduces fatigue from casting.

Buy waders larger than your normal boot size. The air space around your foot allows your feet to stay much warmer due to better blood circulation and room for more insulation.

Save old worn-out waders and cut off the boot section. The boot section makes great slip-on rubber boots and the upper section makes an excellent pair of rubber pants.

CREEL COOLER

Too keep fish fresh in a creel on a hot summer day, carry and use a sponge. Soak the sponge in water and place it in the creel on top of any fish you catch. Dripping water will keep the fish wet, while constant evaporation will keep them cool and fresh. For best results, select a sponge large enough to cover the entire bottom of your creel.

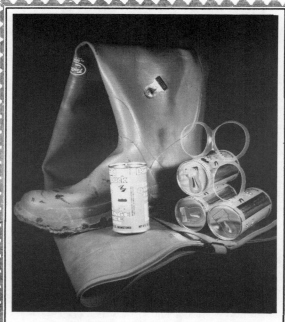

Pull-Tab Boot Repair

Those sticky pull-tabs used on some cans of citrus juice and other drinks can be used in an emergency to patch nicks and punctures in rubber hippers and waders. Of course you will want to have a permanent patch glued or vulcanized on later. But, on the stream, far from regular patching materials, the stick-on pull-tab can do the job.

Stick several of these tabs on the top of your boots now. Then, if barbed wire or a stick causes a puncture, you can transfer one to cover the hole. If the boot surface is clean and dry, the tab will adhere until a permanent repair is made.

Dry Lines and Reels

Get in the habit of removing the spool cover on closed-face spincasting reels after each use so the reel interior and line can dry thoroughly. Not only will this reduce corrosion of interior reel parts, but the line will hold color and strength longer.

EYE-OPENER

Most flyfishermen have been frustrated by a hook eye filled with head cement. You usually find one near the end of the day when you're desperately trying to match the hatch. You can use the point of another hook to clean the eye of a large fly, but that doesn't work well on a small fly. However, many flyfishermen carry fingernail clippers with a stilleto pick which can be outfitted for cleaning small hook eyes. All you need is a small sewing needle and some thread. Just tie the sewing needle on the pick as a short extension. The thread can be reinforced with head cement if you wish. Now you're ready to clean the eye of the smallest hook.

DRY YOUR FLIES

In the past, you may have used Scotchgard to waterproof an article of outdoor clothing, but have you ever tried it on your dry flies? Flies sprayed with Scotchgard remain water repellent much longer than those treated with ordinary flotants, often through several days of hard fishing. Scotchgard requires several minutes to dry, so the ideal time to treat your flies is the night before you intend to use them. After it dries, Scotchgard leaves a white, powdery residue on the fly that can be brushed or blown off.

ERASING LEADERS

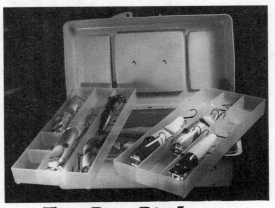

Nothing can ruin the presentation of a perfectly drifting dry fly as quickly as a floating leader. One easy answer to this problem comes in the form of a double-ended eraser. First, drill a hole in the pencil-erasing end and attach a lanyard to secure it to your vest. Next, with a razor blade, slice a thin notch in the end designed for ink removal. Then simply draw the leader through the notch. This removes both the accumulated scum and the shine. Since it abrades only the finish, there is no noticeable loss in strength. Once you have erased your leader from the trout's vision, it will have only your fly on which to concentrate.

Key Ring

STRINGER REMINDER

Ever drown a stringer of fish by forgetting to bring them aboard before you crank up your outboard?

Try putting a key ring around your pull-cord and fastening your stringer to the ring. You'll have to look at the stringer every time you start your outboard.

★

Does the rattle in many fishing lures cause a fish to strike the lure? Fish do strike these rattlers, for sure, but many veteran anglers believe the noisemakers are better in dingy water where visibility is poor, while quieter lures are better in very clear water.

Tiny Box, Big Lures

Tackleboxes with lift-out trays, designed primarily for plastic worms, are great boxes for carrying big six- to nine-inch-long muskie lures. The lift-out trays will hold upward of nine to 12 big lures—usually a sufficient number for a day or a season of muskie fishing. There is still room for snaps, lead jigs and trolling weights. A growing number of fishermen are discovering that several smaller boxes are more convenient than one large one. That way they can pack muskie lures separately from those used for bass or walleyes.

•

An ice chest makes a fine dry stowage container aboard any boat. You can put cameras in the chest, a change of clothes, or anything else you must keep dry.

•

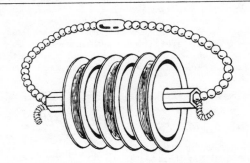

Tippet Spool Holder

Most flyfishermen tie new tippets on their leaders from time to time as they fish. Tippet material usually comes on small plastic spools that are not easy to dig out of a pocket. You can make a convenient holder for the spools from a chain, the plastic body of a large ball-point pen and a pipe cleaner. Tie a piece of string to the chain, and thread the string through the pen body. After inserting the pipe cleaner and crimping its ends, pull the chain through. Now hang the chain from a convenient loop on your fly-fishing vest.

RUBBER FISHING GLOVES

A major problem the winter angler encounters is keeping his hands dry and warm. Wet hands quickly become cold ones, and the angler risks chapping and other discomforts.

One solution to the problem is to wear surgeon's rubber gloves next to the skin, and then pull wool gloves over them. The wool will get wet, but it still retains a lot of warmth.

Surgeon's gloves are available at most drugstores.

Rod Ties

Here's new life for some of those old or out-of-style neckties you have hanging in your closet. Use them as wrappers to protect fishing rods kept in a multirod carrying case. They'll not only cushion individual rods from damage, but also make them much easier to retrieve.

Just sew the small end of a tie shut and it's ready for use. Slip the sections of one rod into the open end, fold down the excess material and secure with a rubber band. Use different colored ties and you'll soon learn to pick out any rod in a case by its wrapper.

CLEANING HANDLES

To remove dirt, grease and slime from cork fishing-rod handles, use an ordinary powdered household cleanser. Dampen a cloth, dip it in some of the powder, and scrub the grips on your rods until they come clean. Not only will it remove the foreign matter from the surface, but the bleach contained in the cleanser will return the cork to its original brightness.

TACKLE-SAVING TIP

When bottom fishing, try this trick to reduce lost gear. Attach a rubber band to the sinker and tie your line to this. When the sinker snags in the rocks, give a yank. The rubber band will break before the line, saving you the hook and bait and reducing the time required to rig up again.—

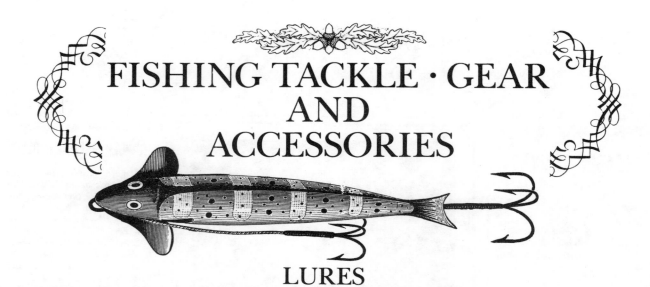

FISHING TACKLE · GEAR AND ACCESSORIES

LURES

A BETTER DOWNRIGGER

Because downriggers are frequently used to troll lures at depths where little sunlight penetrates, a flashy attractor—such as a dodger or cowbell—is often tied into the line to help draw fish to the lure. Some fishermen also fasten an attractor directly to the downrigger weight. It's a trick I have found effective for landlocked salmon, rainbow, brown and lake trout. The attractor can be anything from a silver-dollar-sized Colorado blade to a big ten-inch dodger. A nickel finish is the most popular.

One common way to hook up the flasher is to drill a small hole near the edge of the downrigger stabilizing fin; close a large, quality snap swivel through it, slip a big split ring on the end of the swivel, then attach the attractor.

Some long attractor blades spin in a wide arc, and if the monofilament line is too close it could be cut. So make sure the line is clear of the blade's arc before you begin trolling.

FLASH FOR FISH

Live bait fishermen often use flashing flicker hooks or shiny spinner blades in front of the bait to attract fish. You can achieve the same effect a lot less expensively by attaching small pieces of foil to the hook or by tying thin streamers of foil to the line above your hook.

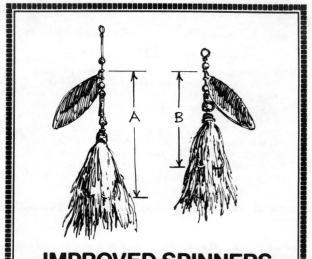

IMPROVED SPINNERS

For reasons not clearly understood, gamefish like lures with revolving blades. They usually hit the blade itself. This means that if the trailing fly or hook is placed too far in the rear, fish miss the business end. So, be meticulously careful of the distance between revolving blade and hook. The shorter the distance, the more fish are hooked solidly. Reduce this gap (A) by using flies with shorter-shank hooks (B) or, in some cases, make entirely new wire shafts that will allow the blade to slide down closer to the fly or open hook.

Painted Sinkers

Bass fishermen are finding that the natural gray of lead isn't always the best color for slip sinkers used ahead of plastic worms. The latest trend is to match the color of the weight to that of the worm, so the sinker will look like the worm's head.

You can buy colored worm sinkers, but to save money, paint your own with automobile spray paints. For best results stand the sinkers on a sheet of newspaper and give them two light coats.

REJUVENATING PLASTIC WORMS

Tom Mann, nationally known lure maker, advised a fisherman who inquired about what to do with faded plastic worms: "Set them where the sunlight can reach each one and the color usually returns."

The fishermen wrote back: "We don't have much sunlight in the winter so I put them near the heat duct and at least three-fourths of them look as good as new. Maybe this will help other anglers."

INCREASED LURE APPEAL

Adding natural scents to lures often triggers strikes from uncooperative fish. Here's one trick walleye fishermen use with the popular Flatfish:

Begin by removing all the hooks, then tie a length of 15-pound-test monofilament to the screw eye that held the belly hooks. To the end of the monofilament tie a No. 4 treble hook. The line should be about two inches long.

Now take a three- to four-inch minnow and carefully fillet one side. When you approach the tail turn the knife blade down and cut through the body. You now have a minnow fillet with the tail attached.

Pin the fillet on one barb of the treble hook; it adds a natural scent and flaps enticingly as the lure wobbles through the water.

SINGLE-HOOK DILEMMA

Regulations limiting anglers to the use of single-hook lures and flies have been hailed as the wave of the future. Unfortunately many spoon and lure casters feel such limitations put them at a disadvantage since the majority of popular lures and plugs come draped with upwards of nine hooks. These computer-designed lures are so finely tuned that removing hooks drastically upsets their movements.

One method I used to meet single hook restrictions in Great Smoky Mountain National Park involved Rebel's new Crawfish plugs. I snipped off the barbed tips of the hooks, then carefully turned the remaining portions inward to the shank. This removed only a small fraction of the hooks' weight. The lure's balance remained intact and performance was not affected by the modification.

Spark Up Your Lures

If you want to add some more sparkle to your plugs or spoons, all you need is some dry-cleaning fluid, masking tape, a spray-can of clear plastic and "glitter" from your local hobby shop.

First, clean the area of the lure to be glittered with the cleaning fluid and mask off. Spray the area with the plastic and immediately, while still wet, sprinkle the sprayed area with glitter and let dry. Caution is recommended to use glitter only as an accent, as too much spray or glitter may hinder the lure's action. The excess glitter can now be rubbed off and the area given a *very fine* coat of plastic spray to give the remaining glitter permanence. Glitter comes in a variety of colors and any excess can be returned to the bottle.

★

If you're going to mark your favorite fishing spots on a chart, use a wax pencil. An ink or felt-tip marker will run and smear if it gets wet.

HOMEMADE FROG HARNESS

There are times when bass want only the real thing—such as a lively frog kicking around in the weeds or brush. Rather than hooking the frog in the mouth or hind leg, many fishermen prefer to use a frog harness. You can make a very effective one from two stout rubber bands, one above the frog's hips, one behind its shoulders. Slip the shank of a double hook between the rubber bands and the belly. The hooks will ride up and be practically snagless. Try a leopard frog, green frog or pickerel frog.

BALLOON TAILS

The undulating action of soft plastic curly-tailed lures and worms has caused the downfall of many fish in the past few years whether in fresh or salt water.

Seeking a method to combine the action-packed tail with hair and feather-dressed jigs and streamer flies, I hit upon a material that is cheap, strong and colorful—party balloons!

Simply use a sharp pair of curved manicure scissors to cut tails to the desired length and width, then tie them on the shank of the hook as you would a standard feather or hair tail. Finish the jig or fly in your favorite pattern.

One word of caution: Do not mix these balloon tails with soft plastic lures. The chemical that keeps the lures flexible will attack the rubber and destroy it.

CHEAP TUBE LURES

Don't throw away worn-out plastic-tube patio chairs. Each one contains a couple hundred potential tube lures.

Cut a piece of tube out of the main seat section and taper one end. Tuck a one-half-ounce sliding sinker into one end, thread heavy monofilament or wire through the sinker, and attach a hook to the bottom end. If you have chosen mono, tie the hook on using an improved clinch knot or a Palomar knot. If you choose wire, you will need sleeves and crimping pliers. Pull the mono back through the sinker until the hook rests against the tube. To the other end of the line tie on a swivel.

DROOP-SNOOT PLUGS

Many manufacturers of fishing plugs recommend bending—carefully—the front eye of their lures to "fine tune" them and make them run true. It can also alter the speed of their action. One Ontario fishing guide, noted for consistent catches of trophy pike, adds a twist to this trick—a twist downward at a sharp angle, that is. He then checks the nose of the plug for cracks or holes and applies a dab of rubber cement where necessary.

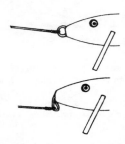

When cast or trolled the plug will run barely beneath the surface. It's deadly to early pike.

Try this technique on one model at a time to make sure it will work. Then, if it works on one, it should do the same on subsequent lures of the same design.

THE EYES HAVE IT

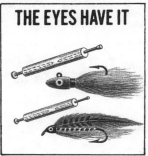

Straight pins and nails are excellent tools for painting eyes on the heads of jigs and flies. The most popular color combination is probably a yellow eye with either a black or red pupil. Simply drive two compatible nails or pins into opposite ends of a three-inch-long wooden dowel. Predrilling holes slightly smaller in diameter than that of the nails will prevent splitting.

A BETTER WORM RIG

Soft plastic worms have been around for more than 30 years. During this time, they have probably caught more bass than any other type of lure—and they have surely missed even more.

Most anglers now use the so-called Texas rig, in which the point of the hook is hidden in the worm. This makes the rig weedless and often fishless.

One of the most successful anglers I know uses a non-weedless rig. He merely threads a worm onto a No. 1, 2 or 4 hook and fishes it without a sinker. He gets lots of strikes and connects almost every time. Moreover, he doesn't have to use a stiff "worm rod" to set the hook. He may hang a few worms up—but he also hangs lots of bass.

★

If you're having trouble getting the distance you need when casting a light lure, let it hang down about a foot from your rod tip. This will increase both your leverage and distance.

THREE-WAY PROTECTION

One-inch lengths of small-diameter plastic tubing, such as clothesline covering, serve three useful purposes when slipped over hook barbs: they keep sharpened points sharp, reduce tangles and protect your pinkies from painful punctures when you root around in overcrowded tackleboxes.

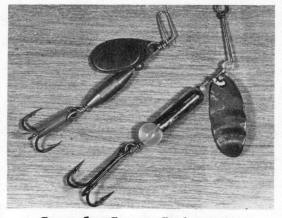

Steady-State Spinners

Spinners are great lures, but unfortunately they have a tendency to rotate as the spinner blade turns. This sometimes twists a line so badly it's unusable at the end of a fishing trip.

If you make your own lures, try using longer than normal wire shafts and make a 45 degree bend in the end of the wire about one to one and a half inches from the line eye. Then fashion the rest of the spinner in the normal manner, threading the blade-holding clevise, the beads and body materials on the shaft and adding a hook to a wrapped eye at the end of the shaft.

The result is that the line will no longer be on the same axis as the spinner blade and the tendency of the entire lure to spin around the axis and twist the line will be markedly reduced, if not eliminated.

JUICING UP JIGS

Most saltwater fishermen have a bucketful of old jig heads from which the feathers or nylon dressing has been stripped by toothy ocean fish. You can easily and quickly repair these expensive lures with just a few matches and a piece of white nylon utility cord (once called "parachute rope", now available in almost any store). Just clip off a piece of rope several inches long, thread the jig hook into it from the rope end and out again at an appropriate point. Work the rope end over the dressing knob found on most jigs, then briefly hold a lit match to the nylon at that point, turning the lure as you do so. The nylon will melt, shrink and adhere tightly to the jig knob. After cooling, fluff out the rope braid with a comb, then trim the fluff to desired size and shape with scissors. Dip the jig head in paint, let dry, and *Voilà*—you've got a brand new lure

Slat Lures

A slat salvaged from a discarded venetian blind is perfect for making featherweight flyrod lures. The metal is lightweight, easy to cut with ordinary scissors and has a curved surface that produces good action. Just draw a lure pattern on the slat with a felt pen, then cut it out. You can use a regular spoon lure as a tracing guide or draw your own design directly on the slat. To finish a lure, file down any sharp edges, and then drill a hole at each end for hook and line attachment. Decorations can be added by using lacquer paint.

LAKE ERIE TROLLING RIG

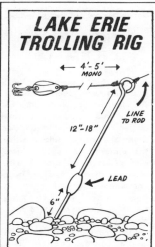

Keeping your lure within inches of the bottom is tough when trolling, specially when you are working deep water that has a rocky or debris-covered bottom.

Lead weight interferes with the full action of most lures and can snag bottom easily or pick up weeds. A sinker on a six-inch dropper and a four-foot leader can wedge itself easily between bottom boulders.

Lake Erie fishermen have a homemade device that facilitates deepwater trolling with no frustrating hangups. They use a quarter-inch-thick metal rod 18 to 24 inches long with a cigar-shaped lead weight soldered onto it six inches from the end. The other end has an eye for attaching the line. A four- or five-foot leader with lure is also tied to the eye.

When fished, the metal rod comes through the water at approximately a 45-degree angle. The bottom end slips and bumps over rocks and other bottom obstructions without hanging up.

Surprisingly, the soldered weight does not feel cumbersome or detract greatly from the fight of hooked fish.

Most Lake Erie anglers carry several of these rods with lead slugs from a half-ounce up to three ounces. (The heavier weights are used for the deepest trolling.)

★

If you need a jig head and find none in your overloaded tacklebox, pinch one or more split-shot onto a single hook just behind the eye.

LURE ALLURE

Looking for the universal fishing lure? Consider the common shad dart. A painted drop of lead molded on a bronze No. 2 O'Shaughnessy hook with a tuft of white or yellow deer hair for a tail, the shad dart will take almost any fish you're after.

I've used it to catch bass and drum in Lake Erie, permit and jack in the Caribbean, weakfish, bluefish and fluke in the Atlantic, and perch and pickerel in Maine. Jigged through the ice, the shad dart will attract big crappies, largemouth bass, and pike. Trolled or retrieved slowly, it'll also catch walleyes,

trout, and an occasional muskie.

Allowed to hang in a river current just off bottom, it'll take fallfish, suckers, rock bass, eels, channel cats, carp, herring and (of course) shad.

You can bait a shad dart, use it with spinners or a wet fly dropper, or fish it by itself. It's simple to make, convenient to carry, and easy to cast. And at only a dollar or two a dozen, it's the cheapest lure on the market, so it won't bother you to lose a couple of darts on the rocks or stumps.

TOO-SHARP HOOKS

Keeping your hooks sharp is essential to success. But they can be too sharp. When sharpening hooks, be sure the point retains enough metal to prevent chipping off while bouncing among the rocks and submerged brush. If the point is needle sharp with very little supporting metal it can easily break off.

To test a hook, pick it up and hold it by the bend with the point resting against a stone, table top or other hard surface. Turn your face away from the hook and apply pressure with just your fingers. If the point breaks you are removing too much metal.

Dress Up Spoon Lures

Long saddle feathers fastened to spoons often make these lures even more appealing to gamefish. Use nylon thread or monofilament to tie on three to five feathers obtained from barnyard roosters. You will find that tying feather tails onto spoons is easily accomplished—as easy as feathering out any other hook, if not more so. Trim off surplus feather material, and apply nail-polish lacquer to cover the finished thread wrapping.

A few feathers added to single or treble hooks seldom interfere with the action of the spoons.

WEEDLESS JIGS

A flexible wire loop that arches over the hook makes jig-type lures more resistant to weeds and underwater debris.

The guard is similar to the nylon line loop devised by fly-tiers for making weedless streamers and wet flies. By substituting flexible wire, the loop guard is sufficiently strong to protect jigs from most weeds and snags, yet it is soft enough to bend aside when fish pick up the bait.

Nylon-coated braided wire of 15- to 30-pound-test is best. It is the kind of wire generally used in leaders for pike. Cut a piece about 2½ inches long (though actual length depends on the size of jig) and fasten under a thread wrapping at the base of a weighted hook. The opposite wire end hangs free until the loop is made by pushing it into the

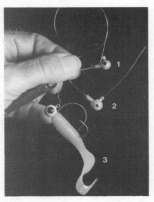

soft plastic grub or worm bait.

The steps in making the loop guard: 1) Thread-wrapping holds braided wire in place; 2) wire is cut to suitable length; 3) loop guard is formed by inserting the end of the wire into the soft bait body.

BELLY DANCER

Have you ever run out of live minnows just as your quarry begins biting at its most frenzied pace? There's a time-tested solution to this dilemma: Kill one of the fish on your stringer, and with a sharp knife cut thin, tapered strips from its belly. Impale the belly strip on your hook at its wide end and fish it either by drifting, or casting and retrieving with slow, gentle twitches.

The fish strip is flashy and flutters seductively in the water, bringing quick, hard strikes from most gamefish. It's also a tough bait that may catch up to a half dozen fish before it needs replacing.

Certain species of fish are better for slicing strips from than others. Tops in the freshwater category is the chain pickerel whose milky-white belly entices all manner of gamefish to strike with a vengeance. Yellow perch are also good, as are crappies. In salt water, the flounder belly is superb at fooling weakfish, fluke, sea bass and croakers.

Cut the strips in lengths appropriate for the gamefish you're after. For salt water, strips two to three inches long are about right. For freshwater bass this is also a good size, but panfish strips should be under two inches.

BAITS FROM BUTTS

The tough, shiny banding that zips cigarette packs open makes for an ideal dressing for flies and lures.

On streamers, it can be used for body material or ribbing. It also adds glitter and attraction to feather and bucktail wings.

You can also use strips of this stuff like bucktail on saltwater spoons, jigs and spinners, and for the bassin' man, it will add appeal to spinnerbaits, and skirts on popping or diving plugs.

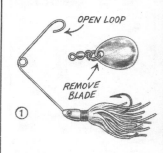

OPEN LOOP

REMOVE BLADE

①

SNAP SWIVEL

②

SNAP-ONS

When the bass are just nipping or swirling at your spinnerbait, a different blade size or color may change their attitude enough to make them engulf the whole thing. Does this mean you have to carry a zillion different spinnerbaits with assorted blade sizes and colors?

Nope. Just use a pair of needlenose pliers to bend open the little loop at the top of the wire arm on the spinnerbait and remove the swivel and blade. Worm the blade out of the split ring and replace the swivel with a snap-swivel. Then put the swivel end of this back on the wire arm and bend the loop closed again. Now clip your blade into the snap end.

Buy yourself a collection of blades in various sizes and colors and keep them in your tacklebox. From now on, when you want to change blades, all you have to do is snap one off and snap another on. It's a lot cheaper and easier to carry an assortment of blades in various sizes than a whole bunch of spinnerbaits.

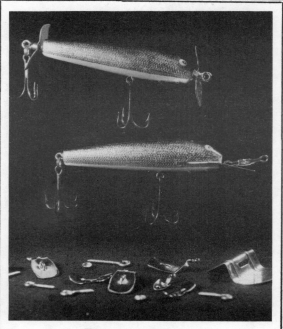

Revamped Lures

Are there plugs in your collection that do not "track" well on the retrieve, or have a poor wiggling action? Are you overstocked with diving models when what you need are more surface lures, or vice versa? Try converting unwanted plugs into some other style.

The photo shows how a diving plug can be revamped into a gurgling, topwater lure. The metal lip, held in place by two screws, was removed, and eye screws, washers and prop-type blades were fitted fore and aft. The lure now is a topflight surface performer.

By changing hardware you can make most plugs play different roles. Even those designed to dive can have their plastic lips cut off and new hardware added to change the zone of action. By substituting diving lip hardware, the reverse is true of surface lures.

The conversion hardware—wiggle disks (lip hardware), eye screws, washers, prop blades, etc.—is available at most sportshops.

Homemade Ice Jigs

To make ice jigs that are truly effective you need a soldering iron, acid core solder and several No. 10 or 12 long-shanked hooks. It takes only a small amount of solder added to the shank of the hook just below the eye. With a little practice you can turn out respectable ice jigs that, when tipped with grub or wax worm, should produce some panfish action. I have had best results when I was using a jig that was painted either red or yellow.

The water hyacinth, *Eichhornia crassipes*, infestation, a severe problem in our southern waters, stems from the International Cotton Exposition held in New Orleans in 1884. The Japanese government gave out plants as souvenirs, which were planted in farm ponds and lakes. Plants escaped into the Mississippi River and its waterways and have proliferated and spread.

SPINNERS AND SPOONS

Spinners and spoons are something no angler can afford to ignore. An assortment should be in every tacklebox. Many are made of plain, smooth-surfaced metal, while others are decorated in various ways. Many are painted with one or more colors on the convex side. Others are fluted and some are hammered. Hammered blades reflect the most light, fluted blades somewhat less light and plain blades the least.

Since we consider the glitter and flash of a spoon its principal attraction, it might be thought that the hammered blades should be the most desirable and that the other two could be dispensed with. Not necessarily so. The strength of the light, the clarity of the water and what the fish are seeking

MANN'S No 21

have a bearing on what will produce best at the time.

On bright days and in very clear water, the spoon that doesn't flash much is usually the best choice. The darker the day and the cloudier the water, the greater the need for a flashy spoon or spinner. Often when fishing in extra-clear water on a very bright day, it is helpful to scour the spoon blade with an abrasive so the finish is dulled and reflects light as would the scales of a natural minnow. More than once I've seen a fish frightened by a flashy spinner strike at one with dull blades.

Size can also make a difference, the general rule is to use smaller spoons for bright conditions and larger spoons for the opposite.

Lure Dispenser

To keep your most-used lures immediately and safely available in the boat, hang them on the *inside* of a smaller, foam-plastic ice chest. This also allows them to dry before being returned to the tackle box. Of course lures that have been used in salt water must be rinsed with fresh before being stored.

NO-TWIST TIE

The method of using two snelled hooks spaced equally apart and tied directly to the line above a small sinker is the backbone of panfishing. Many anglers also use it still-fishing for walleyes, trout, bass, etc. The only drawback is that the snell tends to wrap around the main line, destroying its effectiveness.

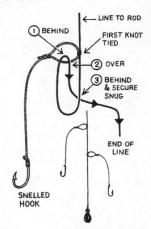

To avoid this condition, first secure the hook snell in place at the desired location with a common knot. Set this knot firmly while pulling the hook snell upward. Before beginning the second knot, pass the line end up through the snell loop. Complete the knot and pull snug. Repeat this same procedure for a third and final knot.

Do not use more than three knots because extra knots will begin to have a reverse effect. With just three, the hook will now stand away from the main line without need of additional conspicuous tackle —presenting the bait in a manner capable of tempting even the fussiest of fish.

★

A tacklebox is unhandy to lug around when traveling light around ponds and streams. Belt kits, available at tackle dealers, are much handier. Also, an old pocketbook with lining removed is quite functional when carried on a shoulder strap. It'll hold lures, tools, spare line and a stringer, plus a lightweight rain jacket.

The Floating Spinner

Many times when walleyes are holding deep they seem to feed only if the bait is presented on a spinner a couple feet off bottom. Jerry Heater, of Suffield, Ohio, has devised a bobber-type spinner that allows him to keep his bait a precise distance from bottom. He assembles all the parts for making a homemade spinner. The only difference is in the wire that the beads and hooks are attached to. He makes it a little longer because in the middle of the wire he threads on a casting bobber.

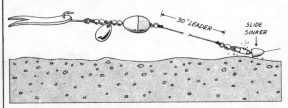

Heater uses two bobber sizes when he constructs this floating spinner. For days when he is drifting very slowly, he uses a spinner that has a bobber about the size of a fingernail. On windy days, or when he is trolling, he uses a spinner equipped with a bobber about the size of an outdoor Christmas tree light. To these spinners he ties on a 30-inch leader. Before attaching his line to the leader, he passes it through a slip sinker. The slip sinker is prevented from sliding onto the leader by a snap and swivel.

The sinker is constantly bumped along the bottom while the naturally buoyant spinner rides above the snags and in full view of the waiting walleye. Because the bottom-bouncing sinker will follow all dropoffs and rises, the buoyant spinner likewise will follow the contours but at a shallower depth.

Fishy Scales

It seems that a doctor was enjoying an afternoon of fishing at a farm pond. The owner of the farm rushed frantically from his nearby house, shouting, "Doctor, doctor, come quick. My wife's about to have a baby."

The doctor replied that he had no equipment with him, and advised the man to take his wife to a hospital, some 20 miles away. After a few minutes of urging, the man finally persuaded the doctor to help.

The doctor delivered the baby, and both mother and child were fine. However, the only scale the doctor had was the one he weighed his fish with.

That baby weighed 31 pounds!

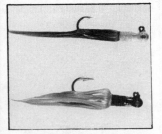

PADDED SHOULDERS

A plastic disk positioned on the hook shank behind the collar of a marabou feather jig creates a "shoulder" that increases the overall silhouette.

Plastic sequins, available at hobby shops, are suitable for ultralight jigs. For larger models simply cut a disk from the soft plastic lid of a disposable food container.

Secure the disk to the shank with a few turns of nylon flytying thread and a drop of head cement.

LINE SIZE DICTATES JIG WEIGHT

Jigs are the most basic fish-getters and will catch every gamefish in either fresh or salt water. Don't use a small jig with heavy line, though. Not only will the lure be difficult to cast, a thick line will destroy the jig's delicate balance and swimming action. Don't use a heavy jig with light line, either. If the cast doesn't snap the jig off, it will likely be lost to a log or rock on bottom. To get the most from your jigs, be sure to match jig weight to line size. Here's a helpful table:

Line Strength	Jig Size
4-lb. test	1/16 to 1/8 oz.
6-lb. test	1/8 to 1/4 oz.
8-lb. test	1/4 to 3/8 oz.
10-lb. test	1/4 to 1/2 oz.
12-lb. test	3/8 to 5/8 oz.
14- to 20-lb.	5/8 to 3/4 oz.

★

MOST FISHERMEN AGREE that it's hard to beat a strip of porkrind as an attractor at the tail of a jig, spoon or spinner. If you have none, substitute the tail of a plastic worm, a flat rubber band, a strip of plastic, or piece of an old rubber glove.

THE VERSATILE JIG

Every angler has a favorite fly or lure, but perhaps the best all-around lure is the simple jig. It can be used for many fresh- and saltwater fish in a variety of presentations, undoubtedly the reason for its popularity. You can swim it, hop it, flutter it, drag it slowly across the bottom, or run it just under the surface.

Jigs can be fished deep or shallow, suspended under a bobber, or flipped into tangles of brush and trees that would foul most other lures.

One particular style of jig should be in every stream angler's kit: the minijig. Made famous by crappie anglers, it is a very effective lure for trout and is easily modified to match stream regulations.

These days anglers often find themselves fishing where regulations require "an artificial lure or fly with a single barbless hook." Plugs, spoons and spinners with treble hooks are hard to modify, but the only requirement on a minijig is to pinch down the barb on its single hook. Then you're ready to go fishing.

The tiny jig closely matches a minnow, one of the trout's favorite foods, and can be cast and retrieved in the same fashion as a tiny spinner or spoon.

Jig Rig

Jigs placed in a tacklebox rattle together, causing even the toughest paint to chip off. Trying to find the style, size and/or color from the resulting tangle of fur and feathers can be a chore.

To solve this problem, I keep my jigs stuck to a small block of plastic foam cut to fit a tacklebox compartment. The foam keeps the jigs separated, organized, and their hooks sharp and clean.

Ordinary plastic foam is okay, but Du Pont's Ethafoam *is better. Used as a packaging material for electronic components, Ethafoam will not crumble.*

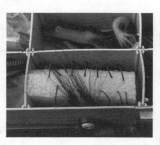

REVERSED SPOONS

To give a wobbling spoon with a treble hook a different action, try this trick. Reverse ends. Remove the tail-end hook and its eye-ring and put it in the front-end hole where you normally tie your line. In this way, the broad end of the spoon becomes the head. Not only do you alter the action, a "reversed" spoon seems to maneuver better through grass and vegetation.

★

When a larger boat passes and throws a big wake, head your bow directly into it. Other approaches can swamp a smaller boat.

ENTICING POLKA DOTS

If you have lures of various colors that just don't produce good catches give them the "polka dot" treatment. That is, add some brightly colored spots.

A flat-headed nail is dandy for stamping on polka dots. A combination of black, yellow, green or red will change the original color scheme and might be just the prescription for better results.

Small vials of lacquer, sold at hobby counters, dry quickly and are ideal paints for decorating lures of all kinds—plugs, spinner blades and spoon lures. If the new color patterns do not net results, stamp on polka dot patterns of a different color.

REOPENING SPLIT SHOT

Here's an easy way to re-open split-shot that has been used. Drill holes in a board to fit the various sizes of shot you use. Make them just deep enough so that the shot will stick up halfway above the surface of the board.

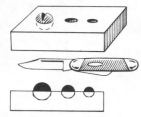

Use a little pressure with a sharp knife and the shot will be open again, ready for use. This prevents cut fingers if a knife slips when you're holding a shot in your hand.

CASTING AID

Using poppers with a fly-rod is great, but casting can be awkward. To remedy this and get better distance, try this:

Drill a small hole in the popper and insert a small BB or buckshot. By drilling a hole just undersized, the pellet will fit snugly with no gluing necessary.

The pellet will not affect the lure's action on the water, but it will extend your casting range by at least 30 feet.

SEEING RED

Here's an old Maine guide trick for catching lunkers. After baiting your hook with a live minnow, tie a few strands of red wool to the eye of the hook. Or you can pretie a few hooks at home. The wool imitates a wounded minnow.

Guides get their wool by

harvesting strands of thread from the shirttails of their shirts.

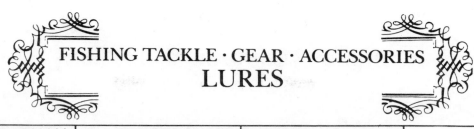

JIG ADJUSTMENT

1. Double line to form 4-5 inch loop—run through eye.

2. Loosely tie single "granny" knot.

3. Twist loop 3-4 times. Bring loop over bend of hook and position just to rear of head.

4. Pull lines toward hook to tighten loop and cinch knot. Trim off end of line.

5. Jig hangs straight because loop prevents knot from sliding forward on eye.

SUNGLASS FLASHER

Check your junk drawer for discarded or out-of-style plastic sunglasses. The lenses can be removed and used as flashing spoons for trolling. Just melt a small hole near the edge of the tapered end of a lens with a heated brad. The lenses can be used to replace lost flashers on trolling sets or you can build new rigs.

★

When you know there are trout but they won't hit *anything*, take a 30-inch piece of 15-pound monofilament, add six spinner blades using clevices to attach them, space them equidistant by using squeeze-on split-shot for separators, add a one-ounce sinker at the head of the leader and your pet fly at the terminal end. Troll in deepest holes and watch the magic happen!

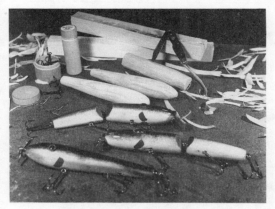

Carve Your Own Lures

Whittling your own plugs is an intriguing hobby. It fills idle time on long wintry evenings and rainy days while camping.

Begin with soft wood, preferably pine, cedar or bass wood. Carve a billet to any size—up to three or four inches long for bass lures, up to six or eight inches for muskellunge.

Cut pieces of aluminum and shape them for front "wiggle disks."

Dip the carved billet in a base paint to seal the pores. Then use a brush or spray-paint to finish the lure in black, white or yellow in combination with green or gold. U upholstery tacks for eyes. Add eye-screws and treble hou and you're ready to go fishing.

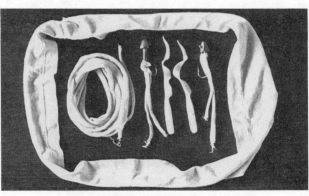

T-Shirt Worms

The most popular bait, with both fish and fishermen, along the rocks and jetties of the Pacific Coast is the jig and seven-inch white plastic worm. Rock bass, ling cod and an array of other hungry predators all like the white worm.

Because the rocks are tackle-grabbers, anglers often run out of worms—it takes one or two dozen to fish a day.

Here is a cheap, quick and simple substitute for plastic worms: strips torn from an old T-shirt. Nick the fabric with scissors in two places, three-fourths of an inch apart, then tear off. The strip will curl up, which is fine. Tear it into lengths about twice as long as a worm. Hook it onto the jig, tie it to the hook shank, or tie it to the line above the jig.

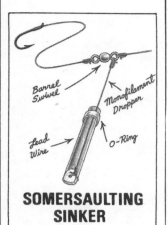

SOMERSAULTING SINKER

You need either three-sixteenths or a quarter-inch-diameter lead wire, rubber surgical tubing that fits tightly over the wire, and monofilament leader material testing two to four pounds less than the main line. Rigging steps are simple, but should be done ahead of time to save fussing when you should be fishing.

• Cut lead wire to the desired length and squeeze one end slightly flat with pliers.

• Punch or drill a small hole through the flattened end, then tie on a short length of monofilament as a dropper.

• Cut an eighth-inch-wide O-ring from the rubber tubing.

• Fold the dropper back against the sinker body, slip the O-ring over the flat end, then roll it to within an eighth inch of the opposite (round) end.

• Tie the dropper either to the front eye of a barrel swivel or to a three-way swivel, with the end of the sinker hanging one to two inches below.

If the sinker hangs up during use, a sharp jerk on the line stretches the O-ring, which causes the sinker to "pole vault" over the obstruction.

Should the sinker jam tightly—between two rocks for example—a steady pull will either cut through the O-ring, or cause it to slide down the sinker and pop off the end. Changing the direction of pull is usually enough to free the weight.

As you lose far more O-rings than sinkers, it pays to carry spares.

PLUG TESTING

After purchasing new lures, especially those that are to be trolled, it is always a good idea to test them before going fishing. All that is needed is a standard baitcasting rod and the use of a local pond or swimming pool. Most lures can be adjusted by altering the eye or scoop, and it is interesting to note that even identical lures will not operate in the same way at the same speed. All lures should be tested, adjusted *and marked* before your prime fishing time.

If some of these lures just can't be adjusted to your satisfaction, strip them for parts and throw the rest away so they won't get mixed up with the good ones.

SPLIT-SHOT JIG

To make on-the-spot weighted jigs, you'll need No. 4 or 5 split-shot and some loose hooks, preferably weedless bait hooks with burred shanks.

Clamp the large shot directly onto the shank behind the hookeye. The trick is to have the lead shot take only a shallow bite, with the larger portion of lead hanging below the shank to act as a keel. This will prevent line from becoming twisted when the jig is retrieved through the water.

The rigged hook is reasonably snag- and weedproof. The added weight does not interfere with the action of curlytail grubs, worms or minnow-shaped baits.

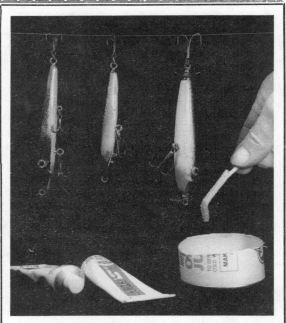

Epoxy Finish for Lures

Punctures caused by sharp hooks or teeth in predator fish allow water to seep into balsa and other wood body lures. The wood swells, causing the enameled finish to crack. You can waterproof and refinish lures with damaged surfaces with epoxy-type glue.

Mix resin and hardener together, then smooth on with a fuzzy wire pipe cleaner or disposable brush. After curing, the new finish will withstand most rough treatment from rocks, teeth and hooks.

WORDS OF WISDOM

I recently asked a sprightly angler in his mid-80s what period of day he considered best for fishing. Without hesitation he replied, "Early mornin's and evenin's are best—but all the hours in between 'em both are just as good."

Weighting Buoyant Lures

Big muskie lures, made of wood, can be weighted to run deeper—a definite advantage when fishing deep water.

Weight these buoyant lures with slip sinkers, the kind used in plastic worm fishing. Drill a hole the same diameter as the sinker in the underside of the lure. Coat with lacquer or varnish, then drive the sinker into the hole.

Decide where it would be best to weight the lure by balancing it on your finger, or by tank testing it with the sinker taped on. When weighted properly, the added weight seldom interferes with the action, but will cause the lure to run deeper—a secret some experts use to get action when others, using the same lure, get no strikes at all.

Worm Welder

Here's a hot tip for worm fishermen: Plastic worms are effective on a wide variety of salt- and freshwater fish, and they are the most economical lures an angler can purchase.

A problem with artificial worms is the softness of the plastic, which tears easily.

Since the worms are inexpensive, the average angler discards a damaged worm. But what do you do if you are wade-fishing half a mile down shore from your tacklebox, and the worm on which you are catching fish becomes so damaged from hook holes and strikes that it won't hang properly—and it's your last worm?

If you have a paper clip, a rubber band and a cigarette lighter, you can "weld" the torn worm.

Even if the worm is torn clear through, the two pieces can be stuck back together.

To make the worm welder, attach the paper clip to the side of the lighter and bend the clip so that one end is directly over the flame.

Heat the tip of the wire, shut off the flame, then use the wire tip as a mini soldering iron to melt the plastic. The hot wire will help to fill in rips and holes, too.

Weedless Jigs

1. Drill a small hole through the soft-lead head. Don't hit the hook.

2. Push a length of stainless-steel .016-diameter wire (available at most tackleshops) through the hole, and wedge it in place with a toothpick.

3. With pointed pliers, grasp the wire and wrap three or four turns around the base of the hookeye.

4. Cut off the wire to a length that just reaches back to the hook point. Bend the wire end at a 45-degree angle to complete the weedless arrangement.

Plain-Jane Lures

Anglers are discovering that drab colors have a strong attraction for many species of fish. For example, West Coast fishermen have known for many years about the fish-catching abilities of unpainted lead-bodied lures or jigs that have become oxydized. Salmon and trout are both known to attack such lures with wild abandon on bright, sunlit days when the baitfish are schooling.

During a recent discussion with a wiley Ontario walleye angler—a chap who garners much envy from fellow fishermen for the size of his catches—he revealed that he uses unpainted jig heads skirted with natural brown deer tail.

"I tie jigs commercially," he said, "but they would never sell—too plain looking." He grinned and continued, "The fancy ones with eye-appeal *sell* like crazy, but those old, plain-lookin' ones *catch* like crazy."

My experiments with unpainted jig heads and natural-colored plastic worms have resulted in excellent catches of smallmouth bass in Ontario waters. Keep the offering small—⅛th ounce heads and two- to three-inch worms—and fish them during the bright part of the day when fish shun bright offerings.

FLEXIBLE HOOK HONE

An inexpensive plastic auto ignition file makes a handy, versatile hook hone. The plastic is coated with a tough abrasive and is sinuously flexible. The file can be cut in half for two hones, making it twice the bargain. Put a hole in one end so you can attach the hone to a safety chain or vest retractor.

The file's flexibility is a real advantage in sharpening both small and large hooks. Since it's coated plastic, it doesn't rust, become brittle and break, give off fish-alarming flashes, or rattle in your fishing vest.

Quick-Change Jigs

Color oftentimes becomes a prime factor in a lure, especially on clear-water lakes and streams. A loaded tacklebox crammed with lures is one solution, but there is a quick, economical way of carrying color changes in your shirt pocket.

Take a trip to the local craft shop and ask for Tinsel-tex in whatever colors you need. Tinsel-tex is chenille wrapped on thin, soft, pliable wire stems. It can usually be purchased by the piece or box.

When a lure color change is called for, wrap the Tinsel-tex over the body, or clip off the old material and add the Tinsel-tex to the now-naked jig. The wire base will wrap and hold in place easily, and the excess can be snipped off.

It is also easy to make a double wrap with this product. Use two pieces to give a more lifelike color pattern to your leadheads, such as green and orange for perch, brown and white for chubs.

Another plus to this chenille-on-wire is that it can be shaped with nail clippers, applying a few snips here and there.

Cork has long been used for making bluegill and bass popping bugs. You can also use this high-floating material to carve realistic imitations of caterpillars, grasshoppers, beetles and ants that will fool the wariest stream trout. A razor blade, emery board, epoxy, hooks and model airplane paints are the only items needed.

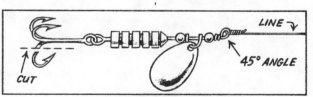

ALTERED BAITS

Spinner baits are effective lures for a wide variety of gamefish. However, they often cause line twisting, which is not only a nuisance but cuts down on casting distance and line life. I solve this problem by turning up the eye of my spinners about 45 degrees. This produces a keel effect on the spinner and reduces line twisting.

You can carry the procedure one step further. When turning up the eye, make sure that two hooks of the treble are in the "up" and one in the "down" position on the shank of the spinner. Then snip off the lower hook with pliers. Bottom snagging is minimized and many lures are saved. Removing the lower hook has little effect on hooking capabilities of the lure.

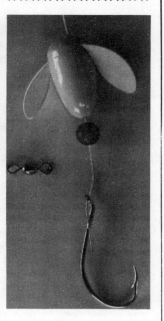

Extra Swivel Catches More Fish

When you're trolling a lure or plug, slips of grass and other little bits of debris get draped on the line, slide down, and inhibit the lure's action. A swivel attached two to four feet above the lure will catch most of the gunk and prevent it from reaching the lure.

Holding Grub Baits

You can minimize the problem of soft plastic grub baits sliding down smooth hook shanks and interfering with the business end of the hook by following the procedure shown above.

(1) Wind six to eight turns of fine-diameter wire around the hook shank. Allow both wire ends to stand upright.

(2) Cover with thread wrapping to anchor the wire firmly in place.

(3) Snip off wire ends to form short barbs or spurs.

(4) Impale the grub onto the hook.

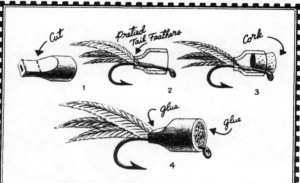

Cigar-Tip Poppers

Ordinary plastic cigar tips are great for making poppers. Just cut the mouthpiece off, insert a hook with pretied tail feathers, then force an oversized cork into the front. Use all-purpose white glue to seal around the cork and fill in the slit in the back (hook end). The popper can be left white or it can be painted.

Hook First Aid

Flies and poppers tied on hooks intended for use in fresh water do not last long when cast into the sea. Their life can be extended greatly, however, if proper precautions are taken. When you're finished using the lure in the briney whip it nearly dry, then submerge it immediately in a pail of fresh water. If you'll be running rough seas to reach fishing territory, line the pail with a plastic bag which can be sealed with a rubber band or a pipe cleaner to keep fresh water in and salt spray out.

At day's end, soak reels and lines in the same water. After two years of using this system my lures and reels show no signs whatever of salt corrosion.

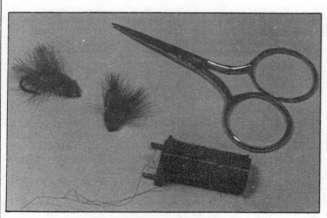

Flytying Wire

A broken radio, clock or almost any electric motor with an electromagnet can be a source for small-diameter copper wire that is ideal for flytying. The wire will often be enameled in useful colors such as red, green, brown or black, or its natural finish may be used.

Multi-Use Jig Holder

Painting enough jig heads to last through a season of hard fishing is a simple task if you use this easily constructed hook-holder. It is nothing more elaborate than two strips of lightweight cardboard stapled together to form a series of individual sheaths into which hooks may be fitted.

The size of the strips will vary in relation to the size and style of hooks being used. They should be wide enough to ensure hooks do not touch or overlap when inserted from opposite sides of the holder, and they should be no longer than twice the maximum reach of your desk stapler. Mine, for example, will staple to a distance of 4½ inches, therefore the strips I use are nine inches long.

A hole is punched through one end of the strips to accommodate a hook formed from a length of coat hanger, or similar wire. The hook, however, is not attached until the stapling is complete.

Strips over two inches in width should have a row of staples down each side, this lends better support to the hooks. Staples should be spaced 1½ times the hook gap —the distance between the point and the shank. This allows hooks to be inserted easily, yet holds them tightly in place until they are pulled out.

Push hooks into individual slots until the collars butt up against the rim. If the heads are collarless leave a slight gap between the cardboard and rear of the heads to prevent a blob of paint from building up and hardening between them.

Once holders are fully loaded, heads may be sprayed or painted individually by brush.

Jig heads are often enhanced by dotting eyes on each side with a small wooden dowel or nailhead. This task can be speeded up by placing the holder lengthwise along a 1-inch-thick board that is slightly narrower than the cardboard and preferably the same length, or longer.

Do all of the heads on one side before turning the holder over.

Unless there is an immediate use for the holders—for they are reusable—simply hang them in an out-of-the-way place with the heads left in position. This is an excellent way to store jigs as there is less chance of the hooks tangling or heads becoming scratched and chipped.

•

A simple way to keep coils of monofilament from unraveling is to twist a plastic-covered closure, commonly used to seal garbage bags, around the coil.

•

Sliding Sinker Trick

A sliding sinker permits fish to take the bait without feeling the drag or weight of the lead. It is difficult, however, to find a sliding sinker in the three- or four-ounce size. An easy method for making a sliding sinker out of nearly any standard type is to run the line through the eye of the sinker; next, thread a small, plastic bead on the line and then tie a swivel to the end of the line. The bead, which can often be found on an old lure, prevents the sinker from slipping over the swivel.

Worm Surgery

At the end of a successful fishing day, the bottom of a plastic-worm angler's boat is likely to resemble the Plains of Troy as described in *The Illiad:* broken, chewed, split and otherwise maimed pieces of once-glistening, perfectly formed new fish baits. It's a shame to bury these once-proud warriors of the water when a few simple moves can put selected bits and pieces back in the front lines again.

For worms that have been split by too many hook sets, simply amputate the bad spot. You'll get a shorter worm, but short worms catch fish, too. Once the cuts have been made, you can also restore them to any size you prefer. Heating two sections with a candle or lighter and then quickly pressing them together will do the job.

You can even run a few bunches of plastic leg material through the body of a beat-up worm at different points to make fish think it is akin to a crab or hellgrammite.

Worms are often damaged at the rear end. With some heat, these too can be back in action. They work even better if you add a different-color tail, one that twists or some other variation.

Bits of ends, namely tails in good shape, can be added on to crankbaits and jigs or made into panfish bugs. Floaters can be used as light-line bobbers or for suspending live baits fished off snells.

Uses for battle-scarred worms are limited only by your imagination. Besides that, worm surgery is fun, especially when your O.R. techniques start paying dividends with fish in the boat.

★

No one has ever proved that bright clothing scares fish, because it doesn't. Movement and sound do. Yet, it has been proved that brightly colored garments can attract bees, possibly because of a resemblance to flowers. So, if bees are a problem, dress dull.

Spinner Making

Making your own weighted spinner lures is easy. Start with a six-inch-long piece of spring wire, roughly .030 of an inch in diameter, for the shaft. Bend an eye on one end. Slide on beads and lead slip-sinker of your preferred weight. Follow with clevis and blade. Bend an eye at the opposite end of the wire shaft to complete the lure.

To prevent those blades of larger size from twisting your line, add a swivel to the upper eye. Use a split ring to fasten a hook or your favorite fly pattern.

For more delicate and accurate deliveries with spinning tackle, feather the line with your index finger as the offering approaches its target. This will slow the lure's course and allow it to drop gently onto the water.

•

Ordinary spinners and spoons can be modified to serve as sonic lures by drilling a few holes into the rear section of the lure or spinner blades (1/8-inch holes in small lures and 1/4-inch in larger ones). The holes create turbulence and bubbling, allow the blade to turn faster at slower speeds, and produce a low hum that will alert fish.

JACKPOT!

A lot of tall tales emanate from Texas, but here's a true one that'll make you shake your head.

Ray Thrailkill, an Amarillo resident, is equally tetched on fishing and playing pinball. One evening he was torn between these desires so he figured out a way to enjoy both.

His sailboat was docked at a Lake Meredith marina where he plied the pinball machines with his buddies. He baited his fishing rig with a lively minnow and left it on his sailboat just outside where he could keep on eye on it. Then he got lost bumping and nudging the little steel ball.

A friend told him his rod and reel were about to be yanked out of his sailboat, so he dashed out and hauled in an 11-pound 5¾ ounce walleye to set a new state record!

He stayed with his fishing and caught two more walleyes, weighing seven and three pounds. When you think of the countless fishermen who have spent lifetimes concentrating all their attention on trying to catch a record fish, well, there's some kind of message here.

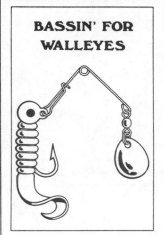

BASSIN' FOR WALLEYES

Most fishermen associate certain lures with certain fish and use them accordingly. For instance, the soft-bodied jig with overhead spinner is usually thought of as a bass lure. However, early and late in the season, when walleyes are feeding in shallow water and can be caught by casting, this lure is a walleye killer. If you're casting over submerged weedbeds, retrieve the lure just above the tops of the weeds. The walleyes seem to prefer white jigs.

★

The narrower the blade on a spinnerbait, the faster it has to be pulled through the water. Bulkier blades, such as the famed Colorado, work at incredibly slow speeds, even while falling freely. Color, vibration and flash are the three critical factors in this lure. Vibration and flash are functions of blade size, shape and coloration. Spinnerbaits may look similar, but it pays to study each one carefully before buying it.

HANDY FISH MAT

Next time you trade in your car or truck, keep its rubber floor mat. Roll it up, secure with a cord and take it on your next camping trip. It makes a great work surface on which to scale or fillet fish. It is quite slipproof. Fish placed on either side won't skid as you work on them. The mat is easy to wash off after using.

FLIES

LOOSE-HAIR GRIP

Occasionally while tying up a batch of my favorite streamer patterns I let my mind wander from the task at hand and suddenly find a clump of bucktail clutched between thumb and forefinger about three steps before it is needed.

Placing the clump on the table usually results in bits and pieces of trimmings adhering to the hair—and what I laid down was not always what I picked up, for the strands of hair seemed to have a will of their own.

I solved this problem by lining the inner jaws of a spring-loaded paper clamp with self-adhesive weather stripping. The sponge-like material has more than enough resiliency to envelop all of the hair and keep it firmly under control.

•

FANCY FEATHERS

Use artist's oil paints to color feathers for flytying. Just mix a few drops of paint with a little thinner in a dish and dip the feather in. The color is permanent, and the oil in the paint adds to the feather's waterproofness. Colors can be mixed to produce any shade.

Easy Streamer

Using four easy steps, you can dress long-shanked hooks into highly effective streamer flies. And any angler, even if he has no previous tying skill, should be able to accomplish it in less than ten minutes. Here's how:

STEP ONE: Use nylon sewing thread to tie on some material for a tail, in this case a generous portion of a duck breast feather.

STEP TWO: Wrap shank with a two- or three-inch-long piece of chenille, or floss, for the body. Stop short of the hook eye.

STEP THREE: Tie in four saddle hackle feathers (found on the cape of barnyard roosters) for wings. Pull off small bunches of fibers from a feather of contrasting color, and tie beneath wings for gills or throat on the fly.

STEP FOUR: Wind on remaining nylon thread to cover all loose ends of feathers. The fly is now complete and ready to be fished.

Red chenille, white wing feathers and brown hackle throat, used here, are suggestive of the famous Thor pattern—a "meaty" looking tie that works wonders on stocked rainbow, brook and brown trout.

A box of very small trout hooks can be easily dropped and the contents lost forever—a costly mistake at today's prices. A small magnet placed inside the box with the hooks will keep the hooks clinging together just in case of such an upset.

CONCENTRATED DYEING

There is now a much simpler way to dye flytying feathers at home. Gone are the boiling pots, simmering pans, rubber gloves, death-defying chemicals and berserk kitchen commanders distraught over the resultant mess. A Mason jar or large-mouthed peanut butter jar, a bottle of liquid fabric dye, a slosh of vinegar and a squirt of dishwashing soap are all that are needed.

The dyeing requires three steps—dyeing, transferring and drying. Pour in the dye, vinegar and soap, and add the feathers. Pour in enough water to fill the jar, tighten the lid, and leave it overnight.

The transfer stage requires plastic salad tongs, or a fork or two. Use them to pearl-dive for the dyed feathers. Another approach is to use a second container to pour the dye into, catching the feathers with cheesecloth or a colander.

After a rinsing, the dyed materials are ready for drying on sheets of newspaper on a flat, undisturbed area.

The dye solution will keep in a jar for several seasons, and after stirring or shaking can be used again.

WEIGHTY NYMPH PROBLEM

If you are tying your own nymphs and weighting some while leaving the lead out of others, there is an easy way to tell them apart. Simply tie the weighted version with a different colored thread.

USES FOR RUBBER BANDS

Don't throw away those rubber bands! Put a few of them in your fishing tackle-box; they can serve a multitude of uses.

Rubber bands can hold fishing rods together in a neat bundle. Slip one end of the rubber band over a rod guide, then stretch it around the rods a couple of times and slip the loop of the other end over another guide. Use at least two bands; one near the tips of the rods and a second near the butt sections.

Hinged lid broken on a small plastic lure box? Wrap a rubber band around the box. It takes only a second to remove and replace it.

Slip a double rubber band around your cigarette lighter and it will help keep the lighter in your shirt pocket when you bend over.

Of course, rubber bands can also be used to hold monofilament line on an openface spinning reel spool.

And if you want to try a unique panfish lure, cut several strips of thin rubber band about three quarters of an inch long and cement them to a Size 12 or 14 treble hook. This makes a fish-enticing "spider."

Eyelet Setting Tip

Tapping a new eyelet into the core of a fly line can be a tricky job. To simplify the task, use a common tool—a mechanic's vise grip. This tool can be adjusted to very delicate tension so that the tip of the fly line can be grasped firmly without damage. Tapping in a new eyelet straight and quickly then becomes easy.

PRISMATIC STREAMERS

Prismatic tape, commonly found in auto parts stores, can enhance the attractiveness of streamers.

The metallic tape comes in a variety of colors, and rather than reflecting just a silver or gold, it creates a rainbow prism of color, considerably more lifelike than standard tinsels.

The tape can be purchased in just about all shapes and sizes, including rolls one-eighth-inch wide that are perfect for winging material. Sections can be purchased from rolls of greater width and pieces can be cut into any size or shape.

The two most effective background colors are probably silver and gold, mimicking baitfish. One combo that I have had good success with in spring is the white marabou tied with strips of red prismatic tape.

Tying instructions are simple. Cut the tape to size before removing the paper from its adhesive backing. The end of the strip you will tie into the head of the streamer needs to be cut fairly thin since it is metal and not easy to work with.

Strip the paper off, using a needle to separate the tape from the backing. Tie-in the tape on the outside of the wing, so the "flash" will be visible to the fish. The adhesive side will stick to the wing and make a sturdy fly.

Fish the prismatic streamer as you would any other, though I have found a stripping action brings out added flash

Fuzzier Nymphs

E.H. (Polly) Rosborough is now past 80 years old and has been tying flies professionally for more than 50 years. He's famous for his fuzzy nymphs, which he makes fuzzier and buggier than ever by simply roughening up the nymph body with a piece of hacksaw blade.

SPARE LEAD-CORE LINE

When fishing the kinds of waters and depths that require lead-core lines, anglers often lose them. To save a lot of wasted fishing time, I always carry a spare.

The best line I have found for this kind of fishing is Gladding Mark V. It comes in 20- and 30-pound test, has a smooth finish, and casts well. Listed in the chart below are lengths of Mark V to balance various rods:

Line No.	Grains	Feet
7	185	15
8	210	17
9	240	20
10	280	23
11	330	27
12	380	32

If you lose a line, your spare, coiled with leader and fly already attached, will get you back to fishing with the tying of only a single knot.

SCORCHING SPUN DEER HAIR

When tying flies with spun deer-hair bodies or heads like sculpins, muddler minnows or bass bugs, try scorching the finished, clipped hair with a match or lighter. This flares and seals the hair making heads and bodies as tight as cork. It also makes them impervious to water. The light brown ash that's left can be brushed away with an old toothbrush.

A Flytier's Helper

As flytiers strive for efficiency, both beginners and advanced "brothers of the art" at one time or another purchase a set of hackle guards. When used with a whip-finisher, these thin metal discs help create a small, neat head, with virtually no hackle trapped underneath.

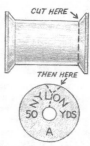

A set of three will cover most hook sizes from No. 28 to No. 2/0; that is about the extent of their coverage. The center hole on the largest hackle guard is too small to accommodate No. 3/0 hooks, and others have a large ringed eye that encourages a dense build-up of larger thread and bulky material ends at the head.

A simple but effective guard can be added to the trio by using an empty foam plastic thread spool. With a razor blade or very sharp knife, make a clean, straight cut completely through the beveled end of the spool. Cut a small V on the outside edge and continue your incision through to the center hole. This slit allows the tying thread to pass to the middle hole as it would with a standard hackle guard.

Unlike conventional guards, held in place by a small sinker or other weight attached to a string, no weight is needed since the homemade guard is secured by the hackle itself. Simply push the guard back until some of the hackle protrudes through the center hole.

Mine has remained on my flytying desk for years now, and has proved invaluable when tying large streamers, hair bugs, or any pattern that utilizes a front hackle in the dressing.

HEAD-CEMENT SOLUTION

Leaving the lid off your head-cement bottle while you tie flies allows the cement to evaporate. After a short time it becomes too thick to penetrate the windings of the fly head. Leaving the lid on means each time you finish a fly, or want to cement an intermediate step, you must unscrew the lid, use the cement, then screw the lid back on.

Garcia Silicote Dry Fly Dressing comes in half-ounce, hourglass-shaped bottles. Within the lid of each is a plastic insert that can be separated from the lid. This insert is large enough and deep enough to fit firmly into the mouth of the bottle without the lid screwed over it.

Stick a bodkin, with a one- to 1½-inch needle, through the center of the plastic insert. Fill the empty Silicote bottle to the neck with head cement. Place the insert over the mouth of the bottle. The bodkin needle should penetrate well into the cement. Each time the bodkin is removed from the bottle the plastic insert will come with it, and a drop of head cement will be on the needle to finish your fly. It is a one-handed operation and the needle and lid are returned to the bottle immediately, preventing evaporation.

Lacquer thinner should be used occasionally to keep the head cement thin and penetrating. Evaporation takes place even in a stoppered bottle, although it takes a matter of weeks instead of days.

Before wading into a stream or pond, fish the immediate area. Many fish that might have been a mere flash of silver to the angler if he had blundered blindly ahead to get to the best water are caught after this step.

TACKLEBOX BOBBIN

Back up your field flytying vise with a quick and inexpensive bobbin. The frame can be bent from No. 8 T.W. electrical wire, a brass welding rod, or even an old coat hanger. The thread spool bearings are cone-style faucet washers and the exit tube is a piece of the spray extension tubing that comes with a can of WD-40. A rubber band over the frame lets you control tension on the thread.

OPOSSUM FUR FLIES

The fur of the lowly opossum is a readily available, inexpensive source of material for those who tie their own flies. In particular, the fur is a fine substitute for the wide variety of hair-wing dry flies developed by Lee Wulff.

Opossum fur is cheaper (a road kill of this widely dispersed nocturnal mammal will provide material for hundreds of flies) than the kip tail, which is the standard material for Wulff patterns. It enjoys several other advantages as well. The opossum's inner fur is soft and pliable, and easy to handle. It is of sufficient length to allow the tier flexibility in fashioning patterns. The floating qualities are excellent, and it takes fly dressings, especially those in liquid form, exceptionally well.

An early morning fog is always followed by a rainless sky.

MONO THREADER

In years past most flytying threads were not prewaxed, and a bobbin could be threaded by a strong sucking breath on the end of the barrel. But today a residue of wax builds up in the bobbin barrel, often necessitating the use of some type of bobbin threader.

A makeshift threader can be fabricated with a length of monofilament and a sharp razor blade. An angular slit is cut in the monofilament a short ways from the end. The mono is fed through the barrel of the bobbin, the thread hooked into the slit, and then the mono/threader pulls the thread out of the barrel. The bobbin is loaded with tying thread and ready for action.

Emergency Head Cement

If you're in the middle of tying trout flies for an upcoming fishing trip and run out of head cement, you can finish the job with Hard-as-Nails, used by women to strengthen their nails. It dries quickly, is waterproof, and is available in drugstores in colors or as a clear liquid. Clear Hard-as-Nails can be colored by mixing it with a lacquer-type paint.

DROP IN THE BUCKET

Flytying cements and rod-wrapping varnishes tend to thicken or dry out without the periodic addition of thinner. Buy a quart of lacquer thinner and transfer some of it to a smaller benchside bottle. Adding thinner is then done easily with a medicine dropper.

•

Most fishermen know that the hours bordering dawn and dusk are the prime times to catch fish. Experts also know that high noon in winter and midnight in summer pay off regularly in bigger fish.

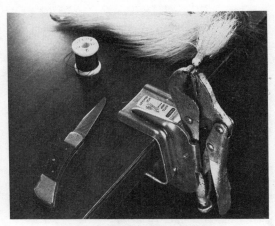

PORTABLE VISE

By placing a Vise Grips pliers in a universal mounting bracket, an angler can have a flytying vise wherever he goes. The jaws of the pliers can be adjusted to hold any size hook and the mounting bracket can be fastened anywhere, even on the side of a boat, for an on-the-spot repair of a favorite bucktail or fly. Most hardware stores carry both tools. The bracket is made by Stanley (part number 84-002). Vise Grips come in a variety of sizes to match your particular style of fishing.

Coffee Break Organization

Any flytier who has more material than can fit in a shoe box has storage problems that require efficient organization.

Some tiers use baby food jars to store their material. That works fine until you try to force No. 8 fingers into No. 16 jars. Others save every empty jar or can they see. This system works fine, but leaves the tying bench and storage area looking like the local landfill.

The solution I've come up with is both aesthetically pleasing and inexpensive. Nestlé's makes Sunrise instant coffee and packages it in three different-sized containers. The jars all have ample openings to accommodate fat fingers.

I am now slowly replacing my landfill collection with a more uniform assemblage of feather-filled glass. While the jars won't help me tie flies any better, they do make it a lot easier for me to locate things.

Free Fly Book

Before tossing out an old worn-out wallet, remember to pull out the section reserved for photos and cards. Compact, self-contained and easy to remove, this unit makes an excellent book for keeping artificial flies.

Items such as wet flies, streamers and even loosely coiled leader can be slipped directly into the clear photo sleeves. Bulkier flies such as nymphs and dry flies can be kept on pieces of foam or other suitable material glued to the inside of the cover flap.

TWO HANDY TOOLS

Two inexpensive but handy flytying tools are found at cosmetic counters. A common pair of tweezers is invaluable for finagling small items such as tiny hooks, diminutive wings and minute flies. The second tool is eyebrow pluckers. Of course, to a flytier's ear, plucking brings to mind the removal of feathers from a prime bird skin, and tweezer pliers are an excellent tool for removing small hackle from a good cape. Eyebrow pluckers can be turned into a "poor man's forceps" and used for other flytying jobs by wrapping a rubber band tightly around the business end of the tool.

★

When fishing below rapids, you'll find trout and grayling in the fast stretches, while bass and walleyes will be in the eddy-water slot and behind big boulders.

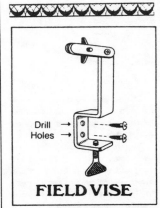

Drill Holes →

FIELD VISE

When you move up the ladder and buy more professional tools than those that were included in your flytying kit, don't throw away the originals. Put them in the bottom of your tacklebox. That inexpensive vise, in particular, just might save the day.

While not entirely suitable as a full-time vise, this simple vise will hold a hook, and it's certainly better than fingers or pliers. To make the "toy-vise" more adaptable under unusual mounting conditions, drill holes as shown and carry several wood screws for easy mounting.

TINY HOOK STORAGE

Sometimes it takes a tiny hook to tempt a big fish into action. Whether fishing with midges or live bait, Nos. 16 to 22 hooks are hard to keep track of and their fine-wire construction makes them delicate as well as difficult to see.

A solution is to imbed them in a big eraser. The large hunk of rubber keeps the hooks together in a cluster where they are more easily spotted by myopic anglers. The rubber prevents the points and barbs from being jostled about, dulling or bending the fine wire. The eraser also prevents moisture from gathering on the metal and thus eliminates corrosion.

The erasers can be cemented into a fly or tacklebox.

Check This

Checkbook covers, whether they are plastic or genuine leather, make good streamer and wet-fly books.

For the fastidious, they can be lined with shearing or clipped sheepskin. But a simple, inexpensive and effective way to line them is with cotton batten pads. One brand is known as Glaze Tex, a flameproof cotton. It is used to drape around the base of a Christmas tree, but available at all times of the year.

Simply cut out rectangular sections the size of the inside of the checkbook cover and attach the material with epoxy or other waterproof glue. The cotton holds the flies securely.

•

King salmon travel as far as 2400 miles inland from the sea to lay their eggs.

Wired Woolly

The woolly-worm tie is one of the all-time greats for panfish and trout. It imitates literally hundreds of worm species, all of which are fish food at some time. It's easy to make, requiring only two materials—chenille and one or two hackle feathers.

If you have the feather (if not, pull one from a pillow) but lack chenille, substitute pipe cleaner. Wind this fuzzy wire around the hook shank. Use thread to tie on the feather and wind spirally over the fuzzy body. Finally, knot the thread over the remaining end of the feather. Now you have a woolly-worm fly ready to fish.

•

Polarized sunglasses cut through surface glare—even when it's raining—and help an angler spot fish. When you are looking for them, remember that you might only see a partial outline. And be alert to any movement near bottom.

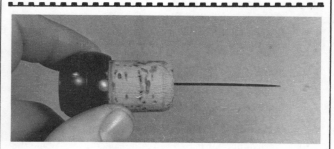

Emergency Flytying Tools

Many flytying tools can be quickly and inexpensively made from household items:

BODKIN: Cork with needle inserted with a pair of pliers.

VISE: Oak spring-type clothespin screwed to a dowel which is set in a wood block. Rubber bands around the clothespin add gripping power. Vise grips welded onto a rod work, too.

HACKLE PLIERS: Heavy coat-hanger wire wound around a pipe and sprung backwards, the ends flattened.

SCISSORS AND THREAD: Family sewing basket, small embroidery scissors that are equipped with pointed ends.

TYING BOBBIN: A quick substitute can be fashioned with rubber bands around the spool of thread to keep it from unraveling.

MATERIAL CLIP: A small spring wrapped around the vise holds tied-in materials such as tinsel out of the way until finally wrapped and tied down.

FLYTYING BACKGROUND

A dark background behind your flytying vise makes it difficult to see the materials you are working with, no matter how good the light. To brighten things up and make hook, thread and materials stand out clearly, clamp a large sheet of white paper under the vise when you set up to tie. It will give you a good background and assure you of a clean, uncluttered area in which to work.

FLYTYING ALTERNATIVES

Many flytying materials are less expensive when purchased in stores or hobby shops. The notions section of a fabric shop will have silver or gold mylar piping in various sizes, extra-fine monofilament for tippets, embroidery floss, packages of movable plastic eyes for deer-hair bugs, and silk thread for flytying or wrapping rods.

Hobby and department stores carry balsa to make poppers and filler-coat for priming as well as jars of enamel paint for finishing the job. Small spools of copper, brass or galvanized hobby wire come in handy, as does soldering wire with its lead content for weighting flies.

Occasionally you find a feather duster made from real ostrich plumes.

During extremely hot weather, try fishing in the cool of the night and during a rain—if there's no lightning. During a cold spell, concentrate on deeper holes and where streams flow into a lake.

HOOKED !

On my first fishing trip to the Klamath River in northern California, I landed a large silver-sided salmon that gave me an exciting 55 minutes as I played him on my dime-store tackle.

Just as I was congratulating myself on this fine haul, an officious-looking character came along and asked me if this was my first salmon. When I told him it was, he stated flatly, "That fish is going to cost you a whole lot of money."

After a few minutes of complete silence while he puffed away on his pipe and I wondered what on earth it was that I had done wrong, he added, "Now you'll be coming up here for the rest of your life."

He was certainly right about that.

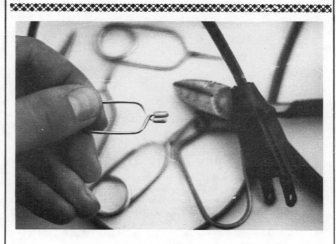

Improving Hackle Pliers

Many flytying hackle pliers are on the market today, varying in quality and price. An inexpensive pair of pliers is usually either too loose to hold the hackle or so tight that it breaks the hackle.

The answer is to find insulated electrical wire the same diameter as the jaws of the hackle pliers. Remove the wire and slip the insulating tube over the business ends of the pliers, clipping any excess off. The insulation provides a firm cushion that holds hackle well without damaging the feather.

WELL-GROOMED FLIES

Various fly and jig patterns call for wings or skirts of such synthetic yarns as polypropylene or acrylic. Most flytiers tease the material with a needle to fluff it out, but the job can be done much faster and easier with a small brush.

A soft-wire-bristle suede brush will make up to a dozen miniature brushes.

Carefully saw crossways between the rows of bristles with a thin-bladed hacksaw or coping saw.

Drill a small hole through the wooden back to accept a length of fishing line to be used as a lanyard fastened to your vest. Then smooth off any rough edges.

EMERGENCY HEAD CEMENT

If you're tying trout flies and run out of head cement, a good substitute is a nail hardener called Hard-as-Nails. It can be found in the cosmetic department of your local drugstore. Hard-as-Nails comes in colors but the clear variety is the most useful for flytiers. It can be colored black by mixing in some ink.

Waxed Fly Heads

Instead of finishing your flies with head cement or lacquer, try this inexpensive substitute: acrylic floor wax. This wax is nothing more than clear, liquid plastic. It makes a durable, lightweight substitute for the cements and lacquers traditionally used for finishing fly heads. It's also cheap and easy to apply with a dubbing needle or small paint brush.

Save the Stems

You have just ended a lengthy session at the tying vise, fashioning everything from steelhead wets to traditional dry flies. A pile of debris sits in front of you, waiting to be swept away. Before you dispose of the rubble, take a moment and pick out all the stripped hackle stems. They have several good tying uses.

When you strip off your best saddle hackle for beard hackle and tailing dry flies, it may be worth your while to put the stems to other uses. Colors such as black, brown and gray make great tails and antennae for mayfly and stonefly nymphs. Durable dry-fly bodies can also be made from stems. Wind a red and a brown stem together for the body of a Red Quill. Try some of the more colorful stems as ribbing over the body of a silver steelhead fly for a little extra color. These are but a few of the ways stems can be used. Undoubtedly there are many others you will come across, so save the stems.

Belt towels made for golfers are great for fishermen. They're handy to wipe hands dry and clean from baits, mud or fish slime. Wading anglers find them especially useful.

Fishing Strings

Old strings from musical instruments are useful to flyfishermen. Tie one to your flytying vise—it makes an easy-to-find wire loop for threading the bobbin. Attach part of a string to your wader suspenders—it will be handy for poking cement out from fly heads. Some light-gauge strings make good wire leaders, having a loop at one end to furnish easy attachment to heavy monofilament.

COAT HANGER FOR BLOOD KNOT

Here is a helpful tool for the tacklebox that can be assembled quicker than the time it takes to read this and costs less than a spoonful of salt.

Cut off approximately 12 inches from the straight length of a coat hanger. With your fishing pliers, bend the wire into a makeshift M, allowing about three inches per portion. Hold the cut ends of the wire and move the center of the M about three-quarters to one-inch higher than the ends. The cut end portions act as the base when placed on a flat surface.

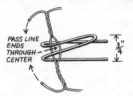

PASS LINE ENDS THROUGH CENTER ↑ 3/4" ↓

To tie a blood knot, hold the two line ends parallel. Slip one of the lines under the raised portion, lift the tool, twirl the tool for as many twists needed for the blood knot, pass the ends through the open center, pull lines tight, and remove tool—presto! A perfect blood knot.

★

Across our nation there are countless ponds that are rarely fished. Make it a point to search these out, and then share your catch with the landowners.

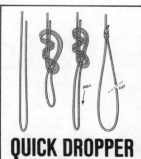

QUICK DROPPER

To tie a dropper in your fly leader when time, light, or know-how prevents the use of a "long-tailed" blood knot, first form a loop about nine inches long in the end of the leader. Then tie a clinch knot in the loop, pull tight, and cut the loop about halfway down one side.

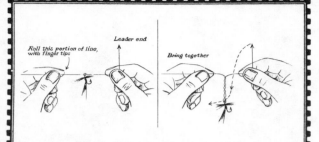

Easy Twist Knot

Here is a quick and easy way to make the twists of the knot that attaches a fly and leader.

Pass the leader end through the eye of the fly. Place the end between the thumb and index finger, exposing approximately one inch at a right angle to main line. Hold the main portion of the leader between your other thumb and index finger, keeping the fly centered.

Using the thumb and index finger that are securing the main portion of the leader, roll the line. Bring both hands together, and lines on both sides of the fly will automatically twist together. Pass the end through the loop at the eye of the fly. Pull at the main portion of the line to tighten.

POSTMAN, BEWARE!

A friend vacationing in northern Wisconsin decided to send some of his catch of fish to his family in Florida. After carefully packing it in an ice-filled refrigerator bag, he wrote on the outside of the package: "If not delivered within three days, forget it."

The Brownell Loop

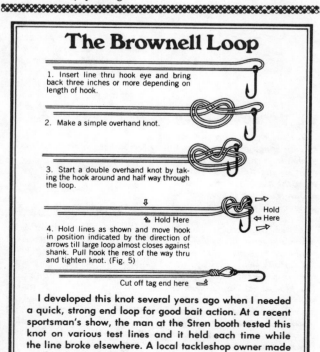

1. Insert line thru hook eye and bring back three inches or more depending on length of hook.

2. Make a simple overhand knot.

3. Start a double overhand knot by taking the hook around and half way through the loop.

⇓ Hold Here

4. Hold lines as shown and move hook in position indicated by the direction of arrows till large loop almost closes against shank. Pull hook the rest of the way thru and tighten knot. (Fig. 5)

Hold Here ⇐

Cut off tag end here ⟿

I developed this knot several years ago when I needed a quick, strong end loop for good bait action. At a recent sportsman's show, the man at the Stren booth tested this knot on various test lines and it held each time while the line broke elsewhere. A local tackleshop owner made similar tests and the knot held.

New Knot, Or Not?

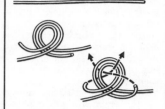

Ever tie the knot illustrated in the accompanying drawings? According to Dr. E. Hunter of Cambridge, England, the answer should be no because he claims that this is a brand new knot and that he discovered it himself only recently.

One knot expert, associated with the British Maritime Museum, supports this claim, "Whether Dr. Hunter has discovered a new knot or simply rediscovered one which has dropped out of current knowledge," says the expert, "he deserves full credit."

Among the advantages claimed for this knot are: that it can be used for anything from fishing line to heavy tow rope; that it transfers tension from one line to the other without twisting, making it great for fishing line; that it does not slip, even to the point of breaking; and finally that it is very easy to tie.

Overlap the two line ends and hold them parallel (figure 1). Twist back the middle to form a loop (figure 2). Then simply pass loose end A through the front of the loop and loose end B through the back (figure 3). To tighten, bring the two ends together and pull against the main ropes.

The extremely useful knot has been christened Hunter's Bend, after its discoverer.

In England *beck* is a small stream; in Scotland it's a *burn.*

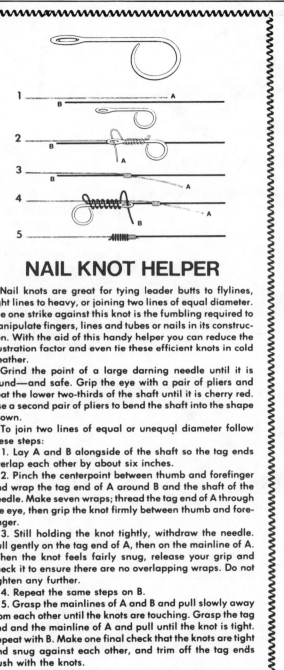

NAIL KNOT HELPER

Nail knots are great for tying leader butts to flylines, light lines to heavy, or joining two lines of equal diameter. The one strike against this knot is the fumbling required to manipulate fingers, lines and tubes or nails in its construction. With the aid of this handy helper you can reduce the frustration factor and even tie these efficient knots in cold weather.

Grind the point of a large darning needle until it is round—and safe. Grip the eye with a pair of pliers and heat the lower two-thirds of the shaft until it is cherry red. Use a second pair of pliers to bend the shaft into the shape shown.

To join two lines of equal or unequal diameter follow these steps:

1. Lay A and B alongside of the shaft so the tag ends overlap each other by about six inches.

2. Pinch the centerpoint between thumb and forefinger and wrap the tag end of A around B and the shaft of the needle. Make seven wraps; thread the tag end of A through the eye, then grip the knot firmly between thumb and forefinger.

3. Still holding the knot tightly, withdraw the needle. Pull gently on the tag end of A, then on the mainline of A. When the knot feels fairly snug, release your grip and check it to ensure there are no overlapping wraps. Do not tighten any further.

4. Repeat the same steps on B.

5. Grasp the mainlines of A and B and pull slowly away from each other until the knots are touching. Grasp the tag end and the mainline of A and pull until the knot is tight. Repeat with B. Make one final check that the knots are tight and snug against each other, and trim off the tag ends flush with the knots.

In matching a fly pattern to a natural insect or an artificial lure to baitfish, think about size and silhouette rather than color. It merely has to be dark or light to represent the real thing. Subtle shading is seldom necessary.

•

An empty bucket makes an excellent tacklebox when you are changing lures frequently aboard a boat. Hang the lures from their rear hooks along the rim, with the bodies inside the bucket. They'll stay untangled and you can get to them easily. At the end of the day stow them properly.

•

Knot Tips: Monofilament line starts to slip inside a knot just before it's going to fail. When tying a knot, moisten the line before cinching it up as tightly as possible. If you are learning a new knot, practice with heavier material first until you know how to tie it.

Fishing I.Q.: Knots

(1) The Blood Knot is also called the _____ Knot.
(2) Spitting on a loosely formed knot before snugging it down will increase knot strength. True or False?
(3) When using the Clinch Knot, as line test increases the number of turns made in forming the knot should be increased. True or False?
(4) The Uni-Knot (described in *Sports Afield* June 1975) replaces the: a. Clinch Knot; b. Blood Knot; c. Nail Knot; d. Palomar Knot; e. All of the above.
(5) The Nail Knot is used to join: a. mono and braided line; b. mono and mono; c. leaders to lures; d. flyline to leader butt.
(6) The Bimini Twist was created to: a. describe a kink in Ernest Hemingway's character; b. give flyfishers a nearly foolproof knot for gut leaders; c. join lines of different diameters; d. make a strong double line.
(7) Loop knots (Buffer, Two Wrap, etc.) can be used in place of the Clinch or Palomar to give lures added freedom of movement. True or False?
(8) The Turle Knot is often used to: a. join lines of different diameters; b. attach flies to tippets; c. form a dropper loop; d. replace snelling.
(9) The Portland or Riffling Hitch is generally used to attach bait hooks to leader. True or False?
(10) The Haywire Twist is most effective when formed in: a. braided wire; b. lead-core line; c. single-strand wire; d. mono.

(10) C.

(9) False. The Portland Hitch is tied behind the heads of some flies to help impart action.

(8) B.

(7) True.

(6) D.

(5) D.

(4) E. The versatile Uni-Knot system can be used in place of not only all these knots, but many others, as well.

(3) False. It's just the reverse: the heavier the line, the fewer turns needed to form a good Clinch.

(2) False. Until recently many fishermen believed lubricating a loose knot with spit would reduce line-weakening friction when the knot was drawn tight and that knots so moistened would form up more perfectly. Sports Afield Angling Editor Homer Circle proved these beliefs wrong by conducting knot tying/breaking experiments with the Du Pont Company (Sports Afield, February 1976, page 104). His results indicated dry-tied knots were superior to moistened ones.

(1) Barrel.

ANSWERS:

LIVE BAIT AND NATURALS

MATCH TRICK SAVES EGGS

Impaled on tiny, midge-sized golden hooks, salmon eggs remain a popular and deadly bait for trout and other gamefish. Despite the relatively high price—from $2 to $4 a jar (and more when you get there)— many fishermen waste this crude caviar. With innocent confidence in last year's supply, they arrive on the water only to find their eggs soft and soured or dried and shriveled— impossible to keep on the hook. Here's a trick that will keep your eggs fresh, moist and firm for several seasons:

At the end of the day's fishing, poke a match down into the eggs with the head protruding above them, but below the mouth of the jar. Light the match head, then quickly screw the lid down tight before the match inside goes out.

The lighted match will burn up all the oxygen within the jar, depriving bacteria of the oxygen they need to break down the eggs. At the same time, a slight vacuum is created, which makes the jar's seal more effective. Treated this way, your eggs could stay fresh for years.

Buzz Baits

Mother Nature provides a freebie in the form of a dandy year-round bluegill bait— wasps.

They are looked on as general pests by homeowners when they use overhangs, utility sheds, attics and the like as brood raising areas. Both paper wasps and mud daubers are guilty, but in the larval stage they are excellent baits for anglers if collected and stored properly.

In order to keep the risk of a confrontation with parent wasps and their stingers to a minimum, larvae collection should be done either during cold periods or at night. Adults are in a more amiable mood then. Paper wasp nests are suspended on a stem from rafters or an overhang, so a broom can be used to brush off the adults and dislodge the nest.

Mud daubers offer a better low-risk factor. The females lay eggs in mud nests just about anywhere that seems handy, sometimes even on the sides of old boxes and buckets. Once the egg is laid on a food cache, the chamber is sealed, and the parent departs. All you have to do is pry the nests loose. They can be stored as is or broken apart, and the sacks holding the larvae placed in a container.

In the late fall and winter keeping wasp larvae in the garage, cellar, or shed works out fine because cool temperatures keep the larvae dormant. However, for warmer months and climes (or heated basements) you need a refrigerator to keep the undeveloped wasps in a less belligerant state. As such, they are one of the best bluegill baits around.

BETTER SPAWN CURE

Ask steelhead anglers how they take care of all that spawn they salvage from hen steelhead and salmon in the spring and fall, and you'll get umpteen different formulas. Most will be based on borax, the approved method for years, although it tends to harden both individual eggs and the skein skin itself in the case of chunk spawn, thus keeping the eggs lumped together. Now there's a better way.

Next time you are browsing through your local photo shop, grab a jar of sodium sulfite (*not sulfate*). Mix it with equal amounts of granulated sugar and noniodized salt.

When you get ready to do a batch of eggs, put them in cold water overnight. The water should be as pure as possible to keep chemical contamination to a minimum. Drain the eggs in a colander, spread them out on a cookie sheet and sprinkle with the mixture (so there is an even coating over all.) After a couple of hours, they will appear to shrivel but not to worry. Prepare as you wish but leave eggs loose. Place the chunks or bags in the refrigerator in Tupperware or a tight plastic container.

When it's time to go fishing, select the amount you want for the trip and place in a jar with just enough water to cover. By the time you reach the river the eggs should swell up again, be nice and firm with no odors.

★

When you have an offshore wind, a small balloon makes a good bobber substitute because it will carry your bait farther out than you can cast.

PARASITE FISH BAIT

While fishing in Wyoming, Dr. Andrew Olson of San Diego State University caught a flannel-mouth sucker with a greatly distended stomach. Inside were three glistening, white, eight-inch tapeworm larvae. He put one on his hook and caught a 14-inch brook trout.

Being a parasitologist, Dr. Olson became interested in the use of parasites as bait. So far, he's had reports of similar tapeworm larvae being used in New Mexico and Montana to catch trout and whitefish.

Dr. Olson has also heard of using a giant intestinal round-worm found in pigs for saltwater bait near Houston, and fish lice (isopods) in Chesapeake Bay. There anglers catch bluefish, pick off the isopods and use these little crustaceans as bait. It's like putting a little crab on a hook, and apparently it works.

Olson has no information on the use of parasitic leeches as fish bait, but says that other leech species are used. "The Minnesota DNR estimates that nearly 60 tons of leeches were harvested from their lakes and ponds in 1978, and sold at a retail value of three and a half million dollars," Olson said.

SHELL OUT FOR FISH

Everything from dog food to chicken guts has been used as chum to attract fish, but did you ever try egg shells? Instead of tossing the shells into the garbage, throw them into a paper bag. After they dry out they can be crunched into tiny chips. Sprinkle a couple of handfuls in the area where you want to attract fish. The chips slowly flutter down, flashing like jewels. To the fish's eye it looks like a school of baitfish. Lake trout fishermen have known about this neat trick for ages, and there is no reason it should not work on other species as well.

CHUMMING WITH BEETLES

One Eastern newspaper recently prefaced a featured article with the heading, "All-Out Beetle Battle." The news article gave an account of the concern shown by people in the U.S. Department of Agriculture, jet airline personnel and the agricultural industry of California, that Japanese beetles, abundant in the East, might migrate by airplane to the West Coast.

These beetles, devastating to many farm crops, entered the United States as grubs in balled roots of imported Asian nursery stock. By 1952 the Japanese beetle was widely distributed along the Atlantic seaboard ranging from Massachusetts to South Carolina and scattered points in adjoining states. It devoured farm crops everywhere.

Bronze and green in color and the size of a large pea, the beetle spends most of its time as a small white grub in the soil where it subsists on roots of various plants. By early July grubs have pupated into adults and emerge from the ground in swarms. It is during July that Japanese beetles hold special significance to fishermen as bait for various fish. Trout, river smallmouth bass and panfish feed heavily on those wind blown into streams and ponds.

One veteran angler skilled at using beetle baits explained his technique. Gathering jarfuls of beetles, he uses them to chum fish into feeding. Beetles are removed singly from the jars and tossed into currents where they are carried over fish holding areas. Only a relatively few beetles struggling on the surface are needed to get fish hopping! Then the angler false casts a bushy bivisible and drops the feathered tie in the midst of the rises. Fish literally fight for his imitation beetle offering.

PORKRIND FORK

To get porkrind out of a jar cleanly, use one of those plastic stirrers you get when you buy coffee in a fast food restaurant. It's just the right size for poking around in a small liquid-filled jar.

Use the stirrer to isolate a single strip of rind. Then, use it again to work the strip up the side and to the top. No more using your fingers and spilling salty preserving liquid all over your tacklebox, or using your knife and risk getting it rusty.

To increase the effectiveness of the stirrer, cut a quarter-inch deep notch into the spoon end with a three-cornered file.

HOPPER SACK

Grasshoppers make good bait for a variety of gamefish, but the frisky insects soon die if kept in a bottle or can. An ideal container is a discarded stocking, which provides good ventilation and cooling. A stocking takes little room in a fishing vest and can be tied to your belt when in use.

JUGGED MINNOWS

When that big picnic jug has served its last outing, turn it into a minnow bucket. The narrow top prevents the bait from jumping out and minimizes water spillage. It keeps the water cooler longer in the summer and prevents freezing in the winter. It's also quiet, doesn't tip easily, and will last almost indefinitely. With all these advantages you might not want to wait until yours gets old to change its assignment.

DISGUSTING BUT..

Crickets, grasshoppers, nightcrawlers and wax worms are all considered dynamite panfish baits by various angling authorities. One unlikely fish enticer that is not so often mentioned in polite angling literature, however, just may be the best of them all. The bait is the larval form of a fly—in other words, the lowly maggot.

Maggots are not newcomers to fishing, having been used by no less an authority than Izaak Walton. Some anglers go so far as to breed and nurture the petite squirmers themselves.

While some anglers relish the bait for panfish, others wouldn't consider using it. Ohio fishermen have found that maggots are extremely productive and have been using the wiggly little tempters for years with success. In fact, one flytier, Jim Eskridge of Rootstown, Ohio, even ties a very popular imitation maggot fly pattern that quickly sells out at a local tackleshop.

As far as most maggot users are concerned, not just any old garbage-can inhabitant will do the trick. The larval flies they use are specially bred and of a larger size than normal household pests.

Flyfishermen have found that tipping a fly with a maggot greatly enhances the lure's attractiveness to the fish they seek. A further bonus is the maggot's tough and durable skin.

UNSCENT YOUR BAIT

Stashed in an accessible corner of my boat is a water and anise oil solution that has helped me land more fish. I have inaugurated a strict code aboard my boat, and it is "all lures must be sloshed around the solution bucket before they hit the water." Much like the anise oil trick spawn anglers use for their spawn flavoring, I feel the water and oil solution washes any unattractive odors from my lures and baits.

PROPER CRAWLER CARE

One of the live baits most widely used by fishermen is the night crawler. It is also one of the most vulnerable to warm temperatures. Most fishermen, whether they buy or pick up their own night crawlers, do not know how to keep them alive and wiggling.

The most important factor in crawler care is temperature. Who hasn't had the experience of a "ripe" can of worms at the end of a hot day's fishing. Crawlers begin to die when the temperature reaches 55 to 60°F. If you can keep the temperature below this mark, you will keep your worms.

You can store your worms at home in any cool place you have handy. An old refrigerator works the best with the temperature setting turned as high as it will go. If you do not have a refrigerator at hand, put them in a cool corner of your basement. This will keep them cool for a number of days. Any bedding on the market, such as peat moss or ground newspaper, is all right. Make sure you add only enough water to barely make the mixture moist and not wet. Crawlers kept cool and in good bedding will last a year or more.

Keeping the crawlers cool does not end when on your fishing trip. Hot sun can wreak havoc on an exposed can of worms. The best container is a small Styrofoam bucket filled with ice water. Just add water, ice cubes and the number of worms you need for the day. The ice cold water keeps them alive and active. As opposed to popular belief, worms will not drown.

Another method is to use a container filled with bedding and a small bag of ice cubes to keep the worms cool.

So stay cool when storing or transporting your crawlers and leave the mess to the other guy.

Keep Ephemeroptera Cool

A small aquarium net and empty pill vials or film containers are great for collecting insects you want to photograph. But photographing a fresh, frisky mayfly can be difficult. Half an hour in the refrigerator, though, will cool any bug capers.

An interesting variation for color shots is to set up the camera and subject in a completely darkened room. Set the camera at the totally open shutter setting. Light is provided by passing a standard drop light around the subject.

Cardboard Bait Storage

Give ice-anglers their choice of baits and they'll scream for corn borers. These tiny worms are dynamite for taking winter panfish; they are tough and outlast similar baits on the hook. There's just one catch: Since the most productive time to harvest them from cornstalks is autumn, keeping them alive for the winter fishing season can be a problem. I have tried keeping them refrigerated in jars of shredded tissue paper, sand and cornmeal. Even storing them in a jar of sectioned cornstalks resulted in a 30 to 40 percent mortality rate; the refrigerated cornstalks invariably developed mold.

Finally, by listening to the advice of an old-timer, I learned the secret of storing corn borers with nearly zero mortality.

Take a corrugated cardboard box and cut it into narrow, several-inch-long strips. Fill a jar with these strips, dump your corn borers in, cap it and pop it in a corner of the fridge. By first ice you'll find your little pets nestled deep in the tiny corrugations and sealed in light webs—dormant, plump and healthy. Hundreds can be stored this way in a pint jar.

When you go fishing, slip a couple of the cardboard strips into your bait container and use them as needed by simply peeling the corrugations back one at a time.

NIGHTCRAWLER DRAWER

The worm is indeed very clever, but he can be outsmarted. Gathering a batch for a fishing trip is easy if you use a little recipe called the "Nightcrawler Drawer."

Mix a spoonful of dry mustard in a cup of water. Pour this solution in worm holes under rocks, old boards and dirt mounds and the worms will quickly flee their homes. Be sure they are completely out of the holes before nabbing them.

KEEPING MINNOWS FRESH

Keeping minnows fresh for several days is sometimes a problem. Professional bait dealers offer these tips.

● Place about ten ice cubes in your bait bucket (preferably of plastic foam) when transporting minnows on a long drive. If the ice cubes are made with chlorinated tap water, keep them in a plastic bag—chlorine can kill minnows.

● Every time you dip for a minnow, replace the bucket lid immediately. This keeps the water cool and oxygenated. Warm water depletes oxygen.

● If the minnows swarm to the surface, the water probably needs changing. Refill only half the bucket each time—a full bucket of fresh water can shock the minnows and shorten the life span. When you add water to the bucket, don't let it increase or decrease the water temperature more than 10°F.

● If you carry fish home in a minnow bucket, wash the bucket afterward with baking soda. This removes bacteria-breeding slime which will consume oxygen that may be in the water.

HALF IS BETTER

Nightcrawlers are excellent trout bait, but sometimes they're too big a mouthful for the frying-pan-size many fishermen seek. If a whole nightcrawler is used, the fish will frequently snip off pieces and never get near the hook.

If you don't have small angleworms and are fishing small brooks or streams with crawlers, try using a half of one. String the head portion on the hook, head right up or over the hook eye. Leave about an inch of the worm to wiggle directly behind the hook. Let it drift downstream, using a light sinker or two. When the drift is complete, "troll" the bait back to you slowly. This frequently teases or provokes a trout into hitting. Use the tail portion in the same manner. Trout often find this soft, still-squirming section to their liking.

The worms go twice as far that way.

GATHER WINTER BAIT NOW

November is the traditional time for ice fishermen to start thinking about Coleman lanterns, miniature rods, ice creepers and such, but most don't worry about their bait needs. There are a few, however, who take advantage of bluebird days to gather tidbits for the hard-water quarry.

Goldenrod grubs are easy to come by. The fat galls on the now frost-browned stems harbor a creamy butterball of a grub that perch and bluegills find hard to resist once the ice is on. Great fields of the stuff can be found just about everywhere. Forget galls with holes—the birds beat you to them. Keep your catch in the refrigerator. To use, all you do is split the gall and remove the worm.

Abandoned wasp nests are another good bet for winter bait. With the adults in hibernation or deceased, collecting is easy whether it is on paper or mud dauber nest. Just break open the chambers, remove the grubs, and place them in a cottage cheese container with a little sawdust or oatmeal. Place the grubs in the refrigerator until it is time to go fishing.

Mousies, the traditional cold-weather winter panfish bait, are the last to be on the bait-shop chalkboard, but are probably abundant now. Prime locales for the get-your-own crowd are cattle barns and canning factories. The little guys with the micelike tails are fly larvae that live in sloppy, wet cattle manure, or in the residue left over from vegetable and fruit-canning processes.

Once permission is obtained, an old bait dealer's minnow net, or coal shovel with the center cut out and replaced with one-eighth-inch galvanized screen, is used to seine the larvae out of the wastes. Storage is the same as that of other larvae: Keep 'em cool.

Safety-pin Shrimp

Sand shrimp are about the best bait available for a lot of ocean fishing. They are a natural food for many bottom-feeding fish, and they have a strong scent that attracts even fish not accustomed to eating them.

But sand shrimp are fragile, nearly impossible to keep on a hook. Their shells and bodies are so soft that brief action from currents or waves knocks them off.

Mustad makes a safety-pin hook, No. 7904, designed especially to hold soft baits like sand shrimp. Use Size 6 for small shrimp, 4 for medium ones, and 2 for the largest. The pin of the hook should run the full length of the back of the bait, leaving the tail and pincers free to move. Some people use a few turns of lead wire, the kind used for weighting flies, to help hold the shrimp.

Getting good bait is only part of catching fish. Keeping the bait on the hook is just as important.

Salamanders, often called waterdogs, are a prime bass bait. Don't use a heavy sinker or it won't swim naturally. The best method is to use a very light spinning rod without any sinker at all.

FLOATING SPAWN SACKS

Many Great Lakes shore anglers now use an ingenious method of presenting spawn sacks when still-fishing for rainbow and brown trout.

While tying the fresh roe up in small squares of nylon, a few chips of Styrofoam are added—either in natural white or painted fluorescent red for increased visibility.

The buoyant bags float up off the bottom, anchored in position by either a small lead weight or a slip-sinker. This appears to offer cruising fish a better target to home in on.

The method is gaining favor with river anglers as well. By adjusting the amount of Styrofoam in proportion to the amount of lead weight used they are able to achieve almost neutral buoyancy between the two. This allows them to skim baits gently over rocky bottoms normally considered too risky to try.

Instead of waiting to work out the proper ratio on the lake or river bank, do it beforehand in a deep sink or bathtub.

It is then a simple matter to wrap each sack in a small piece of aluminum foil and mark it with a wax crayon to signify whether it is high or low buoyancy.

Convenient Bait

A fisherman is always ready to take advantage of a few hours of unexpected free time. He goes out to dig a few earthworms, but it is either too dry to too cold to find them. His favorite bait store is 30 minutes away. Fishing has now lost its appeal. This doesn't have to happen if you would keep the larvae of a moth on hand. These larvae are readily found in bait stores and commonly go by the name of wax worms. The bait has two major advantages. First, it is a dynamite panfish getter. It takes all species of sunfish as well as crappies and perch. Bass and walleyes have even been known to occasionally sample this bait when the larva was on an ice spoon. Second, this bait can be easily stored if it is handled in a proper manner.

Take a baby-food jar and punch several holes in its lid. Either paint the exterior of the jar black, or you can wrap the jar with electrical tape to prevent light from reaching the larvae. Store the jar at room temperature.

Fifty wax worms fit nicely in a baby-food jar and cost a little over a dollar. This low cost, coupled with ability to catch fish and ease of storage, make wax worms the bait of convenience.

GOURMET BAIT

Uncooked fresh or frozen shrimp tails make great trout and steelhead bait (where legal). Many anglers simply peel off the shell and impale the faintly pink flesh on a single hook. Another method involves coloring peeled tails in a bath of food dye. Red and orange are the most productive colors, but yellow and green also work.

Shrimp flesh decomposes rapidly when not refrigerated, but by packing the tails in a container filled with borax spoilage is reduced greatly. The granular powder also sweetens the smell while toughening the flesh with its well-known curing effect.

Although the use of these high-priced crustaceans may seem dollar-foolish in these inflationary times you will be surprised at how little is actually required in the course of a days fishing. When compared to the price of nightcrawlers or roe the cost is actually competitive.

BRIDGE FOR CRAYFISH

You've got to look under aquatic rocks to find crayfish for bait, since this crustacean's defense is to scurry backwards under a rock. However, bait hunters can quickly make a mess of crayfish habitat by overturning all the best hiding spots, leaving survivors prey to smallmouth bass.

Simply by placing a flat rock atop two others to form a small bridge, you can create a crayfish retreat. Man-made bridges might even make it easier to find and catch more crayfish the next time you want bait.

OXYGEN FOR MINNOWS

Laboratory tests conducted by fish culturists in recent years have demonstrated that common household hydrogen-peroxide can be used safely to provide oxygen for small fish. Hydrogen-peroxide releases oxygen by decomposition when it is added to water.

In one test, 25 fry (2cm long) were put into each of two one-quart bottles of water. Then, during a three-day period, 12 drops of hydrogen-peroxide were added to one bottle, and none to the other. The result; 100 percent of the treated fry survived and 100 percent of the untreated fry perished.

In another test, 50 fry were kept in a one-quart bottle and two drops of hydrogen-peroxide were added to the water every four hours. In three days, 86 percent of the fry were still alive and well.

Researchers tested this idea in the hopes of using it to provide small hatchery fish with oxygen during transportation periods. Anglers who use live minnows for bait might also want to experiment with the idea. To be safe, start off by adding only very small amounts of hydrogen-peroxide to a minnow bucket. And remember that it takes about 600 drops of the size used by the researchers to make one fluid ounce. Also, keep in mind that water temperature is very important to minnow survival. Keep the water in a minnow bucket fresh and cool.

Lively Shiners

Shiners are among a trout's favorite meals, but keeping the little fish alive during a long drive to a fishing spot can be a problem. Using an ordinary plastic drinking straw, blow bubbles through the water in the shiner bucket at roughly 15-minute intervals. It will keep the shiners alive and active for as long as eight hours, until you reach fast-running water to place them in.

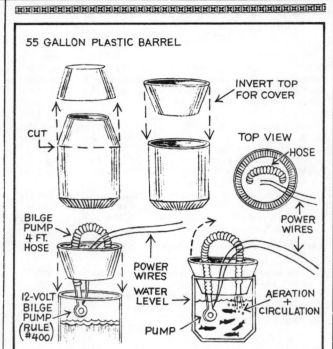

55 GALLON PLASTIC BARREL — INVERT TOP FOR COVER — CUT — TOP VIEW — HOSE — BILGE PUMP 4 FT. HOSE — POWER WIRES — POWER WIRES — WATER LEVEL — 12-VOLT BILGE PUMP (RULE #400) — PUMP — AERATION + CIRCULATION

Instant Live-Bait Tank

For the angler who wants lively baitfish, a storage tank with aeration is mandatory. Bait-keeping systems cost from $100 to $200, but you can make one for less than $35.

Obtain a plastic 55-gallon barrel and wash the interior thoroughly. With a standard carpenter's handsaw, cut the top third of the barrel off, following the molded seam. Get about four feet of flexible bilge-pump hose and a Rule 400 12-volt pump or equivalent. Cut two holes in the top section of the barrel just big enough so the hose will fit snugly, and insert the hose ends. Suspend the pump 18 inches from the bottom of the barrel. Insert the "outflow" flush, leaving space for the pumped water to spill and aerate as it circulates. Also, drill two small holes in the cover to accommodate the power wires.

Power for the pump can be provided by either a 12-volt battery, or the pump can be attached to a power-winch cable.

RECYCLE WORMS

Don't throw away those plastic crawlers that have been chewed to pieces by hungry bass. The pieces can still be useful for catching more fish.

Keep a small plastic bag in your tacklebox for storing pieces of mangled worms. Next time you are out after panfish, sort through this collection. Sometimes a piece of brightly colored worm is just the thing for finicky panfish. Attach it to a hook or jig. With a little practice, you can turn pieces of worms into lures that panfish can't resist.

On Freezing Bait

Frozen bait is quite convenient, but it's of no value if it turns to mush when thawed. This can be avoided by freezing convenient amounts in water. I have found that plastic Ziploc food-storage bags work best. These are sturdier than most sandwich bags and will hold just the right amount of bait. By storing bait in smaller quantities, you never have to thaw out more than you need, and the water keeps it firm and fresh-looking.

GIVE FISH SOMETHING DIFFERENT

You can lead a fish to water, but you can't always make a bass or trout swallow it.

When a worm is wriggling on bottom, about two inches from a fish's mouth, and the fish ignores the bait, try something else.

Look around for other natural bait, native to the area you're fishing, and you may come across what the fish will take.

Lures, worms, minnows, frogs, crayfish and grasshoppers—all effective baits at times—failed in turn to interest a school of smallmouth bass in a clear Quebec stream. Yet a single hellgrammite, found under a streamside log, took a six-bass limit as fast as they could be taken off the hook. When only the bug's tiny head remained on the hook, the final two bass never hesitated in striking it.

Similarly, in an Ontario trout stream flowing into northern Lake Huron, arm-length rainbow trout ignored lures, minnows and worms, but a soft-shelled crayfish, caught beneath stream stones, produced three instant strikes. It seemed these trout simply wanted a stream tidbit after months in the big lake. The next day it might be minnows or worms.

So when fish swim so close to your bait you'd swear they were blind, change your bait and possibly change your fishing luck.

Easy Minnows

Gary Nichols of Klamath Falls, Oregon, doesn't need a net or seine to catch minnows. In a shallow irrigation canal or ditch he submerges a five-gallon bucket on its side and places a sparse tumbleweed in the opening. Then he wades around, frightening minnows so they swim into the weed to hide. Nichols quickly lifts the bucket from the water, and he has his bait. Several bucket sets get him enough minnows to last a year.

NO-SWEAT GRASSHOPPERS

It isn't necessary to work up a sweat or risk heat exhaustion chasing around on a hot summer day to collect a supply of grasshoppers for a day's fishing. Here are a couple of cool alternatives:

Grasshoppers are least active during the coolest part of the day. At dawn, you'll find them clinging to the grasses and plants where they spent the night. Go after them at first light. The best mornings are those when a light jacket or down vest is needed for comfort.

If it's one of those nights when it just won't cool down, get a camp blanket or a piece of burlap about the same size, walk into a meadow and lay the cloth flat on the ground. Walk away about 75 to 100 feet and circle back from a different direction. The hoppers will jump ahead of you, and some will land on the rough cloth, where the spurs on their rear legs will catch. The first two or three passes are the most productive.

Not all species of grasshoppers are found in every meadow. When possible, do your collecting next to the water you'll be fishing so you will be presenting the fish with the kind they're used to eating.

ATTRACT MORE MINNOWS

If you are not having much success in enticing minnows into your trap, try this: Put some cat food in the middle of a six-inch square of cheesecloth, fold up the corners and tie into a small sac. Suspend the bait bag inside of your minnow trap with a paper clip or small piece of wire.

The cheesecloth will prevent your bait from washing away yet will allow small amounts of cat food to disperse through the water, attracting the minnows into the trap.

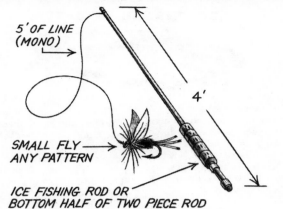

5' OF LINE (MONO)

SMALL FLY ANY PATTERN

4'

ICE FISHING ROD OR BOTTOM HALF OF TWO PIECE ROD

THE FROGGER

Catching a bass or pike on a live frog often creates explosive fishing action.

Here is an inexpensive method for catching frogs that is fun and easy to do. You will need a small artificial fly, five feet of monofilament line, and a four-foot stick (an icefishing rod works well). Put this outfit together as illustrated.

To catch a frog just dangle the fly an inch or two in front of his nose. When he grabs it, set the hook. Instead of spooking nearby frogs, this method draws them in closer.

Look for hoppers around lily pads, logs and weedy shores. Sneak up slowly from behind.

Keep the frogs in a minnow bucket with an inch or so of water and out of the sun.

Fish frogs on a No. 5/0 weedless hook (hooked through the lips). Cast one out into heavy cover, such as in lily pads, and let it hop around.

Frogs are protected in some states (such as the leopard frog in Wisconsin). Find out what the rules are.

FRESHER SHRIMP

Dead shrimp will catch plenty of fish, but the bait is more effective when alive and kicking. To keep them as productive as possible, says veteran Texas fishing guide Forrest West, "keep them uncrowded, well aerated and cool."

West uses an ice chest as a shrimp box. It has a strong lid that can double as a seat, a plug for easy draining, and is well insulated to help ward off the bait-killing heat.

West puts no more than a quart of live shrimp in a 48-quart ice chest. He uses a commercial aerator designed to fit his ice chest.

Many anglers use ice to keep shrimp cool, but in hot weather the ice melts, dilutes the water's salinity and kills the delicate crustaceans as surely as does the heat. West

solves the problem by freezing water in small plastic bottles with secure tops, which can't contaminate the baitbox's salinity. As the bait water warms, he replaces it with another plastic bottle of frozen water.

Some days, even a live shrimp fails to tempt fish. That's when another Texas fishing guide, J. W. Bones, tries his secret trick—brightly colored shrimp.

"I dye the shrimp with food coloring," Bones says. "It doesn't seem to hurt the shrimp—food coloring is an edible substance. Just put some in the baitbox. Red and green have been good colors for me. You'd be surprised how a brightly colored shrimp will turn fish on when they don't seem interested in normal shrimp."

More on Shrimp

Most coastal area fishermen frequently use shrimp for bait, but many anglers living inland are not aware that it is one of the best baits available for panfish and catfish.

Although fresh shrimp is best, frozen shrimp from the supermarket, or even canned shrimp, work quite well.

Shrimp stays on the hook better if peeled. For panfish, shrimp should be sliced crosswise in about quarter-inch segments. Don't just tear off a piece, as the ragged ends make it easier for fish to steal it off the hook.

For catfish, use whole peeled shrimp, with the hook run lengthwise through the bait.

Unused shrimp should be frozen in a container of water to prevent drying out. Soaking shrimp in salt water makes them tougher, but it has a tendency to kill their odor and make them less attractive to fish.

WORM FARM

Discarded felt (not rubber or plastic) carpet padding can be turned into a worm farm. Ir an area not illuminated b lights turn over the soil as one would for a garden. Rake fine and smooth. Cover with the rug padding. Keep well watered, but not flooded, with a sprinkler. After several days, when dark, carefully lift off the wet padding. There will be gobs of nightcrawlers and dew worms on the ground. Replace pad and keep wet for your next fishing trip. The padding will prevent weeds from growing.

GREAT BAIT

Many saltwater fishermen use shrimp and clams as bait with great results. These same baits are also excellent when used in fresh water, however, for big bluegills, crappies, catfish and even bass. Try them and see.

★

Despite inflation, rods and reels of good quality today cost less than they did 25 years ago.

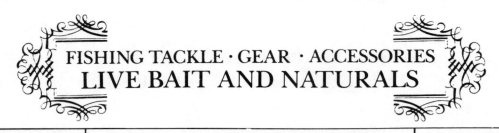
YEAR-ROUND WORMS

"The steelhead are hitting a nightcrawler about 16 inches behind a Colorado Spinner drifted along the bottom! Bring your worms!" calls your frantic fishing friend. But all your worms have gone south for the season. You can prevent this fishing tragedy with an old chest-type freezer. Bury it in the ground, and you'll have generations of worms at minimal expense.

Bury the chest—scrounged from a junkyard or old-appliance center—in your backyard or other convenient place. Drill air holes in the lid. To prevent freezing during the coldest weather, equip the chest with an electric light bulb on a thermostat set between 34 and 36°F; or use a heat tape plug that comes on automatically.

Fill the chest with worms, good earth and peat moss mixed together. Keep the earth moist with periodic watering.

Feed your worms occasionally with coffee grounds, apple and potato peelings and other kitchen discards.

★

A lively minnow will attract the attention of a passing fish far better than a lethargic one. To make your minnows livelier clip off the tail fin. The minnow has to work much harder to maintain equilibrium, thus is more active.

WORM CARE

When mixing worm bedding, it is a good idea to let the mixture stand for 24 hours before adding nightcrawlers. That's because the bedding contains organic compounds that give off heat that can be lethal to your garden hackles.

Once the 24-hour period is past, place your worms on top of the bedding and let stand overnight. The healthy crawlers will find their way into the bedding, while unhealthy and damaged worms will remain on the surface and can be easily picked-off.

DOUGHBALL RECIPES

The most important thing to remember about any doughball recipe is that the dough must be firm and hold together well while being fished. The following recipes are from the U.S. Fish and Wildlife Service:

½ cup plain flour
½ cup plain cornmeal
a little salt
enough water to form a smooth working dough
(cotton is sometimes added to provide strength and consistency)

Mix the ingredients together and drop the dough into boiling water for 20 minutes. When the dough has cooled, work it into the desired shape.

Grated cheese, ground meat or cottonseed meal can also be added before boiling.

2 cups flour
3 cups white cornmeal
1 cup sugar
2 egg whites
1 cup cold water
1 small box anise seed
1 kettle boiling water
1 small sugar or flour sack

Thoroughly sift the flour, cornmeal and sugar together in a large mixing bowl. Beat the eggs and cold water together in a separate bowl until a smooth mixture is obtained. Then add the anise seed and stir. Combine the two mixtures and stir to an even consistency. Add a bit of flour, cornmeal or water as needed to obtain a stiff dough.

Flatten the mass until it is about 1½ inches thick. Place the dough into the cloth sack and tie the sack closed with string. Carefully lower the sack into boiling water. Cook for three minutes on one side, then turn and cook the other side for three minutes. Lower the fire and let the dough simmer for 15 minutes.

Remove the dough from the sack and allow it to cool on a piece of paper. Work the dough until you can roll it into a ball. Place the ball back into the sack, and store.

The bait keeps indefinitely in the refrigerator—the older the better. If the dough becomes dry, a little moisture on the fingers will work it back to consistency.

TROUT TRICK

Trout will be fighting over your bait if you dip a little piece of sponge in sardine oil and hook it on with whatever lure you are using. This works for any trout, any lake, winter or summer.

★

No one can show you the best fishing spots in any public lake as well as a guide who fishes it every day possible. However, there are good and bad guides. Ask around before you hire one, then listen to him because he's your best teacher.

CATCH BAIT SHAD

There is no doubt about it: Live shad catch trophy bass. These baitfish are usually abundant in most waters, so it makes sense to catch your own shad wherever legal and practical rather than pay the bait-shops.

Simply place a few vanilla wafers or some dry dog food into a glass-type minnow trap and submerge it along the bank of a lake or river known to contain shad. After a few hours you should have enough shad for a day's fishing.

SECONDHAND BAIT

Quite by accident, Graham Miller of Brady, Texas, discovered a rather exotic catfish bait. It was a warm fall day, the kind that's perfect for combination hunting and fishing expeditions. The Miller clan was all set for a catfish outing, but they were having trouble locating enough suitable bait.

When Graham used a small-caliber rifle to bag a hefty Rio Grande-strain Texas gobbler (fall turkey season in Texas runs concurrent with deer season), he noted that the bird's crop was bulging with food. His exploratory surgery revealed that the gobbler had been feasting on grasshoppers.

"I couldn't believe how many hoppers were in that gobbler's crop," Miller recalls. "Putting them into a one-pound coffee can would have required some careful packing."

"The grasshoppers were coated with predigestive juices from the turkey's crop. They were kind of gummy, and I figured you could put several on a fishhook and they might stay on pretty good. The upshot is I've never used more effective bait for channel cats."

WORM TIPS

1. Wash your hands before handling worms.

2. Cool the bedding in your container to 50°F. or lower before adding nightcrawlers. Make sure there is ventilation.

3. Use a thermometer frequently to check the temperature of the bedding.

4. Take only the number of worms you will need. Don't overcrowd your portable container.

5. Remove sick or injured worms from the container.

6. Cushion the container from vibration while transporting it.

7. Hook the worms through their heads so that they look natural to the fish.

STINK LURES

Commercial salmon fishermen on the Oregon coast sometimes use a trick to catch fish that may have application for the sportfisherman.

To mask the human scent on artificial baits, and to attract fish, a mixture of condensed milk, rock salt, and ground herring or anchovies is applied to lures.

Spoons, plugs, and other lures are dipped in the mixture before being placed in the water. The ring of grease which forms on the inside of the container holding the mixture is rubbed into streamer flies or it is applied to lures.

To prepare the scent, pour three cups of rock salt into a quart of water and stir thoroughly. Next, mash eight or ten herring and mix them in the solution. Add two 13-ounce cans of condensed milk and mix it with the other ingredients. The solution is then ready to use, and it will keep well without refrigeration.

SPRING YOUR BAIT

Fishermen often have a problem keeping soft baits on the hook. It is frustrating to hear the plop that follows a cast—the sound of the hook going one way and the bait another.

There is a solution for this problem. Take a ballpoint pen apart and save the spring. It is just the right size to run over the barb of the hook and up to the shank. The coils of the spring provide something to press the soft bait into, thus keeping it on during casts.

Doggone Good Bluegill Bait

Poke holes in a dog food can and attach it to an overhanging limb above the water. After flies have done their work, maggots will begin to drop off the can and into the water. Then you'll be able to load up on bluegills at that spot.

WORM KILLER

When traveling to a favorite fishing spot, cushion your worm container to reduce vibration and shock. Vibration can kill worms, and uneven distribution in the container makes them nervous, which causes shock. Solve the problem by placing the worm container on the car seat, a boat cushion, or on anything that will absorb the vibrations.

MINNOW NET KINK

Increase the efficiency of your minnow net by putting a bend in it, as shown. Just turn the wire handle down 90 degrees, then push the net back on line. The forward-positioned net makes it much easier to trap a baitfish against the inside of an open-top bucket.

SMORGASBORD BAIT

If you've offered the fish several kinds of bait and they won't bite, try a smorgasbord. Saltwater anglers use this trick often. The Eastern Shore Sandwich is a favorite black drum bait composed of half a crab and a clam strapped with a rubber band to a large hook. A popular combination bait for flounder and sea trout consists of a thin tapered strip of squid and a live minnow.

It works in fresh water too, with a minnow and worm on a single hook. Other good combinations include crayfish and worms, hellgrammites and minnows, crickets and grasshoppers, crickets and worms, and nymphs and worms.

Breaded Bait

When freezing minnows in a plastic bag, roll them in cornmeal first. This enables you to break them apart easily without thawing a whole bag for just one or two minnows for bait.

WALNUT WORMS

Worms and night crawlers are probably the country's most popular fishing bait, but digging for worms is still a chore. Here's an easy way to get those worms out of the ground without digging.

Gather a few handfuls of walnut shells and let them soak in a bucket of water for a day or two. Then select a spot known to contain worms and pour the walnut solution on the spot. The mild mixture irritates the worms' bodies, forcing them to the surface of the soil where they can easily be picked up by hand. (Be sure to rinse them with clean water immediately.)

GIVE BAITS A CLIP JOB

Sometimes large, frisky live baits—such as chubs in fresh water or mackerel in salt water—can present bait-control problems to fishermen. Big baits may swim too strongly, too fast or, in the case of bottom fishing, may drag terminal gear into snags.

An easy way to decrease the speed of a large bait is to clip the lobe tips off its tail. Generally, cutting off one-quarter to one-third of each tail lobe will significantly slow the swimming speed of the bait and still allow an enticing action.

At times, this little trick can even produce *more* strikes, because the bait acts like a cripple, working harder to keep swimming.

TASTY TRAP

Popcorn is perfect for baiting minnow traps. It floats for a long time and eliminates that slimy, soggy mess that bread becomes.

Leeches for Bait

Leeches make a fine bait because they never seem to quit moving and squirming on the hook. The problem is to get enough leeches with which to tempt fish. Here is a simple and effective way: Place a soup bone inside a large fruit or tomato juice can, the top of which has been removed. Set the can with open end up about an inch under the surface of the water known to harbor leeches. They will congregate on the bone and are easy to pick off. A piece of beef or pork liver may also be used. Place the liver in the can and set a stone on it to keep it from floating away. Do not set it in fast water as leeches prefer little or no water movement.

Strawberry Carp Bait

There is no doubt that the lowly carp is a long way from being a popular fish in this country. But those who like to catch and eat carp are a very avid group. If you have ever hooked onto a big one, you know what a battle and what a thrill a carp can give.

Here's a recipe for carp bait that's easy to make.

2 cups cornmeal
3 tbsp. sugar
½ tsp. salt
1 pkg. strawberry gelatin
2 cups water
1 tbsp. vanilla

Mix together the dry ingredients, then add the water and vanilla. Stir well, until the gelatin is dissolved.

Cook over a low to medium flame, stirring constantly, until the mixture is quite stiff. Form into balls. Then all you have to do is press a ball of carp bait onto a hook and go fishing.

Limnology is the study of lake and pond life.

FISHING BOATS
AND
EQUIPMENT

FISHING BOATS AND EQUIPMENT

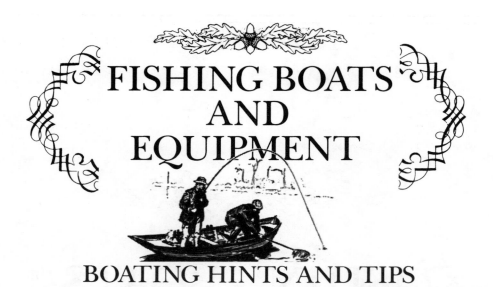

BOATING HINTS AND TIPS

BOAT FLAGGER

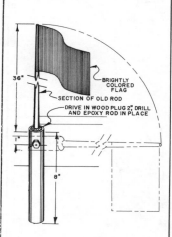

36"

BRIGHTLY COLORED FLAG

SECTION OF OLD ROD

DRIVE IN WOOD PLUG 2". DRILL AND EPOXY ROD IN PLACE

1"

8"

Anyone who has ever backed a boat trailer onto a launch ramp to pick up a boat knows that at times it can be difficult. When a trailer is backed down the ramp at many launch sites it disappears—at a certain angle on the ramp the back of the car blocks it from view. When the driver cannot see, it is easy for the trailer to go in the wrong direction.

A simple remedy for this dilemma is to mount on the trailer a tilting flag pole and brightly colored flag that the driver can see when the trailer disappears. The flag pole automatically tilts out of the way when the boat is cranked onto the trailer and springs back up when the boat is launched.

An effective and rugged tilting flag pole can be made with a minimum of tools, material, and expense by following the accompanying drawing.

RULES TO LIVE BY

There are a dozen boating rules that should never be broken, according to the Coast Guard:

1) Learn how to swim.
2) Don't overload—the more people, the more risk.
3) Each passenger should wear an approved life jacket; check the law.
4) Position boaters carefully to prevent falls.
5) Know proper first aid. Carry a first-aid kit.
6) Carry all required safety equipment such as fire extinguishers, bailing bucket, magnetic compass (know how to read it).
7) Obey all boating regulations such as courtesy to other boaters. Don't cut in front of other boats. Accidents are caused by clowning and by drinking.
8) Don't smoke while refueling.
9) Stay out of swim areas.
10) Don't overpower.
11) Don't second-guess the weather. If it looks bad,

head for shore fast.
12) Don't make high-speed turns.

A Basic Skills course is suggested for all boat owners. Call the Coast Guard Auxiliary for a listing of classes.
The following safety tips will help ensure a fun day:

● Check with the harbormaster for weather near port *and* destination. Leave word of your destination and time of return.
● If the boat is small (outboard), try to travel in pairs. The buddy system can save you in case of trouble.
● If your boat overturns, *stay with it.* Your chances of pickup are better staying with the more visible boat.
● Learn to read the wind. A wind of 8 to 12 knots indicates a nice day. From 12 to 15 knots, cold and wet; from 15 to 20 knots, rough seas; more than 20 knots is considered dangerous. If whitecaps are building, the wind is 12 to 15 knots.

HUB GREASE

If you ask your mechanic to install grease fittings in the dust caps on your boat trailer hubs, you'll be able to fill the bearings and hub centers with grease. It's the simplest way to keep water from washing away bearing grease while launching and shouldn't cost more than a few dollars, grease and all.

FLAT BOTTOM IN A PICKUP

A square-bow, flat-bottom johnboat can be carried in the bed of a pickup truck with the tailgate down, but loading and unloading the boat can wreak havoc on your paint job. Movement of the boat in transit can scratch the paint, too. To prevent this, all you need is a length of heavy sheet plastic as wide as your johnboat and about two feet longer. Put one end of the plastic on the tailgate, allowing enough at the front to overlap the bow, then rest the bow on the sheet. Pull the front flap of plastic up over the bow, leaving the greater length hanging down and trailing on the ground. Keep the weight of the boat on the bow and push the boat into the truck. It will slide in easily, pulling the plastic with it. Push the boat all the way to the front of the bed—the flap of plastic over the bow will help protect the front wall. Then secure both sides of the stern to the truck with heavy rubber tie-downs or ropes. The boat will slide out as easily as it went in, usually pulling the plastic sheet back out.

Outboard Fuel

Most outboard motor breakdowns are caused by avoidable fuel problems. Never save outboard fuel from one season to the next—gasoline degrades with time. Always disconnect the fuel line and run the outboard "dry" before taking it from the water. Adding fuel conditioner (sold by the major outboard companies) to the last tankful of the season will prevent any remaining gasoline from damaging the motor.

CHILDREN'S LIFE JACKETS

A life jacket, like an extra paddle or a landing net, is rarely appreciated unless needed.

For children weighing less than 30 pounds, a Type II Personal Flotation Device (PFD) is recommended. Designed to keep the child floating upright, leaning backward slightly with head above the water, the life vest should fit properly and be worn at all times. The Kindergaard Life Vest, developed for infants and small children, features an aquafoam collar that holds the head above water more effectively than other PFDs. The inner-tube-type collar eliminates the need for crotch straps.

The effectiveness of any PFD depends largely on the way parents prepare the youngster for the unexpected. Have a practice drill. The child should float in shallow water while wearing the vest. Most children weighing less than 50 pounds on land weigh seven pounds or more in water and need an equivalent buoyancy aid.

Because of the weight distribution of children and their tendency to panic if capsized, parents should train the child to behave calmly during make-believe rescue. A life line of three to four feet attached around the waists of mother and child can add an extra measure of safety and security.

As a child grows, body weight distribution and buoyancy requirements change. Prior to each boating season, test the support of life vests. Make a game of holding hands and assuming the fetal position as an exercise in conserving body heat and maintaining confidence in water.

•

When choosing a canoe or boat paddle remember lightness is okay if it has stiffness, too. If a paddle is too flexible it loses efficiency.

Propeller Protector

Propeller protectors are available from some manufacturers and are well worth the investment. However, some boaters who run their craft on rivers where the bottoms are strewn with rocks and debris fashion their own propeller protectors from pitchforks.

Bracketry is formed to fit around the outboard's lower housing and welded to the pitchfork. The complete unit is installed by bolting the brackets together and around the drive housing. This rig is easy to remove and reinstall as desired.

BOAT-HOLE PATCH

Last year I discovered something to patch those tiny holes that mysteriously present themselves in my aluminum fishing boat. To cover them, I squirt hot thermal glue into the hole and spread it out on both sides of the surrounding surface. It has worked extremely well and takes just a few seconds to apply. The surfaces and hole must be completely dry, and the hot glue spread out evenly and thinly to about the size of a silver dollar over and around the hole.

END SHEAR-PIN PROBLEMS

Ever shear a pin on your outboard motor and then frantically discover the spare was in another tacklebox back home?

Here's a simple solution that will end shear-pin frustrations forever. Tape three or four spare pins on the inside cover of the outboard motor using heavy-gauge nylon or duct tape that won't soften and unstick. One caution: be sure and tape spare shear pins where they won't fall into the flywheel or other moving parts. On my Evinrude 4-horse outboard, the best place is on the lower right rear corner, but there is ample room within the head cover of all popular make outboard engines.

You can go a step further and tape spare cotter pins and a propeller nut inside the head cover. This should take care of any accidental dropping of other key parts while changing the shear pin.

ANCHOR ROPE DEPTH INDICATOR

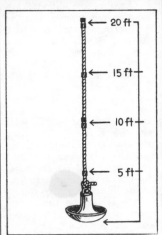

My depthfinder is far from sophisticated, but it gets the job done and is very inexpensive.

With the aid of two felt-tipped markers (red and black) I marked my anchor rope as follows: A single red mark around the rope at five feet, a red and black mark at 10 feet, a single red mark at 15 feet, two black marks at 20 feet, a single red and two black marks at 25 feet and three black marks at 30. Use the color code red for every five feet and multiples of black for 10 feet.

I can feel the anchor touch bottom, and while the line is taut I can get my depth reading.

THWART BOAT HEISTS

The increase in condominium and townhouse homes is causing an increase in boat and trailer thefts. Local police departments say anglers and sailors are forced to park their boats, temporarily or permanently, in front of the condo complexes because of a shortage of garage or storage facilities. Nighttime boat heists are the result.

Police and insurance agencies suggest that you remove one of the trailer wheels and block the trailer level. This tactic definitely slows up or discourages would-be thieves. If you're on the road, the blocking procedure is good insurance when bunking overnight in a motel.

River Rafting

Contrary to traditional rowboat technique, river-runners row facing forward, bow first, looking downstream to see any obstacles the river presents.

The basic *push stroke* (pushing forward on the oars) is used only for easy maneuvers by rafters, although it's a favorite of hard-shell boats that move faster. For quick response and making speed in a raft, use the *power stroke*: pull backward hard on the oars, with the raft angled stern first in the direction you're going.

A raft can be turned by pushing or pulling on one oar, but for quick, sure pivoting use the *double-oar turn*: to spin the raft left, pull hard on the left oar while you push on the right. Reverse for a right turn.

Beginning oarsmen should test rowing skills on lakes first, to develop the fundamentals and gain confidence. Then move on to easy streams with sluggish currents as you become adept at maneuvering the raft or driftboat forward through flat water and riffles, then back and forth across the river (*ferrying*). Gradually move to rougher rivers. A good way to learn is to follow an experienced oarsman, matching the *line* he sets stroke for stroke.

With a good boat and a season of practice, you can escape the limitations of bank-plunking to explore new, otherwise inaccessible backcountry.

Cushioned Oar Grips

Oar handles become rough and hard on the hands after being exposed to the elements for several seasons. To avoid this problem, cut lengths from a discarded bicycle inner tube and slip them over the oar handles. This not only provides a smooth surface but also cushions the grips. If an old bicycle inner tube isn't readily available to you, stop in at a local bike shop.

Boat Polish Saves Energy

Costly energy can be saved by polishing exterior surfaces of aluminum and fiberglass boats. Polished surfaces slip through water with less resistance than those that are pitted and corroded. Hence gas and electric motors can push boats faster with less fuel consumption.

Check the exterior, particularly the bottom of your boat, annually. If corroded, pitted and rough to your touch, use steel wool, followed by an application of aluminum polish to remove all corrosion. A fresh coat of resin applied on the underside of fiberglass boats makes them "slippery" and helps to save fuel.

SILENT ANCHOR PULLEY

A simple anchor pulley mounted to the bow or stern of a boat makes raising and lowering the anchor considerably easier. The only problem with such devices is that they usually squeak and clatter, thus alerting any nearby fish or wildfowl to your presence. Even when periodically lubricated, they still fall short of being totally silent.

There is a practical and economical alternative. You need a large U-bolt, a few nuts and washers and an old-style glass or porcelain fencepost insulator (there are still many of these old insulators lying around most farms).

Slip the insulator on a U-bolt, drill a couple of holes to accommodate the bolt, and tighten it to the mounting surface. (The insulator is not meant to spin—it should remain stationary.) The anchor rope will slide freely in the insulator's groove, and the anchor lowers and raises as effortlessly as with a pulley, especially once the rope is wet.

★

Many reservoirs around the nation have deep drawdowns, lowering pool levels as much as 50 feet. Strangely, you usually find fish at the same depths, during each season, as when the water is high.

Prop Gauge

Next time you buy a new motor, remove the propeller and make an impression of it in cement. Then should that prop get bent, you'll have a perfect mold for checking the repair job.

To make the impression, press the prop into a shallow pan filled with stiff mortar. Remove the prop, rinse and wait five minutes to see if the impression remains rigid and clear. If it sags, level the mixture and try again. When you're satisfied that you have a solid impression, set the pan aside and let the cement dry thoroughly.

When you do routine maintenance on your motor, remove the prop and test it in the mold. If it is bent, simply tap it back into shape right there in the mold. Use a mallet and tap lightly.

FUEL TANK PROTECTOR

To help keep an outboard motor fuel tank from rusting on the bottom, and also to prevent it from rattling on the bottom of your boat while underway, slit a piece of discarded garden hose along its length, fit it around the bottom lip of the tank, and trim the ends for a neat job.

PADDLE SAVVY

What's the best length for a canoe paddle? It's supposed to come to your chin, right? Forget it. All that palaver comes from the Maine Guide Era when all paddles were the long beavertail design. Today paddles come in more styles and shapes than you can imagine. So how do you fit one? Try different lengths until you get one where you can dip the entire blade in the water without having to lean out. If you are paddling with only half the blade, you have only half a paddle. If you're going for long cruises pick a paddle with a narrow blade—five or six inches. But if you like whitewater work, blades of eight and nine inches grip the water better.

Free Boat Bumpers

Don't throw away any bottle-type plastic containers, particularly the softer ones—they make great dock bumpers or fenders for small boats.

The bottles can be sealed tight by coating the cap with epoxy and screwing it back on, thus creating a positive seal.

The handles on the containers are great for attaching a short line to it and then to a small boat or the dock.

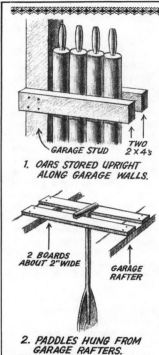

1. OARS STORED UPRIGHT ALONG GARAGE WALLS.

GARAGE STUD — TWO 2 x 4's

2 BOARDS ABOUT 2" WIDE — GARAGE RAFTER

2. PADDLES HUNG FROM GARAGE RAFTERS.

Oar Storage

To a boater few things are more frustrating than hearing a loud crunch when backing out of the garage and discovering you've just run over a brand-new $50 ash oar. Or to uncover a canoe paddle that has warped during the wet winter months.

Your equipment can be protected and kept neatly out of the way with an inexpensive storage system that can be put together in just minutes.

For oars, nail a short piece of 2×4 on both sides of the garage wall studs. Then stand each oar upright between these two support boards.

Paddles can be conveniently suspended from garage rafters by nailing two board scraps close enough together to insert a paddle handle sideways. Then rotate the paddle so that its T-shaped handle rests over the boards.

Safety does not require that you wear a life preserver all the time you are fishing, especially on a hot day. Put one on when you are running from place to place, or when you approach what might be a hazardous situation.

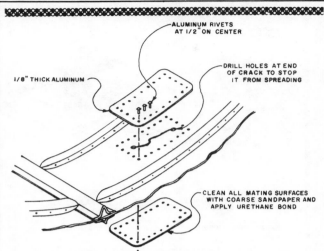

ALUMINUM RIVETS AT 1/2" ON CENTER

1/8" THICK ALUMINUM

DRILL HOLES AT END OF CRACK TO STOP IT FROM SPREADING

CLEAN ALL MATING SURFACES WITH COARSE SANDPAPER AND APPLY URETHANE BOND

Patching Aluminum Boats

A few years ago I purchased a two-person aluminum boat for $25. The "good deal" is the reason I called it a two-person boat: It took two to operate it—one to run the motor and the other to bail. But patching my bargain boat was no problem and took less than an hour. Now I could sell it for close to ten times what I paid for it.

The first step is to drill a hole at all ends of the split or crack—a one-quarter-inch hole is about the right size. Use a rubber mallet to reshape the damaged area.

Next cut two patches of equal size from a one-eighth-inch sheet of aluminum. They should extend at least one inch on all sides of the crack. Use a fine-toothed plywood blade on a radial arm saw or a table saw. Round off the corners of the patches and shape them to conform to the contour of the boat. Position the patches over and under the crack, and drill a hole at one end through them and the boat. Place a rivet through the hole. Drill a second hole at the opposite side of the patches and place a rivet through

them, too. With the two rivets holding the patches, drill additional holes around the edges on about one-half-inch centers.

Be sure the rivets are aluminum or they'll corrode. They should protrude through the inner patch, boat and outer patch about the same length as the diameter of the rivet.

Clean and rough up the mating surfaces of the patches and the boat with coarse sandpaper. Liberally apply Dow Corning Urethane Bond to the patches and the boat. (There are other adhesives that will work equally as well, but I have experience with Urethane Bond and know it will do the job and last a long time.)

Work fast, before the adhesive sets. Place the rivets through the holes and peen them over with a hammer. Hold a second hammer on the head of the rivet while flattening the other end to form a second head. Keep the head of the rivet even with the patch while peening. Do a good job, and the patched crack will never leak again.

SOAP STOPPER

To stop a small leak in a fuel line or tank, use a bar of hand soap. Just rub the bar back and forth over the leak. The hole

or crack will quickly fill with soap paste and stop the dripping. The plug will hold for several days, giving you plenty of time to make the necessary permanent repairs once you return home.

TRY A BAILING SPONGE

Cans may be fine for bailing boats, but if you want to keep your craft really dry use a sponge. It'll pick up that last little bit of water that you never seem to get with an old tin, no matter how you bend the lip. What's more, it'll hold just as much water as a can.

Ideal for the job is a piece of soft upholstery sponge at least 2x6x8 inches—or any size that's easy for you to wring out. I find new uses for it every time I step into a boat. It'll wipe a seat dry after a heavy dew or rainshower, clean the deck after boating a fish and, if nothing else, it sure softens up those hard bench seats you find in some boats. Try sitting on a tin can for comparison.

CARPET FOR BOATS

Carpet samples and swatches made of synthetic fibers, like those left over from recarpeting your home or purchased from carpet stores for nominal cost, are ideal for boating use. They serve well under tackleboxes and gas cans to reduce noise and protect the boat bottom. Shag or other fluffy carpeting helps flyrodders since it will hold the coils of flyline stripped onto a deck and prevent them from blowing around.

Carpet swatches can also serve canoeists as knee pads and they help deaden noise from an anchor in the anchor locker or in the bow of the boat.

STRINGER SHEAR PIN

Let's say you shear a pin and there is not a spare in the boat. In your tacklebox an emergency remedy is awaiting. Take out your chain stringer, and snip off a piece of the wire on one of the links used to hold fish. Fit this piece of heavy wire into the shear pin slot of your prop, and you will be able to limp home.

TRY TUBING

For boaters who do their own wiring, here's a tip to make the job look factory-done—and safer.

Where several wires are strung together, from battery to switch, lights, motor ignition and electric-powered accessories, encase them in lengths of bicycle inner tubes.

You don't have to buy new tubes. We know a dealer who gives them away. The badly punctured or blown tubes are of no use to him.

The rubber cable thus formed eliminates taping the wires together at intervals, protects them from weather and accidental bangs and bumps that could cause shorts, and looks neat.

Where several lengths are needed, use either clamps, heavy rubber bands and/or cement to join the sections.

Increase Your Anchor's Holding Power

Buddy Grucela, who guides for shad and bass on the Delaware River around Easton, Pennsylvania, has designed an ingenious anchor for holding a good-sized boat in a brisk current over a rocky bottom. He uses a large swivel snap to fasten four feet of heavy chain to a standard mushroom anchor. Easily procured from a junkyard or a scrap-iron dealer, the chain boosts the anchor's weight and holding power, provides convenient handles for lowering and raising, and gives extra leverage when an anchor jams in rocks or snags. When he brings it aboard, he coils the heavy chain on a bed of old foam-rubber pads so it doesn't rattle around or dent his boat. In calm water, he simply unsnaps the chain and uses the mushroom anchor by itself.

MATERIAL DIFFERENCES

Here's how experts rate the materials that canoes are built from today:

Wood and canvas: Costs are almost double that of boats built from modern materials, but if you can find a good used one don't hesitate to buy it. Although not as strong as other materials, plenty of handsome old-timers have passed the century mark of service.

Aluminum: This has been the workhorse material since its introduction some 40 years ago. Light, tough, strong, inexpensive and requiring low maintenance, aluminum is what most of America's canoes have been built of. Bad features are unimaginative shapes, noise, hot and cold on bare feet. For river-running, aluminum bottoms hang on rocks other materials slide over. They can be handsomely painted but most aren't.

Fiberglass: Most modern shapes and whitewater kayaks and canoes are made of reinforced plastic. Easily repairable by amateurs, plastic boats are light and strong. They are more slippery over rocks than aluminum. They come in gay colors and a variety of lengths, styles and shapes.

ABS: This plastic comes in a bewildering variety of brand names. It's the same stuff that football helmets are made of. Incredibly strong and tough, it's the most slippery boat material there is. Inherent flotation does away with space lost to air tanks or flotation blocks. They command a premium price comparable to wood boats.

Kevlar: This light and strong DuPont fiber replaces woven glass cloth in plastic boats. Since Kevlar is stronger in lighter weights than glass, it can cut boat weight by about 20 percent, with a cost premium over regular plastic by about 20 percent.

BOAT BEACON

The long-stemmed boat light, used in the stern for night boating, doubles as a handy beacon when towing a light utility trailer. The lighted lamp guides you at night when backing up or parking the trailer. During the day, the tall stem is easily seen through the rear window and reveals how the trailer is responding to your steering.

Check state laws about towing a trailer at night on the highway with this lamp lit. Off the highway, the lighted lamp is a great aid.

Long-stemmed lights are available with either a bracket or C-clamp for fastening to a boat. The bracket type is best for fastening to the trailer body.

A BETTER CANOE MOUNT

An electric motor will move a light canoe along at a good clip. Typically, it is fastened on a mount attached near the stern, or on the stern itself if the canoe has a square one. But for the angler there is a better way to mount an electric motor—one that requires neither a motor mount nor a square stern.

A canoe is vulnerable to the wind. More than once I have had gusts hit mine broadside and swing it off course. Then a fishing friend showed me how to mount my electric motor on the gunwale near the bow. Located just to the rear of the bow seat, it pulls the canoe along instead of pushing it, making it less vulnerable to the wind. It is easy to operate from the bow seat.

Since most electric motors can pivot 360 degrees in their swivel the side mount is no problem. On most canoes it will probably be necessary to place a short piece of wooden board on the inside to provide a sturdier clamp for the motor and to prevent damage to the gunwale.

To help balance the load, the battery that supplies the power can be located toward the stern.

LOCK SAVER

It's a good idea to rig a chain between trailer lock and trailer. Then if you forget to relock it, you won't lose an expensive padlock. All that's needed is a six-inch length of chain and a screw or rivet. A good choice is the type of chain commonly used to hang fluorescent fixtures. It fits snugly around the lock's U-shaped bolt. Paint the chain to prevent rust.

INSTANT ANCHOR

When packing a small raft into a remote lake, hauling along an anchor is out of the question. An easy answer is to include a nylon stuff bag and a length of cord in your pack. Put a few rocks into the bag when you're ready to fish and you have an instant anchor.

OUTBOARD CRADLE

If you're one of the millions of sportsmen who take to the outdoors in a pickup truck, you probably have trouble stowing your outboard motor so it won't bang around in the bed of the truck.

Take heart! Yet another use for old tires has been found. Simply lay the heavy (top) end of the outboard in the ring of an old tire and your troubles are over. The motor will be nestled on the rubber cushion and you will arrive at your destination without a scratch on the housing—not to mention no bent shift levers or control handles.

RECYCLE TRAILER TIRES

A good way to shelter an expensive boat or camper trailer lock from rain, snow and dirt is with a section of worn-out trailer tire.

Use a hacksaw to cut a section to fit—for most needs, a quarter or fifth of a tire is plenty.

The tire's natural shape will keep it securely in place over the trailer coupler.

HAVING GOOD CONNECTIONS

Any boating angler who gets a lot of use out of his electric trolling motor has probably discovered the need to periodically replace the spring-loaded clips that attach to the battery terminals. After prolonged use, these wear out and fail to provide enough bite for good electrical contact. Sometimes nothing happens when you flip your motor on, or upon arriving at the lake, you may discover that your battery didn't take a proper charge.

To prevent either of these things from happening, simply wrap a heavy-duty rubber band round and round the front portion of each clip on both motor and charger. This works, and replacing the rubber bands once a season is far more economical than buying new clips.

ANCHOR BAG

An old bowling ball bag is perfect for storing and transporting a small boat anchor. Built with a reinforced bottom, it can take and carry the weight of an anchor easily. It also has plenty of storage space on top that can be used to pack an anchor line. Secondhand bowling ball bags can often be bought at garage sales and flea markets for just a few dollars.

INFLATABLE BOAT ANCHOR

A common problem faced by anglers in an inflatable boat is that of wind drift. To maintain a stationary position, the boat must be anchored from either end. However, most commercial anchors are not built with the inflatable in mind—their design and sharp edges make them difficult to handle and capable of puncturing the craft.

The answer is an empty one-gallon jug, such as a plastic detergent container.

Fill the jug to the top with pea-gravel, then add water for extra weight. Replace the cap and tie on the desired length of anchor rope. Presto: You have a safe, inexpensive anchor for an inflatable boat. The shape of the plastic jug prevents punctures and it rarely drags weeds up from the bottom of a pond. The approximate weight of the anchor when it is filled is 15 pounds.

★

Two anchors are needed to hold a boat in proper position, broadside to the hole you plan to fish. If you are caught with but one anchor, however, tie it on the upwind gunnel at the point where it balances best against the wind pressure.

POTTED ANCHOR

An anchor in a boat is a necessity, but it can also become a nuisance by banging into the sides of the boat and stowed gear. A simple and inexpensive answer is a large plastic flowerpot. This is both flexible and durable enough to hold a heavy cast-iron or lead anchor. If the pot can't be wedged into a convenient anchor-storing corner, it can be fastened with bolts or screws. As a bonus, the pots are already equipped with drainage slots.

BETTER ANCHOR LINE

Many West Coast saltwater anglers are switching the nylon anchor ropes in their small boats for flat webbing of the same material. The reason for turning to the more expensive webbing is simple—both mooching and strip casting for salmon, or bottom-jigging, call for frequent moves. The wide, soft texture of the webbing is easier on wet hands than narrow-diameter rope. I also use ⅝-inch width webbing in my canoe, both as an anchor rope and for lining in fast water.

Cartop Boat Cushions

Aluminum boats carried on exposed metal cartop racks sound like rumbling thunder every time you go over a pot-hole.

Deaden this sound by covering the carrier rods with heavy-duty radiator hose. These slip easily onto most metal carrier rods. If not, slit and tape pieces in place.

There is an advantage to not damaging hoses during installation: They can be used as spares for fixing radiator hose blow-outs that sometimes occur on the highway.—

STORING ALUMINUM BOATS

Though this information's on the level, the way you store your aluminum boat or canoe should *not* be, according to technicians at Grumman Boats. Level storage might permit meltwater or condensation to puddle inside hollow extrusions used for ribs, thwarts and gunwales. Freezing can cause expansion and split the extrusions.

Such damage can be expensive and difficult to repair. But the cure is easy: Simply make sure that one end is slightly higher than the other—about an inch or two—so water can't collect.

It isn't a bad idea to make sure that one *side* is higher by a like amount. Don't cover the hull, but let it rest on wooden sawhorses. Wet canvas and ropes can cause pitting.

The cleaner the metal and the fewer things in direct contact, the better the hull will come through the rigors of the winter. That goes for lashing it down to the sawhorses—remember wet ropes against the metal hull?

QUIET ANCHOR

A plastic antifreeze jug filled with rocks makes a quiet and inexpensive anchor. The cap can be wired on to keep it from falling off, and the handle is convenient for tying on the anchor rope.

FISH COOKERY
AND RECIPES

FISH COOKERY AND RECIPES

CARE OF CATCH

Fast Fish Cleaning

Here's a quick and easy way to clean trout for the skillet. Hold the fish upside down in your hand and make a semicircular cut from A to B and a straight cut through the skin only from C to D (see illustration). Place your thumb into the AB hole and your index finger in the CD hole. Pinch the thumb and index finger together and grasp the fish with your other hand. Now roll the thumb/index-finger hand toward the tail.

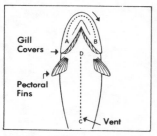

Gills, pectoral fins and viscera are removed in one operation, leaving only the blood vein to be removed by deftly running your thumbnail up the body cavity.

Fish Clean-up

Next time you have a mess of fish to clean, get some salt and toothpaste. Before you start, wet your hands and dip them in the salt. It will help you hang on to those slippery little devils, especially the smaller ones. When you are done, wash your hands with the toothpaste to remove the fish odor.

FISH CARE

Just as a deer that's killed quickly, with one clean shot, will taste better than one that has run for miles, so a fish landed quickly and killed instantly will taste much finer than one fought for an extended period of time and then allowed to flop around in the cooler until it slowly expires.

In fact, it's even more important to dispatch fish quickly, because they undergo more prolonged physiological stress during the fight that causes a heavy release of decay enzymes into their systems. Even when kept on ice, the enzymes work at decaying the flesh, because fish are cold-blooded. However, icing them down does reduce the rate of decay substantially.

Fatty fish such as tuna and bluefish are particularly vulnerable to decay, since the fats in fish are polyunsaturated and become rancid faster than the saturated fats found in red meat.

The Seafood Rx

It is a myth that eating fish will increase brain power. However, seafoods may prevent some cardiovascular problems in humans.

The American Medical Association reports that eicosapentaenoic acid (EPA), a fatty acid found in fish, marine oils and perhaps seaweed, may guard humans against coronary thrombosis. EPA originates in phytoplankton, the microorganisms that nourish all ocean creatures.

During the 1970s, Danish researchers studied Greenland Eskimos who eat large amounts of fish and other marine products high in EPA, because it was known that Eskimos have a low incidence of heart attacks.

More recently, investigators at the University of Oregon Health Services Center put volunteers on a 10-day diet of salmon, a fish rich in EPA. The results? The diet lowered plasma cholesterol levels by up to 17 percent in healthy persons. For patients with high blood lipid levels, cholesterol levels dipped by 20 percent. Also, triglyceride levels fell by as much as 40 percent in healthy volunteers and by 67 percent in hyperlipidemic patients.

It's too early for any solid conclusions from the EPA study. The researchers aren't yet sure about EPA effects on atherosclerosis or cardiovascular disease. They only know that the fatty acids lower blood fats and affect function, reducing the tendency of thrombosis.

BROWN-BAGGING TROUT

Years ago trout fishermen kept their catch cool all day long by putting their fish on beds of damp moss in wicker creels. Though these were bulky and burdensome they did keep trout fresh.

Modern trout fishermen usually opt for cotton flyfishing vests that have creel pouches sewn into the back. But it doesn't take long for the sun to dry out a fish protected by nothing more than a sheet of cotton material.

Vic Stewart, a fellow angler who specializes in trout fishing in the Great Smoky Mountains, has found a solution. Tucked away in his creel pouch is an ordinary large, brown grocery bag. After his first catch he dresses the fish, soaks the bag in cool stream water and places the trout inside. The bag is rolled up and returned to the creel, having absorbed enough water to feel damp.

This brown-bagging method will keep trout cool for hours even in the hot sun.

BONELESS BREAM

Here is a quick method for preparing "boneless" bream. Even small, stunted fish can be used. Fillet or scale/skin and gut and run the fish at least twice through the smallest gauge meat grinder you have. Putting it through twice ensures that even the tiny "feather" bones are completely chopped up. Now prepare and cook as you would salmon croquettes. The same method also works for small carp.

EASY FILLETING

If you experience trouble slicing your fish cleanly along the backbone when you fillet them, try a trick Jim South of Clintwood, Virginia, showed me a couple of fishing seasons ago.

Jim places the fish belly down straddling the crack between the boards of a picnic table—or any board-top table used for cleaning fish. He carefully lines one edge of the fish's backbone with the edge of one of the boards, and using the edge as a guide and the crack as a recess for his knife, neatly slices off the fillet. The board on the other side of the space serves as a guide in removing the other fillet.

Jim does not cut through the skin at the fish's tail. Instead, he flips the fillet over, and using the still-attached skin as an anchor, runs the thin fillet knife between the skin and the flesh to clear the fillet.

FISH FLIPPER

It is always a pleasure to watch a skilled camp cook flip pancakes. The feathered counterpart of the camp cook is the anhinga, found in the Everglades and marshlands of surrounding states. The anhinga is a sizable waterbird very expert at catching fish, which make up most of its diet. It is not dismayed by sunfish with their sharp spines. The bird flips the spiny victim into the air and swallows it as it turns headdown, fins and spines neatly folded.

SKIN THEM

Its not the flesh that causes many fish-eating enthusiasts to reject a platter of pan-fried bass. What really turns them off is the unappetizing skin. The black bass is one freshwater game fish that definitely needs its outer covering removed before entering the skillet.

TRANSPORTING FROZEN FISH

Baseball Hall of Famer Ted Williams and his long-time Canadian fishing guide, Roy Curtis of Blackville, N.B., Canada, have a unique method of packing salmon and trout for transport.

Freshly caught, these fish are quickly gutted and prepared for quick-freezing. Curtis then puts them in cold storage wrapped in a cellophane or common trash bag. Once frozen stiff, he prepares them for transport by wrapping each fish with a single layer of newspaper and then with a final blanketing of common house insulation, paper side out. Curtis wraps the insulation tight by applying strips of masking tape around the outside and making an easy-to-handle package. Wrapped this way, salmon and trout will keep four days before showing signs of thawing.

Boneless Pickerel

Some fishermen prefer to pass up the feisty chain pickerel, even though it is one of the most spectacular topwater battlers around. What turns most people away from them are the hundreds of tiny *Y*-shaped bones embedded in their otherwise tasty flesh.

A quick and easy method of preparing boneless pickerel is described here:

The fish is scaled, then filleted in the usual manner by cutting behind the head and lengthwise down the backbone with a fillet knife, thus freeing the meat from the carcass in a whole slab.

Lay the fillets skin side down and make a series of cuts one-quarter inch apart in the flesh, down to the skin but not through it. The severing of bones will be audible during this operation.

Another series of cuts made along the length of the fillet will complete the process.

The fish can be baked, broiled or breaded and fried. Those annoying bones are effectively dissolved during the cooking, resulting in a delicious meal of flaky, white meat.

GIVE SCALES THE BRUSH OFF

I recently learned something as I watched two anglers dress out their limit of eight coho salmon taken from the Campbell River in British Columbia.

It was not the fellow who wielded the knife that attracted my attention, but his companion. Her job was to scale the gutted fish—a task she performed so quickly and thoroughly I was amazed. Her scaler was a long-handled wire brush, the type used for cleaning rust and corrosion from metal surfaces.

Holding each fish by the wrist of the tail, she gave a few brisk scrubs, flipped the carcass, and was finished in a fraction of the time it takes normally.

Her brush had stainless-steel bristles, something to consider if you decide to try this ingenious method of fish scaling.

Frozen Fish

Icefishermen catch more bluegills than other species of fish, but bluegills can be a real problem to clean. That's because if placed on the ice after being caught, they oftentimes come back to life when taken into a warm house for cleaning. This makes for fish that flip, flop, and stick your hands with sharp spines.

A quick solution to this problem is to drop your bluegills into a bucket of warm water just before cleaning. The sudden temperature change will kill the fish quickly.

Even fish that are already dead yet partially frozen can be quickly thawed for easier cleaning using this method. Remember to leave fish in the warm water only a minute or two or the flesh may become mushy.

Camp-Cooking Hints

- The handles of iron skillets get hot. If you thoughtlessly grasp one without a protecting potholder or towel, plunge your hand into cold water and hold it there until the sting subsides.

- When cooking over an open fire, wear long pants or jeans. They are safer, comfortable and more practical than shorts or bathing suits.

- Half a can of beer mixed with an equal amount of tomato paste and heated makes a good sauce for strong-flavored fish.

- An empty tuna can is useful when making meat patties for buns. Use the open end for cutting them into circles, the closed end to gently flatten them to uniform thickness.

- Test boiling potatoes with a skewer or toothpick instead of a fork. It makes fewer holes, which cause watery potatoes.

- To prevent green discoloration between the yolk and white of hard-boiled eggs, cook at a temperature below boiling and cool promptly.

- To remove excess grease from the top of soup or broth, drop a lettuce leaf into the pot. Discard after the grease has been absorbed.

- Use a potato masher to separate ground beef when browning it for spaghetti (or other) sauce.

- Keep one ice tray full of frozen sweet milk to use in cold milk or milk-chocolate drinks. These cubes chill the drink without diluting it.

- Add a spoonful of olive oil to boiling water before adding pasta to prevent its sticking together or to the pan.

- If you have a number of fish to scale and/or fillet, rub a little cooking oil or shortening, or even bacon drippings, on the backs of your hands. When the job is finished dried scales, slime, etc., will wash off easily.

CANNING FISH

When I lived in northern Virginia, one of the blessings was the annual herring run each spring in Occoquan Creek and other streams that emptied into the Potomac River. Although herring are great-tasting fish, the chore of picking bones from the cooked fish was enough to try severely the patience of any otherwise sane soul. In addition, there was the greater problem of how to preserve a large quantity of fish to savor the delectable flavor many months after the run is complete.

Most families in the area salted them down in tubs or barrels. This preserved the fish for a good length of time, but we didn't like the extreme salty flavor, and in addition, there were still the bones to contend with. So, my wife and I searched for a better method and decided to pressure cook the fish. The results were so good that we now use this method to can and preserve different types of bony fish that we don't want to freeze. Using this method almost all bones are dissolved, with the possible exception of the backbones in large fish which may be discarded when the jar is opened.

Clean the fish thoroughly, wipe dry and cut into chunks or lengths that will fit into pint jars. Fill jars to within one inch of the top and adjust lids. Place jars in a pressure canner and cook at ten pounds pressure for approximately one hour and 40 minutes. Remove cooker from heat, and after cooling store jars away from sunlight or heat. (Note: Required pressure pounds and cooking time vary from cooker to cooker. Be sure to read the instructions very carefully.)

When a jar is opened, the fish are seasoned to taste and warmed. Our favorite method is to make fish cakes which are delicately fried to a golden brown in an open cast iron skillet.

LITTLE IRISH CHOWDER

If the fishing has been exceptionally good and I've had my fill of fried and boiled trout—or if the fishing has been really lousy and I haven't caught a thing—I like to cook up a thick potato-based chowder for a satisfying hot meal. It's easy to make, cooks up quickly and can be partially prepared ahead of time. The basic recipe will serve four.

1 6-oz. pkg. Betty Crocker Hash Brown Potatoes
4 tbsp. dehydrated vegetable flakes
2 tsp. dehydrated chopped onions
1 tsp. salt
¼ tsp. pepper
6 tbsp. flour
1 qt.-sized envelope powdered milk

Place all ingredients except the powdered milk in a quart freezer bag. Twist top and toss to mix well. Tie off the bag for storage in your grub box or backpack. At camp, add chowder mix to a pot with six cups of cold water and set aside to soak for about 30 minutes. In the meantime, fry several strips of thick-sliced bacon for each person, and prepare a batch of biscuits. While the biscuits are baking, hang a pot over the fire and bring contents to a boil. Move the pot to less heat, and simmer for eight to 10 minutes. Stir occasionally to prevent scorching. Set pot aside and dissolve powdered milk in one cup of cold water, then add to chowder. Stir well and heat until steaming, but *don't boil.* Ladle into bowls and serve.

Chowder Variations
Backpacker's Chowder: Double the amount of powdered milk (for extra protein) and increase the dehydrated vegetables and onions to suit. Add one or two tablespoons margarine or bacon grease.

Clam Chowder: Reduce water by one cup and add two small cans of minced or chopped clams, including juice, just before adding the milk. Heat until steaming, but don't boil.

Fish-Camp Chowder: Reduce water by one cup and omit the powdered milk. When chowder begins to boil, add about one pound of boneless fish, cut into chunks, and a one-pound can of tomatoes that have been cut into chunks. Bring to a boil again and simmer seven or eight minutes.

THESE FISH DON'T LAST LONG

Want a great fish-eating treat? Here's how professional fishing guide Bob Snook does it on the banks of Oregon's Rogue River. He fillets a salmon or steelhead (a big trout will do) and cuts the fillets into chunks four to five inches long.

Snook builds a fire and lets it die down until the coals are just right. He tests them by holding his hand a few inches above the coals and counting, "One hippopotamus, two hippopot—" About then the coals get too hot, and he jerks his hand away. Two hippopotamuses are just about right. One is too hot; three is too cool.

Snook places the pieces, flesh side down, on a grill just off the coals and cooks them until they're done about one-fourth of the way through—you can tell when the pink meat turns tan. He flips the fillets, places a dab of butter on each and sprinkles them with lemon pepper, and cooks them until done. The skin will char, but the meat won't burn.

BAKED STRIPED BASS

1 striped bass weighing about 5 lbs.
2 medium onions, thinly sliced
4 or 5 ripe tomatoes, thinly sliced
½ cup chopped parsley (or celery leaves)
1½ tsp. salt
½ tsp. black pepper
½ tsp sweet basil leaves, crumbled

For baking the fish should be left whole. Remove scales and fins. It is best to leave the head and tail. When the fish is to be stuffed the backbone may be removed if this can be done skillfully. Any stuffing can be used: however a simple vegetable stuffing is easy and gives excellent results.

When the fish has been cleaned and readied turn the oven to 450° F. Line a baking pan large enough to hold your fish with a double layer of heavy duty foil. Butter the foil well.

Quickly rinse the fish and wipe it dry. Stuff with the vegetables laid in layers, dotting each layer with bits of butter and sprinkle with chopped parsley. Sprinkle tomato layer with sweet basil. Salt and pepper the filling. Close the opening with small skewers or large toothpicks. Rub the skin with butter and place in the foil-lined pan. Bake, allowing ten minutes for each inch measured through the thickest part (about 30 to 35 minutes). Test with toothpick before removing fish from oven. When fish is done, pick it up on foil and slide onto hot platter. Remove skewers and place lemon wedges around edge of platter.

If fish is larger than can be easily baked or a smaller amount is wanted substitute two large steaks for a whole fish. Place stuffing between them.

Smoked Redfish

3 pounds redfish (approximately)
¼ pound butter
3 cloves garlic, minced
juice of a lemon
salt, pepper and paprika

Melt butter, add garlic and sauté gently for a minute or two. Add lemon juice and remove from heat. Double a piece of heavy-duty foil and turn up the sides to form a pan a little larger than the redfish. Score the sides of the cleaned fish by cutting deep Xs into the meat. Sprinkle with salt, pepper and paprika on both sides. Pour one-fourth of the butter mixture into the foil pan, place fish on top and pour another one-fourth of the mixture over it. Place foil pan on the grill of a covered barbecue smoker over medium-hot coals. Cover loosely with a sheet of foil and replace lid of smoker. Cook 45 minutes to one hour, basting occasionally with the remainder of the butter mixture. Do not turn fish. Test for doneness with a fork—it should sink to the bone with little resistance.

Crawfish Stew

6 pounds live crawfish
1 large onion
2 cloves garlic
1 stalk celery
½ cup lard or shortening
⅔ cup flour
1 pint water
Salt, red pepper and black pepper to taste

Wash, scald and clean the crawfish. Chop onion and celery. Mince garlic. Heat lard, add flour, stir until brown. Add onion, celery and garlic, then crawfish. Stir until stew looks a little greasy. Add water and simmer 20 minutes. Season with salt, pepper and red pepper to your liking. Serve the stew hot.

CRAWDAD BOIL

In late September and early October, when water temperatures reach 50° F, crayfish become active, and they can be caught with a length of string and a chunk of leftover breakfast bacon. They make a great camp meal for hungry sportsmen.

Raid the spice rack for the following:

¼ cup mustard seed
¼ cup coriander seed
2 tbsp. dill seed
2 tbsp. whole allspice
1 tbsp. ground cloves
4 dried hot red chilies, stemmed and crumbled
3 medium-sized bay leaves, crumbled

All of this equals about one cup of mix and will easily fit into a sandwich bag, which in turn will fit into a hip pocket to tote along for the makings of a campfire feast.

To three quarts of water, add 3 tbsp. or so of the mix. Bring the water to a boil over high heat, then cover and reduce heat to boil for 20 minutes.

Rinse the crawdads in fresh water. When the mix has boiled its allotted time, add the live crawdads and boil uncovered for five minutes until they turn bright red.

Remove the meat by gripping the tail between the thumbs and forefingers of both hands and applying pressure to crack the shell. Crawdads taste very similar to lobster.

This is also a great boil for lobster, crab and shrimp.

BASS COOKERY

The Young Housekeeper's Friend by Mrs. Cornelius gives this recipe for stuffed baked bass: First, make a cracker-crumb stuffing out of finely crumbled crackers, seasoned with salt and pepper and a sprinkle of cloves, and moisten it with a beaten egg. Stuff the body cavity of the fish with this mixture, and sew it closed. Place in a baking dish, sprinkle with nutmeg and crumble a few crackers over the fish. Drench with melted butter and bake for one hour. Take your bass directly from the oven to table, and serve it in the same dish in which it was prepared.

She further recommends, "If a fresh fish of any kind is left of dinner, it is a very good way to lay it in a deep dish and pour over it a little vinegar, with catsup, and add pepper or any other spice which is preferred."

Cobia Parmesan

4 lb. cobia steaks, cut ¾ to 1 inch thick
1 lb. cooking margarine
3 tbsp. lemon juice
1 tbsp. Worcestershire
1 tbsp. crushed basil
¼ tbsp. thyme
¼ tbsp. marjoram
celery salt
black pepper

1 6-oz. can tomato sauce or pureé
1 3-oz. can grated parmesan cheese

Melt the margarine in a saucepan and add the other seasonings. Heat just enough to make the margarine bubble and let this mixture get acquainted for 30 minutes, stirring frequently so it doesn't burn. Put the fish steaks in a greased baking pan and pour the seasoned margarine over it. Bake in a 325°F. oven 1½ hours, basting often. Now pour the tomato sauce over the fish and cover heavily with the grated cheese. Place in oven, turned to broil, just long enough to melt and brown cheese.

Pike Caviar

Anglers may wish to experiment with this unusual and delicious German recipe for "pike caviar." It is based on approximately one pint of eggs.

Salt the egg sacs heavily, place in a covered bowl and refrigerate overnight.

Scrape eggs from the membrane with a dull table knife, place in a strainer and rinse well with cold water.

Drain and pour into a large mixing bowl.

Stir slowly with a wire whisk and add one teaspoon of salt.

Add one teaspoon of sunflower or peanut oil and beat the mixture quickly for at least one minute. Continue beating as four more teaspoons of oil are added at one-minute intervals.

Add one teaspoon of dry mustard, and a pinch each of thyme and flaked parsley.

Continue beating quickly until the mixture takes on a light, fluffy consistency. You will probably be surprised to note the contents of the bowl expand in volume quite a bit during this process.

Add Spanish onion diced into micro-fine pieces and serve with either fresh bread or hot toast.

FAST AND FANCY FISH

About 2 pounds fish fillets (bass, crappie or perch but not trout)
½ cup French dressing
2 tablespoons margarine
2 tablespoons cooking oil
1 small onion, chopped
1 lemon
Tartar sauce

Heat margarine and oil in a large skillet over moderate heat. Dip the fish fillets in the French dressing and add them to the skillet. Sprinkle onion over fillets. Cook three to four minutes, turn and repeat. Serve with lemon wedges and tartar sauce. Serves four to six.

A good substitute for tartar sauce can be made by adding pickle relish to salad dressing.

FISH SOUFFLÉ

Prepare a seven-inch soufflé baking dish (any straight-sided dish will do) by greasing it with butter and dusting with flour. Make a collar for it by wrapping a piece of aluminum foil (shiny side out) around the outside. The collar should extend three inches above the top of the dish to hold any soufflé that gets overly ambitious.

Preheat the oven to 325°F as you mix the following:

3 tbsp. butter
3 tbsp. flour
1 cup milk
1 cup cooked, flaked fish
¼ cup finely chopped raw carrots
¼ cup finely chopped celery
2 tbsp. pimento
3 egg yolks, beaten
3 egg whites, beaten until stiff
1 tbsp. lemon juice
salt, paprika, parsley

Melt the butter in a double boiler and sprinkle in flour. Stir the mixture until it forms a smooth paste, then slowly add milk, stirring until the sauce is smooth and thick. Remove from heat and stir in fish, carrots, celery and pimento. Then, mix in egg yolks and season mixture with lemon juice, salt and paprika. Try to have the ingredients at room temperature before folding in egg whites and a small amount of parsley.

Place soufflé inside another baking dish that contains two inches of water and bake for 35 minutes. Garnish with parsley. Serves two to four.

Salmon And Sour Cream

Like sour cream? Try your salmon steaks this way.

Lightly salt two or three steaks about two inches thick. Put them into a baking pan or dish. Mix two cups (one pint) sour cream, two or three tablespoons finely chopped onion, one tablespoon lemon juice. Spoon this mixture over the salmon steaks and bake in a 350° F. oven for about 30 minutes.

FISH CASSEROLE

2 pounds boneless fish fillets
2 cans condensed cream of celery soup
3 cups milk
10 small potatoes peeled and halved
7 tablespoons diced ham
5 tablespoons diced onion
6 slices American cheese
4 tablespoons grated cheese

Coat inside of two-quart casserole dish lightly with oil then lay in fillets. Place potatoes along the sides. In a saucepan heat and mix soup, milk, onions and ham, then pour over fillets and potatoes. Sprinkle on grated cheese and bake in a 200°F oven for three hours. Then lay cheese slices on top and heat until melted. Any sort of fish can be cooked in this fashion. Serve bubbling hot with a loaf of rye bread and white wine.

KIPPERED SALMON

Any species of salmon can be kippered. Cut fish into four-inch squares about two inches thick. Or if preferred, salmon can be cut in halves. (Save leftover pieces for canning or pickling.)

For each five pounds of fish mix together one tablespoon salt, three teaspoons brown (or raw) sugar, one-fourth to one-half teaspoon black pepper. Sprinkle mixture over both sides of fish. Let stand overnight in a cool place. Drain fish and place on racks in smokehouse, skin side down, over glowing coals and charred wood. It takes about an hour to dry and glaze the salmon.

For kippered salmon, smother the coals to a heavy smoke with chunks of applewood or peeled alder. You need enough to burn about 48 hours. Place the rack 18 inches from coals; for cold-smoking about four feet.

Kippered salmon should be refrigerated and used within a relatively short time. If salmon is to be kept for weeks or months, the use of additional salt and longer smoking time is necessary. The fully smoked salmon must be wrapped against moisture and stored in a cool, dark place.

FISH CAKES

No matter how carefully you cut the meat from the bones of fish, you will still leave some attached to the backbone. I found, though, that you can scrape the meat off the vertebrae with a spoon or a knife and use the bits of flesh in a variety of ways. Here is one of them.

Scandinavian Fish Cakes

1 cup raw, chopped fish (any species)
1 cup milk
1 egg
2 tbsp. potato flour (or dehydrated potato flakes)
1 tsp. salt
¼ tsp. nutmeg
1 tbsp. minced onions (optional)

Put all the ingredients except the fish in a blender and spin until thoroughly mixed. Add the fish and blend until the mixture is a smooth consistency. Shape the batter into silver-dollar-sized cakes about three-eighths of an inch thick, or into one-inch balls, and fry them in butter or shortening until they are brown. Serve the cakes hot, alone or with a white sauce.

Refrigerated, they keep well. When hungry I simply warm the cakes by frying them in butter.

TASTY TIDBITS

Those fortunate enough to have eaten walleye cheeks are usually totally in agreement that they are the most delicious part of the entire fish. Walleyes, however, do not have a monopoly on these delicacies. Almost any fish of decent size has a tender scallop of meat located behind each eye on the cheeks. They can be easily removed by making two adjoining cuts (see illustration) and simply scooping the scallop out with your thumbnail. As the scallop pops from the cheek, pinch it between thumb and forefinger and pull it free of the tab of skin that is still attached to the head.

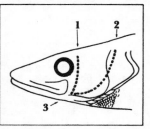

1. Slice straight down behind the eye.
2. Draw bottom of second cut in toward the first cut.
3. Force thumbnail into the bottom of the V and pop the scallop out. The skin will pull free.

In our house the cheeks are frozen in water until enough are hoarded for a feast. Deep fried in smoking-hot peanut oil for just a few moments produces pure ambrosia that has to be tasted to be appreciated.

★ ★ ★

BRANDIED FISH

On your next fishing jaunt, take some brandy along. Not only can you use it for "medicinal purposes," you can also prepare an out-of-this-world marinade for barbecuing your catch. Mix equal parts of brandy and melted butter, and soak fish in it for about 30 minutes. Barbecue the fish in aluminum foil on a rack over the campfire. You won't believe that anything that simple can taste so wonderful.

CRAWFISH ÉTOUFFEÉ

3 pounds fresh crawfish
1 stick margarine, or cooking oil
6 onions, finely chopped
½ cup celery, chopped
½ tsp. tomato paste
½ tsp. cornstarch
½ cup cold water
Salt, pepper and red pepper to taste
¼ cup onion tops and parsley, minced

Parboil and peel crawfish. Set tails aside. Mix margarine or cooking oil with chopped onions, celery and tomato paste in heavy pan. Cook, uncovered, over medium heat until onions are translucent. Add crawfish tails. Dissolve cornstarch in the ½ cup of cold water and gradually add to crawfish, stirring constantly. Season to your taste with salt, black and red pepper. Bring to a boil over medium heat and cook, uncovered, for about 15 minutes. Add onion tops and parsley. Mix well. Serve with hot, freshly cooked rice. This recipe serves 4 or 5.

Salmon Indian Style

Clean, wash and fillet salmon while your cook fire is burning down to coals. Cut straight boughs of alder or willow about 20 inches longer than your fillets. Split these at the thick end. Cut four smaller sticks or twigs. Cross the twigs X fashion on either side of the salmon fillet. Place these in the split end of the alder or willow bough and tie ends together to hold the fillet. Push the end of the bough into the ground close to the coals. Cook until salmon is well done, turning occasionally. When done remove the bough, leaving the fish in the crossed sticks. Salt and pepper the fish to your liking and brush on melted butter.

PUT A SUNFISH ON YOUR MENU

Don't shun the sunfishes because of their tiny bones and fishy taste. It's easy to avoid both by skinning and filleting them, and it's quicker and simpler than scaling and gutting.

First, lightly make the outlined cut shown in Diagram 1

with a small, razor-sharp knife. Next, use a small pair of pliers to peel back the skin gently but firmly, scales and all, from point A to point B. (Don't use needle-nosed pliers; it tends to puncture and tear the skin.)

Remove the skinless fillets, as in Diagram 2, by sliding your knife first along the backbone and then down and out at point C. Now turn the fish over and repeat the steps. After a stringer or two, you'll be cleaning a fish a minute. This method makes even a four-inch bluegill worth keeping. The fillets freeze readily.

Sunfish fillets are rich in protein and low in calories and cholesterol. My family likes to eat them, panfried and golden-brown, with our fingers, like french fries.

For variety, my wife uses this delicious recipe, which serves four:

SUNFISH ITALIAN (RED)
1 lb. sunfish fillets
2 scallions sliced thin
1 green pepper sliced thin
1 small jar of spaghetti sauce
1 chopped tomato
½ cup water
½ cup white wine
pinch salt

Combine scallions, pepper and sauce. Cover and simmer for 10 minutes. Add fish, salt, tomato and wine. Simmer, covered, for six minutes. Ladle over rice and rim with parsley.

Finally, when you're all done skinning and filleting your sunfish, plant their little carcasses deep in your tomato patch or rose bed. They make terrific fertilizer for your garden.

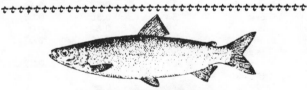

BAKED CISCOES

10 ciscoes, filleted
1½ tbsp. lemon juice
2 cups heavy cream
1 cup light cream
1½ tsp. flour
1 tbsp. butter
salt and pepper
buttered toast

Quarter the fillets. Place fish pieces in a buttered flat baking dish. Sprinkle with the lemon juice. Heat butter and flour in saucepan. Add the 2 cups heavy cream and the cup of light cream slowly. Bring to boiling point, stirring constantly. Pour sauce over fish and sprinkle with salt and pepper. Bake at 325° about one hour. Serve fish and sauce on (or with) buttered toast.

If fish is being cooked at camp, undiluted evaporated milk may be substituted for the cream.

Fish can be covered and slowly simmered in a heavy pan instead of baked.

Other freshwater fish may be cooked in the same manner.

FISH LOAF

After filleting your catch, don't throw away the backbones. A fair amount of meat is attached to these bones and can be used to make a delicious fish loaf. Begin by either baking the backbone scrapings in a 350° F oven or by steaming them over boiling water until they are cooked. While the fish is cooking, gather the following ingredients:

1 cup toasted bread cubes
1 small onion, diced
2 stalks celery, diced
1 tsp. salt
1 egg, beaten
½ cup tomato sauce
¾ cup grated cheddar cheese paprika
1¼ cups cooked, flaked fish (from the scrapings described above))

Mix all ingredients except paprika and ¼ cup of the grated cheese in a large bowl. Work in the flaked fish until a uniform texture is attained. Spoon the mixture into a 9×5-inch breadpan and shape it into a loaf. Spread the remaining grated cheese over the loaf and sprinkle paprika on top. Bake the loaf at 350° F for one hour. Let it cool five to 10 minutes before cutting.

Since some fish have a very mild flavor, you might want to add a little zip to the loaf by adding some chili peppers or sprinkling in a dash of hot pepper sauce.

While fish loaf makes an excellent main dish, it is also very good as an open-faced sandwich. Cut a one-inch-thick slice from a cold, cooked loaf and place it on a piece of fresh bread or an English muffin. Sprinkle on a small amount of grated cheese and broil until the cheese melts. Or, you may prefer to substitute a few tablespoons of your favorite sauce for the cheese.

FISH COOKERY AND RECIPES
RECIPES

FREEZING FISH

How long can you store fish in the freezer before spoilage begins? Home economists say it all depends on the species of fish and its fat content. Some species can be frozen for as long as six months, while others begin to lose flavor after two months.

The fat in fish is high in polyunsaturated fatty acids whose chemical structure make fish vulnerable to spoilage or flavor loss, no matter how carefully wrapped.

If you bring home fatty fish such as bluefish, salmon, Pacific ocean perch or mackerel, they should be eaten within two months, even when frozen at 0° F. Striped bass and sea trout should be eaten within three months. Lean fish, such as cod, halibut and flounder, can last up to six months.

CUTTING FISH STEAKS

When cutting steaks from round-shaped fish such as salmon, don't mash the fish while trying to cut through bone. This usually happens when you place a fish on its side before cutting. Lay the fish on its belly instead so that the backbone is facing up. Cut straight down, and more often than not the knife will find its own way between the vertebrae of the backbone.

PARASITES: good enough to eat?

Parasites, or fish disease, are usually harmless to both the fish and fish eater, but in rare cases they can infect humans. Just last summer two anglers contracted tapeworms after consuming marinated, uncooked walleye. For this reason, whether you are preparing a raw fish dish or pickling fish, you should always be aware of common parasites found in freshwater fish.

FOOD VALUES OF FISHES

Have you ever wondered about the nutritional value of certain species of fish you may have caught? It is interesting to note that allied species have different food values. Listed here are four of the more popular domestic foods that can be used as a yardstick for comparison. Note: All values are based on a three-and-a-half-ounce serving.

ITEM	CALORIES	OZ. OF PROTEIN	OZ. OF FAT
Sirloin steak	288	0.55	0.86
Ham	259	0.47	0.79
Chicken (fried)	165	0.85	0.12
Ground beef	177	0.72	0.35

FISH - Freshwater species, wild (not hatchery or commercially grown)

ITEM	CALORIES	OZ. OF PROTEIN	OZ. OF FAT
Bass, largemouth	104	0.66	0.10
Bass, smallmouth	109	0.67	0.11
Bass, striped	196	0.76	0.29
Bass, white	98	0.63	0.08
Catfish, bullhead	84	0.57	0.06
Catfish, channel	103	0.62	0.11
Crappie	79	0.59	0.03
Perch, white	118	0.68	0.14
Perch, yellow	91	0.68	0.03
Pickerel	84	0.66	0.02
Walleye	93	0.40	0.04
Salmon, king	222	0.67	0.55
Salmon, pink	119	0.71	0.14
Salmon, silver	153	0.73	0.27
Shad	170	0.66	0.35
Trout, brown	101	0.68	0.07
Trout, lake	168	0.64	0.35
Trout, rainbow	195	0.76	0.40
Whitefish, lake	155	0.66	0.29

Saltwater Fish & Shellfish (wild—not commercially grown)

ITEM	CALORIES	OZ. OF PROTEIN	OZ. OF FAT
Bluefish	117	0.72	0.12
Butterfish	169	0.62	0.34
Clams	54	0.30	0.03
Cod	78	0.62	0.01
Crab (steamed)	93	0.60	0.07
Flounder (baked)	202	1.05	0.29
Haddock	79	0.64	0.004
Halibut	100	0.73	0.04
Kingfish	105	0.64	0.11
Lobster	91	0.59	0.07
Mackerel, Atlantic	191	0.67	0.43
Mackerel, Pacific	159	0.77	0.26
Ocean perch, Atlantic	88	0.63	0.04
Ocean perch, Pacific	95	0.67	0.05
Oysters (raw)	66	0.30	0.12
Pollock	95	0.71	0.03
Red snapper	93	0.70	0.03
Sardines	311	0.73	0.86
Scallops	240	0.49	0.70
Sea bass	96	0.75	0.02
Shrimp	91	0.64	0.03
Swordfish	118	0.68	0.14
Yellowtail	138	0.74	0.19

FAVORABLE FISH FATS

A diet of fish may reduce the risk of cholesterol build-up. Research by Dr. William Harris and Dr. William Conner of the University of Oregon found that eating fish decreased the level of harmful cholesterol, which is a factor in hardening of the arteries, and increases the level of beneficial cholesterol that protects people against heart attacks by preventing blood clotting in the circulatory system. They put ten healthy volunteers on a diet of salmon, fruits, vegetables and grains for four weeks and found a significant change in the blood cholesterol that prevents clotting and blood vessel damage.

A significant factor was the calorie restriction in the amount of fats consumed. Fats make up over 40 percent of the total calories in a normal diet, and an ounce of fat contains 270 calories compared to 120 calories in an ounce of carbohydrate or protein.

About 75 percent of the calories in untrimmed sirloin steak or hamburger are fat, compared to 2 percent for cod and perch, 5 percent for catfish and tuna and 9 percent for salmon, trout and sardines. Fish oils are more beneficial than animal fats, with high-quality protein, vitamins A and D.

KEEPING FISH

If the fish cannot be eaten within two days, freeze it. Double wrap the fish in plastic wrap or bags to prevent freezer burn, and spread fish packages out near the cooling elements for quick chilling.

Thawing is actually where much flavor loss and texture deterioration occur, rather than in the freezing. Decide at least a day ahead of time if you want to have fish and thaw the package out slowly, in the refrigerator, for 12 to 24 hours.

Ice crystals should melt slowly. Rapid defrosting at room temperature causes these crystals to break down the delicate fish flesh.

FISH COOKING TIME

Researchers at the University of Delaware College of Marine Studies suggest this simple, reliable method for determining how long to broil large fish fillets or steaks:

Measure the fillet at its thickest place and allow 10 minutes cooking time for each inch of thickness. Add an extra five minutes to the overall cooking time if you wrap the fish in foil or cover it with a sauce. Double the overall cooking time if the fish is frozen. It's done when you can flake it easily with a fork.—

GOURMET FISH BATTER

Chances are that in your kitchen you have three of the four ingredients needed to make the quickest and most delicious fish batter recipe ever concocted. Concocted with tender loving care by professional chef and fishing guide Stan Nelson of Litchfield, Minneapolis, this fish batter will draw friends like geese to a cornfield.

1½ cups of flour
1 tsp. salt
1 tsp. baking powder

Mix in enough inexpensive white wine (not cooking wine) to create a pancake-batter consistency. Salt and pepper the fish fillets and dip them in the batter. Deep fry in hot cooking oil (vegetable oil is preferred).

Lemon Butter

If you plan to cook fish on your next trip afield, mix up some lemon butter at home and store it in a chip-dip container for use later. The butter can be melted in the container and used to dip fish in or to pour over a cooked fish. For one container of lemon butter mix the following ingredients:

6 tablespoons butter
½ teaspoon salt
½ teaspoon pepper
2 teaspoons lemon juice
When ready to serve, blend and heat.

TROUT CREPES

While few will argue that the best trout is panfried and fresh, sometimes you may want to try something exotic. The following recipe is easier than it looks and tastier than it sounds.

PLAIN CREPES
¾ cup flour
⅛ tsp. salt
3 beaten eggs
2 tbsp. melted butter
¾ cup milk (more or less)
butter to brush the pan for each crepe

Beat flour, salt and eggs together with a wire whisk or egg beater until batter is smooth. Add butter and mix thoroughly. Add milk until batter has the consistency of heavy cream. Let stand a few minutes and beat once more.

Heat a six- or seven-inch crepe pan (a heavy skillet will do) and brush with butter. Pour in about 2 tbsp. of batter and tilt pan so the bottom is covered completely. As soon as edges begin to brown or bottom appears dry, loosen edges, flip and cook other side until slightly golden. Makes about 12 crepes. Store in waxed paper or aluminum foil until needed. They can be made ahead and frozen, or refrigerated and then reheated when they are filled.

TROUT FILLING
2 tbsp. minced onion
4 tbsp. butter
4 tbsp. flour
1 cup milk
1 cup chicken stock
2 tbsp. white wine (optional)
salt and pepper to taste
2 cups cooked, boned trout
½ cup chopped mushrooms
½ chopped, cooked green pepper

Sauté onion in butter until golden. Stir in flour, then milk and chicken stock. Stir and simmer until thickened. Add wine, salt and pepper. Set aside ½ cup of this sauce.

Add trout, mushrooms and green pepper to remaining sauce. Simmer briefly, then fill and roll crepes. Tuck in the ends and place in a shallow baking pan. Glaze with reserved sauce. If you are home, broil for a few minutes. Otherwise, warm on any heat source. Serves four to six.

(A quick version of this recipe can also be made by substituting canned cream of mushroom soup for the milk, chicken stock and mushrooms.)

SEASONED FISH

Many fish that have a strong flavor—such as large black bass, bonito, yellowtail and skipjack—are often discarded because one or more members of the family express a dislike for them. These objections may be overcome by seasoning fish fillets or steaks about one inch in thickness with an old hickory liquid smoke or an all-purpose soy sauce. Apply the seasoning generously to both sides of the flesh with a basting brush. Place the seasoned fish on a double thickness of aluminum foil with the edges turned up to form a shallow pan and place on the bottom of the oven or on top of the broiler. Depending upon the amount of seasoning desired, brush the top side of the fish while baking, as it is turned several times to prevent sticking to the aluminum foil. Bake with moderate heat until the flesh flakes readily when pierced with a fork.

The flesh from wild game animals or birds may be seasoned in a similar manner to the delight of those who dislike the natural flavor.

GOURMET FISH CAKES

Nobody in your family likes fish? Maybe it's the way you cook it. Try something new. Use the basic recipe below and see if you don't have more fish eaters than you ever imagined.

1 lb. skinned, boneless fish fillets
1 lb. shredded white potatoes
1 egg
½ tbsp. bacon grease (per skillet)
salt
cheese (optional)
bacon (optional)

Peel, eye and shred enough potatoes (about four medium size) to make one pound.

Cut the fish fillets into small pieces and put through a meat grinder or an electric mixer. If you don't have a grinder or blender, poach the fillets and flake with a fork.

Mix fish and potatoes in a bowl with the egg and salt. (If fish were poached, add two tablespoons of water.) Make into three- to four-ounce patties about one half to three fourths of an inch thick and fry in bacon grease in a large skillet over medium heat. Fry for five minutes per side or until golden brown. Remove and serve as fish cakes or place between bread, toast or hamburger buns and serve as sandwiches.

For a gourmet touch, melt some cheese on top of the patties before removing them from the frying pan.

Like onion or garlic? Chop fine and add to the main ingredients. No need to sauté it if you keep the fish cakes thin.

Having special guests? Prepare fish cakes as directed above; remove from frying pan, add cheese and wrap with rare bacon. Broil in oven to crisp bacon. Serve as entree.

FISH COOKERY AND RECIPES
RECIPES

FISH COOKERY, 1869

"Fish cannot be made a constant substitute for butcher's meat without considerably impairing the muscular, and perhaps the mental, force . . ."

This blunt statement comes from the "Fish and Its Preparation" chapter of a book called *The Philosophy of Housekeeping* by Joseph Lyman, published in 1869.

Lyman does, however, acknowledge that "when freshly caught and properly cooked," fish is quite suitable for certain groups of people. Among these are "invalids, jockeys, prisoners, soldiers and those whose occupations are sedentary."

Try some of his recipes:

1. To prepare smaller kinds of freshwater fish, cut three or four slices of salt pork, then soak overnight. Fry the pork until crisp, then remove it, keeping the fat hot. Roll the fish in flour or cornmeal and lay in the pork fat. Cook five minutes on each side, then remove quickly. Lyman's tip: "The finest of fish can be utterly ruined by allowing the flesh to become soaked with rancid or burnt fat."

2. To cook fresh shad, salmon or mackerel: Since these fish have a definite flavor all their own, they must be "unmixed with baser matter" and broiled. Use no fat or pepper, just a pinch of salt and a few drops of lemon juice. Put the fish in a folding wire gridiron ("the cost of a good one is about 70 cents"), then broil until crispy on the outside. Tip: "Cooling is fatal to enjoyment."

3. To bake flounder, halibut or turbot, melt four ounces of butter in a baking dish, sprinkle in a teaspoon of flour, then stir. Add a pinch of salt and pepper, nutmeg, chopped parsley, two or three chopped mushrooms and three pounds of fish. Pour a glass of vinegar over this mixture. Cover and bake in a moderate oven until done. Tip: "Very flavorful for breakfast."

CLASSY COOKING

Korbel vintners of California, producers of champagne, have sent us these recipes for fish that Almanac readers might enjoy experimenting with for a real taste treat.

CHAMPAGNE FISH GRATINEE
1 onion, finely chopped
2 tbsp. minced fresh parsley
4 oz. mushrooms, sliced
½ cup dry bread crumbs
4 fish fillets
salt and pepper, to taste
¾ cup champagne
½ cup shredded mozzarella cheese

In a greased baking dish, place half the onions, parsley, mushrooms, and bread crumbs. Place the fish fillets on top. Season with salt and pepper and cover with the remaining vegetables. Pour the champagne over this mixture.

Bake in a 375°F oven ten minutes. Sprinkle with the remaining bread crumbs and the cheese. Bake 15 minutes longer. Serves four.

Crawfish Jambalaya

3 pounds (about) crawfish tails
½ cup butter
2 tablespoons flour
6 onions, shredded (green), chopped parsley, chopped onion tops
Salt, black pepper and red pepper to taste
3 cups cooked rice

Melt butter and add flour. Brown a little. Add onions and simmer until soft; add fat from crawfish heads. Simmer another few minutes then add tails, parsley and onion tops and seasonings. Cook 15 minutes. When ready add hot cooked rice.

OVEN-BAKED CHAMPAGNE SOLE
1 onion, thinly sliced
2 fillets of sole (or other firm white fish), 6 ounces each
½ cup champagne
salt and pepper, to taste
½ cup butter, softened

Spread the onions in a greased baking dish, just large enough to hold the fish in a single layer. Place the fish over the onions. Add the champagne and season with salt and pepper. Bake the fish, covered, in a 400°F oven for 15 minutes.

Strain the cooking liquid into a saucepan (keep the fish warm). Cook until reduced to two tablespoons. Add the butter and stir until melted. Serve the sauce over the fish. Serves two.

BARBECUED FISH IN FOIL
For each portion:
1 small, whole fish or fish fillet or steak
salt and pepper, to taste
1 slice lemon
1 bay leaf
1 tbsp. butter
3 tbsp. champagne
1 sheet aluminum foil

Place the fish on the foil and raise the sides slightly. Season with salt and pepper and place the lemon and bay leaf on the fish. Dot with butter and sprinkle with the champagne. Seal the foil well. Cook over hot coals for about 40 minutes.

TURTLE A LA KING

6 hard-cooked eggs
2 tablespoons butter
2 cups light cream
Dash of pepper, allspice and nutmeg
½ teaspoon salt
2 cups cooked turtle meat, chopped

Remove egg yolks from the whites, carefully cutting the whites in quarters lengthwise. Press yolks through a sieve, then cream with the butter. Scald the cream in a double boiler, add the seasonings. Beat in the egg yolk mixture. Add the turtle meat and heat thoroughly. Serve hot garnished with the reserved egg whites.

BATTER-FRIED BLUEGILLS

Oil for deep frying
½ cup flour
2 tbsp. cornstarch
½ tsp. salt
¼ tsp. pepper
1 egg yolk
½ cup water
1 egg white
1 pound (about) bluegill fillets, (or other sunfish)
1 lemon

Combine the flour, cornstarch, pepper and salt and sift together onto a plate or piece of waxed paper. Beat the egg yolk and water to a smooth cream then incorporate the flour mixture a few tablespoons at a time. Just before using the batter, beat the egg white until stiff enough to stand in peaks when lifted on the beater. Scoop the egg white into the batter and fold it gently with a spoon or spatula.

Heat the oil in a heavy kettle. Pat the fish fillets dry with paper towels or damp cloth. Pick up fillets with tongs and dip into batter and carefully drop into the hot oil. Deep fry for four or five minutes, turning them as they brown. This will require about three minutes. As they brown, transfer to paper towels or brown paper to drain.

Arrange fillets on warm platter and serve them at once accompanied by wedges of lemon.

BLUEGILL CANAPÉS

What do you do with little bluegills? Many simply throw the little critters off to the side as a treat for raccoons or some wild animals, or they take them home for fertilizer in the garden.

Those little three- and four-inch bluegills are tasty, even if they do lack meat. Fillet them, skin them, and boil them in water for three to four minutes. Chill them, and then cut them into strips, put them on ice, and serve for a panfish cocktail—just as you would prepare a shrimp cocktail.

-134-

FISH STEAKS PEKING

1 egg white
3 teaspoons cornstarch
2 pounds of fish steaks
2 tablespoons cooking oil
½ cup chicken broth
¼ cup dry sherry
1 tablespoon dark corn syrup
¼ teaspoon salt

With a fork beat egg white and one teaspoon of the cornstarch until blended. Dip fish steaks in this mixture, coating all sides. Heat oil in a large skillet over medium heat. Add fish and sear on both sides, about two minutes. Remove fish from skillet. Stir broth, sherry, corn syrup, remaining two teaspoons cornstarch and salt in skillet and bring to boil over medium heat, stirring constantly until thickened. Return fish steaks to skillet and cook about two minutes on each side until done. Remove from skillet and pour sauce over steaks. Serves four.

Catfish Stew

2 pounds (about) skinned catfish fillets
5 slices bacon
1½ cups onion, chopped
1 28-ounce can tomatoes
1 8-ounce can tomato sauce
3 cups potatoes, peeled and diced
2 Tbsp. Worcestershire sauce
¼ tsp. Tabasco sauce
Salt and pepper to taste

Cut fillets into 1½-inch pieces. In a heavy Dutch oven, fry the bacon over low heat until crisp. Drain on paper. Crumble and set aside.
Add the onion to Dutch oven, cover and cook about five minutes or until tender. Stir in the remaining ingredients except bacon and fish pieces. Bring to a boil and simmer 30 minutes over moderate heat. Add bacon and catfish, cover and gently simmer for ten minutes or until fish flakes easily. Serve with hard rolls, toast or corn muffins. Serves five or six.

POACHED SALMON

1 salmon, 4 to 6 lbs.
1 small onion, cut into chunks
1 celery rib, cut into chunks
1 carrot, cut into chunks
2 bay leaves
½ cup dry white wine (optional)
parsley or watercress sprigs
lemon and/or lime slices

Put enough water into a large roasting pan or fish poacher to cover the salmon. Add the onion, celery, carrot, bay leaves and white wine to the water.
Cover and bring to a boil. Lower the heat and simmer for 15 minutes. Place the salmon on a rack or in a double thickness of cheesecloth and lower it into the bubbling water. Bring the water back to a boil, then lower the heat until the water is slowly bubbling.
Cover the pan and poach the fish for 10 minutes per inch thickness. (Measure the fish at the thickest place on the back to determine cooking time.) Most salmon will require about 25 to 30 minutes. Be sure the water is bubbling before starting to time. The fish will flake easily on the back when it is cooked.
Lift the fish from the liquid and place on a heated platter. Strip off the top skin and garnish with greens and lemon or lime slices. Serve immediately, or cool and serve. Serves five to eight.

NOVA SCOTIA FISH CHÓWDER

According to Buck Doming of Roanoke, Virginia, if you're served steaming-hot fish chowder while fishing aboard a Nova Scotia charterboat, this is how it's made.

2 pounds haddock (or any whitefish) fillets
3 large cans Carnation milk
3 large diced Idaho potatoes
¼ pound butter
3 large onions, sliced
yellow cornmeal

Dip fish fillets in yellow cornmeal. Cook in frying pan in Crisco until done.
Place potatoes and onions in pan with just enough water to cover, add salt and pepper, and cook seven or eight minutes, or until potatoes are done. Add butter while potatoes are cooking. Do not pour off water.
Break the cooked fish into chunks and add to potatoes and onions. Add Carnation milk and heat. Do not boil. Serves 14 bowls.

FISH STOCK

If you're like me you hate throwing away any part of a gamefish (except the gills and viscera). After filleting a fish, I always save the backbone and head to make stock for soups and casseroles.
To prepare basic fish stock, toss the heads and backbones into a pot, cover with cold water (do not add any flavorings yet), and bring to a boil. Lower heat, cover and simmer for one hour, skimming off any scum that comes to the surface. Let cool and then strain through cheesecloth into plastic containers, one cup per container. Freeze stock for later use. Discard the heads and backbones.
I use fish stock to make rice soup: For each serving bring four tablespoons of rice to a boil in one cup of fish stock. Salt and pepper to taste. Add a pinch of thyme, one heaping tablespoon of diced onion, and one half of a garlic clove. Cook until rice is done.
Try adding one cup of fish stock to a packet of dried onion soup, boil and serve.
You can use fish stock instead of water in any dish where the flavors are compatible.

ARMENIAN BAKED FISH

3 lbs. whitefish (any white-fleshed bland fish may be substituted)
3 fresh tomatoes or 1 small can tomatoes
1 clove garlic, mashed
1 tbsp. flour
1 cup water
4 tbsp. minced parsley
½ cup olive oil
juice of 1 lemon
1 tsp. salt
½ tsp. pepper

Fillet and rinse fish. Spread the fillets, skin side down, in a buttered baking pan.
Cover fish with the tomatoes, garlic and the flour mixed with the water. Sprinkle with parsley. Season with salt and pepper. Pour oil and lemon juice all around fish. Bake at 325° for 20 to 40 minutes, depending on the thickness of the fish. Spoon pan juices over the fish several times while baking. May be served hot or cold. Garnish with sliced lemon. Serves six.

FISH CHOWDER

Fish fillets,* two pounds
cornmeal
vegetable oil
3 large diced Idaho potatoes
3 large sliced onions
salt
pepper
¼ pound butter
3 large cans evaporated milk

Dip fish fillets in yellow cornmeal. Fry in vegetable oil until done. Remove fish from pan and drain on paper towels. Put potatoes and onions in four-quart pan with just enough water to cover, add salt and pepper. Cook seven or eight minutes or until potatoes are done. Add butter while potatoes are cooking. Do not pour off water. Break the cooked fish into chunks and add to the potatoes and onions. Finally, add canned milk and heat. *Do not boil!* Season to taste. Serves about 14 bowls.
*Any fish fillet such as walleye, cod, smallmouth or pollack will make a fine chowder.

Pickled Salmon

4 to 5 pounds salmon
2 quarts vinegar
1 ounce whole peppercorns
1½ tsp. grated nutmeg
1 tbsp. salad oil

Wrap salmon in washed cheesecloth or lightweight muslin and simmer in salted water to cover for 40 to 45 minutes. Lift from kettle and drain well; wrap in dry cloth and refrigerate.

For the pickle use one quart of water in which the salmon was cooked, the vinegar, peppercorns, nutmeg and mace. Boil this mixture in a tightly covered kettle for a few minutes. Cool. When cold pour over salmon, which has been placed in a glass dish or jar. Pour the oil on top of the pickle and place the dish or jar in a cool, dry place or in the refrigerator. This will keep for weeks if no one with a six-pack and a loaf of rye happens to be around.

RAINBOW TROUT MONTANA

4 rainbow trout (or 4 pounds)
½ tsp. paprika
1 tsp. salt
¼ tsp. pepper
½ cup (about) yellow stone-ground cornmeal.

Wipe cleaned trout with a damp cloth. Blend paprika, salt and pepper in a cup or small bowl, rub trout inside and out with mixture. Spread cornmeal on a sheet of waxed paper; roll trout in it.

Add cooking oil or cooking oil and butter, to heated skillet until about a half-inch deep. Heat but don't allow to smoke; brown fish about ten minutes, turn and fry other side five or six minutes or until done. Place on platter, surround with watercress and sprinkle with chopped parsley.

Hot biscuits, sliced tomatoes and pan-fried potatoes complement the meal.

Butterfly 'Em!

At intervals throughout the spring and summer months a species of grunion (*Leureshis tenuis*), commonly referred to as "surf fish," obeying the age-old laws of nature ride the waves to the beaches along the Pacific shore. A bold run, with the proper net, into the breaking fish-laden waves will be rewarded with the makings of a gourmet fish fry. These fish keep well frozen, so you might as well make enough runs to make the wetting worthwhile.

To prepare surf fish for frying, remove heads and tails, cut down the belly, end to end, and remove entrails. With thumb and forefinger pull off all the small fins—a quick, sharp jerk does this cleanly. Using both thumbs open the fish, supporting the back with fingers, and press gently but firmly on the backbone, moving its full length. This will allow the tiny backbone and ribs to be lifted out. Care should be taken not to sever the skin along the back. When you have finished you'll have a butterflied fish. Continue until the number needed are finished, stacking them flat. Allow six to ten fish for each person to be served. Store in the refrigerator until wanted. Partially freezing the fish helps to facilitate the bone removing chore; or partially thawing if fish have been frozen.

Prepare the remainder of the meal and set the table before frying the fish.

In a brown bag put one cup flour for each 24 to 30 fish, ½-teaspoon salt and ½-teaspoon paprika. Pepper if you wish.

Heat oil for deep frying. Drop five or six fish into the bag with the seasoned flour. Shake. Remove the fish one at a time and carefully lower into the hot oil. Cook until a light golden brown. This requires only a short time—a minute or two to the side. When done remove to a heated platter and keep warm. Repeat until all fish are cooked. French fries can be cooked in the hot oil immediately following the fish, or better, at the same time in another kettle or skillet of hot oil.

Serve fish hot with wedges of lemon. Accompany with a large tossed green salad, the fries, buttered toast and a dry white wine.

Catfish With Mushrooms

2 medium catfish
1 cup sliced mushrooms (puffballs may be used)
1 medium onion, finely chopped
2 tsp. fat or bacon grease
Salt
1 cup bannock or biscuit crumbs
½ cup vinegar added to ½ cup water

Remove heads from cleaned fish and rub salt in the body cavities. Place side-by-side in center of heavy-duty foil folded double, or two pieces one atop the other. Foil should be lightly greased.

Melt fat in a frying pan. Add mushrooms, onion and a generous sprinkle of the vinegar mixture. Fry until onions are lightly browned. Add remaining vinegar water and the crumbs. Set aside to cool. Stuff fish with the cooled crumb mixture and roll loosely in foil, sealing well. Place the packages over coals and cook for 25 to 30 minutes; turn once. Test for doneness. If not cooked to your liking, reclose and return to heat for a few minutes, being careful not to overcook.

CARP IN BEER

4 pounds (about) carp fillets cut in serving-sized pieces
salt
3 cups beer
2 onions, thinly sliced
1 bay leaf, or 5 juniper berries
1 lemon, sliced
1 tablespoon flour
1 tablespoon sugar
pepper

Sprinkle fish lightly with salt and allow to stand for one hour.

Place fish in saucepan, pour in beer and add onions, bay leaf or juniper berries, lemon and a generous sprinkle of pepper. Simmer gently over moderately low heat until fish flakes easily. Remove fish to hot platter.

Cream flour with enough butter to make a soft paste and stir into broth. Add sugar and simmer until thickened. Pour sauce over fish and serve. The amount of butter and flour may need to be adjusted according to the amount of broth you have left. Serves four.

Fish Boiled In Parchment

2 pounds boneless fillets
2 tablespoons butter
2 tablespoons minced onion
1 tablespoon minced parsley
1 tablespoon lemon juice
salt and pepper

Dampen two sheets of parchment and spread out flat. Brush with oil. Cut fish into serving pieces and portion equally on each sheet of paper. Place one teaspoon each of butter and onion on each serving and sprinkle with parsley, lemon juice, salt and pepper. Gather edges of papers and tie securely. Place in boiling water and cook 15 minutes. Remove fish to hot platter, taking care not to lose any of the juices. This method enhances the flavor of any fish.

BAKED STRIPED BASS

1 lb. onions, sliced
6 tbsp. olive oil
½ cup currants
½ cup pine nuts
¼ tsp. cinnamon
¼ tsp. allspice
1 tsp. salt
¼ tsp. pepper
4 tbsp. chopped parsley
2 tbsp. lemon juice
½ cup tomato sauce
¼ cup dry white wine
1 lemon, thinly sliced
1 striped bass, about 3 lbs.

Scale and clean the bass. Fillet it butterfly style so the fillets remain attached to each other. Wash and place in a baking dish.

Sauté onions in oil until transparent. Add currants, pine nuts and seasonings, stirring all the while, then add parsley and lemon juice.

Fill fish with the sautéed mixture, spreading evenly.

Mix the tomato sauce and wine, then pour this over the closed fish. Put lemon slices on top. Bake at 375° F for about 45 minutes, or until the flesh flakes with a fork. Excellent when served cold as a buffet dish. Makes six servings.

EASY FREEZING

Old-time salmon and trout gourmets know that the best-tasting fish are cleaned just before cooking. So if you have the facilities, keep your fish on ice, *without gutting*, then freeze as soon as possible, again *without gutting*. When ready to cook, thaw the fish, gut and cook.

FINE FILLET KNIFE

A grapefruit knife makes an excellent fillet knife for fish. It has a serrated edge for easy slicing, plus a downward curve in the blade that conveniently fits the contours of a fish. A grapefruit knife is also more economical—one costs about half the price of conventional fish fillet knives.

MAPLE LEAF TROUT

4 trout, 10 to 12 inches
2 tbsps. maple syrup
⅓ cup milk
¾ cup cornmeal, seasoned with salt and pepper
2 tbsps. butter
2 tbsps. cooking oil

Dry the cleaned trout with paper towels. The heads may be removed. Mix the maple syrup and milk in a shallow dish and dip the trout in the mixture, allowing some to seep inside the stomach cavity.

Roll the trout in cornmeal, coating the skin thoroughly. In a large, heavy frying pan, heat the butter and oil over medium-high heat. Fry the trout for 5 minutes on each side until they are nicely browned and flake easily when probed with a fork at the thickest point on their backs.

Serve immediately on a heated platter. Serves four.

PINE SMOKED TROUT

The simplest method of getting a nice smoky flavor when cooking trout is with a wire holder. Be sure that it will hold the trout securely so it can be turned over—like the type made to hold hot dogs or hamburgers.

Cut several pine boughs, place them on your campfire and lay the holder with your trout directly on top. Light the pine boughs. The fire will sear, cook and smoke your trout in about a minute before burning itself out. Turn the holder over to sear the other side, add a couple more pine boughs and light your fire again. Naturally, if the trout are bigger, you'll need a bigger fire so the fish cook longer. I have found that a couple of pine boughs and less than a minute for each side is perfect for half-pound trout.

Easy Baking-Powder Biscuits

The sun has set and the campfire is glowing—it's the perfect time to set up a reflector oven and make some baking-powder biscuits. It is no trouble to brew up a batch: Put two cups of flour in a pan, add four teaspoons of baking powder and one teaspoon of salt. Work in two tablespoons of shortening, melted to make it go faster. To this crumbly mixture add enough milk (or water) to make a stiff dough. Form the dough into dollar-sized chunks, drop on the greased reflector oven, and place it close to the fire.

TEN MINUTES AN INCH

The most difficult part of cooking fish is being certain when they are ready to serve. Too much or too little cooking can very well result in a tasty meal becoming unpalatable.

The Nevada Department of Fish and Game has this suggestion, devised a number of years ago by the Canadian Department of Fisheries. They found that the best rule in cooking fish whether by frying, baking, broiling or poaching, is to cook ten minutes for each inch of thickness. For frozen fish, there's no need to thaw, just change to 20 minutes per inch. If cooking in foil is your specialty, add five to ten minutes to the total. The method works especially well for baked fish. It is recommended to bake at 425° to 450°F. for the calculated time.

CANADIAN FISH CHOWDER

On our northern lake camping trips we always plan a hearty chowder for dinner at least once a week. The following recipe was acquired on Canada's Lake Nipigon about 30 years ago. It is a simple one-pot meal.

4 medium potatoes
2 medium onions
1 carrot
4 slices bacon
1 lb. fish fillets
1 13-oz. can Milnot or condensed milk
1 can cream-style corn
salt and pepper

Dice the vegetables, add salt and pepper, barely cover with water, and simmer until tender. Dice and add the bacon and simmer 10 minutes. Dice the fish into bite-sized pieces, add, and simmer 10 minutes. Add the Milnot or condensed milk and simmer 10 minutes. Add the corn and simmer 10 minutes while stirring frequently to prevent sticking. Serves four.

Cheap and Delicious

The common white sucker, whitehorse—call him what you may—will never enter the record book for its dazzling display of bait spitting and tail dancing, or as the filet mignon of fish flesh. However don't knock'em before you taste'em. Taken from cold, clean water, they are a taste delight when ground and formed into patties.

Pattie preparation is quite simple. After running the skinned chunks or fillets through the grinder, form firm patties and roll in seasoned bread crumbs. Then fry in hot grease or oil until golden brown.

Doesn't that sound good? Cheap too. Have you priced canned salmon lately?

ODDS AND ENDS

ODDS AND ENDS

FACTS AND TIPS

YOUR OWN FISH POND

A fishing pond can be a source of pride, joy and personal fulfillment. Consider the possibility of transforming a stretch of land into a pond capable of supporting fish, birds and mammals.

Contact the local office of the Soil Conservation Service (SCS), where there are specialists in fish-pond planning and construction work. A good reference book is *Creative Fishing* (Stackpole Books, Cameron & Kelker Sts., P.O. Box 1831, Harrisburg, PA 17105) which deals with all phases of pond planning, building and management.

Locate an acre or more of land with a reliable water source, such as a spring or stream; or select a suitable area which retains run-off.

Construction features of the pond and dam can be discussed with the SCS. Under certain circumstances, the federal agency can assist with construction or management costs. In addition, the SCS can recommend ways of building the pond to make maximum use of the natural slope of the land and cut down cost.

Decide the type of fish best suited to the climate, water quality and fishing preference. A fisheries biologist from the local conservation department can recommend the most suitable fish for your specific area. The Bureau of Sport Fisheries and Wildlife will provide advice and at times furnish fingerlings for stocking under certain conditions. Check with your local game and fish department about stocking ponds under the Farm Pond Program.

FISHING SIGNS

The Idaho Department of Fish and Game is using the new International Symbol signs on waters with special fishing regulations. Other states soon may follow suit.

CLOSED TO ALL FISHING

OPEN TO FISHING

NO MOTORS WATER

CATCH-AND-RELEASE
Artificial flies or lures with single barbless hooks are required.

WILD TROUT WATERS
Release trout under 13 inches. Use artificial flies or lures with single barbless hooks.

FLYFISHING ONLY
Only artificial flies, flyline, flyrod and fly reels may be used.

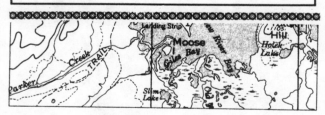

Two-Season Maps

Sportsmen who regularly pore over maps for hours during the hunting season rarely break them out before a fishing excursion, yet a map could spell the difference between success and failure.

Maps show the angler places he will want to explore, such as oxbows and the mouths of feeder streams.

The river width in conjunction with the gradient—easily determined by checking the map contour lines—may dictate whether to float or wade a certain section.

In either a lake or stream situation, maps will give you an indication of possible access points so you can decide whether a foot or vehicular approach would be better.

Put-in and take-out points for a float trip can be clearly marked on a map. This could spare you, particularly in bad weather, a lengthy and miserable wait while your fishing partner drives down from an upstream location to find you at day's end.

TAXIDERMIST TIPS

Alaskan taxidermist Hunter Fisher has Ten Commandments to be followed to ensure that your trophy makes the journey from stream to his hands in the best possible condition.

1. Do not use nets or gaff hooks. Beach your trophy or use a tailer.
2. Do not use rocks, clubs or knives to dispatch your trophy. Mother Nature will do just fine without you.
3. Do not clean your trophy. A fish in the round will ensure a more lifelike mount.
4. Do not use plastic bags to carry home your trophy. Wrap it in a wet T-shirt or other soft cotton cloth.
5. Do not wrap your trophy in grass or leaves. They tend to discolor or leave imprints on the fish.
6. Do not attempt to skin your trophy. This should be entrusted to the skilled hands of a taxidermist.
7. Do not keep your trophy frozen too long. The longer it stays in the freezer, the harder it is to work with.
8. Do not misdirect Mother Nature. If your trophy is a hook-jawed spawner, attempting to make a fresh-run fish out of him will result in a silly looking, hook-jawed silvery fish.
9. Do not ask for the meat from your trophy. Trophy fish are caught and kept for the memories, not table fare.
10. Do not rush your taxidermist. His skills were honed with years of patience, and pressuring him will have an effect on your finished mount.

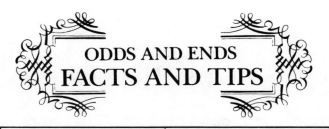
FISH TAGGING

The famous naturalist-painter John James Audubon is thought to have been the first person in the United States to band birds. In the 1830s he tied silken threads around the legs of songbirds.

The tagging of fish took longer to develop. It wasn't until 1873 that an angler tagged Atlantic salmon in the Penobscot River in Maine.

However, because of the complexities involved, fish tagging was relatively untried. By 1910 it is estimated only 100,000 fish had been tagged nationwide. By 1933 the total had grown to less than 500,000. Programs were handicapped by the lack of efficient types of tags for the majority of fish species. Early studies were mostly utilized to learn migration habits.

Over the years tags have been made out of every conceivable type of material including silver (best), bone, brass, leather, nickel, rubber and plastic. Tagging spots on various species have been on the gill cover, in the back muscle, in front of the back-fin. Fish have also been identified by notching certain fins or the jaw.

Tagging now plays an important role in fisheries management, providing vital information on parent streams of anadromous fish, racial studies of fish on feeding areas and nursery areas, age and growth rates, mortality rates, and speed and migration routes, survival and growth of transplants and survival rates of hatchery transplants.

★

Old riverbeds, canals or stream channels are regular routes used by fish in man-made lakes. You can find them by using a flasher sonar and by consulting topographic maps obtainable at your county engineer's office. These are good spots for fishing.

What's Fishing Success?

Jim Chapralis, an internationally known fisherman and editor of the PanAngler, a fishing newsletter, has analyzed what determines fishing success. Here are his thoughts:

Forty percent depends on weather. Usually you have no control over weather. Storms, floods, winds and a dozen other meteorological aberrations can ruin your chances.

Twenty-five percent of the credit should go to the guide. Reasons Chapralis, "Certainly the guide gets more than 25 percent of the blame if the fishing is lousy. We should gracefully assign him that much if it's good." He says that as a rule if a camp has ten guides a couple of them will be outstanding, and a couple would be considered poor. The rest will be average.

Thirty-five percent depends on fishing skill. Here's how he breaks that down:

Proper equipment. Matching your equipment to the demands is the first important step. Beginners' most common mistake—purchasing inferior equipment to save money.

Equipment Preparation. Sharp hooks, properly tied leaders, rods checked, reels lubricated.

Knowledge of Species. The more intimately you know the quirks of your quarry, the more you'll fool them.

Casting Ability. Often this is a vital necessity. Examples: snook fishing in mangroves, bass along a grass line, rising trout.

Fish-Fighting Ability. The skill of the strike and knowing exactly how much pressure can be applied lets the expert catch fish that others lose.

Positive Fishing Approach. "All the famous fishermen—the Aptes, Sosins, McClanes—simply know they are going to catch big fish. They never lose their alertness."

How important is luck? Well, says Jim, you more or less have to luck out on weather. Often you luck out getting the good guide or the bad one. Often whether the fish rises to your lure or another's depends on luck. But overall luck plays a lesser role. Proof? Look at the consistency of the great fishermen. Day in day out, they always produce. Can they be eternally lucky?

FISH SHRINKAGE

You've heard about how a possible record was missed because a fisherman didn't get his fish weighed for several hours. Well, it's not nearly as critical as imagined. Here's a handy shrinkage chart you might want to retain for settling arguments:

FISH WEIGHT, POUNDS	AFTER 6 HOURS		AFTER 12 HOURS	
	Lbs.	Ounces	Lbs.	Ounces
1	—	15½	—	15
3	2	13¾	2	13
7	6	10	6	8
10	9	8½	9	6
15	14	4¾	14	1
20	19		18	12
30	28	9½	28	2
40	38	2	37	8

These tests were made after fish had been removed from the water and left in open air. If you keep your fish in water, or moistly wrapped in, say, burlap, the weight loss should be negligible because most of it comes from dehydration.

BLUE-RIBBON STREAMS

Montana's trout streams are famous the world over. Fishermen speak of the state's "blue-ribbon" waters—the Madison, West Gallatin, Big Hole, upper Missouri, Yellowstone and Rock Creek—in reverent tones, and all hope to someday wade these waters.

In 1959 the U.S. Bureau of Sport Fisheries and Wildlife, now known as the Fish and Wildlife Service, undertook a survey of the Missouri River Basin. Part of the survey was a report entitled "A Classification of Montana Fishing Streams," in which streams in the state were divided into five classes on the basis of their relative value for recreational fishing. The best streams, those with "national" value, were termed Class I, the next-best Class II, and so forth down to Class V. A map was part of the report, and on that map the streams were colored according to the old "country fair" format—blue for Class I, red for Class II, and so on. It's thought that a state publicity man came up with the term "blue-ribbon" to describe the blue-colored Class I streams, and "blue-ribbon stream" became a part of Montana's—and the nation's—trout-fishing vocabulary. "Blue-ribbon" just has more of a ring than "Class I."

SUPER CLEANER

Carry some pipe cleaners in your fishing vest and tacklebox. Keep them on the workbench. They're great for cleaning out the slots in a jackknife. They're fine for holding coils of fish line in proper order. Wrap one around a hook, and you have a wooly worm that will take fish. When cleaning your outboard motor's spark plugs, use one to wipe out the inside after cleaning. Run one back and forth between a gun barrel and the magazine for a good cleaning job. Pipe cleaners will sub for ties on bags, such as refuse bags. Use them for temporary shims on loose reel seats, etc. And of course, they do clean out pipes, too!

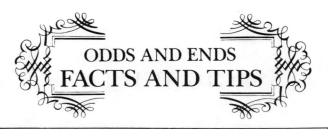
Beneficial Burlap

One of the most useful items on a hunting or fishing trip is the clean burlap bag. In a pinch, one bag filled with rocks and tied at the top makes a substitute boat anchor. Hooked to the side of the boat, it can be used as a live bag for fish. In camp, food can be placed in the bag and tied to a high tree limb to keep it out of the reach of raccoons and bears.

A burlap bag makes a fine cooler. Place perishables in a waterproof container and wrap this in water-soaked burlap—evaporation keeps the food cooler.

Fish can be wrapped in wet burlap to keep them fresh and cool on the trip home. You can keep gamebirds or animals cool the same way, taking care to protect the feathers, hair or flesh from direct contact with the fabric.

Burlap bags may be hard to find in this day of plastic. Usually grain elevators and feed stores in farm areas have them. Bulk burlap can also be purchased from plant nurseries, where it is used to wrap and protect roots of trees and shrubs.

AMEN

Parson Joseph Seccombe is credited with writing the first American work on sport. Originally a sermon delivered to a group of fishermen and entitled "A Discourse Utter'd in Part at Ammauskeeg-Falls in the Fishing-Season, 1739," the work was published in Boston in 1743. The sermon was a defense of the innocent pleasure and proper recreation of angling, for such pursuits were "necessary for the better support of the body and the soul." Well spoken, Parson Seccombe.

★

A foul-weather suit is a must even when it isn't raining. Use it as a windbreaker to keep you from chilling when running to and from fishing both early and late in the day.

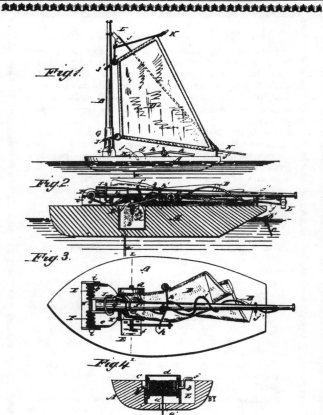

Fig.1

Fig.2

Fig.3

Fig.4

Oddball Fishing Tackle

During the late 19th century thousands of patents were issued relating to fishing tackle. The genius and originality of the inventors of these items are clearly evident, however misguided. One of the inventions that deserve top honors was a fishing float devised by R.W.E. Aldrich that was constructed in the shape of a boat, featuring an anchor, a folding mast with sail (whose significance was paramount), and a fishing reel installed amidships. To use the float, the hook was baited, a length of line drawn from the reel, and the mast locked in a horizontal position by a trip bar attached to the reel. According to the inventor, when a fish took the bait, the sail would pop up, giving free play to the fish and signaling the bite! It was recommended that the bottoms of the floats be painted green to resemble leaves of water plants and not frighten the fish.

Diehard Fisherman

Emil Ambos was an avid angler to put it mildly. The Columbus, Ohio, man lived for the sport. Being aware that life was fleeting, he gave much thought to leaving a monument that was befitting—one that depicted his life. Not for him the impressive marble or granite columns on his grave. Nor weeping cherubim, gentle lambs of limestone, solemn crosses, or flying angels. Should you visit Green Lawn Cemetary in Columbus you will see a life-sized figure of Emil Ambos happily surveying his peaceful surroundings clad in a complete fisherman's outfit. Emil Ambos isn't dead—he's just gone fishin'.

NEAT OILER

Many reels and other items of outdoor equipment are equipped with small holes that are designed to be oiled with either a nozzle-equipped tube of oil or a bottle cap equipped with a piece of wire as an oil dropper. Unfortunately, the oil we are using or prefer to use may not come in one of those containers that will let us do a neat job. A paper clip makes a perfect substitute and has the added advantage that its normal function allows spare clips to be attached to many pieces of equipment, even trays in tackleboxes, where they will be handy for instant use

To use, straighten out one end of the clip. Dip the straightened end in the oil and transfer the drop it picks up to the spot to be oiled. This method can also be used on pressure type oil holes such as found on Penn saltwater reels. Use two paper clips, one to push in the spring-loaded ball to hold it open, the second to transfer the oil as to a regular hole. This seems to do a neater job than the nozzle-type containers normally used on these pressure holes. The regular-sized clip works better than the jumbo size, probably because the wire of the regular clip is about the same size as used in oil bottles.

Dandy Fish Scaler

Almost everyone in these United States drinks soda pop, so it is quite simple for anyone to come up with one of these free fish scalers. You can even make them to size for the type of fish in your area, whether small bass or big bluefish. The number of bottlecaps used will depend on the size of your scaler. Puncture a hole in the center of each cap from the inside and screw each cap to the board. Do not snug screws down as the caps will clean scales faster if they float free.

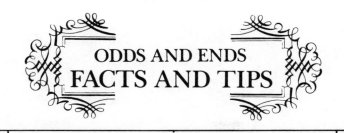

FISH FRY

A rather fishy story emerged recently from the Dayton Power and Light Company. Officials of the Ohio utility swear that the cause of a power outage was a 14-inch smallmouth bass.

It seems that at 12:29 a.m., the fish knocked out an electric transformer 30 feet in the air on a power pole. However, the fish was helped on its subversive mission by a huge owl. The owl apparently caught the fish and then landed on the electric transformer. Both owl and fish were fried.

DP&L Chief Don Butts said, "My crewmen took a photo of both the bird and fish to confirm the cause of the outage, and their sobriety."

ADDED INSURANCE

A short while after the death of a close friend I was approached by his widow and asked if I would like to have any of his "old fishing stuff."

I spent the next couple of evenings gathering his rather extensive array of tackle, lures, and flytying material together. I was amazed at the amount of gear he had acquired in some 40 years of pursuing the sport, but the real surprise came when I finally figured out the approximate worth of the equipment.

The outcome was a series of small advertisements with local newspapers and outdoors groups that resulted in my friend's widow receiving a respectable sum of money for what had seemed valueless.

This spurred me on to cataloging my own collection of fishing gear, firearms, boating equipment, even the outdoor books in my modest library.

My family has been well briefed on the list and the probable value of its contents should I suddenly depart for wherever the place is to which unrepentant anglers are summoned.

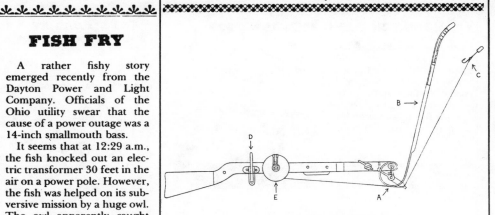

...A Catapult Rod?

In 1915, Francis Phillips was granted a patent on a catapultlike casting rod. It was a rifle stock device with a strong coil spring (A) at the muzzle end. A long arm (B) of the spring held the terminal tackle (C) and was bent back along the top of the stock. A latch (D) held the arm under tension of the coil spring. When the trigger was pulled, the arm catapulted the line out over the water. A reel (E) retrieved the line.

There is no record of the device having been manufactured.

Wake-Up Magic

The first night out on our fishing trip with Grandpa we discovered we had forgotten his old alarm clock. "Never mind," he said, opening the oatmeal box. "This will get us up."

He stepped outside and tossed a generous supply of the cereal on top of the camper. With the first streak of daylight we awoke to what sounded like hailstones. A flock of noisy birds was having breakfast on our metal roof.

HAND TOWEL HOLDER

Catching a nice fish is a great moment but it can often be followed by an unpleasant one when you try to get the slime off of your hands.

Paper towels aren't a good cure for this problem—they always blow away or accumulate as trash. A regular hand towel is generally somewhere in the car or tacklebox while you are downstream. A pair of blue jeans or an old T-shirt will take only so much slime before "gangrene" sets in.

The simplest solution is to have a towel with you, but there are options. The old standby I once used was a golf bag towel with a grommet and shower curtain hook in it. Technology has now brought us the magic of Velcro.

Velcro can be sewn onto any towel, with the other half sewn on your fishing vest. A slip-on loop with one side of Velcro fastener on it can be worn on the belt and the towel hooked on, always at your side for ready use.

A bass fisherman from South Carolina I know has Velcro glued onto his boat hull in several places so there is always a towel within reach. They don't blow away when he takes off down the lake looking for another hotspot.

ST. PETER'S FISH

As a fisherman, I had been curious as to what kind of fish was used in feeding the biblical 5000. The man who taught me to flyfish, who was a man of the cloth, said the fish were similar to the bluegill.

The fish, dubbed St. Peter's fish, are tilapia. They are panfish that resemble bluegills. However, they grow much larger—up to five pounds—and their spawning is quite different: They are mouth breeders.

Using its mouth, a tilapia male prepares a small saucer-shaped depression in the soft pond bottom. The female deposits the eggs, and he fertilizes them. She then scoops up the eggs and carries them in her mouth for 10 to 14 days until the fry hatch and are large enough to care for themselves.

These fish are found in northern Africa and the Middle East and have been introduced to some southern states in this country. In ancient times tilapias were usually caught by nets similar to some seines still used today.

Fishing is important in the New Testament and is mentioned quite often. At least seven of the 12 disciples were fishermen, and Bethsaida, the home of Peter, Andrew and Phillip, means a place of nets or fishery.

The sign of the fish became the sign of the early Christians. According to one source, these early Christians had a secret sign by which they could identify themselves. When a Christian met someone along the way, he would quietly draw a single arc in the earth. If the stranger were Christian, he would complete the sign of the fish by simply adding a reversed arc.

★

Lantern users should tape extra mantels under the fuel tank or reservoir where they are always available.

BAITED BREATH

Here's a sneaky trick described in *Game Fish of the Northern States of America* by Robert Barnwell Roosevelt, published in 1862: "A boy having caught a sun-fish, runs his hook through its nose and out of its mouth, covering the point with a lively worm. Other sun-fish seeing their fellow have all to himself a fine, fat worm which he seems unable to master, collect around him, and by their number attract the bass, who dashes in among them, and while the rest make off, swallows the one with the worm, and of course himself falls prey to the ingenious young fisherman."

★

When you see the wake of a feeding or cruising fish, cast well beyond where the fish is working and bring the lure rapidly past, not at, the fish to trigger a strike.

MOUNT OR RELEASE

Modern taxidermists are so efficient they have fiberglass molds of almost any size for popular sporting species. Fiberglass is far more durable than a natural mounting, yet some say, "It's not real."

I believe the new mold is far better than the real thing because 1) it looks just as natural, 2) it is impervious to moths and bugs, and durable for handling or moving and 3) you didn't need to kill a prized specimen to get your mount.

How much more sensible to weigh and measure your trophy fish and release it to live on. Then, just tell the taxidermist the dimensions of your whopper and he can duplicate it for you.

FIN PROTECTION

If you've caught a trophy fish and intend to have it mounted, be sure to coat the fins with Vaseline petroleum jelly before packing the fish for transport. This will keep the fins from drying out and breaking while your trophy is on its way to the taxidermist.

HOOK, LINE AND SUPERSTITION

The average fisherman has more knowledge, skill and equipment than ever. But for days when the best lures and favorite fishing spots yield nothing but frustration, here are some fishing superstitions that may help assuage your pain:

In some parts of England, fishermen believe that to make fish bite you should remove an eye from the first one you catch and throw it into the water. It will look for other fish and draw them to your boat.

* * *

To bring them luck, fishermen in Northern Ireland always spit in the mouth of the first fish they catch.

* * *

Sit with your feet crossed while fishing, and you will catch a lot of fish.

* * *

A good time to fish is when the moon is on the wane. But if you see a new moon while you're fishing, look at the first coin you take from your pocket. If it's heads, you'll have good luck. If it's tails, you will catch no more fish.

* * *

According to American Indian legend, a hook that has already caught fish will bring good luck.

* * *

Some fishermen in England consider it lucky to quarrel with their families before going fishing.

* * *

Fishermen of Brittany take a cat with them when they go fishing. Cats love fish and can scent them from afar.

* * *

In Iceland, fishermen will not sing while fishing. And some anglers consider it unpardonable to whistle.

By holding a fish upside down, you keep it from squirming and so can remove the hook more easily.

MANICURE'S MANY CURES

A woman's container of manicure equipment isn't the sort of place you'd expect to find fishing and hunting gear, but the fact is that several hand-care products are quite useful in the outdoors.

"Hard As Nails" nail polish puts a tough coating on rod windings and fly heads. In its several colors, it can be used to dress up old lures and a coating of clear polish will prevent shiny surfaces from dulling or corroding.

Oily nail-polish remover quickly penetrates and lubricates frozen metal parts. Use it to free stuck ferrules and screws in reels or guns.

A double-grit fingernail emery board sharpens hooks and shines up lures. It's also ideal for cleaning corrosion and dirt from hard-to-reach places like electrical contacts and spark plugs.

Vaseline Intensive Care hand lotion affords ample protection against chapping, cracking and drying of your face and hands. Should you forget to use it at the start of the day, it will soften and smooth dry skin after your day afield is over.

STRIPERS BY REMOTE CONTROL

On a spring day in 1982, Alex Oswald and Ron Grove cruised to the edge of a no-boating zone on Raystown Lake near Huntingdon, Pennsylvania, and looked dejectedly into the off-limits area where hundreds of large striped bass boiled the water on a feeding spree. Casting as far as they could, Alex and Ron still couldn't come near the fish. So they returned home and adjourned to the workshop, where they designed and built a battery-operated, three-foot motor launch-equipped with a row of clothespin lure releases.

Then they went back to Raystown Lake, anchored again on the legal side of the marker buoys, and piloted their toy boat into the school of stripers by remote control. At that point, they jerked the lures free of the clothespins and retrieved them through the feeding fish.

Using this remote-control technique, Alex and Ron began to catch their limits of striped bass—some up to 19 pounds—with cheerful regularity until the state fish commission got wind of their success from rival fishermen and ruled the toy motorboat "an illegal fishing device."

Alex and Ron appealed that decision, claiming that all they had done, really, was invent a more efficient way to cast. District Magistrate James Kyper agreed with them and reversed the commission's decision. "These guys should get a medal, not arrested," he said. "It's an ingenious idea. I think the other fishermen are just jealous."

★

Do you really know what your lures look like to a fish? Most of us just guess from boatside observation. If you really want to fish intelligently, don a pair of goggles, sit on the bottom of a swimming pool and have a buddy reel your pet lures past you. Then you'll know what they look like to a fish and maybe understand why some catch more fish than others.

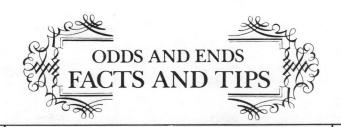

Insight Better Than Hindsight

Back in 1881, the Rev. Myron H. Reed, an enthusiastic angler, ventured this prediction:

"This is probably the last generation of Trout fishers. The children will not be able to find any. Already there are well-trodden paths by every stream in Maine, New York and Michigan. I know of but one river in North America by the side of which you can find no paper collar or other evidence of civilization; it is the Nameless River.

"Not that Trout will cease to be. They will be hatched by machinery, and raised in ponds, and fattened on chopped liver, and grow flabby and lose their spots. The Trout of the restaurant will not cease to be. He is no more like the Trout of the wild river than the fat and songless reed-bird is like the bobolink. Gross feeding and easy pond-life enervate and deprave him.

"The Trout that the children will know only by legend is the gold-sprinkled, living arrow of the Whitewater—able to zig-zag up the cataract, able to loiter in the rapids—whose dainty meat is the glancing butterfly."

An Angler's Dozen

While on a meandering fishing and camping trip in northwestern Quebec, my partner and I stopped off at a roadside tavern where we struck up a conversation with a colorful French Canadian woodsman.

As we drank a cold beer he amused and enlightened us with tales of the local fishing, pointing out many of the areas on a smoke-darkened map that appeared to have been on the wall for many years.

"Here you catch beeg Dore (walleye)—and Brochet (pike) as long as your leg," he said, tracing the outline of a fair-sized lake with a work-calloused finger.

"How about specks?" asked my partner, using the common Canadian name for brook trout.

"Specks? Truite? Hah! I tell you, you goin' to catch specks till your arms get tired in dis reever here where she come into de lake."

"Big ones?" my companion asked, his interest fully aroused.

The wiry little man took a long swallow at his beer and wiped the moisture from his droopy moustache with the back of his hand. Leaning across the table toward my friend he said, "Beeg? By golly, de las' time I was dere de feesh were so beeg it only take eight of dem to make a dozen."

CAJUN FISH PROPHECY

During the spring of 1941, while I was living in Houma, Louisiana, my next-door neighbor, A. J. Boudreaux, invited me to go fishing sometime with him in the bayou country.

About two weeks later, around 4:00 a.m. I heard a knock on my window—the signal we had agreed on. I dressed and walked over to Boudreaux's back porch. The kitchen door was open and he had already poured coffee for two. When we finished it and the warm, tasty doughnuts—both of which play a major role in Cajun hospitality—Boudreaux said, "Let's go into the living room and see how the fish bite today."

Not knowing what to expect, I followed him into the next room and watched him drop three or four flakes of oatmeal into a goldfish bowl. Four or five little fish swam around leisurely and ignored the food.

"Go home and go back to bed. The sac-á-lait ain't gonna bite today, my friend," Boudreaux announced with certainty.

"Boudreaux," I said, "next time see if the darned fish will bite before you wake me up!"

"Oh," he answered, "I j'es wanted you to see how I know when to go to fish."

Two weeks later I was again awakened by Boudreaux's knock on the window. I dressed, went next door and, over the usual coffee and doughnuts, the Cajun informed me "the fish are really gonna bite today!"

The confident fisherman had all the necessary equipment packed and the bateaux hooked to his car. In great anticipation of the bountiful catch awaiting and with the complete assurance provided by Boudreaux's prophetic goldfish, we struck out for Little Bayou Caiou. Upon arrival we launched the bateaux, cranked up the one-cylinder outboard and headed for the promised jackpot.

It might serve all you fishermen well to keep a bowl of goldfish handy to try old Boudreaux's "sure-fire test" before launching your boats or baiting your hooks. We really did load the bateaux with sac-á-lait that day!

ANGLER RECOGNITION AWARDS

When you catch a braggin'-sized fish, have it weighed before cleaning or mounting. It just might earn you an award from your state conservation department.

Many states have angler award programs. Weight, not length, is generally the determining factor for an award. Any fish matching or surpassing an established minimum weight is eligible for a citation.

Regulations and weight limits vary from state to state, but usually the following conditions must be met: The fish must be taken from public waters by rod and reel; it must be weighed on a certified scale; a photo of the fish must accompany the citation application. Check with your state conservation department for application procedures.

TRIP TIP

A friendly camper recently showed me a quick method for measuring distances on a map.

Bend a pipe cleaner or a piece of soft copper wire along the proposed map route, then straighten the cleaner or wire and measure it against the scale-of-miles chart in the corner of the map. This saves adding up all those short distances between small towns and remote crossroads and results in a fairly accurate reading of the mileage.

WELCOME ABOARD

An ingenious method of fishing used by the Chinese requires a rowboat with a white-painted board along one side. The board slopes from the gunwale to the surface of the water at an angle of about 45 degrees. For some reason, upon seeing this board gleaming in the moonlight, fish cannot resist the temptation to leap over it—and right into the boat.

Biting Bug Remedy

The mosquito and blackfly problem has been solved for me with a homemade remedy from a French-Canadian guide I met in the woods of Quebec.

He mixes two squares of camphor with a pint of olive oil and says it works for him every time. He should know, for the area where he guides has swarms of mosquitoes and blackflies so thick they can almost bleed one to death.

Be A Stinker

I live in Southern California, which has a more than healthy mosquito population, and I often go fishing and hunting along the lower Colorado River which has even more, but I have not had a mosquito bite in over two years. My secret? When I know I'm going to be in a heavy mosquito area, I prepare myself a few days beforehand by taking a daily dose of a cheap vitamin B complex. Aside from the dietary benefits of the vitamin, this practice causes the skin to emit an odor, undetectable to humans, that really repels mosquitoes and other bothersome insects. Vitamin B, such as the common supermarket brands, is cheap and a season's supply costs only a couple of dollars. There is no danger that you will take too much, as the body does not store this vitamin and any excess is passed off in the course of normal digestion. The one thing to remember is to start taking the vitamin a few days before you know you'll need it. This gives your system time to start producing the repellent odor.

★

Always take raingear with you when going fishing. In fact, it's not a bad idea to carry two outfits. The second one is for the comfort of your partner who usually forgets his.

HEARD 'ROUND the POTBELLY STOVE

In a good fishing camp it is not enough to share equally in the work . . . each must offer to do more.

●

One of the pleasant things about middle age is losing a fine fish and not losing one's temper.

●

The people I've met who say they "used" to fish can never give a good account of why they stopped. Neither can they explain the meaning of their existence.

●

I would rather fish with a friend and catch nothing, than to have good fishing in bad company.

●

There is good evidence for the theory that fish catch men and that the reason the one takes the other home is that the latter has a weight advantage.

●

Fish are held together with bones. Without the bones they would be invertebrates and therefore no more difficult to catch than earthworms. So it is that when I meet someone who fusses about eating fish because they are "bony" I must assume they do not understand the nature of things or have been poorly reared.

●

There are only two kinds of fishing: good and great. Great fishing is when you catch fish.

Skeeter Itch

Don't blame the mosquito for the itching bump that results from its bite. You cause all that discomfort yourself.

There is no poison in a mosquito bite. The saliva the female injects beneath your skin contains a protein foreign to your body, which promptly produces an antibody to combat it.

As the antibody attacks the protein, histamine is liberated. It is this histamine that raises a welt and causes the skin to itch.

Fish-Odor Remover

For years I have tried to find an easy but effective way to remove fish odor from hands, kitchen utensils and pans. I have four sons and a husband who fish, and the smell is often pretty strong. I have used soda, salt, detergents, bleach and Grease Relief with only fair results.

Finally, I tried Octagon laundry soap on my hands after skinning an especially oily bass. The odor washed off.

The soap also cleans old black pans without removing the "seasoning." I use the soap on hands, scaling board, fish bags and knives.

FISHING TRIVIA

● Nobody knows who the first fisherman was, but Persia is credited with being the first country to recognize the food value of fish nearly 3000 years ago when the Persians introduced it into their national diet. However, fishing in America dates back a lot farther than that, for remnants of fish nets over 10,000 years old were found in caves near Great Salt Lake, Utah.

● Historians claim that the reel existed in crude form before the year 1300 in China. And though Izaak Walton is honored as having written the first authoritative book on fishing, another Englishman by the name of Thomas Barker, known as the "Father of Salmon Poaching," wrote *The Art of Angling* some two years before Walton's work.

● Modern fish management is about 35 years old, but one of the earliest regulations put into effect was in Virginia, when in 1678 the practice of attracting fish with lights was outlawed.

● The first fish commission was established by Massachusetts in 1856 and the first fish hatchery to breed salmon was an experimental lab in New York City in 1864.

● In 1887, Michigan appointed the first fish warden who also doubled as a game warden.

Water is considered fresh when its salinity is less than 0.5 parts per thousand (ppt). If it contains between 0.5 and 30.0 ppt, it is brackish. Sea water salinity is between 30.0 and 40.0 ppt.

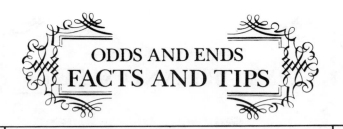
VINTAGE FLYRODS

Increasing interest in older bamboo flyrods often leads to questions regarding identification and relative age. These rules may be of help in determining the approximate age of an old bamboo rod.

1) *Very early rods sometimes had fewer than the common six strips—usually four.*

2) *Early rods (ca. 1865-1885) were sometimes planed round instead of showing a polygonal crossection.*

3) *Loose ring guides were popular prior to the 1890s. About that time the familiar snake guides came into use. Some older rods, however, may be rewound with snake guides.*

4) *Before the 1890s cork was not used much as a handgrip material. A grip of wound rattan or cane was often used from the 1870s through the early 1900s.*

5) *Patent dates are often found on ferrules or reel seats.*

6) *Although lack of a name does not necessarily reduce the value of an old flyrod, the prestigious makers frequently stamped their names on the reel-retaining ring or the butt cap.*

THE BUZZBAIT STORY

Although the noise-making surface lure known as the buzzbait did not become nationally popular until the last six to seven years, it has been catching trophy bass for over 20 years.

The original buzzbait, currently marketed under the trade name Lunker Lure, was patented in 1962 by Haskall (Hack) Jackson of Marion, Illinois. Jackson was a bass fishing coal miner who, with his wife and son, hand fashioned lures on the kitchen table and sold them out the door to an impressive line of local bassing men who took lures even before the paint dried.

By 1965 the Lunker Lure sold for $2.50, an outlandish price for a single lure of that time. But Jackson suffered no shortage of buyers, and he sold every lure his family could produce.

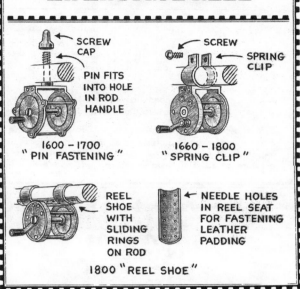

HOW TO DATE AN ANTIQUE REEL

SCREW CAP
PIN FITS INTO HOLE IN ROD HANDLE
1600 – 1700 "PIN FASTENING"

SCREW
SPRING CLIP
1660 – 1800 "SPRING CLIP"

REEL SHOE WITH SLIDING RINGS ON ROD

NEEDLE HOLES IN REEL SEAT FOR FASTENING LEATHER PADDING

1800 "REEL SHOE"

FISH HOOKS

A modern fishhook is essentially a needle, bent and barbed. Steel needles were invented by the Chinese and were first produced in quantity in Europe by the fourteenth century. British needle manufacturers added fishhooks to their product lines about 1560. Modern fishhook manufacturing began in Norway in 1832 with the founding of the famous Mustad Company in Oslo.

In the last century most hooks were fabricated in England and Scandinavia. Making them by hand was a tedious process, involving cutting, precision chiseling, annealing, grinding and shaping steel wire, then tempering the hooks with dry heat, oil and hot sand. The tempering was touchy, since too much heat resulted in brittle hooks, and too little caused them to be soft and easily bent. The process was mechanized in the United States in the early 1900s.

COLLECTOR'S COLLECTOR

Many anglers enjoy collecting books about their favorite sport, and fine collections have been assembled by fishing enthusiasts. As far as is known, however, none can match the truly remarkable collection of angling books made by Daniel Butler Fearing, an 1882 graduate of Harvard and one-time mayor of Newport, Rhode Island. Fearing collected nearly 12,000 books and pamphlets in 20 languages. Fearing's great collection was donated to the Harvard Library in 1914.

•

If you travel out of the country for fishing, make copies of the two pages in your passport that contain your photo and basic information. Carry them in another part of your baggage. Should you lose the passport, the stats are invaluable in helping you to get a replacement quickly.

Although there were anglers of the Izaak Walton variety in colonial America, wholesale methods of catching fish flourished. A fenced-in enclosure in a waterway easily gathered the fish, aided by enormous nets, with sinkers on one edge and floats on the other. Crowds of fishermen created a festive spirit, with much revelry and intoxication.

Shad abounded—up to 3000 were taken per haul. They sold for one to two cents apiece, so inexpensive that they were sometimes ignored and salmon selected from the net instead. People of means ate shad secretly, to avoid arousing suspicions of their not possessing a substantial pork supply.

Colonists may have imported the art of spearing fish with a harping iron or gig from England, although it is more likely Indians coached them. Virginians and Marylanders speared with resolute determination, plunging into the water on horseback from river shoal beaches. Wielding flaming birch-bark torches, Connecticut River fishermen waded into the water and grabbed the lampreys.

SIDE PIECES CUT GLARE

Excessive wind or glare from light reflected off water can burn your eyes and cause fatigue and eyestrain. Cut leather side pieces to fit your sunglasses or regular eyeglasses. The basic shape is a rounded rectangle, with two slits cut near the top for sliding the leather pieces on over the bows of the glasses.

•

Soap and a stiff brush, or steel wool soap pads do a neat job of cleaning and restoring cork rod grips.

CHILL FACTOR

Wind Speed (MPH)	35	30	25	20	15	10	5	0	−5	−10	−15	−20	−25	−30	−35	−40	−45
5	33	27	21	19	12	7	0	−5	−10	−15	−21	−26	−31	−36	−42	−47	−52
10	22	16	10	3	−3	−9	−15	−22	−27	−34	−40	−46	−52	−58	−64	−71	−77
15	16	9	2	−5	−11	−18	−25	−31	−38	−45	−51	−58	−65	−72	−78	−85	−92
20	12	4	−3	−10	−17	−24	−31	−39	−46	−53	−60	−67	−74	−81	−88	−95	−103
25	8	1	−7	−15	−22	−29	−36	−44	−51	−59	−66	−74	−81	−88	−96	−103	−110
30	6	−2	−10	−18	−25	−33	−41	−49	−56	−64	−71	−79	−86	−93	−101	−109	−116
35	4	−4	−12	−20	−27	−35	−43	−52	−58	−67	−74	−82	−89	−97	−105	−113	−120
40	3	−5	−13	−21	−29	−37	−45	−53	−60	−69	−76	−84	−92	−100	−107	−115	−123
45	2	−6	−14	−22	−30	−38	−46	−54	−62	−70	−78	−85	−93	−102	−109	−117	−125

(Wind speeds above 45 mph have little additional chilling effect.)

Source: U.S. Commerce Dept. (National Oceanic and Atmospheric Administration)

Most outdoorsmen, with the possible exception of those in south Florida, wouldn't think much about venturing outside when the thermometer reads 35° F. But if the wind is blowing, that could be a serious mistake. A 20-mile-per-hour wind combined with an air temperature of 35° F. translates into an effective temperature of 12° F.

WARM, DRY HANDS

Steelhead fishing, duck hunting, or bass fishing: They're all done in the rain. We huddle up in layers of down and wool, protected by hip boots, rain pants, slickers and sou'wester hats. But what do we do for our hands? We can't wear gloves if we're trying to feel the subtle take of a steelhead mouthing eggs, or of a bass picking up a plastic worm. We can wear them when we shoulder our favorite shotgun, but they are clumsy, and we shoot better if we don't.

To give your hands a break, roll up a terry cloth towel and put it in a three-pound coffee can with a plastic lid. Keep it under the boat seat or the bow deck. When your hands get wet and cold, pull out the towel and dry them off before you put them under your shirt or in your pockets to warm up. They will thaw out twice as fast. To give them a real treat roll a glowing hand-warmer in the center of the towel. After a soaking rain shower, or after you've gotten your hands wet pulling decoys, wipe your hands and face with the towel, then hold onto the warmer for a few minutes. Your hands will be ready to go back to work in half the normal time.

If you are wearing gloves, drying your hands before you put them on will help keep your hands warm all day. The coffee can will make a good emergency bailing can, too.

★

Thousands of words have been written about why we fishermen fish. Add two more benefits: 1) no TV to watch and 2) no telephone to answer.

BEWARE OF HYPOTHERMIA IN SPRING

Sportsmen are well aware of what frigid conditions can do, but many ignore the fact that hypothermia can strike when it's sunny and 50°F. Hypothermia is deceptive—it occurs when there is a subnormal temperature within the central body. This results when an individual is exposed for a prolonged period to cold, freezing wind, snow or chilling rain or is dumped into water 50°F or colder.

Spring temperatures in the 40s and 50s can be deadly and are often more threatening since they are deceiving. The temperature may be 50°F, but a strong wind combined with the cool temperature from the ground can produce a wind-chill factor well below freezing. A cold rain makes conditions even worse.

Sportsmen are prime candidates for hypothermia in the spring. So be prepared for just about anything. Wear several layers of clothing.

A good warm wool cap and mittens or gloves should be worn on any outing in the early spring. The groin and the sides of the chest are two other areas where body heat is lost quickly. Don't forget insulated boots.

Carry some food and hot liquids with you. Chocolate is a quick energy source. Hot chocolate, coffee and soup are good warming fluids. Carry dry matches to start a fire.

Hypothermia can strike the unwise boater on a nice spring day. You can't last more than 10 or 15 minutes in cold water.

Should someone in your group begin showing symptoms of hypothermia, warm him as quickly as possible. Dizziness, disorientation, drowsiness and slurred and slowed speech are the first symptoms. When the temperature of the heart, lungs and brain reaches 90°F, unconsciousness may occur.

Time is the important factor. Get the person covered with as many blankets or articles of clothing as possible. Warm him by a fire. Make him eat something and drink hot fluids. Never give him alcohol. Get him to a doctor or hospital as soon as possible.

BEWARE OF FROSTBITE

Aside from thin ice, a hole fisherman's greatest threat is frostbite. It is a skin condition similar to a burn and is caused by a combination of subfreezing temperature, humidity and wind. Staying out too long is inviting disaster.

Most often affected are the ears, the tip of the nose, fingers and toes. If you ice-fish alone, it's a good idea to carry a pocket mirror to see how your nose and ears are doing as the day wears on. Should any exposed skin appear yellow-white, waxy, and cold and hard to the touch, get out of the cold. A car is a good place to warm a frostbitten area because it can be done gradually. Don't massage the affected area; rather, keep it cool until returning blood circulation thaws it from within. Applying heat directly to the frostbitten area before the circulation returns can result in clotting the blood in the blood vessels, causing that part of the skin to die, turn black and fall off—a phenomenon known as dry gangrene.

Common sense should keep the winter fisherman out of trouble. If your hands or feet get numb, or you feel a burning sensation on any exposed area followed by numbness, it's time to quit.

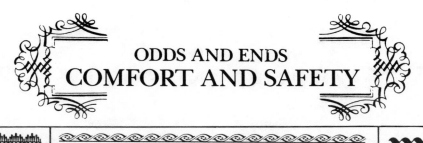

ODDS AND ENDS
COMFORT AND SAFETY

WINTER WADING DANGER

Late season steelheaders, striper fishermen and duck hunters face a seldom-anticipated danger when they wade deep.

Because of the bone-chilling cold, it is common practice to layer clothes: cotton long johns, insulated tops and bottoms, heavy wool pants and shirts, all topped by a bulky parka.

These garments preserve warmth because they trap air, but that same protective air creates an unusual amount of buoyancy inside a pair of chest waders. If you wade to within inches of the top, your purchase on the bottom of a bay or stream bed is virtually neutralized, and you are thus at the mercy of waves and currents.

A wading staff offers some insurance against being swept off your feet, but beyond that, the safest solution is extreme caution when you wade deep in the winter.

AVOID CHAPPED LIPS

Chapped or sunburned lips are an annoyance, and people have tried everything from dishwashing liquid to boot grease to protect themselves. Items such as these may work, but the taste can be awful at best, and some should not be ingested.

A good lip balm is butter. If your lips are already cracked, the salt may sting a little, but it will prevent further drying and splitting.

Catsup (if thick enough) and mayonnaise can also be used, but they might sting because of the acids they contain.

★

When one of two fishing partners hooks a fish, it's smart for the other to cast behind the fighting fish. Most of the time there is another fish following the hooked one.

THE OUTDOOR BODY AS BAROMETER

The next time you feel irritated enough to ram your fist through the wall of your tent or camper, take a look at the sky. Chances are bad weather is on the way if it hasn't already arrived.

Dr. Michael DeSanctis of Minnesota's Buffalo Mental Health Center believes that as much as one-third of the population is abnormally sensitive to weather changes. When it turns from fair to foul they can suffer lethargy, dizziness, headaches and depression.

Weather-sensitive individuals tend to have short-lived changes in mood, energy levels and pain tolerance. You can put the blame on ions. Air ions affect the production of serotonin—a hormone that affects sleep cycles, sexual arousal and emotions.

DeSanctis claims negative ions, which are associated with

pollution-free air, high altitudes and improving weather phases, can reduce anxiety, promote faster reaction times, and increase one's vigor.

What strikes DeSanctis, a clinical psychologist, is how collective weather variables have gone largely unnoticed by traditional psychologists and psychiatrists, e.g., Freud, Rogers, Piaget and Skinner.

"All I'm saying," DeSanctis concludes, "is that there is a significant amount of variance in behavior associated with weather."

EMERGENCY CLOTHES

You won't use them often, but if you've ever fallen into an icy trout stream above your waders or gone hunting or fishing on a cold, rainy day, you can appreciate the value of always having a complete change of clothes tucked away in the car.

Take an old pair of pants, shirt and socks that you seldom wear, plus a set of underwear and some spare shoes and wrap them in a plastic garbage bag. Tie the bag tight with a metal twist-on tab and stash it away in your trunk or the back of your camper, where it will always be available when you need it.

SPECTACLE PRESERVER

A long, skinny balloon, partly inflated and tied to both ear pieces on your glasses, makes a comfortable strap to hold them in place when you're on the water. If you should happen to knock them off, the air in the balloon will cause them to float, preventing a costly trip to the optometrist.

QUICKSAND

Quicksand is fine sand suspended in water. It may look like smooth, dry sand, but the water underneath lubricates the grains and allows them to flow easily. There is nothing mysterious about quicksand—it acts as any thick liquid would, and if you react sensibly you can escape it.

Quicksand has no power to suck you under, but frantic struggling to free the feet creates a forceful downward movement that causes the sand first to move away, then quickly return to pack around the legs. The result is a firmer and deeper hold on the body. Further struggle repeats the process until the body is engulfed completely.

If you get caught in quicksand, fall backward and lie face up, flat on the surface. You will float. Don't hold up your arms—let them rest on the surface. Roll slowly to firm ground, or turn onto your stomach and do a slow breaststroke. By moving slowly you will *swim* to safety.

To avoid getting caught, look for quicksand in riverbeds, washes and run-off areas.

Seasickness Cure

Traditional medication to ward off seasickness includes nonprescription drugs as Dramamine or meclizine. Both, however, can cause side effects such as severe drowsiness. Now the U.S. Coast Guard has discovered new drug combinations that work much better at preventing the dread mal de mer—and they are almost free from any unpleasant side effects. The two drugs, both staples on every druggist's shelf, are promethazine HC1 (an antihistamine commonly known as phenergan) and Ephedrine, a well-known decongestant. Both should be taken at least one hour before sailing.

Tests by the Coast Guard on ten recruits in heavy weather aboard a 44-footer showed no signs of seasickness after they had taken the two-drug combination.

★

The main difference between a fisherman who just fishes and one who catches fish is concentration. This means being constantly aware of what's happening at the end of the line.

GROUNDING ON WATER

Lightning kills more people each year than do tornadoes, hurricanes or floods. Boaters are particularly vulnerable to lightning strikes. There is a precaution you can take—a simple grounding system to protect the boat. Run a No. 4 copper wire from a metal rod, installed at the highest point on the boat, to one square foot of copper flashing dangled in the water or attached to the hull below the waterline.

PAIN KILLER

A fast-acting remedy for the pain caused by the spine of catfish is meat tenderizer powder sprinkled directly on the wound, or make a poultice of it on cloth and apply that. The tenderizer also is effective with Portuguese man-of-war stings.

SUMMER -- DEADLY KILLER

According to the National Oceanic and Atmospheric Administration (NOAA), winter is the only season that claims more lives through its harsh conditions than summer heat waves. There are four heat disorders: knowing both the warning signals and how to treat the disorder can save a life.

HEAT ASTHENIA

Symptoms—Easy fatigue, headache, heavy sweating, high pulse rate, shallow breathing, poor appetite, insomnia.

First Aid—Move to cooler, dryer environment, drink plenty of fluids and take a salt tablet *only if your diet allows it!* Rest before moving on—then take it easy.

HEAT CRAMPS

Symptoms—Painful spasm in voluntary muscles (legs, arms, side, etc.), pupils dilate with each spasm, possible heavy sweating, skin cold and clammy.

First Aid—Firm pressure on cramping muscles, warm wet towels, three or four doses of salty water at 15-minute intervals.

HEAT EXHAUSTION

Symptoms—Profuse sweating, weakness, vertigo, skin cold and pale, clammy with sweat; pulse is thready, blood pressure low, possible vomiting.

First Aid—Move to cooler environment immediately. Bed rest, salty water. Get medical help as soon as possible.

HEAT STROKE

Symptoms—Weakness, vertigo, nausea, headache, heat cramps, mild heat exhaustion, excessive sweating, sweating stops just before heat stroke, temperature rises sharply, pulse is bounding and full, blood pressure elevated, delirium or coma common, skin flushed at first, later ashen or purplish.

Heat Stroke is a killer!

First Aid—Without delay summon a doctor or get the victim started to a hospital. Even a short delay can be fatal. Also, move the victim into a cooler environment, reduce body temperature with iced bath or by sponging. Use extreme caution not to send the person into shock. Continue the treatment while moving the victim to the hospital.

Every person who enjoys the outdoors should memorize these symptoms and the first aid treatment. Lives may depend on it!

Warmth When Needed

A pair of soft cotton jogging pants has more uses to the outdoorsman than to a jogger.

They can be worn around as comfortable camp pants, or when evening chill sets in they can be drawn quickly over regular pants—much easier than undressing and putting on long johns. They make excellent pajamas when the sleeping bag is not quite warm enough.

A fisherman can put them on under his waders, or draw them over a pair of pants. They are warmer and also absorb moisture.

The hunter can wear them over his pants in the morning until he has walked off the morning chill. Then he can tuck them into his daypack until the afternoon wind comes up, or until he decides to take to an evening stand.

BUZZ BEGONE

Mix this concoction to repel mosquitoes:

4 tbsp. talc
1¾ cups cornstarch
2 tbsp. eucalyptus oil

Combine the talc and cornstarch, then add the eucalyptus oil. Stir until it is thoroughly absorbed. Dusted on clothes and skin, it acts as a repellent. You can store it in a glass, metal or plastic container.

THE <u>REAL</u> OUTDOOR DANGERS

The Upjohn Company recently surveyed outdoorsmen to discover the kinds and frequency of the dangers and accidents they encounter. See how close you can come to ranking these in the order Upjohn's sample reported: *contaminated water; insect bites; poison ivy; wasp stings; sunburn; food poisoning; getting lost; traumas like near drownings, major falls, violent storms or bear attacks; deep cuts; embedded fishhooks; broken bones; snakebites; sprained ankles; sunstroke; burns other than sunburn and blisters.*

Answer: *Insect bites 95%; sunburn and contaminated water tied at 77%; wasp stings and blisters tied at 70%; deep cuts and traumas tied at 52%; poison ivy 45%; embedded fishhooks and sprained ankles tied at 43%; burns 32%; getting lost 16%; broken bones 14%; food poisoning 10%; sunstroke 8.4% and snakebites 4.8%.*

Most of the percentages represent occurrences within the past three years, but Upjohn extended the reporting time for four of the dangers—embedded fishhooks, broken bones, getting lost and food poisoning—to a lifetime of outdoor recreation.

Interestingly, once in the wilderness, you're over 15 times more liable to be attacked by a water-dwelling parasite than to be bitten by a snake, and most snakebites could be avoided by leaving snakes alone.

BUG OFF

Vitamin B may well prove to be the perfect bug chaser. Scientists believe that it creates a body odor that repels even the worst biting bugs. Mosquitoes, blackflies and chiggers actually avoided volunteers who had taken B-complex capsules. Unfortunately, it doesn't seem to help everyone. But before your next trip into fly country, take some B. It may work for you.

DROWNPROOFING

Hundreds lose their lives each year because they can't swim. Two life-saving in-the-water rules give outdoorsmen a better chance of surviving:

First, *learn to swim.*

Second, *learn "drownproofing,"* a technique that protects people who get into trouble due to panic and exhaustion. According to Dr. Reagh C. Wetmore, who teaches the method at Boston University, "It is the best way to stay alive in water for long periods of time without artificial aids, and anyone from four to 70 can learn the method."

The basic principle: Make the most of your body's natural buoyancy by *floating face-down in a relaxed dangling position* instead of using up energy to keep your head above water. Wetmore says, "You come up for air every 10 seconds or so. Clothes, currents, undertows and tides all lose their fearsome aspect."

Drownproofed people should be able to survive 24 hours at sea unless there are hazards such as concussion or cramps. If you experience these, "you *can* survive with just one arm or leg working," Wetmore says.

Find out where drownproofing is taught: Check your local Red Cross or the Ys.

RESCUE

Hundreds of fishermen, hunters, hikers and campers will get lost this year. Most will make it back okay, but an unlucky few will wander aimlessly until they die.

If you become lost, think of the word RESCUE and what the letters stand for:

R RELAX, never panic. Running around only uses up energy and further disorients you.

E ELEVATION. Find a hill or higher ground. Don't aim for some promontory miles away. Just get higher so that you have a better view of the situation.

S SIT DOWN. Use your map, compass, the sun's position and anything else at your disposal to get oriented. Most of the time, you will be able to right yourself. If you still can't figure out a way back, give thought to backtracking.

C CHOOSE a *course* of action with a *cool* head. If you haven't reoriented yourself, make camp. If you know which way's out, be sure you can make it back before sunset. If not, spend the night and rest.

U UTILIZE everything at your disposal. If you make camp, collect enough firewood for the night. Make a comfortable bed and signal with your knife or mirror as long as the sun allows.

E ECONOMIZE on your supplies. Drink water and eat, but save enough for a possible long stay. If your county has a search-and-rescue team, a smokey fire usually spells rescue in the morning. Save food for breakfast—they may have a long hike out.

★

RAINSUITS are fine for keeping your body dry during a sudden downpour, but what about soggy feet? Simple. Just carry a couple of plastic bags and two rubber bands. Slip one over each shoe and pull up under the rainsuit legs.

DEADLY CIGUATERA

Ciguatera (poisoning by eating certain species of fish), is on the rise. The disease which can sometimes be fatal has spread from the Caribbean to south Florida, and increasing numbers of fish species now carry danger of the disease. Formerly only barracuda were considered too dangerous to eat, especially in larger sizes. Now such popular species as grouper, snapper, cobia, amberjack and king mackerel have been known to poison people who ate their flesh. The disease does not affect the host fish and results from a buildup of dinoflagellates eaten by smaller reef fish on which the predators feed. Ciguatera symptoms are vomiting and diarrhea, followed by tingling then deadness in the mouth and lips, aching joints, weakness in the limbs and pain. A victim's temperature is reversed, hot seems cold and cold hot. How can you avoid ciguatera? Feed a piece of suspect fish to the cat and watch what happens is one way. Or you can follow the Bahama formula since larger fish are more likely to carry the poisons—"shorter than your arm, can do no harm"—and hope for the best.

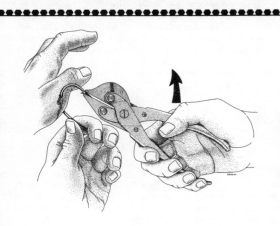

EASY HOOK REMOVAL

A large stainless-steel hook accidentally embedded in a fisherman's flesh can cause a serious and extremely painful wound. However, the task of removing such a hook is not as difficult as might be assumed from the strength of the hook steel. To break off the hook point and barb, grasp the hook point up to the barb in the groove of fishing pliers, while holding the hook shank firmly in the other hand, as illustrated. Bend the hook point directly away from the hook shank with a sharp, firm motion of the pliers and the point and barb will break off surprisingly easily. The barbless hook can then be removed from the wound.

BLACKFLY RELIEF

Hungry blackflies torment man and beast alike, but anglers are the most susceptible near fast-flowing streams, a favorite haunt of these insects.

Although numerous commercial and homemade fly repellents are available, none are 100 percent effective. In most cases, a fisherman's only recourse is to dress in tightly knit pants tucked into high boots, and to wear a headnet, gloves and a tightly knit shirt with long sleeves.

Unfortunately, most shirts have slits at the wrists, and blackflies are most resourceful in finding the tender skin exposed by these openings.

To solve this problem, cut off the feet on a pair of old socks (lightweight nylon is preferred). Then slip the leg sections onto your arms, elastic ends first, much like putting on wristlets. The tubes should cover the slits, and the elastic tops will keep them in place. This also eliminates the need for you to wear a long-sleeved undershirt.

WADING NEAR 'GATORS

Most sensible outdoorsmen know you shouldn't feed bears, no matter how friendly they appear. And few outdoorsmen would feed an alligator—unless inadvertently. In a recent incident in Florida, however, an angler did just that.

Lothian Ager, a specialist with the Freshwater Game and Fish Commission, was wading and bass fishing in Lake Kissimmee. Ager had several bass on the stringer tied to his belt. As he waded he felt the stringer sort of snag occasionally, and thought it was hanging on bottom cover. After an especially persistent snag he tugged on the stringer and the snag tugged back.

He looked down and saw an alligator's head surface. "It looked as big as an ironing board," he later reported. He left the bass with the alligator.

STRESS KILLS FISH

Sportsmen mean well when they release fish to live on, but many of them die. The reason is shock, or infection, from improper handling. Here are important tips:

1) Wear a glove. Hand acid causes fungus, fungus kills.

2) Never hold a fish such as pike by its eye sockets.

3) Grasp and paralyze by gently pressing in gill flaps while removing hooks.

4) Do not throw, toss, or drop a fish onto water. Release it gently.

5) If a fish is too pooped to maintain equilibrium, or balance, aerate it by opening its mouth and moving it back and forth in water until fully revived.

APPETIZING FISH NAMES

In its infinite wisdom the Oregon Legislature has ordained that a name change would enhance the desirability of certain fish with unappealing identities. It reasoned that fish lovers would hardly break down supermarket doors or wait in long lines at restaurants to obtain cowcod, or members of the rockfish family long known as widow, bank, speckled, yellow-eye, bocaccio, vermilion, speckled, yellowtail and olive.

From now on these fish are commercially christened as snappers, and sold as such. Sablefish now legally masquerade as black cod or butterfish. Hake has been elevated to Pacific whiting.

Strange Fish In Our Waters

Ever wonder how strange exotics and potentially dangerous fish get loose in our waters? Some 47 of them now exist around the United States, 26 of which live in Florida.

The problem is more acute in the Sunshine State, especially southern Florida where many tropical species can exist. There some $115 million are taken in by the tropical fish industry and some 250 fish farms ship about 25,000 boxes of live aquarium types weekly to pet shops around the nation.

Although illegal, when some operators go out of business, or get stuck with certain species, they dump them into the nearest canal or pit. Once these fish get into the Everglades, they can swim north to Georgia without leaving fresh water. The toothy piranha and the weird walking catfish are two species that have authorities concerned.

A special laboratory is being set up in Gainesville to identify and control such exotics. Fortunately, most of these imports are tropical species that cannot exist in waters below 60° F., so their northward movement is restricted by Mother Nature.

GIANT SALMON

Smilodonichthys Rastrosus, an extinct North American salmon living perhaps 5 million years ago, was a giant among salmon species. Fossil heads and other body parts of Smilo tell us of a salmon that swam the Pacific coastal waters along with *Oncorhynchus* (Pacific salmon) that would dwarf the largest chinook. Average size for Smilo was about six feet four inches with weights somewhere between 250 and 350 pounds. That means that this salmonid was two to three times the size of the largest of our living salmon species, the chinook, which at its heaviest rarely goes over 90 pounds.

I

First Trout Hatchery

The year was 1864. The murderous war between the states was drawing to its agonizing finish. But Seth Green's mind was on trout. Logging had ruined one stream after another in northern New York State where he lived. Yet some streams, freed from pressure because of the war, were coming back. Trout would live in them again—if fish could be found to restock them.

To fill this need Green bought property on Spring Creek in Caledonia, a small community 20 miles southwest of Rochester, and started the nation's first trout hatchery. It was so successful that in 1868 when the New York Fishery Commission was founded—with Green one of its three commissioners—it purchased the hatchery and voted $10,000 to finance its programs.

Seth Green's hatchery, much modernized, remains in use today, rearing between 80,000 and 100,000 pounds of trout and salmon yearly. An expansion program is underway to double its capacity. The hatchery is open to visitors.

FAST FISH

The top speed for a human runner is about 20 miles per hour. How does he compare with fish? Well, remember that water is about 700 times more resistant than air, then marvel at the speeds of our finned friends. Here are those that have been studied and timed for sustained runs, not spurts:

SPECIES	SPEED MPH
SAILFISH	70
SWORDFISH	60
WAHOO	37
TARPON	35
SALMON	30
DOGFISH	30
BONEFISH	22
PIKE	20
BASS	12
BLUEGILL	1.25

And in case you might think a fish's fins are the secret to its speed, that's not so. With all fins removed, including the tail, fish still can propel themselves through the water with rippling undulations of their bodies.

GARISH GARS

Gars of several species are common inhabitants of the quieter waters in the southeastern United States. These primitive predators are unlike other scaled fishes in that their scales are diamond-shaped and do not overlap. They fit closely together like bathroom tiles.

What a Worm!

A tiny fish tapeworm with the long name of *Diphyllobothrium latum* grows up to 30 feet in length when it infests the body of a human. You can get this parasite by eating uncooked fish. Smoking or pickling is no preventive, and raw herring eaters have the highest infection rates.

Freezing fish for 48 hours at 14°F. (−10°C) kills the larvae. To be absolutely safe, thorough cooking of all fish is recommended. Okay you raw-fish eaters, remember that 30 feet is a long worm!

WALLEYES DON'T RATE

Walleyes entered the Columbia River system, first showing near Grand Coulee in Washington, about 30 years ago. They have slowly worked on down the Columbia and are now being caught regularly above Portland. But availability and acceptance are two different things.

Recently a creel checker for the Oregon Department of Fish and Wildlife found a steelhead angler who had just taken a nice walleye near the mouth of the Sand River. Not at all impressed with some trashfish from the Midwest, the steelheader was going to toss it aside when the ODF&W man intervened.

This walleye weighed two and a half pounds and was 18½ inches long. In other parts of the country these fish are prized as the *best* tasting fish, but obviously they still don't rate among anglers in this area.

FLATHEAD CONTROL

Chemicals and nets aren't the only antidotes for rough fish. The flathead catfish eats bullheads and other less desirable species, and is an efficient predator in lakes that are overcrowded with stunted fish. That's why the Minnesota Department of Natural Resources has launched a heavy flathead stocking program in several lakes and rivers in the southern half of the state.

Although the program is pegged as experimental, biologists expect the flatheads to be a major element in control efforts. Better yet, flatheads provide good eating and plenty of sport. They can reach a length of five feet and scale in at 100 pounds and over.

Lucky Drum

The drum is unique among fishes in that it is capable of making a distinctive sound in or out of the water. I have heard this rather odd sound many times; it's similar to a bullfrog muffled in an echo chamber.

This fish, a distant cousin to the croakers, has a very large air bladder and lower throat bones covered with coarse, blunt teeth. A combination of these two features permits it to make that deep, croaking sound.

But this ability to "talk" is just one of two oddities of the drum (or sheepshead, gaspergou, gray bass, croaker, grunter, or whatever it is called where you live). The other is its so-called "lucky stones." These two stones are ear bones located on either side of the head, slightly back of and above the eyes. Each has a distinguishable "L" etched on it. Superstition has it that if you remove these bones from a drum and carry them in your pocket they will bring you luck.

They've never helped me—not when it comes to catching fish anyway.

Predators are not used to being charged by their prey and respond by moving out of the way. That's why it is critical to present a bait or lure in a natural manner and allow it to swim past the fish as if it were trying to get away. If your offering moves toward the quarry or comes up from behind, the fish will invariably spook and regroup.

Whirling Disease

One of the most devastating diseases of trout and Atlantic salmon is the Whirling Disease (*Myxosoma cerebralis*). Fish catch it from spores released from feces and decomposing fish. It affects the brain and causes the fish to lose balance and whirl, a form of piscatorial vertigo that is fatal.

Whirling Disease was first reported in Germany in 1904. It next appeared in Denmark in 1926, then in France in 1952. In succeeding years it infected fish in 11 countries.

Troubled Rockfish

Things aren't going too well for the rockfish, or striped bass as it's called above the Mason Dixon line. A research project of the University of Maryland's laboratory at Horn Point near Cambridge, Maryland, made these dismal findings:

"Less than 50 percent of eggs stripped from captured wild females and artificially fertilized actually became fertile. Under normal propagation 95 percent of the eggs would be fertile.

"Of the fertile eggs only 10 to 20 percent are hatching. Normally an 85 percent hatch rate can be expected.

"Three days after hatching only 1 percent of the fry survive. And almost all of these show some element of deformity."

Scientists think that what is happening in their hatchery is also happening in the huge spawning rivers of the Chesapeake where most of the rockfish come from. "Males appear to be marginally fertile," says Dr. George Krantz, hatchery director. Krantz suspects the presence of heavy metals or pesticides is the culprit and he is working on tests to determine this.

GRAYLING, MICH.

During the 1800s Michigan boasted a tremendous grayling population. In a town named Grayling, the Manistee River was known for its famous grayling habitat, where it was easy to catch a hundred or more such fish in a single day. Often two or three could be taken at a time with as many flies.

The last of the Michigan grayling were seen in the Otter River in 1932 after an attempt to save this species failed.

Today there are isolated grayling populations, some of them healthy, in Montana, Wyoming, Washington, Idaho, Colorado and Oregon, but the most spectacular grayling fishing is found north of the Canadian border.

ODDS AND ENDS
FISH FACTS

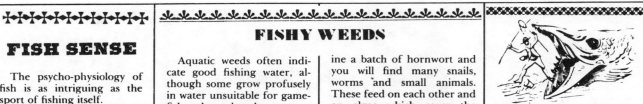

FISH SENSE

The psycho-physiology of fish is as intriguing as the sport of fishing itself.

John Herrick, a fishing guide in Minnesota's Boundary Waters Canoe Area Wilderness, claims that "Fish take the path of least resistance. They're like all nature. They want to survive, but not just survive—thrive. They want it as easy as possible. They learn how to prey. They know what easy prey is around. They don't live in a lake ten years, eight years, five years and not learn what easy living's all about, and pursue it. They go on the accessible food base."

Although most fish cannot hear airborne sounds, they hear—with their whole bodies—sounds in the water. They have systems of pores that are supplied with tiny organs responsive to changes in water pressure; nerve fibers connect the organs to the brain. Thus a fish's lateral line is his whole sound system.

"Perhaps the most important objective of a fish small enough to be a prey for bigger fish is to make no sound at all," according to Donald E. Carr in *The Forgotten Senses*. "Fishes accomplish their swimming with a lack of hydraulic noise unbelievable to a hydraulic engineer . . ."

Fish experience stress.

"In a school of fish," Herrick said, "once you catch a fish and reel it up—all know there's a problem. There's stress everywhere. Many times a northern pike will pick up on that, and come in. Fish give off vibrations in the water."

They also smell. They have noses that can smell food, return to their place of origin (like salmon) by following scents, and react to sex signals, the body odor of other fish and to odors of alarm.

A fish also has a talent for tasting. Taste buds on the body and barbels of fish unerringly locate food.

Finally, fish speak. If you submerge an underwater microphone you will hear grunts, rattles, snaps and honks.

FISHY WEEDS

Aquatic weeds often indicate good fishing water, although some grow profusely in water unsuitable for gamefish; others clog the water to such an extent that fish shun the area.

However, hornwort and curled-leaved pondweed are two of the fishy ones that lake and pond fishermen should learn to recognize.

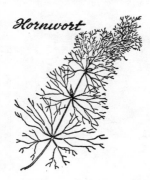

Hornwort is a good food producer and shelter for fish. It is fair as a shade weed, an excellent oxygenator, and grows on hard bottoms since it needs slight root anchorage. It usually is found well out from shore in from two to eight feet of water. Sometimes it grows to the surface but does not push above it. Examine a batch of hornwort and you will find many snails, worms 'and small animals. These feed on each other and on algae which cover the plants. That's why hornwort stands are frequented by gamefish.

Curled-leaved pondweed is a very good food producer that gives shade and shelter and is also a fine oxygenator. It usually grows in water from one to five feet deep. The leaves seem to be relished by certain aquatic larvae and snails. There are about 40 North American species; most grow wholly submerged except for their flowers, which bloom in June and July. It is one of the most important fish weeds.

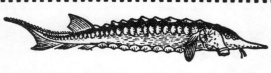

Heaviest Freshwater Fish

Weighing in at authenticated weights of 2000 pounds, the white sturgeon is the heavyweight of freshwater fish. Once pulled from the Snake River by mule teams and block and tackle, over-commercialized fishing has seriously reduced its numbers. They may no longer be kept from this river system. In the Columbia River where their numbers are healthy, the minimum size at which they may be kept is 36 inches; the maximum is six feet.

Sturgeon are also the oldest-living of freshwater fish. An eight-foot specimen may be over 100 years of age. They do not become sexually mature until their 16th year at which time the females start producing the gourmet's delight— caviar. A 300-pound female may carry as many as 50 million of these eggs which sell for hundreds of dollars per pound.

Superior Fish

Fish may be more sophisticated than you'd ever believe. They have a better sense of taste than animals and superior to man's basic taste of sweet and sour. In some species of fish, the whole body has a sensitivity to taste.

Not only that, many fish have a better sense of smell than terrestrial animals and many have a built-in "radar" system, either in the lateral line that runs down the center of their body, or in their dorsal fin. The "radar" helps them travel in dark or murky water and helps them find food.

SEAWEED AND FISHING

The return of California's once-depleted kelp beds is good news for saltwater fishermen. In recent years, marine biologists have determined that giant kelp, a brown seaweed found in dense mats in coastal Pacific waters, is vital to the survival of countless sportfishes.

It seems that barren ocean bottom can only support 100 pounds of fish per acre, while a comparable area covered with giant kelp maintains three times that much. In addition, as many as 90,000 juvenile fish per acre use the kelp beds as safe havens during the early stages of their lives.

Kelp forests off the California coast once covered well over 100 square miles. Today, changes in water temperature, pollution, and a population explosion of sea urchins (which chew their way right through the plants) have greatly reduced the giant kelp beds.

Several projects are currently underway to restore kelp to much of its former range. As an extra bonus for fishermen, when kelp plants are reestablished over soft sand bottoms, the area turns into a fishing hotspot.

FISH AND THE ICE AGE

Fish found in your area may have been influenced by movements of giant glacial sheets from 8000 to 10,000 years ago.

Muskies, for example, are found in cool waters throughout the Midwest—and are even native to mountain rivers in North Carolina, Virginia and Tennessee. But they are not found in similar waters in New England. The reason is glaciation. Muskies originated in southern Europe and eventually entered America through the lower Mississippi drainage. They moved into waters in the South and Midwest when glaciers blocked their entry to other suitable habitats.

Chain pickerel and northern pike took a different route. Also native to Europe, these fish spread to North America through a northern route. Biologists believed they moved eastward through brackish marshes that lined the exposed land bridge across the Bering Sea and then made their way across the top of North America, eventually ending up in river systems. Melting glaciers may have created new freshwater routes for them.

Other fish were also influenced by these changes. Landlocked salmon, for example, are now native to a handful of lakes in northern New England. They are the remnants of Atlantic salmon populations that were trapped in these lakes thousands of years ago.

DATED FISH

Age of fish can be determined from growth bands formed by ear stones or "otoliths," which are made of the same substance as seashells. According to Cornell University marine biologist Edward Brothers, ear stones enable a fish to hear. Differences in their thickness, density and protein content are clues to changes that occur in the life cycle of fish. They are similar to the growth bands or annular rings of a tree trunk.

Age Your Fish

The age of your trophy is readily determined by the annual growth rings on the scales. However, there are other indications that a fish is approaching old age and living in its twilight years:

1) eyes sunk more than usual in sockets
2) cheek regions concaved due to muscle atrophy
3) discolored areas infected by fungus
4) leathery tight skin due to lack of fatty tissue
5) large head in comparison with the body
6) decrease in stomach size and girth
7) no fresh scars on lower caudal fin, indicating that it hasn't been fanning a nest during spawning

Most of these mature fish, many of lunker size, are seldom caught by anglers. They die and sink to bottom where scavengers dispose of the body. They are seldom found washed up on shore.

Most fish are dark on top and light colored along the belly. It's called countershading and is an effective method of camouflage. The blending of color eliminates a distinct break in the body, makes the fish look flat rather than solid, and protects it by causing the fish to match the bottom.

A Fish by Any Other Name...

Mudblower or honey fish—which would you rather eat? The National Marine Fisheries Service would like to know.

Concerned by dwindling numbers of some of the more commercially popular fish, the Fisheries Service has spent seven years and nearly $500,000 on a study of how to get the public to willingly consume such delectable yet odiously named fish as the gag, grunt, ratfish and hunchback scorpion. So far, all the evidence points to the necessity of renaming these species: monikers such as butterfly and sunshine fish are currently being considered.

Research monies have included a $63,000 contract to a Chicago firm to rate these fish on their "edibility profiles." Yet, despite extensive public polling and in-depth testing at the Army's food research lab in Massachusetts, the Service has so far been stumped in its efforts to prove that a hogsucker by any other name would in fact taste sweeter.

FISH-KILL CULPRIT

A protozoan parasite which becomes highly active in cold water has been pinpointed as the cause of widespread fish kills along the southeastern Louisiana coastline during the winter of 1977-78.

Speckled trout, redfish, sheepshead, drum, mullet and other species were observed floating in Lake Pontchartrain, Lake Borgne, Lake Robin, Oak River, the Ship Channel and other major water bodies east of the Mississippi River.

J. Burton Agnelle, secretary of the Louisiana Department of Wildlife and Fisheries, said fisheries biologists working with Dr. John Plumb, fish disease and parasitology expert from Auburn University, found that the parasite attacks the gill tissues of the fish. This causes abnormal mucous secretions which clog the gills and lead to suffocation.

Fish weakened by the condition also become susceptible to skin lesion bacteria, the experts stated.

FISH TALK

Everyone knows that porpoises "talk." Fishermen who have spent the night below the hull of a boat have been kept awake by the grunts and croaks of fish. Now scientists with sophisticated sound-sensing equipment have discovered that all fish talk, especially at breeding time. The male minnow or shiner, the species commonly used as bait for large gamefish, calls a female with a shrill shriek; she answers with a similar shriek. When his nest is threatened, he bellows like a miniature elephant to warn off the intruder. The creek chub is one of the most talkative of freshwater fish. A fish hears with its inner ear, also with its air-filled swim bladder which regulates the depth at which it swims. It also makes its sounds with the same bladder by manipulating muscles surrounding it. Trout and bass talk, too. Someday there may be a tape recording that will call fish to your bait.

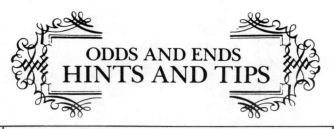

PRESERVE A MAP

Topographic maps are among the few things that grow in value as they are used. They become laden with useful information plotted on them by their users: new trails and campsites, good fishing spots and productive hunting areas. However, they soon fray. To prevent this and keep the paper in good condition, you should mount them on cloth. The most common type is unstarched, bleached muslin sheeting.

To mount a map, first spread a piece of cloth, a bit larger than the map, taut over a smooth, flat surface (a board or worktable will do) and fasten it along the edges with tacks about four inches apart. Apply flour-and-water paste or wallpaper paste on the back of the map with a brush, and then wait for a minute or two until the paper softens. The paste should be the consistency of canned applesauce; if it becomes lumpy, strain it through cheesecloth. Apply another coat, and quickly lay the map on the muslin. Wipe the map with a damp sponge or cloth, applying light pressure to smooth out any creases or ripples.

If you want to prevent features from disappearing in the foldlines, follow this procedure before applying paste to the map: Draw lines on the back where the folds will be made. Cut apart on these lines and soak each piece in water. Apply paste to the back of each piece, and lay them in the proper order one-eighth inch apart on the cloth. Then clean and smooth out the map.

Do not remove the map from the board until it is thoroughly dry—it should take at least a day. Do not place it in the sunlight while it is drying; the sun will bleach it. When it is completely dry, trim off the excess cloth.

Another mounting method is with backing cloth, which can be attached to the map by ironing it on. Art and photographic stores or stores specializing in framing usually carry it.

MEASURE BEFORE RELEASE

Once in a great while we take a trophy fish on a fly and release it without getting a picture of it, or even an accurate idea of its size. The next time you hook such a fish, lay it gently in the shallows and measure it with your leader, the fly still attached. Then cut the leader at exactly the fish's length. Over the years you will build a collection of chewed flies with various lengths of leader attached, each with a story behind it, something to be preserved forever in a display case instead of in your memory.

FISHING PHOTOS

Here are a few pointers to make certain your photos are as interesting to viewers as they are to you.

Pictorials—those pictures showing a favorite lake with the sun setting in the background—look better with a person in them doing something that leads the eye into the photo.

Frame your pictures. Use trees, weeds or rocks in the foreground and midground of the picture to lead the viewer's eye. If there is nothing in the foreground, especially if the sky is cloudless, hold a tree branch overhead so it drapes into the top of the photo.

Use a wide-angle lens for close-quarters shots to take in more information.

Try to photograph your subjects in motion. Under low-light conditions, where shutter speeds must be slow, have the subject exaggerate his motions—stretching way out to net a fish or holding a netted fish high in the air with the water streaming out. These pictures don't require the subject to move, yet they indicate action.

Catch fishing rods in motion, even under low-light conditions, by snapping the picture just as the rod stops one motion and begins another, such as the transition between forecast and backcast.

Photograph jumping fish by bringing them to the boat as soon as they are hooked, never allowing them the chance to fight. When the fish is close enough to focus on, let it have some line. It will still be lively and put on a show.

Capture a flyline in midcast by placing the fisherman between the photographer and the sun. The sun will reflect off the airborne line.

For a still-life, arrange the fish on a plain background and have some fishing gear near the fish to indicate its size. Use a fishing creel, the butt section of a rod with the reel showing, or perhaps a landing net. Wet the fish with water to give it a freshly caught look.

A polaroid filter cuts through the surface glare when photographing fish in the water. This filter is very effective in photographing a fish coming into the landing net.

USE A THERMOMETER

Different gamefishes prefer different temperatures, but they all react similarly to changes in water. Colder water slows them down while warmer water means increased activity.

So, to find the species you are after, determine the depth where the temperature is ideal and fish there.

Should the overall temperature be warmer than optimum, use smaller lures that can be retrieved more rapidly to trigger strikes. When the overall temperature is colder, use larger lures and fish them s-l-o-w-l-y.

Here are the ideal ranges (Fahrenheit): largemouth bass, 60°-75°; smallmouth and spotted basses, 60°-72°; crappie, 55°-75°; bluegill, 65°-75°; walleye, 50°-75°; trout, 50°-65°; and northern pike, 55°-75°.

FISH APLENTY

To find out how many fish were in Kentucky's Lake Barkley, biologists partitioned off a 209-acre embayment with an artificial barrier and rotenoned the area. The number of fish in the embayment was phenomenal. A total of 3.1 million were found, averaging out to over 15,000 fish per acre. However, 92 percent of the fish were non-game species including shad, drum, carp and buffalo. The rest were gamefish, mostly largemouth bass and crappies. The weight of all of the fish in the embayment was over 90 tons.

So, biologists estimate that there are approximately 868 million fish weighing about 49 million pounds in Lake Barkley. The data from this study will be used to help calculate fish populations in similar bodies of water.

★ ★ ★

If your fishing time is limited, then pick the two best hours of the day. These are the hour beginning with dawn, and the hour before dusk—the times when the bigger fish are on the prowl.

IMPROVED HOMES FOR TROUT

Timberline Reclamation, of Bozeman, Montana, is a firm that specializes in improving trout streams. Rich McIntyre began the business three years ago because he "saw a need for a professional organization involved with aquatic reclamation." He has improved trout habitat in several states and in New Zealand.

A typical stream improvement procedure involves an initial study that includes water and habitat analysis, assessment of insect populations and a fish survey. The client then decides whether or not to opt for a master plan that outlines engineering details for stream improvement and may cost as much as $10,000. Improvements include bank stabilizers, vegetation enhancement, stream deflectors and dams.

After completion of a project, fishing often gets better within a year.

HAY FOR FISH

Where legal, sinking brush in a lake or pond is a proven way to build a fishing hotspot. To make this area even more productive, dump a few bales of spoiled hay in and around the brush. Grubs and other insects breed inside the rotting hay and gradually fall out. This provides food for fish and helps keep them in the vicinity. Spoiled hay is often sold in garden supply stores under the label *mulch hay.* It can also be purchased directly from farmers for a modest amount of money.

Plastic worms can be repaired very easily when they become torn or pull apart: Apply a match flame to a tear until it melts together, or heat the ends of separate segments and hold until the joint cools. You'll have a "new" worm. You can also make some intriguing and often effective lures by sticking together odd pieces of worms.

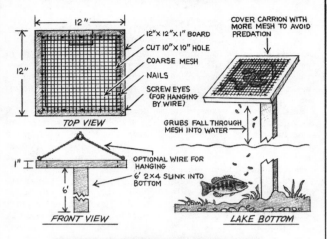

12" · 12"×12"×1" BOARD · CUT 10"×10" HOLE · COARSE MESH · NAILS · SCREW EYES (FOR HANGING BY WIRE) · TOP VIEW · FRONT VIEW · 6' · 1" · OPTIONAL WIRE FOR HANGING · 6' 2×4 SUNK INTO BOTTOM · COVER CARRION WITH MORE MESH TO AVOID PREDATION · GRUBS FALL THROUGH MESH INTO WATER · LAKE BOTTOM

FISH FEEDING STATION

Brush and logs sunk in the water have always provided shelter and feeding areas for fish. Here is another method of drawing fish to an area.

First, hang a small, screened platform (12×12-inch of coarse mesh) from a tree branch over the water or mount it on a six-foot pole sunk into the bottom. Once positioned, place some meat scraps or rotten fruit on the platform and cover with more coarse mesh.

Flys will lay eggs on the carrion, and in a few days maggots will be falling from the platform into the water. Bluegills, crappies and bass will appreciate your efforts.

Obviously, this is a warm-weather project. Add more meat or fruit to the platform once in a while to insure a continuing supply of food for the fish.

VIDEO YOUR HOTSPOTS

A video camera can improve your fishing success on some lakes and streams. During periods of low water, take shots of likely fish-holding cover and structure that would normally be hidden from view. Such cover would include sunken logs, stumps and rocks. When filming, be sure to include a landmark in the scene so that you can locate the structure in high water. Also, making notes will help you tell what's what, where, how far and so on.

Ordinary water-level fluctuations of many streams and lakes can reveal quite a lot, but the real payoff comes when man-made impoundments are drawn down for one reason or another. And new impoundments under construction, including farm ponds, offer a unique opportunity to film the entire bottom.

VERSATILE VANILLA

One of the most effective odor neutralizers is right on your kitchen shelf—and it's not baking soda. Try artificial vanilla extract. When you return from a camping trip, sprinkle a few drops of the extract on a paper towel, then wipe the insides of your ice chest and rinse. Presto—no more fishy smells! Pour a bit of this fragrant liquid into plastic canteens and water jugs, too, so they'll be fresh for your next outing.

Also, you might want to stash a bottle in the camp kitchen. It's a quick remedy for fishy hands.

Clean-Up Hints

Tired of your hunting and fishing duds looking like something the cat dragged in? These simple tips can help get them clean again:

● Apply meat tenderizer with cool water on blood stains. Let it set for 30 minutes or so, and then sponge the spot clean and wash as usual.

● Boil underwear, socks and T-shirts in water with a little lemon juice. They'll come out white again.

● Use warm vinegar water to remove perspiration odor.

● To remove berry stains, stretch the clothes over a bowl and from a height of two feet or so pour boiling water down through the stain. Then wash as usual.

● Spray-starch white tennis shoes to keep them looking white.

● Soak chewing gum spots in white vinegar, or rub with egg-white, before washing. If that doesn't work, try freezing the offending garment and then chip or scrape the gum off.

● Dry mildewed clothes in sunlight, then add a half cup of Lysol to the wash water.

● Loosen stubborn zippers by rubbing them with graphite from the "lead" of a pencil.

MAKE-A-LIST TIP

In your haste to get out on the lake, have you ever run off and left something of importance behind—oars, life jacket, thermos, etc.?

A simple remedy to the problem is to sit down and make a list of everything you could possibly need for your outing and stick it up on the wall of your garage or in a place where it's easily noticed, such as your vehicle's windshield or door. Then, before starting each trip, just run down the list to be sure that you have not forgotten anything.

EASY SCALE REMOVAL

A long-time Pacific City, Oregon, dory fisherman has a simple and effective way of removing those pesky scales from the salmon you catch.

All you have to do is put the cleaned, whole salmon on the grass, ground or driveway, and adjust the nozzle of the garden hose to a fairly sharp, concentrated stream.

Place the salmon on the ground with the head away from the nozzle and the tail nearest to it.

Hold the stream of water low enough so that it goes underneath the scales. The water's force leaves your salmon denuded and much more pleasant to work with, especially if you're planning to slice the fish either for freezing or for use while fresh.

If the salmon is still moist, or has been packed in ice, the scales can be removed even more readily. But if it has been out of water for some time and hasn't been iced, the stream of water, in a matter of minutes, will handily de-scale your catch.

★

Although sonar flashers are great for reading bottom contours, maybe you can't afford or don't care for one. Old-timers did pretty well with a sparkplug on a string to find bottom holes and drop-offs.

Small Scaling

Small panfish are great eating, but scaling large numbers of them can be a tedious chore. The job is easier at home if the fish are partially frozen.

A method that will work in the home as well as in camp is scalding. Submerge the fish in boiling water for a few seconds. This loosens the scales and they will come off easily. You can prepare several fish at a time by stringing them on wire or twine.

Using an icepick and a scaling board makes the chore easier, too. Put the icepick through the fish's head to hold it on the board and scale away.

WATER-DOWN MAPS

In the art of angling it's beneficial to know the underlying structure of the waters you are fishing. Locators of all makes and descriptions tell the depth and dropoffs and even show the hardness of the bottom. However, almost all fishermen have yearned to put on a scuba outfit and see the bottom with their own two eyes for added dimension.

Well, this can be accomplished very easily and without the expense of diving equipment. During the autumn months, many reservoir water levels are lowered. Sometimes the water drop is in the double-digit range. The wise fisherman is able to stand on dry land and look over many of the areas that he fishes in the spring and summer.

With a piece of paper and pencil, sketch or map out each and every rock, stump and dropoff. These fish-holding structures and the bottom they rest on should be charted.

When the water returns to its normal level, you won't have to guess what structure your locator has picked up. A quick check of your "water-down" map and the answer is there.

Marsh Anchor

Bass anglers who fish the marsh reservoirs along the Texas and Louisiana coasts often are hampered by strong winds off the Gulf. A good anchor is a must for these shallow waters, which average less than three feet deep.

Since the marsh bottoms are layers deep in rotting vegetation, conventional anchors designed for small boats cause problems. The mushroom, Danforth, and navy anchors hold flatbottom aluminum marsh boats well enough, but the bottom vegetation accumulates on conventional anchors and causes a mess when it comes time to weigh anchor.

So, shallow-water fishermen along the Gulf have developed what they call a "marsh anchor" to better suit their unusual needs. It is usually made from a heavy metal rod about two and a half feet long. An eye is bent in one end, or else welded onto the rod. The anchor rope, attaching the rod to the boat, is attached to this eye.

Cast like a spear, the marsh anchor imbeds itself in the boggy bottom and holds a light boat surprisingly well. Because of the long, slender shape, it does not collect vegetation and is easily cleaned before being brought aboard.

TRANSPORTING TROPHIES

Some of the damage claims against trucking companies this year will be filed by hunters and sportfishermen whose once-in-a-lifetime trophies are disfigured or destroyed in transit. What can you do to better the odds of your trophy's safe arrival?

If your taxidermist plans to ship your trophy freight collect, talk to him about crating.

Insist on a sturdy crate, such as a framework of 2×4s covered with three-eighths-inch plywood, even if it means paying extra for materials.

For most trophies, the additional weight of a better shipping container adds nothing to the freight charges. And it could prevent your prize buck from becoming an insurance check.

TACKLEBOX DRYER

If you've ever overlooked your tacklebox sitting open during a light drizzle or had an active fish splash water into it, you know it's going to need to be dried out completely. A job that no fisherman looks forward to. It's tedious work to hand dry all those lures and wipe the moisture from all the cracks and corners of an intricate tacklebox.

There's a better way. It takes less time and does a more thorough job to use your wife's hair dryer, aiming it at the trays and equipment. This will even dry out the cork padding in the bottoms of the trays.

Note: Some plastic gear may be damaged by excessive heat, so use the machine on the "Style" setting if it has one, or "Low" if it doesn't. Also, this trick won't work if salt water has been splashed into your tacklebox. Then everything must be washed with fresh water.

Natural Refrigerator

Peat, or sphagnum, moss is usually found in compact, green and purple mats along the banks of streams, the surface of bogs, and around small lakes. It has long been valued for its spongelike ability to retain water. Peat also has a preservative ability. Bodies recovered from peat bogs as long as 100 years after death were still in good shape.

The moss maintains a uniform temperature all year long and is often used as a natural refrigerator. Food will keep underground for long periods under the moss. Game and fish stored under it will stay cold until packed for the trip home.

ODDS AND ENDS
WEATHER

WEATHER WISDOM

1. You really can smell bad weather coming. The high atmospheric pressure present during fair weather literally holds down odors. As the barometer drops, the lowering pressure liberates smells both fragrant and foul.

2. Another sense heightened before a storm is sight. The relatively stable air of good weather is laden with dust particles giving a haze to the horizon. As a front moves in, the haze is blown away and distant objects look sharp and clear.

3. Your hearing too, is increased when a tempest is brewing due to the lowering of cloud cover that acts as an acoustical barrier bouncing back sound waves.

4. If you find dew on the ground when you roll out of your sleeping bag, it probably won't rain that day. Dew is condensation caused by the chilling of the air after the sun goes down. If there is cloud cover to hold in heat or a wind circulating warm air over the ground, dew cannot form.

5. A pale sunset is created by sun rays reflected through water droplets—which will probably reach you sometime tomorrow.

6. The delight of sailors, a red sunset, occurs when the sun is seen through a dust-laden atmosphere in fair weather.

7. A halo around the sun or moon is one of the most reliable indicators of rain. Halos are formed by light shining through veil-like cirrostratus clouds. These clouds are forerunners of a storm front.

8. An east wind has been justly damned since biblical times as a sign of bad weather. In the northern hemisphere an east wind (NE, E, or SE) is indicative of a low-pressure system that brings violent weather.

WEATHER FORECASTING

Predicting the weather is an imprecise art. Yet an ability to anticipate weather changes, particularly in areas of extreme climatic conditions, is important to hunters and anglers.

Wind—Rapidly shifting winds indicate an unsettled atmosphere and a change in weather is likely.

Clouds—A general knowledge of clouds and the atmospheric conditions they indicate can help you predict the weather.

Cumulus: "Wool-pack" are huge masses of white billowy clouds that generally are a sign of good weather. They are a bright white when opposite the sun and dark with bright edges when between you and the sun. Height or altitude varies.

When cumulus clouds begin to build vertically, forming massive thunderheads, they should be considered storm clouds. When you see dark anvil-shaped cumulus clouds moving your way, it indicates an approaching thunderstorm. These are called cumulo-nimbus clouds.

Cirrus: These are the "feather" clouds and are usually seen on a sunny day. They are the highest of cloud formations, about five or six miles high. Cirrus clouds are generally a sign of fair weather. In cold climates, however, if cirrus clouds begin to multiply and are accompanied by building winds blowing steadily from the north, they are a sign of an oncoming blizzard.

Stratus: They are known as "spread sheet" clouds. Low-lying, solid coverings of dark clouds like a horizontal sheet of fog generally mean drizzle or rain.

Cirro-cumulus: Sometimes called a "mackerel sky." They are small flakes arranged in groups or lines resembling fish scales—a warning that precipitation can be expected in 12 to 15 hours. These clouds generally mean calm seas.

CLOUD TYPES

Cumulus

Cirrus

Stratus

Cirro-Cumulus

WEATHER WARNINGS HELP

Birds, campfire smoke and cottonwoods can serve as weather warnings for the outdoorsman.

When a low-pressure system (falling barometer) begins, small birds and bats will fly at lower elevations. Some believe this is because they are sensitive to low pressure, but more likely it is because the insects they seek are hugging the earth then.

Smoke from a campfire will stay near the ground during the onset of a low-pressure system. So when smoke rises it is an indication of good weather.

Trees in the cottonwood family are also a good indication of fair weather turning foul. As an atmospheric low moves into an area, the alders and cottonwoods will show the undersides of their leaves.

These weather warnings will generally occur two to 12 hours in advance, sufficient time to pull your slicker and boots from the closet.

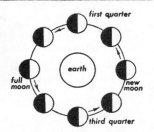

MOON MONTHS

January	*Winter or Wolf*
February	*Trapper's or Snow*
March	*Fish or Worm*
April	*Planter's*
May	*Mother's or Flower*
June	*Stockman's*
July	*Summer*
August	*Dog Days or Sturgeon*
September	*Fall*
October	*Harvest*
November	*Hunter's or Beaver*
December	*Christmas*

WIND SPEED

If you've ever wondered how fast the wind is blowing here are a few tell-tale signals that have long been used by farmers, guides, Indians and other outdoorsmen, including professional meterologists. Nature's signs may not be as accurate as mechanical wind-monitoring devices, but your own observations will give you a rough guesstimate.

When leaves rustle, estimate wind velocity at four to seven miles per hour. If branches move, and dust, snow or leaves are raised, figure on 13 to 18 mph. If most waves show whitecaps, estimate the wind at 25 to 31 mph.

ANIMAL FORECASTS

Animals have long been thought of as nature's meteorologists. Here are some ways in which they are supposed to foretell weather:

♦ *Cows lying in a field signify rain.*

♦ *A thick coat on a woolly bear caterpillar is a forecast of a hard winter.*

♦ *Bees stay near their hives if rain is imminent.*

♦ *When the groundhog sees his shadow on February 2, it means six weeks more of cold weather.*

♦ *Crickets that chirp quickly are harbingers of warmer days.*

♦ *Flies bite more often before a rainstorm.*

♦ *Squirrels work more feverishly storing nuts before a harsh winter.*

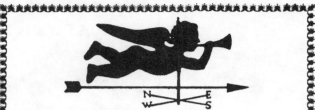

WEATHER PROVERBS

Do you know why that old adage "If a goose flies high, fair weather; if a goose flies low, foul weather" is true? It's because with fair weather the optimum density for flight is higher in the sky than in bad weather, when the best flying condition is closer to the ground. Birds are very sensitive to the aerodynamics of flight and act accordingly.

———

"The squeak of the snow, the temperature will show" is based on the fact that cold air creates high frequencies of sound waves. That's why you get the squeak of a boot or tire on snow in frigid weather.

———

"Ditches and manure piles smell stronger before a rain" because low pressure creates more hydration (wetting) of molecules, which aids the sense of smell, be it of a man or a hunting dog.

———

Fish bite better just before a rain because low air pressure makes fish food on the bottom rise to the top. The fish follow it—right up to the bait you are then using.—

LOCATING HIGHS AND LOWS

Low-pressure areas usually bring unsettled weather conditions, while high-pressure areas generally bring fair weather. Because of the great impact weather has on outdoor activities, it is useful to know whether a high or low front is approaching.

You can determine the location of a high or low front without a barometer or current weather forecast. Stand with your back to the wind and then turn right about 45 degrees. Your back is now to the wind, and the low pressure area is to your left and the high to the right.

Since highs and lows move in a generally eastward flow, whatever weather condition is to your west will probably move over you.

These rules do not hold true for local breezes, such as sea breezes; and highs and lows may become stationary or dissipate before they reach you. However, these tips can be valuable in making your personal weather forecasts and planning your outdoor ventures.